Foreword

By Professor Richard Toye

'I cannot forecast to you the action of Russia,' said Winston Churchill, in a radio broadcast made a few weeks after the outbreak of World War II. 'It is a riddle, wrapped in a mystery, inside an enigma.' That delightful Churchillian phrase made it into the dictionaries of quotations, but it is often forgotten that the then First Lord of the Admiralty went on to suggest that the riddle perhaps had a key: 'That key is Russian national interest.'

It was a remarkably understanding, even forgiving, comment, given that it was made by a die-hard anti-Communist at a point when the ink was barely dry on the recent Nazi-Soviet Pact. It spoke to Churchill's realisation that, if Hitler were to be defeated, cooperation between the British Empire and the USSR would at some point surely be necessary, even if it was far from clear how that might be brought about.

In fact, the key to the riddle of Churchill's seemingly paradoxical attitudes to the Soviet regime is to be found in his own understanding of the Russian national interest. In spite of his hatred of Bolshevism, and the threat he believed it posed to the very fabric of civilization, by the 1930s he had come to the conclusion that Stalin was a rational actor who could be expected to behave like the leader of a traditional Great Power.

This did not mean that Churchill's attitude to Communism had mellowed, simply that Stalin, unlike Hitler, could be relied upon to make tough bargains and stick to them, provided he saw that his negotiating partners also meant business. Seen in this light, the 1946 'iron curtain' speech showed continuity with Churchill's wartime attitudes, not a breach with them. Circumstances had changed, but if the Western powers talked tough enough, the Soviets could be made to see sense. As Anthony Tucker-Jones puts it in this important new book, 'Churchill never saw the Soviet Union or Communist China in the same light as Nazi Germany. He always felt that both countries would see reason if they were brought to the negotiating table.'

Tucker-Jones places some of the blame for the outbreak of the Cold War at Churchill's feet. Try as he might, the now-ageing statesman could never quite shake off the 'war-monger' label. This was due in part to his impetuous attitudes in the present, but was also attributable to the persistent memory of his passionate, some said deranged, support of the Whites during the Russian civil war. It should be acknowledged, though, that Churchill faced a series of hideous dilemmas in his dealings with the Soviets, as for example over the fate of Poland. If the outcomes were often far from optimal, it must be remembered that sometimes, even as Prime Minister, he was no more than a helpless onlooker as tragedy unfolded.

By focusing attention on a poorly understood but vitally important aspect of Churchill's career, Tucker-Jones has performed an important service. *Churchill Cold War Warrior* should be read, not only as a commentary on the ironies of history, but also as an essay on the potential and the limits of power.

Professor Richard Toye
Exeter University

CHURCHILL COLD WAR WARRIOR

CHURCHILL COLD WAR WARRIOR

WINSTON CHURCHILL AND THE IRON CURTAIN

ANTHONY TUCKER-JONES

FRONTLINE
BOOKS

CHURCHILL COLD WAR WARRIOR
Winston Churchill and the Iron Curtain

First published in Great Britain in 2024 by

Frontline Books
An imprint of
Pen & Sword Books Ltd
Yorkshire – Philadelphia

Copyright © Anthony Tucker-Jones, 2024

ISBN 978 1 39904 745 6

Typeset in 9.5 / 11.5 pt Palatino by SJmagic DESIGN SERVICES, India.

Printed and bound in the UK by CPI Group (UK) Ltd.

Pen & Sword Books Ltd incorporates the imprints of Pen & Sword Archaeology,
Atlas, Aviation, Battleground, Discovery, Family History, History, Maritime, Military,
Naval, Politics, Social History, Transport, True Crime, Claymore Press, Frontline
Books, Praetorian Press, Seaforth Publishing and White Owl

For a complete list of Pen & Sword titles please contact

PEN & SWORD BOOKS LTD
George House, Units 12 & 13, Beevor Street, Off Pontefract Road,
Barnsley, South Yorkshire, S71 1HN, England
E-mail: enquiries@pen-and-sword.co.uk
Website: www.pen-and-sword.co.uk

or

PEN AND SWORD BOOKS
1950 Lawrence Rd, Havertown, PA 19083, USA
E-mail: uspen-and-sword@casematepublishers.com
Website: www.penandswordbooks.com

Contents

PART FIVE: ONCE MORE TO WAR

PART SIX: FADING GLORY

PART SEVEN: ESCALATING TENSIONS

Introduction

Winston Churchill is internationally famous thanks to his successful wartime leadership during the Second World War. It was his decisiveness and resilience during the dark days of Dunkirk and the Battle of Britain in 1940 that really sealed his reputation and his place in the history books. What many people do not realise is that he became Prime Minister for a second time in the troubled 1950s. This was when the Cold War was really beginning to gather momentum. During this time he faced two key challenges. The first was countering the emerging global Communist threat posed by the Soviet Union and China. His second was managing the slow process of dismantling the British Empire in a dignified manner. He was not entirely successful with either task. As a Cold War warrior he proved unable to stop the spread of Communism nor to defuse tensions with the Soviet Union and China.

Post-war he is best known for his historic prophetic speech in Fulton, Missouri, where he employed the term 'Iron Curtain' foretelling the coming Cold War. However, it was Churchill who sowed the seeds for this, by foolishly agreeing to spheres of influence in Eastern Europe with Joseph Stalin in 1944. As a result, Eastern Europe and the Balkans were lost to Communism and Europe was partitioned. Only Greece was saved and that was after a protracted civil war involving British troops. This makes Churchill's Iron Curtain speech rather paradoxical if not downright hypocritical. Likewise, Stalin was given a free hand by the Allies in Manchuria and Korea when he belatedly entered the war against Japan in 1945. Korea was partitioned and four years later Mao Zedong's Communist forces triumphed in China. The subsequent Korean War showed that the Cold War was anything but cold.

During Churchill's second term as prime minister from October 1951 to April 1955 he was forced to don the mantle of warlord once more. Times though had changed. When he was premier in the Second World War he presided over Britain at its strongest. Through his second term he had to watch it rapidly lose its world power status to America. The main conflicts he oversaw included Cyprus, Egypt, Kenya, Korea, Malaya and Sudan, all of which placed a terrible burden on Britain's diminishing military resources. Churchill inherited responsibility for countering the ongoing Communist insurgency against British rule in Malaya.

He appointed General Sir Gerald Templer as High Commissioner there and Templer's determined strategy eventually bore fruit. This became the gold standard for future counter-insurgency operations around the world. The Mau Mau Rebellion against British rule in Kenya broke out in August 1952. This was countered by General Sir George Erskine using the very same tactics developed by Templer. The employment of largescale internment in both Kenya and Malaya inevitably opened Churchill to much criticism over human rights abuses.

In the Middle East Churchill had to accept that Britain's influence was waning. The Egyptian military coup in 1952 was followed by terror attacks against the British presence in the strategically vital Canal Zone. This forced Britain to withdraw, setting in train events that led to the disastrous Suez Crisis in 1956 and the end to British rule in Sudan. The redeployment of British troops from Egypt to Cyprus in 1954 also fuelled a nationalist guerrilla war by the Greek Cypriots. With limited resources Churchill had to contain the situation there.

Notably though, Churchill refrained from escalating Britain's involvement in the Korean War, which witnessed large-scale American, Chinese and international intervention. This was the first major confrontation between the Western democracies and the Communist camp following the Berlin Blockade in 1948. The Chinese conquest of Tibet also occurred while he was in office. Although Churchill committed to Britain's independent atomic bomb, he lived in fear of a nuclear war. He was dismayed when America threatened to use the bomb in Korea and Indochina. The enormity of the nuclear arms race became apparent when the atomic bomb, a city killer, was replaced by the hydrogen bomb that could wipe out entire countries. Churchill became a voice of caution and reason.

He was also prime minister during the early stages of France's colonial wars, notably in Indochina and Algeria. Although Britain helped restore French authority in Indochina and Dutch authority in Indonesia at the end of the Second World War, Churchill declined to offer further military assistance. Instead he stood by while French forces suffered a humiliating and decisive defeat at Dien Bien Phu. This sowed the seeds for the Vietnam War that sucked in America, China and the Soviet Union which really brought the Cold War to a boil.

Just after Churchill resigned due to ill-health, Britain and France attacked and occupied the Suez Canal. America and the rest of the world were furious at this last gasp by two failing imperial powers. Both countries were obliged to withdraw. In Europe the Hungarians revolted unsuccessfully against Communist rule, and the bush war commenced in Rhodesia with Nationalist guerrillas fighting for black majority rule. Churchill's hoped-for Cold War legacy was never achieved. He wanted to get the Soviet Union around the negotiating table in the belief they would soften their confrontational stance with the West. President Eisenhower would not play ball as he was not prepared to trust the Soviet menace. In his retirement years Churchill could only watch as Cold War tensions escalated. To his dying day he resolutely refused to believe that he had a hand in drawing the Iron Curtain across Europe or starting the Cold War.

Prologue

Time to Go

Winston Churchill was sitting in a wicker chair in the grounds of Chartwell, lost in thought. His right hand was holding a cigar to his mouth which he was absent-mindedly chewing. He may have been idly wondering where Rufus the poodle had disappeared to. Winston had good reason to worry about the dog known as Rufus II. His predecessor years previously had been killed by a bus while his master was attending the Conservative Party Conference in Brighton. Churchill had been distraught and had him buried in the grounds of Chartwell. Rufus II proved a sickly animal subject to alarming spasms, but Winston was greatly attached to him. He was regularly photographed with the faithful poodle at his side. Fortunately for him Rufus II got on well with Gabriel, his wife's Siamese cat, and their numerous other animals. At least there was harmony amongst the Chartwell menagerie.

There were much more important matters to ponder. By the mid-1950s Churchill had the weight of the world on his ageing shoulders. After the loss of India under Clement Attlee's post-war Labour government, he was trying to salvage what remained of the British Empire by converting it into the Commonwealth. This involved offering independence with dominion status, whereby newly independent nations continued to recognise the British monarchy as head of state. In the face of a rising tide of nationalism and republicanism this was a difficult task. Furthermore, after the Second World War, with the division of Europe between the democratic west and the Communist east, this unwelcome polarisation spread around the world fuelling the Cold War. The combination of Communism and nationalism had become a dangerous and intoxicating cocktail in Indochina and Korea. The conflicts there had threatened to bring the world to the brink of world war.

Churchill cherished a dream that if he could just get the Soviet leadership around the table along with the Americans, as he had done during the Second World War, then everything could be resolved over a nice dinner and drinks. 'Churchill had warned the world about the "Iron Curtain"', observed his youngest child Mary, 'now he felt his last task was to assist the "thaw" in international relations.'[1] Churchill stirred in his chair and rested his left hand on his walking stick. He needed it to get about these days. It was a warm day and he was wearing a hat to keep the sun from his bald head. He was oblivious to those around him, lost in silent reverie. Churchill had been agonising over something for months, something that he had continually put off. For a moment he glanced at the house.

Chartwell had been the family's home since 1922 and was his sanctuary from the hurly-burly of political life. Although the Churchills also owned a house in London, Chartwell was where Winston came to think, write and paint. As it was only an hour from the capital it had regularly hosted the great and the good at weekends. Many a happy family Christmas had been spent there as well. 'Winston greatly enjoyed conducting guests on the "Grand Tour", wrote Mary, 'He and the less young and active would drive in the demobilized army jeep while the rest of us followed at our own pace.'[2] He liked to show off, according to Mary, his 'farms, cattle sheds, pigsties, and the market garden.'[3] The guided tour would culminate with his artist studio at the bottom of the orchard.

Although it gave him much pleasure Chartwell proved a terrible money pit. The place was subjected to extensive renovations and building work over the years. Sarah, Winston's second daughter, recalled, 'All these endeavours were not achieved without considerable and sometimes costly mistakes.'[4] Clementine his wife was less keen on the place because she had warned from the start that it would be a financial burden. James Wood, Churchill's accountant, despaired at the expense of it all. 'Winston, like many others,' he observed dryly, 'finds it more pleasant to pay for the pleasure of farming than he would to pay the inland revenue.'[5] Churchill took mischievous delight in calling him 'Mr Accountant Wood' to distinguish him from his proof reader Charles Wood who he dubbed 'Mr Literary Wood'.[6]

Churchill also enjoyed staying at Chequers, the official country residence of the Prime Minister of the day. It too offered seclusion outside London and he used it as an extension of 10 Downing Street, the Prime Minister's official city residence. At Chartwell, one of his favourite places was on the terrace overlooking the lakes, which were frequented by a friendly heron and black swans. He once said, 'I bought Chartwell for that view.'[7]

Churchill was not alone that day. Sitting on the grass besides him, knees bent and ankles crossed, looking decidedly uncomfortable, was his protégé, close friend and loyal ally Anthony Eden. The latter was tied to Churchill by blood as well as politics. He was married to Winston's only niece Clarissa Churchill, who was the daughter of his late brother Jack. Mary noted the marriage was an 'event which created a considerable stir both inside and outside our family.'[8] Eden was twenty-three years older than Clarissa, but they were happy. Winston and Clementine had been fully supportive of their union.

Out on the lawn Churchill was attired in one of his trademark siren suits, essentially a boiler suit or overalls. Eden, in contrast, was wearing formal pinstripe trousers, tie and black jacket. He wore no hat to shield his silver hair. He was hardly dressed appropriately to be sitting in a field. To balance himself Eden was clasping his right wrist with his left hand. His only concession to comfort was the cushion Churchill had loaned him. It was an incongruous sight, caught by a photographer. The younger man symbolically seated at the very feet of his political mentor. There was deep significance in this. Why had Eden not been offered a chair and been made to sit on the ground? After all he was a distinguished and accomplished politician in his own right.

The pair had been through thick and thin together during the Second World War when Eden had been part of Churchill's War Cabinet serving as Foreign Secretary. They had regularly been photographed together. Eden the debonair First World War veteran had long been considered a potential leader in waiting. This was highlighted when he was appointed Foreign Secretary for the first time in 1935 at the age of just thirty-eight. When Churchill became Prime Minister five years later he summoned Eden to fill the same role once more. Although Attlee, the Labour leader, served as Churchill's Deputy Prime Minister in the wartime coalition government, in party political terms Eden was really Churchill's de facto second-in-command. He was the crowned prince and everybody knew it.

After the war, Eden was Churchill's heir apparent in the Conservative Party for ten long years. When Churchill was elected to serve as Prime Minister for a second time in 1951, it was widely expected he would last a year before handing over the reins of power. The Conservatives needed him to win the election; after that they would put him out to pasture. This, though, did not happen and by 1955 Churchill and Eden's relationship was increasing fractious. Even the Labour Party felt Churchill was well past his prime. 'He was increasingly becoming a misfit,' noted future Labour Prime Minister Harold Wilson, 'in the rapidly changing Britain of the post-war world.'[9] President Eisenhower also noted privately, 'Churchill should begin planning his farewell address.'[10]

Eden had found himself stuck in the role of Foreign Secretary once more. There was now a growing sense of bitterness between him and Churchill, with each suspecting the other of betrayal. Up until that point they had buried any petty differences for the benefit of the party and the country. There was the Cold War to be fought and an Empire to be saved. Eden, though, was conscious he was losing his window of opportunity if he was to reach the pinnacle of his career. In recent years he had been seriously ill, and he was fast approaching sixty so was hardly in his prime. 'To any parliamentarian, and there is no camaraderie, irrespective of Party, to compare with that of parliamentarians,' observed Harold Wilson, 'it was a tragic period.'[11]

The public and the media had become bored by the issue. 'Even the press now began to be tired of speculating on W.'s resignation,' said John Colville, Churchill's Private Secretary, 'except for the *Daily Mirror* which has a personal vendetta against him.'[12] Churchill had also been stung by Malcolm Muggeridge's *Punch* magazine which had been cruel in its treatment of him. 'They have been attacking me,' he lamented to Lord Moran, his doctor. '*The Mirror* has had nothing so hostile.'[13] Muggeridge rather unkindly likened Churchill to 'a bookie'.[14] Churchill knew he had nothing left to gamble with. Both his political credit and his health were all used up. Muggeridge had actually meant this as a compliment as he felt it was better than being 'a clergyman' and 'sentimentally virtuous'.[15]

Churchill had done all he could to safeguard Britain's place in the world. However, the truth was that he had played a part in fuelling the Cold War. It was Eden who had failed to save Greece from Hitler in 1941. Fatefully Churchill, in order to save Greece from Communism three years later with the German withdrawal, promised Stalin control of Eastern Europe. This was a deal with the devil which had sown the seeds for the Iron Curtain and the partition of Europe. Churchill now wanted to do his utmost to try to remedy the situation before he stepped down. He was stymied in this not by the Soviet Union but by America. Furthermore, his second premiership was marred by ill health and waning powers of concentration. To be fair he was an old man, who should have been enjoying his retirement.

By early 1955 Churchill had promised to go, but to Eden's despair he kept changing his mind. Eden's Principal Private Secretary, Evelyn Shuckburgh, noted in his diary, 'There have, however, been a number of last-minute efforts by the Old Man to escape the inevitable.'[16] Eden needed time to prepare for a general election, and the longer Churchill put it off, the worse the situation became for him and the Conservatives. 'I am increasingly compelled to take account of these distasteful economic factors,' acknowledged Eden, knowing that he could not put off an election.[17] There were also unresolved issues in Cyprus, Egypt, Kenya and Malaya that urgently needed dealing with. Tensions between Egypt and Israel were mounting after the Israelis accused Egyptian forces in Gaza of sponsoring terror attacks.[18] This threatened war in the Middle East. In Europe, East and West Germany were about to embark on rearmament, ending any hopes of a neutral unified state.

Churchill, staring out across the grounds of Chartwell, knew in his heart it was time to go, but he felt he still had more to offer. Also the historian in him was looking at his legacy. No one could dispute his remarkable achievements during the Second World War, but he had not been elected, he was an emergency appointment. Subsequent electoral defeat had made him more determined than ever to prove a point, which he did in 1951. Although the Conservatives recognised they needed younger blood, Churchill wanted to cling on until he achieved one last grand gesture for the history books. He even half-hoped to die while still in post to avoid the steady decline of old age.

It was not to be. Finally, in February 1955, he informed Eden he would step down on 5 April that year. Churchill's own sense of mortality had been brought home by the recent death of his sister-in-law Nellie, who had died at the age of sixty-six from inoperable cancer. Between Nellie's bouts of treatment, Clementine had her come and stay with them at Chartwell to recuperate. She had endured a tough life; her husband Bertram Romilly died in 1940 and Esmond, one of her sons, had been killed on a bombing mission the following year. Her other son Giles, a Communist journalist, had been captured in Norway while reporting on the war and ended up in Colditz. 'Poor Nellion,' said Churchill sadly to his wife.[19] He missed having her about the house. Mary recalled, 'Winston was always devoted to "Nellinita" as he [also] called her.'[20]

It was time for Eden to shoulder full responsibility for the challenges facing the country. After much soul searching Churchill agreed to stick to this departure date. 'They will be weaker when I am gone,' he told Lord Moran. Then in an act of gross ingratitude added, 'Anthony's foreign policy has not been very successful.'[21] He very unfairly blamed Eden for failing to orchestrate a three-power summit between Britain, America and the Soviet Union. This though was not Eden's fault. President

Eisenhower had made it clear he saw no point in talking to the Communist bloc in light of its ongoing hostility towards the West. John Colville recalled, 'W. began to form a cold hatred of Eden who, he repeatedly said, had done more to thwart him and prevent him pursuing the policy he thought right than anybody else.'[22]

Churchill had hoped he could do business with Soviet Premier Georgy Malenkov, Joseph Stalin's successor. Malenkov offered the tantalising chance that the Soviet Union might mend its ways and become more amenable to the West. He wanted to improve the standard of living in the Soviet Union, and that could not be achieved while Moscow was spending a fortune on weapons. It was a bold step. However, on 8 February 1955 he was forced to resign. 'Yes, they are isolating Malenkov and then they will strangle him,' Churchill informed Lord Moran. 'No, my usefulness where Russia is concerned is gone. I wanted to give Malenkov a chance, and he has vanished.'[23] The loss of Malenkov and Eisenhower's intransigence was a blow to Churchill's long-held aspirations. His faith in the jovial-looking chubby-faced Soviet apparatchik was wholly misplaced as the man was a career Stalinist. Malenkov was replaced by Nikolai Bulganin with Nikita Khrushchev lurking in the background. They also were lifelong Stalinists.

The unfortunate Eden, as Foreign Secretary, was only responsible for British policy towards those countries outside the Commonwealth and the Empire. The latter were the responsibility of the Colonial Secretary Alan Lennox-Boyd and his predecessor Oliver Lyttelton. They had served Churchill well. In Kenya the British military were just gearing up for a final push against the rebellious Mau Mau, while in Malaya a government was being formed to negotiate an end to the decade-old Communist insurgency.

Churchill had once relished the challenge of strategic problem-solving, but now it was time to let someone else have a go. Eden seemed eminently qualified for the job. Churchill though was about to hand Eden a tainted legacy. Just days before he stepped down, Cypriot nationalists bombed the Cyprus Broadcasting Service near Nicosia airport, heralding their armed campaign against British rule. Military facilities across the island were also attacked. Churchill was to blame for this as he had refused to grant Cyprus independence. Eden would very quickly find himself forced to boost the British garrison from 1,100 men to 27,500. Much worse was to come. Churchill's long-delayed military withdrawal from the Suez Canal had greatly aggravated Anglo-Egyptian relations and brought the situation to crisis point.

Winston shifted in his chair in the grounds of Chartwell once more and puffed furiously on his cigar. Nothing happened; it was extinguished. He had a habit of only smoking half before he let it go out. Reaching into his pocket he produced a box of matches and struck one down its side. He lifted the flame to the end of the cigar, puffed again, and his head was briefly shrouded in smoke. He looked to his left at Eden, briefly smiled then nodded. That was it then; Eden was to be Prime minister. It was definitely time to go. 'At the age of eighty,' said Sarah Churchill, 'he had decided it was time to relinquish the burden of being Prime Minister of England and retire to his beloved Chartwell.'[24]

Beforehand he would dine with his other close friends, Tory grandee Harold Macmillan and Field Marshal Bernard Montgomery, and let them know. He also wanted to spend some time at Chequers and 10 Downing Street one last time. 'We shall want to say goodbye to everyone,' said Clementine in one of her notes to her husband.[25] Winston summoned Eden and Lord Butler and made a rather perfunctory announcement, 'I am going and Anthony will succeed me. We can discuss details later.'[26] Privately Churchill had forlornly confided to Lord Butler, 'I feel like an aeroplane at the end of its flight, in the dusk, with petrol running out, in search of a safe landing'.[27]

When Churchill resigned on 5 April 1955, he and Eden were photographed together again. There was no warmth in their expressions. Both men sat rigidly. Churchill looked cross, while Eden had an air of melancholy. It was almost as if Churchill held Eden responsible for the Cold War, whereas he was, not his long-suffering protégé. In reality it was Churchill's Iron Curtain as much as it was Stalin's. He had presided over the rise of Communism and the end of empire. Eden tried to be magnanimous. He and Clarissa sent a note of goodwill just before the Churchills embarked on a holiday to Sicily. 'This is just to send the warmest love from us both to you and to Clemmie,' Eden wrote from Chequers, 'with every good wish for the journey and for sunshine.'[28] Despite all their difficulties it was heartfelt.

Harold Macmillan feared that Churchill's departure was much too late. When it came to Eden's apprenticeship he observed, 'It may really be that he has been Prince of Wales too long.'[29] The unfortunate Eden faced two major challenges, only one of which he survived. On 26 May 1955 he fought a general election in which he dramatically increased the Conservatives' majority. Egypt, though, was to be his downfall. Now that almost all British troops had gone, Suez was vulnerable to Egyptian plans to nationalise the Canal. Prime Minister Eden would last less than two years before the Suez Crisis and the disastrous Anglo-French invasion of Egypt terminated his long-awaited premiership. His mentor had lasted much longer and made a bigger impact.

List of Illustrations

1. The Big Three, Churchill, Roosevelt and Stalin at Yalta in early 1945. (Photo by US National Archives and Records Administration)

2. In the summer of 1945 the Big Three got together at Potsdam, this time with Truman replacing Roosevelt. (Photo by US National Archives and Records Administration)

3. After the defeat of Germany the British people did not want to go forward with Churchill. (Wartime poster via Author's Collection)

4. Britain in July 1945 rejected Churchill and voted in Clement Attlee and his Labour government. (Photo by Dutch National Archives)

5. Churchill took his electoral defeat badly but refused to retire from politics. (Photo via Public Domain)

6. In 1946 Truman encouraged Churchill to make his now famous Sinews of Peace speech at Fulton, Missouri. (Photo by US National Archives and Records Administration)

7. Churchill's only post-war trip to Latin America was in 1946 when he visited Cuba. (Cuban National Archives)

8. Attlee oversaw the hasty British withdrawal from India and Palestine. (Photo via Public Domain)

9. It was always doubtful that India's Hindus, Muslims and Sikhs could live peacefully together post-independence. (Photo by Inter Services Public Relations Directorate, India)

10. Churchill supported Muhammad Ali Jinnah's desire for a separate Pakistan. (Photo by Ministry of Information & Broadcasting, Pakistan)

11. Churchill blamed Lord Mountbatten for Britain's rapid scramble from India. (Photo portrait by Allan Warren)

12. Ultimately Churchill held Jawaharlal Nehru responsible for India's bloody partition. (Photo by US Embassy, New Delhi)

13. Churchill at the Congress of Europe in 1948. He wanted unity in the face of the Soviet threat. (Photo by Fotocollectie Anefo Reportage)

14. The Berlin Blockade and the subsequent airlift heralded the Cold War. (Photo by National Museum of the US Air Force)

15. In the late 1940s President Truman pledged America would help to protect democracy from Communism. (Photo by US National Archives and Records Administration)

16. Mao Zedong with Joseph Stalin in Moscow in December 1949. (Photo via Public Domain)

17. The outbreak of the Korean War announced the Cold War going hot in Asia. (Photo by US National Archives and Records Administration)

18. The commitment of British forces to Korea was very small due to limited resources. (Photo by US Army Signal Corps/US National Archives and Records Administration)

19. General Douglas MacArthur wanted to use the atomic bomb in Korea to stop the Chinese. (Photo by US National Archives and Records Administration)

20. The Bulldog is back. Churchill weakened Attlee's government in 1950 and defeated it the following year. (Photo via Public Domain)

21. The handsome Anthony Eden served as Foreign Secretary twice under Churchill. (Photo by US Army Signal Corps/US National Archives and Records Administration)

22. Churchill with Eden, Dean Acheson and Harry Truman in January 1952. (Photo by US National Archives and Records Administration)

23. During his second premiership Churchill had to contend with guerrilla wars in Malaya and Kenya. (Photo via Public Domain)

24. Kenyan nationalist leader Jomo Kenyatta was arrested in 1952. (Photo by Israeli National Photo Collection)

25. Churchill did not want to relinquish control of the vital Suez Canal to Egypt. (Photo by Author's Collection)

26. Dwight D. Eisenhower became US President in January 1953. (Photo by Eisenhower Presidential Library)

27. Georgy Malenkov succeeded Stalin in 1953. (Photo by Dutch National Archives)

28. In 1953 Churchill had British Guiana's left-wing Chief Minister Cheddi Jagan arrested. (Photo by Dutch National Archives)

29. Churchill and Eisenhower at the unsuccessful three Power Summit in Bermuda in December 1953. (Photo by Tupelo)

30. After the use of the Atomic Bomb against Japan, Churchill did not want it ever deployed again. (Photo by US National Archives and Records Administration)

LIST OF ILLUSTRATIONS

PART ONE

OUT IN THE COLD

Chapter 1

A Deal with the Devil

'Winston never talks of Hitler these days,' noted Lord Moran, Churchill's doctor, in August 1944, 'he is always harping on the dangers of Communism. He dreams of the Red Army spreading like a cancer from one country to another.'[1] Churchill, ever since the days of the Russian Revolution and subsequent Civil War, had made no secret of his hatred of Communism. It was opposed to everything he held sacred and Britain and America's alliance with the Soviet Union had been simply one of convenience. In the closing months of the Second World War foremost in Churchill's mind was the Communist threat posed to Greece, Italy and Yugoslavia.

This issue was worrying Churchill when he visited liberated southern Italy to meet with senior Allied commanders and local politicians. While in Naples on 12 August 1944 he first met with the Yugoslav Communist partisan leader Josip Broz Tito. 'I was very impressed with him,' said Field Marshal Harold Alexander, the Allied commander in Italy. 'He was a fine and very friendly man.'[2] Britain had backed Tito's war effort against the Germans with weapons and advisors. Now that his Communist forces were gaining the upper hand, Churchill was beginning to regret championing Tito's cause. Churchill urged Tito to reinstate King Peter of Yugoslavia once the Germans were defeated. It is very doubtful that Tito took any notice of Churchill extolling the virtues of a constitutional monarchy rather than a republic. Then in Rome Churchill met with Georgios Papandreou, Prime Minister of the exiled Greek government. 'The PM is sorely perturbed about Greece,' observed Lord Moran. 'His mind is full of forebodings about what will happen when the Germans leave Athens. The Communists will seize power, and he is resolved to thwart their purpose.'[3]

Churchill was similarly worried about the fate of post-war Italy. Following the Allied landings on mainland Italy in September 1943, the Italians sought an armistice and dictator Benito Mussolini fell from power. In response to the defection of his once staunch allies, Hitler swiftly occupied northern Italy where he installed Mussolini as head of the puppet Repubblica Sociale Italiana. This plunged the country into civil war. In the south the Communist, Christian Democrat, Liberal, and Socialist parties formed the National Liberation Committee which cooperated with the new Italian government. The latter was insistent that King Emmanuel III could not remain head of state because of his long association with Mussolini and fascism.

Italian Communists in the occupied north created the Liberation Committee of Upper Italy with the Garibaldi Brigades operating as their military wing. These attacked not only Mussolini's fascist supporters and the German occupiers but also anti-Communist organisations. As far as the Communists were concerned they were not just at war with the fascists and the Germans, they were also conducting a revolutionary war to defeat capitalism. These northern Communists were led by Luigi Longo, a Spanish Civil War veteran who was well versed in violence. He and his supporters were not fighting for Italy and democracy, but for Moscow and Communism. This was highlighted when Stalin sent Palmiro Togliatti, one of the founders of the Italian Communist party, back to Italy after eighteen years of exile in the Soviet Union. Togliatti was soon liaising with Alexander Bogomolov, the Soviet Ambassador to Italy, and General Solodovnik, the Soviet representative on the Allied Control Mission in Italy. Despite having been banned for two decades during Mussolini's rule, the Italian Communist party rapidly emerged as a force to be reckoned with.

Churchill visited the Vatican on 23 August and had an audience with the Pope. Afterwards he met with the Italian cabinet which included Togliatti. Harold Macmillan, Britain's Minister Resident in the Mediterranean, was of the view, 'Togliatti is torn between loyalty to Moscow and to Italy. The former will prove stronger...'[4] Churchill hoped to use his friendship with Stalin to dissuade the Soviets from causing further mischief in Italy and Greece. He knew there was little he could do about Yugoslavia. When Churchill flew back to London on 29 August he arrived with a temperature of 103 degrees and was immediately sent home. It did not take him long to recover. The following day his Private Secretary John Colville recorded, 'The PM was better and did a certain amount of work in bed.'[5]

'On 31 August Mr Churchill, somewhat disenchanted by his meeting with Tito,' wrote Foreign Secretary Anthony Eden, 'sent me a minute remarking upon our responsibility for supplying Tito with arms with which he could subjugate Yugoslavia.'[6] Eden was rather annoyed by this as his Foreign Office had been warning for months against such an eventuality. 'I have certainly never lost sight of this danger,' said Eden in his reply to Churchill, 'which has arisen largely because our policy towards Yugoslavia has had to be dictated on grounds of short-term military expediency rather than those of long-term political interest.'[7] Eden then wrote to Tito asking him to form a broad-based government ready to assume control of Yugoslavia once the Germans were gone. Tito responded by flying to Moscow to hold talks with Stalin. The Red Army would support his accession to power.

Romania, also once a staunch Nazi ally on the Eastern Front, declared war on Germany on 25 August. The Red Army moved into Bucharest unopposed six days later. Field Marshal Alan Brooke, British Chief of the Imperial General Staff, noted in his diary, 'Romania out of the war and Bulgaria tumbling out next. The Germans cannot last much longer.'[8] The Bulgarians, while they had not committed troops to the Eastern Front, had taken part in the brutal Axis occupation of the Balkans. They changed sides on 5 September 1944 and allowed the Red Army to enter Sofia ten days later. This defection cost Bulgaria dearly as the Germans swiftly overwhelmed the Bulgarian 1st and 5th Armies in Macedonia and Serbia. 'The Bulgarian situation is very unsatisfactory, even alarming,' wrote Harold

Macmillan. 'I fear the F[oreign] O[ffice] have "missed the bus" again.'[9] This meant that the Red Army was now in a position to easily intervene in Greece and Yugoslavia. While Churchill was prepared to sacrifice the latter, he felt beholden to the former.

In the meantime, next stop for Churchill was Canada and the second Quebec conference, where he was to meet US President Franklin Roosevelt and the combined chiefs of staff.[10] Although Canadian Prime Minister Mackenzie King was hosting the two leaders he was not invited to the key discussions which commenced on 12 September. Amongst the most important topics was the division of post-war Germany into occupation zones controlled by America, Britain and the Soviet Union. Churchill wanted to add France to the list, but Roosevelt was not receptive.

It was in Quebec that Churchill was made aware of the Red Army's advance into Bulgaria. Foreign Secretary Anthony Eden sent a message informing him of the developments in the Bulgarian capital. 'This Russian move has created an entirely new situation,' explained Eden, 'since even if they do not penetrate into Greek territory their presence in the Balkans is bound to produce strong political reactions.'[11] By this he meant that the Greek Communists would be encouraged to seize power. Eden then urged Churchill to send British troops to Greece as soon as possible. Churchill immediately agreed and two British brigades were earmarked for deployment to Athens once the German garrison had departed.

'Already the Greeks are restive and the Communist members of the Papandreou Government may easily resign,' wrote Harold Macmillan.[12] As soon as the Germans began to withdraw from the Greek islands and the Peloponnese the Communists started massacring soldiers and civilians alike. In occupied Thrace Bulgarian troops found themselves in danger of getting into a shooting match with Greek guerrillas who wanted to take control. For Churchill and Macmillan, it was very frustrating that Papandreou's government, which was in Italy, could not move immediately to Greece. Papandreou felt he should travel to the mainland even if he could not get into Athens.

Eden joined Churchill in Quebec on 14 September and when he saw Roosevelt remarked in his diary, 'Thought he looked very drawn.'[13] John Colville, Churchill's Private Secretary, recalled, 'The PM told me he fears the President is now "very frail"'.[14] In contrast, when Eden dined with the senior delegates that day he noted, 'W[inston] looks much better and Mackenzie a very fit old man.'[15] Eden tried to get Churchill and Roosevelt to recognise General Charles de Gaulle's French Provisional Government. De Gaulle and his supporters were by now firmly ensconced in liberated Paris. Neither though were keen. 'W[inston] did however,' said Eden, 'go so far as to say that he would rather have a de Gaulle France than a Communist France...!'[16]

President Roosevelt and American democracy accidently did Europe a great disservice. Churchill travelled to Moscow on 9 October without his trusted ally, where he and he alone foolishly sowed the seeds for the Cold War. Roosevelt tried to head this eventuality off but he was singularly unsuccessful. Churchill wanted Roosevelt to accompany him, but he was facing a presidential election the following month. 'The PM was unable to hide his irritation,' recalled Lord Moran. 'The Red Army, 'he said scornfully,' would not stand still awaiting the result of the election.'[17] In particular, Churchill, having failed Greece and Poland once before, was determined not to do so a second time. Churchill told Moran that he had decided to 'go it alone.'[18]

In America the US Democratic party, concerned about Roosevelt's failing health, insisted he drop Henry Wallace, his lacklustre vice president and replace him with Senator Harry Truman of Missouri. Although Roosevelt was on the campaign trail, seeking to defeat the Republican candidate Thomas Dewey, he sought to offer Churchill his best wishes. Initially he drafted a message wishing Churchill every success, but his trusted advisor Harry Hopkins opposed sending it on the grounds Churchill might think he was acting with America's authority as well. Instead, Roosevelt sent Stalin a clear warning. 'I am firmly convinced that the three of us, and only the three of us,' he said firmly, 'can find the solution to the still unresolved questions.' Roosevelt then made Churchill's position perfectly clear, 'In this sense, while appreciating the Prime Minister's desire for the meeting, I prefer to regard your forthcoming talks with Churchill as preliminary to a meeting of the three of us.'[19]

This was clearly a case of wishful thinking on the part of Roosevelt. Stalin's agenda was very simple. He was determined to create a security buffer in Eastern Europe and the Balkans to prevent Germany from ever invading the Soviet Union again. As far as he was concerned the Red Army had been doing all the hard work since 1941. Now that the Germans were being driven back everywhere on the Eastern Front, in his view the spoils had been won in Soviet blood. John Colville noted in his diary that Churchill was determined to go to Moscow, 'because he wants to discourage any idea that the UK and USA are very close ... to the exclusion of Russia ... and that there is no tendency to leave her in the cold.'[20]

Roosevelt was well aware of Churchill's developing plans and was not happy with them. At the end of May 1944 he was displeased to be informed by Churchill that the British had proposed to Moscow that the Soviet Union take the lead in Romania while Britain took the lead in Greece. Anthony Eden had made this offer to the Soviet Ambassador on 5 May. Eden sought to justify his actions saying, 'My suggestion was a limited one, intended to confine as far as possible the conflicts which were already developing between Russian policies in the Balkans and our own.'[21] Eden was well aware of 'the danger of a link-up between pro-Soviet movements in Yugoslavia, Albania and Greece.'[22] 'I hope you may feel able to give this proposal your blessing,' Churchill wrote in a telegram to Roosevelt. 'We do not of course wish to carve up the Balkans into spheres of influence.'[23] He naively went on to reassure Roosevelt that this would only be a wartime arrangement and would not affect any post-war settlement. Averell Harriman, the US Ambassador to the Soviet Union, had also learned of this when he stopped to see the Prime Minister while on the way back to Washington.

Churchill's initiative was designed to safeguard British interests in the Mediterranean, but as far as Roosevelt and the US State Department were concerned it created a dangerous precedent. Roosevelt responded to Churchill tersely, 'I think I should tell you frankly that we were disturbed ... I hope matters of this importance can be prevented from developing in such a matter in the future.'[24] In his reply Churchill pointed out that Stalin was in a position to do whatever he wanted in Romania and that Britain had lost 40,000 men in 1941 trying to save Greece. If Stalin was not discouraged from supporting Greece's Communists then they would take power as the German occupiers withdrew. He also warned it was important to prevent Yugoslavia from descending into civil war. Roosevelt though had no enthusiasm for seeing the deposed royal families reinstalled in either country.

Churchill was thinking in terms of 'spheres of action' whereas Roosevelt considered them as 'spheres of influence.' It was the Soviets who had first raised the issue of spheres of influence in the summer of 1943. Churchill warned on 3 September 1943 that there should be 'no question of our disinteresting ourselves in any part of the world for out of this might immediately come the cause of a new war.'[25] This was Churchill's first warning of the potential for an armed standoff with the Soviet Union and the coming of the Cold War. By early August 1944 Churchill was under a great deal of stress regarding the Red Army's sweeping victories on the Eastern Front. 'Good God, can't you see that the Russians are spreading across Europe like a tide;' he snapped at Lord Moran, 'they have invaded Poland, and there is nothing to prevent them marching onto Turkey and Greece!'[26] It was instructive that he had used the word 'invaded' and not liberated.

Although Churchill conducted extensive shuttle diplomacy during the Second World War, he was annoyed by Stalin's constant reluctance to meet outside the Soviet Union. Just before he flew to Moscow Churchill grumbled to Sir Alan Lascelles, King George VI's private secretary. 'Next time we must get Joe Stalin to meet us somewhere – perhaps at the Hague,' said Churchill, 'though he is always miaowing about his health, and pretending that he is too sick to travel.'[27] The truth was that Stalin never felt safe.

For the future of Europe, it would have been better if Churchill had waited until after the US election. For Stalin it offered him an opportunity to divide and rule the Western allies. If he could wring concessions from Churchill then all the better. This meant that the fate of eastern Europe hung in the balance. To make matters worse there was a sense that Bulgaria, Hungary and Romania as former Nazi allies deserved everything they got. The British in particular were unhappy that the Bulgarians were increasingly hostile to their military mission, which included officers being placed under house arrest in Grecian Thrace.

Elizabeth Layton, one of Churchill's secretaries who formed part of the British team that went to Moscow, found Stalin cut an intimidating figure. 'Marshal Stalin was much shorter than I had thought, and the twinkle in his eye looked, somehow, all too knowing,' she wrote. 'Bundled up in his long Army greatcoat, he reminded me of a rather wicked-looking stuffed doll.'[28] Layton was right; although Stalin would launch a charm offensive during the visit he had no intention of bending to Churchill's wishes. Years earlier Stalin had told his inner court, 'The question of borders will be decided by force.'[29]

Churchill and Stalin discussed the future of Poland as the plan was to readjust the country's borders once the war was over. Poland was to lose its territory east of the Curzon Line to the Soviets.[30] In compensation it would get Silesia and part of East Prussia from Germany, while the Soviet Union gained the Prussian capital of Königsberg. Prussia was seen as the heart of German militarism. Indeed, as far as Churchill was concerned, 'Prussia was the root of all evil.' Britain and America had also agreed to Stalin's claims on the Baltic States.[31] Churchill wanted a democratic Poland. However, he knew full well that after the defeat of the Polish uprising against the Nazis that summer, it would be relatively easy for Stalin to impose a Communist government.

Anthony Eden was not optimistic. 'I was not hopeful for the outcome of our mission,' he noted. 'The Russians had already grabbed the territory they wanted, so the Curzon Line was no longer a real issue. It was what happened in Poland that mattered.'[32] By this he meant whether they could get the London-based Polish government in exile and the Polish Communist National Committee in Lublin to work together. The problem was that both parties detested each other. The Poles in London opposed adoption of the Curzon Line, while the National Committee accepted it. Stalin knew that with the National Committee backed by the Soviet Polish 1st Army waiting in the wings, it was only a matter of time before Poland's Communists took power. John Colville, who had remained in London, jotted down in his diary on 9 October, 'A disturbed night owing to demands from Moscow that the Polish Ministers shall at once fly there for conversations; and the Poles don't want to do so except on conditions.'[33]

Churchill then tried to trade Romania as a sphere of Soviet interest in return for Britain having a say over Greece's future. Britain was after all a key Mediterranean power. Stalin knew full well that Churchill was haggling from a position of weakness. Nonetheless, he smiled and said, 'that Britain should have the first say in Greece.'[34] He had baited his trap, but he need not have bothered as Churchill proceeded to acquiesce to Stalin's wishes. Churchill began to write what by his own admission he called the 'naughty document.'[35] On it he ranked five European countries according to the Allies' priorities. At the top Romania was assigned 90 percent to Russia, Bulgaria 75 percent to Russia, Greece 90 percent to Britain, while Yugoslavia and Hungary were deemed 50-50. Notably no mention was made whatsoever of Albania, Czechoslovakia, Germany or Poland.

The list was passed to Stalin who, after examining it, ticked the countries with a blue pencil as if he were marking a child's homework. As far as Stalin was concerned Churchill had just agreed to the Sovietization of the Balkans and parts of eastern Europe as long as he kept out of Greece. Churchill immediately realised it was a diplomatic error to write all this down. 'Might it not be thought rather cynical if it seemed we disposed of these issues,' he said, 'so fateful to millions of people in such an off-hand manner? Let us burn the paper.'[36] When this was translated Stalin smiled and replied, 'No, you keep it.'[37] He hardly needed Churchill's piece of paper when the Balkans were already within his grasp. Offering Greece as a scrap from the table was hardly a big price to keep the British happy. Furthermore, Stalin was probably well aware that at some point Greece's Communists would make an attempt to seize power in Athens. Stalin rightly suspected that Churchill was negotiating without Roosevelt's agreement. Notably Averell Harriman, the US Ambassador, had not been present for the percentages talks. To allay Churchill's concerns, Stalin had slyly observed that Roosevelt 'demanded too many rights for the United States of America, leaving too little for the Soviet Union and Great Britain.'[38]

7

Churchill knew that the strength of the well-organised Communist partisans in Albania, Greece and Yugoslavia meant that there was a good chance they could take power.[39] He suggested to Stalin that something should be done to stop Greece and Yugoslavia descending into civil war. Churchill pointed out he did not support the return of the region's monarchies unless they were wanted. This was an academic undertaking as they were certainly not wanted in Albania or Yugoslavia. He also asked Stalin not to stir up the Communists in Italy. Stalin happily agreed to all this, claiming he had no influence over Italian Communist leader Togliatti. He then claimed that Togliatti was 'a wise man, not an extremist, and would not start an adventure in Italy.'[40]

As far as Stalin was concerned Churchill's 'naughty document' was an amusing attempt to negotiate what was already a *fait accompli*. Nonetheless, the next day Anthony Eden found Vyacheslav Molotov, his Soviet counterpart, haggling over the percentages. Most notably he wanted 75/25 percent for Hungary and Yugoslavia. When Eden protested, Molotov said he would accept 60/40 for Yugoslavia or trade 50/50 for the latter in return for 90/10 for Bulgaria. 'Finally I told him that I was not interested in figures,' said Eden.[41] He felt having a say in Bulgaria and Hungary was more important than Romania and Yugoslavia.

When Eden briefed Churchill the Prime Minister was dismayed, realising he had made himself hostage to fortune. 'Winston rather upset by my report,' noted Eden. 'I think he thought I had dispelled [the] good atmosphere he had created the night before. But I explained this was the real battle and I could not and would not give way.'[42] Also on 10 October Harriman informed Roosevelt that he thought Churchill was offering to 'work out some spheres of influence with the Russians.'[43] Roosevelt responded to Harriman instructing, 'such steps as are practicable should be taken to insure against the Balkans getting us into a future international war.'[44] By this stage Roosevelt was aware that British troops had arrived in Greece.

On 11 October Eden again found himself trying to fend off Molotov's haggling over percentages. Churchill, who had forgotten about Albania, now offered 50/50 – this was something Enver Hoxha the Albanian Communist leader would have scoffed at. He had no intention of allowing his country to become the puppet of an outside power ever again. Field Marshal Alan Brooke, Chief of the Imperial General Staff, who was part of Churchill's delegation, noted that night, 'During dinner a salute was fired for the capture of Cluj, a wonderful display of fireworks which were reflected in the Kremlin windows.'[45] Cluj was a city in northwestern Romania, from where the Red Army could threaten Hungary. Shortly after, the Hungarians announced an armistice with the Soviet Union. In response the Germans occupied Budapest to stop them from defecting. Only a week earlier on 6 October the Soviet-backed Czechoslovak 1st Army Corps and the Red Army fought their way through the Dukla Pass and onto Czechoslovakian soil.

Churchill, realising he had committed a strategic blunder, wanted to send Stalin a memo to better reflect his intentions. 'These percentages which I have put down,' he wrote 'are no more than a method by which in our thoughts we can see how near we are together, and then decide upon the necessary steps ...' Churchill went on to conclude, 'Let them work out their own fortunes during the years that lie ahead.'[46] When he showed his draft to the US Ambassador, Harriman warned him that Roosevelt would disavow it. In consequence Churchill never sent it to Stalin, hoping that this was an end to the matter.

Churchill sent a telegram to the British War Cabinet trying to justify his actions. He argued that the percentages had merely been discussion points and were not intended to establish 'spheres of influence.' The Foreign Office were horrified by talk of the 'naughty document' and Lieutenant Colonel Ian Jacob on Churchill's staff suggested that certain passages be exercised from the record. He warned that they should not 'give the impression to historians that these very important discussions were conducted in a most unfitting manner.'[47] Reference to the 'naughty document' was duly removed. Interestingly Anthony Eden in his memoirs only ever made two references to the 'percentage' agreement.

Churchill was completely beguiled by Stalin. 'I have had very nice talks with the Old Bear,' he wrote to his wife on 13 October. 'I like him the more I see him. They respect us here and I am sure they wish to work with us.'[48] However, he clearly knew he was out on a limb, as he added, 'I have to keep the President in constant touch and this is the delicate side.'[49] Although Churchill messaged Roosevelt on a regular basis, he preferred to discuss the presidential elections. 'Although I hear the most encouraging accounts from various quarters about United States politics,' wrote Churchill. 'I feel the suspense probably far more than you do…'[50]

Stalin knew that Churchill liked the finer things in life and laid on sumptuous banquets despite the austerity being experienced by wartime Moscow. 'Luncheon and dinner usually lasted two hours each,' noted Elizabeth Layton. 'Each meal would be of about ten courses.' One such repast included caviar, chicken, fish and pork dishes. All of which was washed down with copious quantities of cognac, vodka and wine. Marian Holmes, another of Churchill's secretaries, also recorded 'hospitality was amazing… caviar and vodka for breakfast… huge buffets… We were entirely spoiled.'[51] Churchill, who was not in the best of health, was regularly late to bed and as a consequence had a late start the following day.

As for Poland, the London Poles, much to Churchill's frustration, steadfastly refused to accept the adjustment of the frontiers. As a result, they became an irrelevance to the future of their country. Churchill riled against Prime Minister Stanislaw Mikolajczyk, the leader of the London Poles. 'You are no Government if you are incapable of taking any decisions,' snapped Churchill. He then threatened him, 'I don't know whether the British Government will continue to recognize you.'[52] This effectively meant that Churchill had abandoned Poland to Stalin. Churchill then unwisely criticised the Polish leadership with the Soviet leader. 'Where there were two Poles,' Churchill told Stalin, 'there was one quarrel.' Stalin found this amusing and responded, 'Where there was one Pole he would begin to quarrel with himself through sheer boredom.'[53]

A key sticking point for Mikolajczyk and his delegation was that they would not agree to the city of Lvov, just east of the Curzon Line, becoming Soviet. Churchill and Eden tried to persuade them that Poland would be territorially compensated at Germany's expense, but it did no good. In the end Churchill lost his patience. 'I will have nothing more to do with you,' he cried. 'I don't care where you go. You only deserve to be in your Pripet Marshes.'[54] Calming down he then offered to go to Stalin and ask if they could keep Lvov. This though was only on the condition that if Stalin said no, the London Poles would agree to the Curzon Line. Predictably they refused his offer. Churchill had desperately wanted them to power share to temper the Polish Communists, but Poland's future was sealed. The London Poles' position was completely undermined when Polish Communist leader Boleslaw Bierut informed Churchill and Stalin, 'We are here to demand on behalf of Poland that Lvov shall belong to Russia.'[55] 'The Poles' game is up,' Churchill despondently told Lord Moran, 'Neither side will give way.'[56] Poland was destined to become a Communist state along with the rest of Eastern Europe and most of the Balkans.

Churchill either genuinely believed he was making progress with Stalin or was simply putting a brave face on things. On 16 October he wrote to brief King George VI saying, 'The Prime Minister and Mr Eden in their various talks with Marshal Stalin and [Foreign Minister] M. Molotov have been able to deal with the most delicate problems in a frank, outspoken manner without the slightest sign of giving offence.'[57] Lord Moran noted how intransigent the Soviets were being. He commented to Churchill that morning, 'Russia would have things all her own way in Europe after the war.'[58] The Prime Minister considered this for a moment and then replied, 'Oh, I don't think so.' He seemed to think that the fate of Stalin would determine Europe's future. 'When this fellow goes you don't know what will happen,' added Churchill. 'There may be a lot of trouble.'[59] On 18 October the news reached Moscow that Soviet troops had pushed deep into Czechoslovakia; once again the city was treated to a firework display.

Churchill left Moscow the following day in high spirits. On his departure Stalin gave him a number of gifts, one of which was a vase depicting a 'Hunter with bow against a bear.' The symbolism of this could not be lost. 'There is some fable about some hunters going out to shoot a bear,' observed Field Marshal Brooke, 'who on the eve of the shoot became so busy arguing about the sale of the skin… they forgot to shoot the bear!'[60] Eden recalled more chillingly, 'I became more wary of the advantages the Soviets might seek in a weakened and divided continent.'[61] John Colville met Churchill at RAF Northholt three days later noting, 'He arrived, well and cheerful'.[62] Churchill felt it had been a fruitful trip and seemed blind to what he had done in regard to the futures of Albania, Bulgaria, Greece, Romania and Yugoslavia. He optimistically told his wife, 'We have settled a lot of things about the Balkans and prevented hosts of squabbles that were maturing.'[63]

Sir Alan Lascelles dined at 10 Downing Street on 23 October with some of Churchill's senior staff. Later he scribbled in his diary, 'Their verdict on "Tolstoy" (the code-name for the conference) was that it was 100 per cent successful, except for the Polish end of it, and even that was sixty per cent successful.'[64] Four days later Churchill informed the House of Commons that Britain and the Soviet Union 'have reached a very good working agreement about all these countries, singly and in combination, with the object… of providing, as far as possible, for a peaceful settlement after the war is over.'[65] On 31 October he touched on the matter again in the Commons. 'Immense successes have rewarded strenuous Russian military efforts,' he said, 'and skilful Russian and Allied diplomacy.'[66]

Churchill had been at pains not to discuss spheres of influence with Stalin, but he had done exactly that. As far as Stalin was concerned, he was one step closer to turning Eastern Europe and the Balkans into one big security buffer for the western Soviet Union. If he could install Communist governments that would be bastions of Soviet ideology then all the better. The seeds had been sown for the creation of the Iron Curtain and the Cold War and Churchill had played a major part in it. By this point the Red Army was about forty miles south of Budapest, though it was not until mid-February 1945 that the city was finally in Soviet hands.

Harry Hopkins cabled Churchill on 8 November 1944 to inform him that Roosevelt had won the US presidential elections for an unprecedented fourth term in office. The popular vote had been very close with 25 million to 22 million. However, in the Electoral College Roosevelt had defeated Dewey by 432 to just 99. Churchill sent a message of congratulations that said, 'It is an indescribable relief to me that our comradeship will continue and will help to bring the world out of misery.'[67]

Clearly Stalin had duped both Churchill and Eden. The latter, although tired from his long trip, dined with the King on 8 November. 'He was amusing about Moscow,' recalled Sir Alan Lascelles, 'and said that Stalin had promised Winston and himself that he had no intention of trying to "Communise" any country outside [the] USSR.'[68] It beggars belief that Churchill and Eden believed him. Lascelles added, 'He promised to send the King some of the spoils from Moscow – a tin of caviar and a bottle of vodka.'[69] The irony was that Stalin had ended up with all the spoils. Two days later Churchill wrote to Eden, 'At this time every country that is liberated or converted by our victories is seething with Communism. ... Only our influence with Russia prevents their actively stimulating this movement, deadly as I conceive it to peace and also to the freedom of mankind.'[70] Churchill clearly overestimated his influence. The Soviet leader was holding all the cards and when he next met Churchill and Roosevelt he continued to do so.

In late 1944 the Allies, largely as a pragmatic move, agreed that the Liberation Committee of Upper Italy should administer northern Italy once the Germans left until the arrival of the Allies.[71] The committee also agreed to hand Mussolini over to the Allies should they capture him. Secretly though, the Communists and Socialists decided to execute Mussolini without trial should he fall into their hands, which is exactly what happened the following year. Communist leaders Togliatti and Longo were also planning to launch an insurrection that would begin in Milan. Italian apathy towards the war would ensure this did not happen. There would be no popular rising.

Churchill remained very determined to save Greece. After the German withdrawal there was no strong central government in Athens. Various factions were vying for power. Harold Macmillan, Britain's Minister Resident in the Mediterranean, backed Archbishop Damaskinos becoming Regent in an effort to prevent the return of the divisive King George. Churchill and Eden arrived in Athens on Christmas Day and threw their support behind the Archbishop, which included the commitment of British troops to secure the Greek capital. Churchill left three days later and on 11 January 1945 a truce was secured between the Communist and royalist guerrillas. 'Greece's troubles were by no means over,' wrote Eden after their trip, 'but at least the Greek people would now have a chance to choose their destiny without fear.'[72]

Chapter 2

We Seemed to be Friends

By the time Churchill got to Yalta in the Crimea in February 1945 to meet with Roosevelt and Stalin, the fate of Poland, the rest of Eastern Europe and the Balkans was largely a done deal. Stalin knew exactly where he stood with Churchill and was little concerned about pleasing Roosevelt. Churchill still thought it was vital to try and sway Stalin towards the merits of holding elections in the liberated territories. He wanted the conference to last as long as possible so they could thrash out a firm agreement. Roosevelt, who was very ill by this stage, was not amenable to a prolonged meeting. This annoyed Churchill greatly. John Colville noted on 10 January 1945, 'He is disgusted that the President should want to spend only five or six days at the coming meeting between "the Big Three"'.[1]

In a state of irritation Churchill cabled Roosevelt, 'I do not see any other way of realizing our hopes about World Organization in five or six days. Even the Almighty took seven.'[2] The best the long suffering Roosevelt could do was agree to a preliminary get together with Churchill on Malta. The pair met on 2 February. 'My friend has arrived in best of health and spirits,' reported Churchill enthusiastically in a telegram to his wife that day.[3] 'It was quite obvious that he was a very sick man,' observed Churchill's daughter Sarah in contrast, 'His appearance gravely distressed my father and, indeed everyone.'[4]

Secretary Elizabeth Layton, who was part of Churchill's team, was indeed shocked by Roosevelt's appearance. 'He looked much aged,' she noted. 'This was even more apparent at closer quarters; he appeared frail and haggard.'[5] There was clearly no hiding Roosevelt's failing health. 'He seems to have lost so much weight,' observed another secretary, Marian Holmes, 'has dark circles under his eyes, looks altogether frail'.[6] Lord Moran was even more damning, 'I only give him a few months to live.'[7] The fate of the world was in the hands of three ailing men, as neither Churchill nor Stalin were in the best of health.

Churchill and Roosevelt met twice to discuss how they would handle Stalin. Anthony Eden, who was in attendance at lunch, reported, 'Pleasant but no business whatsoever done.' He adds that dinner 'was no more successful than the luncheon.'[8] A very vexed Eden confronted Harry Hopkins, 'pointing out that we... had so far neither agreed what we would discuss nor how to handle matters with a Bear who would certainly know his mind.'[9] Although Eden held talks with

US Secretary of State Edward Stettinius and Hopkins, nothing was settled. Eden, when the British and American delegations flew to Yalta early on 3 February, was concerned that there was a 'void' between them.[10] According to Sarah Churchill the British delegation felt that Roosevelt's frailness had brought an end to the 'easy understanding' that had existed between him and her father.[11]

Once again Stalin planned to ply his guests with the best food and finest wines that the Soviet Union could offer. Furthermore, they would be housed in luxurious former royal palaces. The only snag was that Saki airport near Simferopol where the British and American delegations landed was 80 miles from Yalta and the wrong side of the Tauride Mountains. Churchill was not in the best of moods when he arrived, having developed a very high temperature during the flight. Rendezvousing with Roosevelt at the airport he was dismayed by the President's condition. 'He was a tragic figure. You only had to look at the photographs,' said Churchill. 'He could not get out of the open car, and I walked at his side while he inspected the guard.'[12] Churchill was annoyed about the additional long journey they faced. 'This drive will waste a whole day and another precious one on the way back,' he grumbled loudly to his daughter.

Sarah Churchill was soon desperate for the toilet and was thankful when they stopped halfway through their journey to Yalta. 'We were led into a small room,' she recalled, 'groaning with food and wine and a smiling [Foreign Minister] Molotov.'[13] Unfortunately they had already stopped off for sandwiches and soup, so no one was really hungry except for Churchill. 'It is always the same,' said Lord Moran. 'Caviar, smoked salmon, suckling-pig and the rest, with their sweet champagne.'[14] The American delegation, no doubt because of the condition of Roosevelt, chose not to stop and sped on.

The long journey may have been a deliberate ploy so that the delegates could witness the terrible destruction the Germans had inflicted on the Crimea. This would help harden British and American attitudes when it came to dealing with post-war Germany. Harry Hopkins complained that 'we could not have found a worse place for a meeting if we had spent ten years looking for it.'[15] Churchill uncharitably characterised the region as the 'Riviera of Hades.'[16] 'At Yalta, the "Nice" of the Crimea, the whole of the sea-front had been burned down by the Germans,' recalled journalist Alexander Werth just after the liberation.[17]

The Crimea had been wrecked twice during the war. First during the German conquest in 1942 and again two years later when the Red Army liberated it. Churchill and Hopkins were right in sensing that this was an unhappy place. Not all the inhabitants had been pleased to see the return of Soviet rule. Stalin was determined to punish those who had collaborated with the occupation and this included the Muslim Crimean Tartars.[18] Alexander Werth, who toured the region, recalled 'the Tartars looked on, morose and scared.'[19] They had good reason to be. In all about 200,000 Tartar men, women and children were forcibly deported east immediately after the liberation. Stalin conducted a similar policy in the Caucasus. Rather than arrest the guilty he decided to hold entire races responsible. Some of the desolate villages Churchill and Roosevelt passed may have been a result of the deportation. There certainly seemed to be no shortage of soldiers in the Crimea. 'The whole hundred miles of road,' observed Sarah Churchill, 'was lined every two hundred yards with Red Army men and girls who sprang to salute.'[20] Most of the delegates preferred to enjoy their champagne and caviar rather than acknowledge they were being hosted by a police state.

The conference took place at the Livadia Palace. Roosevelt was housed there, while Churchill stayed at the Vorontsov Palace. 'Within were accommodated the Prime Minister, the Foreign Secretary, Field Marshals Alexander and Maitland-Wilson, the three Chiefs of Staff, General Ismay and various others,' said Elizabeth Layton.[21] The Soviet delegation took up residence at the Yusupov Palace. This policy helped Stalin to divide and rule the two western leaders, especially as both liked to see him separately. The palaces were empty and Stalin had furniture flown in from Moscow. The plumbing though was at best rudimentary; the Vorontsov Palace only had a single bathroom and three washbasins. The British and American delegations soon found that the palaces were rife with bedbugs. 'Despite these glamorous surroundings,' wrote Elizabeth Layton, 'this was the least enjoyable of the conferences I attended.[22]

On 4 February, the first day, Stalin drove to see Churchill at Vorontsov. 'We had the world at our feet,' said Churchill happily. 'Twenty-five million men marching at our orders by land and sea. We seemed to be friends.'[23] Churchill should have appreciated that Stalin would never forgive Germany and its Axis allies for the appalling destruction wrought on the Soviet Union. 'We have already lost four million soldiers...' Stalin told Churchill, 'and the war is not yet won.'[24] Field Marshal Alexander was flabbergasted by this and later asked the War Office to check the figure. 'Anything up to four and a half million,' came the reply.[25] Stalin also saw Roosevelt separately, who rather worryingly told him 'the British were a peculiar people and wished to have their cake and eat it too.'[26] This immediately signalled to Stalin that Britain and America were not in accord. 'Winston is puzzled and distressed,' said Lord Moran. 'The President no longer seems to the PM to take an intelligent interest in the war.'[27]

The opening sessions of the conference were largely concerned with the progress of the war on both the Eastern and Western Fronts. Then the dismemberment of Germany was discussed, including granting France an occupation zone in Germany along with the 'Big Three.' This could be created by dividing up part of the British and American zones. However, both Roosevelt and Stalin were not keen on inviting France to become part of the Allied Control Commission for Germany. Roosevelt had no time for de Gaulle, who he felt was a potential dictator, and Stalin felt the French did not deserve a place at the table.

Stalin wanted massive war reparations from Germany. Churchill was averse to this realising, that the deprivations of the Versailles Treaty following the First World War had fostered deep resentment that helped bring Hitler and the Nazis to power. Roosevelt dropped a bomb shell when he announced the 'United States would take all reasonable steps to preserve peace, but not at the expense of keeping a large army indefinitely in Europe... That was why the American occupation was limited to two years.'[28] As far as Roosevelt was concerned America did not have an open cheque book to ensure European security. Not unreasonably he felt it was time for Europe to accept responsibility for keeping the peace. This panicked Churchill because he felt the French were incapable of shouldering the burden of protecting western Europe alone, which meant Britain would have to maintain a field army on the continent, potentially permanently.

Roosevelt on the issue of Poland supported the Curzon Line, though felt the Poles should keep Lvov. There was also much discussion about Poland's revised western border. Churchill though was not so much concerned about the frontiers as a guarantee of free elections. Britain and France had after all gone to war in support of Poland, so it was vital that Britain at least saved face politically. 'To Britain, Poland is a question of honour,' agreed Stalin, 'to the Soviet Union it is a question of both honour and security.'[29] Stalin pointed out that the Lublin government had as much legitimacy as General de Gaulle's government did in Paris, much to Roosevelt's displeasure who felt the latter lacked Allied approval. The Soviets were now calling it the Polish Provisional Government and it was in power in Warsaw.

Churchill did all he could to argue for the inclusion of the London Poles, but it did little good. He sent his Labour Deputy Prime Minister Clement Attlee a message saying, 'We are having a hard time here. Poland will be very difficult.'[30] US Secretary of State Stettinius was well aware that it would be almost impossible to squeeze any concessions from Stalin. 'As a result of the military situation,' he astutely observed, 'it was not a question of what Great Britain and the United States would permit Russia to do in Poland, but what the two countries could persuade the Soviet Union to accept.'[31] This would essentially be nothing.

Furthermore, Britain and America, still fighting the Japanese in the Far East and the Pacific, needed to keep Stalin onboard with his promise that once Germany was defeated he would declare war on Japan. This inevitably would make Japan's position untenable in Manchuria and northern China. In order to get Stalin's military assistance Roosevelt was prepared to let things slide over Poland. He was also prepared to give away Japanese territory. In a secret session with Stalin on 8 February he agreed Stalin could have the southern half of Sakhalin island off the east coast of Siberia, the Kuril Islands, the port of Dalian and Port Arthur in return for attacking Manchuria. This would give the Soviet Union complete control of the Sea of Okhotsk and a sizeable foothold in the Yellow Sea. A written agreement was made without consulting the Chinese Nationalist leader Chiang Kai-shek. William Bullitt, the former US Ambassador to the Soviet Union, declared scathingly, 'No more unnecessary, disgraceful and potentially disastrous document has ever been signed by a President of the United States.'[32]

This had serious ramifications. Stalin would undoubtedly back Chinese Communist leader Mao Zedong once Mao's alliance with Chiang against the Japanese came to an end. If the Red Army took Japanese-occupied Manchuria and northern China then Stalin could easily hand these areas over to Mao's forces. 'Molotov told General Patrick Hurley,' noted Stettinius, 'that the Soviet Union was not interested in the Chinese Communists; these weren't really Communists anyway.'[33] It seemed hard to countenance that Stalin would not want a Communist ally in Asia to counter American and British influence post-war.

On the night of 8 February, during dinner at the Yusupov Palace, Churchill warned, 'We now have a chance of avoiding the errors of previous generations, and making a sure peace.'[34] Field Marshal Brooke, who was attending the various

15

chiefs of staffs' meetings, found the event interminable and boring. He was trapped between General Aleksei Antonov, who could not speak English, and Harriman, who he disliked immensely. The constant toasts meant that the food was cold by the time they got to it. 'Stalin was in very best of form,' recalled Brooke, 'and was full of fun and good humour'.[35] The highlight of the trip for Brooke was being able to tour the old Crimean War battlefields, especially Balaclava, scene of the infamous Charge of the Light Brigade.

The following day Stalin agreed that British and American observers could witness the proposed elections in Poland.[36] However, he rejected Churchill's call for a three-power commission to monitor Polish voting. 'The Poles are an independent people,' insisted Stalin, 'and they would not want to have their elections supervised by outsiders.'[37] He also agreed that Stanislaw Mikolajczyk and his supporters could take part. Likewise, Stalin gave assurances that he would persuade Tito, the Yugoslav Communist leader, to hold free elections open to all political parties. In return Churchill agreed to repatriate all Soviet prisoners taken by British forces who had been fighting for the Germans. Stalin secretly planned to exterminate all those who had hoped to gain independence from the Soviet Union, especially the Cossacks and Ukrainian nationalists serving with the German Army and the Waffen-SS.

This agreement was one of the more shameful episodes of Yalta. The Allies though were reliant on Soviet goodwill to help repatriate around 125,000 British and American prisoners of war previously held by the Germans. Britain and America handled Soviet prisoners taken in Europe differently and as a result the issue was largely a British one. To the north the British 21st Army Group, until September 1944, sent Soviet prisoners to camps in Britain. The US 12th Army Group fighting in the centre held them in liberated France while the US 6th Army Group to the south had sent them to British camps in North Africa. The Americans did not initially distinguish between the 21,000 Soviet prisoners held in France from the German ones, as they were all in the same uniform. The Americans, knowing they needed to do something with them, signed up to repatriation.

'The atmosphere was very friendly and informal,' recalled British diplomat Pierson Dixon on the afternoon of 10 February. 'In the middle of the meeting A[nthony] E[den] and Molotov broke off to sign the Prisoners of War Agreement, which had been concluded only a few minutes before.'[38] The following day in London, Attlee, chairing the War Cabinet, approved it. At the end of the war over a million Soviet citizens would be forcibly repatriated by the British whether they wanted to go or not. Regarded as traitors to Mother Russia, the Gulag or firing squad awaited all of them.

Throughout much of the conference Roosevelt was distant and unfocused. His mental faculties were waning and it was cruel to drag him all the way to the Crimea. The truth was that he was often almost comatose but his senior staff could not admit he was no longer up to the job. Besides, Roosevelt like Churchill did not want to miss out on the action on the international stage. For him perhaps he hoped that this might be his last hurrah. Nonetheless, his chain of thought was often all over the place. 'The president is behaving very badly,' Churchill complained to Lord Moran on the morning of 11 February. 'He won't take any interest in what we are trying to do.'[39] Eden was of a similar view, noting, 'I do not believe that the President's declining health altered his judgement, though his handling of the Conference was less sure than it might have been.'[40] Roosevelt tried to put a brave face on things when he wrote to his wife Eleanor on 12 February, 'I am a bit exhausted but really all right.'[41]

Churchill knew that his friend and closest ally was seriously ill but seemed to make no concessions. He later acknowledged, 'at Yalta I noticed that the President was ailing. His captivating smile, his gay and charming manner, had not deserted him, but his face had a transparency... and often there was a faraway look in his eyes.'[42] Churchill was very rattled by Roosevelt's lack of support over Poland, and talk of appointing custodians for the world's colonies. Churchill assumed that the latter was a reference to the British Empire and was furious. 'It was plain at Moscow, last October,' noted Lord Moran, 'that Stalin means to make Poland a Cossack outpost of Russia, and I am sure he has not altered his intention here.'[43]

For public consumption and the history books, Churchill, Roosevelt, and Stalin agreed to the 'Declaration on Liberated Europe.' This pledged to help the freed countries of Europe 'to solve by democratic means their pressing political and economic problems.'[44] This was in keeping with Churchill and Roosevelt's 1941 Atlantic Charter which recognised the right to self-determination. 'This too, though admirable in intention,' remarked Anthony Eden, 'was soon to be denied by Soviet action.'[45] Stalin was happy with it as long as Communist governments were 'voted' into power. In the case of Poland they were already in place and disinclined to cooperate with the other parties. On 14 February Churchill left the Crimea. 'The end of Yalta told him,' wrote Sarah Churchill sadly, 'that free men would once again be enslaved by obtuse and interminable recriminations and by the rise of a new tyranny.'[46]

Initially the response in America was good. Eleanor Roosevelt reported to her husband, 'We seem to be almost united as a country in approval of the results of the Conference.' Then she added with delight, 'All the world looks smiling!'[47] John Colville in London concluded that Britain had got everything it wanted at Yalta. 'We seem to have won most of our points,' he observed rather optimistically, 'and the PM has won another great personal success. He was tireless in pressing for this conference, in spite of Roosevelt's apathy, and deserved most of the credit for what has been achieved.'[48]

In contrast King George VI found the reports from Yalta highly confusing. 'I find in my daily reading of Cabinet papers and Foreign Office telegrams, besides the daily papers (Press),' he wrote in his diary, 'that it is almost impossible to keep a clear mind....' He then added with an air of pessimism, 'These negotiations are the foundations of the future peace of the World and will they ever be ratified.'[49] Sarah Churchill observed, 'At that time no one knew that Stalin was falsifying his promises.'[50] Roosevelt soon realised that he had been fooled. 'Though Franklin had felt confident of being able to work with Stalin when he left Yalta,' wrote Eleanor Roosevelt, 'not long after he got home he began to feel that the marshal was not keeping his promises.'[51]

The fear of Communism in the Mediterranean was not very far from British minds. On the way home Churchill and Eden stopped off in Athens and saw

Regent Archbishop Damaskinos and Harold Macmillan, British Minister Resident in the Mediterranean. Macmillan had helped negotiate the truce that ensured a pro-British government remained in power. Although the Greek civil war was very far from over, Stalin surprisingly honoured Churchill's percentages agreement. Churchill was mobbed by 50,000 Greeks in Constitution Square. 'One American journalist described it later as like a pre-war Hitler demonstration, which it certainly was not,' said Eden.[52] The festive mood of the crowd put Macmillan in mind of 'a football match, or a race meeting in peace-time'.[53] Churchill was just grateful that progress was being made to keep the Communists from taking over. 'Let party hatreds die. Let there be unity,' he told the gathered masses. 'Let there be resolute comradeship. Greece for ever! Greece for all!'[54]

While in Athens, Eden and Macmillan's conversation, after discussing the situation in Greece, turned to the Italians who wanted Allied status and increased financial assistance. 'Italy is a British interest, in the sense that we do not want to see an important Mediterranean power in dissolution or in a state of permanent revolution,' Macmillan told Eden. 'We do not want to see Italy break up and/ or "go Communist"'.[55] This was something that both Eden and Churchill were in agreement on. Everything had to be done to ensure the Communists did not take power in Italy. For the Allies and the Italian government, it would be vital to reassert control of northern Italy once Germany was defeated to prevent the Communists from creating a power base there.

Regardless of what Stalin had said at Yalta, at the end of February he orchestrated a coup in Romania that resulted in a Communist government taking power. Stalin ordered King Michael to replace pro-Western General Nicolae Radescu with the pro-Soviet Petru Groza. Radescu, fearful for his life, took shelter in the British legation. When the Foreign Office moved to lodge a strong formal complaint Churchill stopped them, arguing 'We really have no justification for intervening in this extraordinarily vigorous manner for our late Romanian enemies thus compromising our position in Poland and jarring Russian acquiescence in our long fight for Athens.'[56] He later took the same position with Bulgaria and refrained from protesting about the imprisonment of fifteen Polish leaders in Moscow at the end of the war. 'In Romania, the Romanian Government started off well, and Michael was praised after their liberation,' King George VI noted in his diary. 'Now orders from Moscow have come to work up agitation against them and to form a minority Communist government.'[57]

The King, in light of his Prime Minister being such an ardent royalist, was dismayed by Churchill's stance over Romania. 'Poor Michael and his mother Zitta [Queen Helen] in Romania have been having a very worrying time from the Russians...,' he wrote to Queen Mary. 'I feel so differently towards them, than the attitude taken up by the Government. The latter say Romania was an enemy and is now in the Russian sphere.'[58] Roosevelt, likewise, decided it was inappropriate to complain about Soviet dealings with Romania as the Red Army's lines of communication ran through the country. In other words, their actions were justified.

In London Churchill's dealings at Yalta did not go unopposed. In a vote in the House of Commons at the end of February twenty-five Members of Parliament voted against the Curzon Line as Poland's new eastern border. Thirty other MPs refused to vote. Churchill knew that thanks to his percentages agreement with Stalin in October 1944, and British military intervention in Greece, he could hardly complain about Soviet actions in Romania. 'This again would lead to comparisons between the aims of his actions and those of ours,' Churchill warned Roosevelt. 'On this neither side would convince the other. Having regard to my personal relations with Stalin, I am sure it would be a mistake for me at this stage to embark on the argument.'[59] Churchill still seemed to believe he could trust Stalin and evidently did not want to back him into a corner. He admitted to Roosevelt that it might be seen 'that you and I by putting our signatures to the Crimea settlement have under-written a fraudulent prospectus.'[60] Churchill appreciated that in the face of a divided Germany and the creation of a Soviet bloc Britain and America could hardly leave France to defend western Europe alone. Roosevelt though had made it clear he did not want American troops lingering in Europe once Germany was defeated.

Sadly, Roosevelt lost the battle with his failing health on 12 April 1945. 'President Roosevelt died in the afternoon,' John Colville recorded in his diary. 'The news did not reach the PM till midnight, but I gather he was very distressed.'[61] 'I have just heard the grievous news of President Roosevelt's death,' said Churchill in a telegram to his wife the following day.[62] Clementine was touring the Soviet Union but managed to briefly talk to her husband by telephone from the British Embassy in Moscow. 'He was a staunch friend of the country,' wrote King George VI, 'and Winston will feel his loss most of all in his dealings with Stalin.'[63] These were to prove prophetic words.

Roosevelt's death was a deep blow to Churchill, though his close relationship with the US president had been waning as Britain and America's post-war policies began to rapidly diverge. Vice President Harry Truman immediately assumed the office of President. Anthony Eden attended Roosevelt's funeral in Washington on 14 April as Churchill's representative. Churchill had intended to go but at the last moment changed his mind. Eden was slightly alarmed to learn from Harry Hopkins that Truman 'knows absolutely nothing of world affairs'.[64] Eden also attended the groundbreaking San Francisco Conference, which led to the United Nations Charter and the creation of the United Nations.

Subsequently, after the euphoria over Hitler's suicide on 30 April 1945 and Germany's unconditional surrender eight days later subsided, the reality of rebuilding the defeated country and ending the war with Japan began to sink in. Although Churchill had successfully led Britain to victory over Nazi Germany, he continued to fret about the spread of Communism in Europe. Even before the war ended *The Times* newspaper picked up on a broadcast by the German Foreign Minister in which he warned, 'In the East the iron curtain... is steadily moving forward.'[65]

Churchill sent Truman a telegram on 12 May 1945 outlining his concerns, especially as the American, British and Canadian armies on the continent would soon start to draw down their strength. 'I have always worked for friendship with Russia, but like you,' said Churchill, 'I feel deep anxiety because of their misinterpretation of the Yalta decisions, their attitude towards Poland, their overwhelming influence in the Balkans... and above all their power to maintain very large armies in the field for a long time.'[66] Churchill went on to ruminate about what would happen in the next few years if the French did not step up. Turning back to the Soviet Union he added, 'An iron curtain is drawn down upon their front. We do not know what is going on behind.'[67] He then urged that they should meet with Stalin as soon as possible.

That same day Truman pointed out that Tito had occupied territory in Carinthia and Venezia Giulia in northeastern Italy. This meant Britain and America had to decide whether they should permit their Yugoslav ally to indulge in land grabs. His view was that Field Marshal Alexander should move to fully secure the Italian port of Trieste to head off Tito's claim on the city. 'Truman, full of bellicose views and ready to be rough with Tito,' wrote Field Marshal Brooke. 'Winston delighted, he gives me the feeling of already longing for another war!'[68] Harold Macmillan felt 'the Americans gave us full support with great humour, although with sometimes embarrassing zeal.'[69]

Previously Alexander, once through the Po Valley in Italy, hoped to strike northeast through the Ljubljana Gap to reach Vienna and forestall the Red Army. To achieve this, he needed Trieste as a base of operations. However, Tito's Communist partisans beat General Freyberg's New Zealand Division to it, arriving in the city on 30 April. Churchill was furious the Communists had got there first and made no secret of it. That day Field Marshal Brooke recorded in his diary, 'An unpleasant Cabinet with Winston in a bad mood. In spite of the fact that Alex had made the greatest advance he had yet brought off, he was abused for not having taken Trieste!'[70]

Although Freyberg entered Trieste two days later, took the surrender of the German garrison and secured the docks, there remained the thorny issue of the presence of Tito's men. Following Germany's surrender the Allies no longer needed Trieste, but were not happy leaving it under Tito's control.[71] Churchill knew the situation needed to be handled sensitively or Britain could find itself at war with Yugoslavia. Nonetheless, he agreed with Truman that it would be unwise to allow Tito to get his own way. The worry was that Stalin would take ownership of Trieste as a measure of the Allies' resolve. The loss of Trieste would also be a future source of friction between Italy and Yugoslavia.

Nonetheless Truman, realising that getting 'rough' with Tito might involve the Red Army, sent Churchill a telegram cautioning he 'could not dream of asking America to start hostilities unless the Yugoslavs attacked first.'[72] It is important to appreciate that the partisans who arrived at Trieste were not some sort of rag-tag guerrilla organisation. By this stage Tito had 800,000 battle-hardened, uniformed men under arms, organised into four armies with seventeen corps controlling over fifty divisions. Picking a fight with such a force would have quickly led to extensive bloodshed.

Churchill held Stalin directly responsible for the situation at Trieste and wanted him to know it. He launched into a tirade while lunching with Feodor Gusev, the Soviet Ambassador, at Downing Street on 18 May. Churchill wanted the 'Big Three' to meet again and warned, 'either we shall achieve an agreement on future cooperation between our three nations, or the Anglo-American community will become united in opposition to the Soviet Union.'[73] Gusev sat slack-jawed at this apparent threat. Churchill though was only warming up, saying, 'We are full of grievances.'[74] When Gusev enquired what these were, top of Churchill's list was Trieste, this was followed by the Soviet refusal to allow the Allies into Berlin, Prague and Vienna. Then to Gusev's further surprise Churchill announced, 'I have ordered the demobilization of the Royal Air Force should be delayed.'[75] When Gusev reported this meeting to Moscow he added, 'Churchill was extraordinarily angry, and seemed to be making an effort to keep himself under control.'[76]

It was clear Churchill had helped create a monster when Tito began demanding the repatriation of fighters from the Serbian Chetniks and the Croatian Ustasha who had escaped to Italy and Austria. Tito saw them as traitors and enemies of the state. Although both organisations stood accused of collaborating with the Axis to differing degrees, they were also virulently anti-Communist. This had fuelled their hatred of Tito's forces and led to civil war during the occupation. Tito was particular keen to get his hands on Dragoljub Mihailović the Chetnik leader, who presented a potential threat to Communist rule.

Churchill was to attend one last conference as a member of the 'Big Three', but beforehand he faced a general election on 5 July 1945 that would bring an end to his wartime coalition government. He had promised Attlee an election once Germany was defeated. The count had to be delayed three weeks while the ballot papers from the British armed forces were flown back to Britain. In the interim the country was run by a Conservative caretaker government. Whilst out electioneering Churchill unwisely likened Socialism to the Gestapo, an intended slur against the Labour party that won him no friends. Furthermore, service personnel were ready for a change when they came home. 'Many who voted Labour had the impression that they could vote Labour and still have Winston Churchill,' wrote Sarah Churchill. 'This they were to learn was not to be so.'[77]

Interestingly not all Labour politicians thought the election should have been held then. Ernest Bevin, who served as Minister of Labour in the Coalition government, made his feelings on the matter perfectly clear to Conservative peer Lord Butler, who briefly took over from him before the election. 'Churchill ought not to have broken up the Cabinet coalition,' Bevin told him crossly, 'He should have run at any rate till the end of the Japanese war and then we would not be in this position.'[78]

While still awaiting the results, Churchill got together with Truman and Stalin to thrash out the final details of post-war Europe at Potsdam to the southwest of Berlin on 17 July. He took Clement Attlee with him, knowing full well that Attlee might shortly be the new Prime Minister. Churchill and Truman met for the first time the day before. 'I called on him the morning after our arrival,' Churchill later wrote, 'and was impressed with his gay, precise, speaking manner and obvious power of decision.'[79] Mary Churchill wrote to her mother reaffirming her father's impressions, 'He told me he liked the President immensely… He says he is sure he can work with him.'[80] Churchill was in part buoyed by the news that the first American atomic bomb had been detonated at Alamogordo in New Mexico. 'Everything has opened well so far,' said Churchill in a telegram to his wife, 'but of course we have not reached any of the serious issues.'[81]

Top of the agenda though was the division of Germany as well as the unconditional surrender of Japan. Churchill had not given up on the Poles and informed Stalin and Truman that he attached 'great importance to the early holding of free elections in Poland which would truly reflect the wishes of the Polish people.'[82] Churchill brought up the vexed subject of Yugoslavia, claiming it was now 99-1 against Britain. Stalin countered, arguing it was 90 per cent Britain and 10 per cent Yugoslavian with nothing for the Soviet Union. He added, 'The Soviet Government often did not know what Marshal Tito was about to do.'[83] Stalin also complained that America had no right to call for a change of governments in Bulgaria and Romania when he had stuck to his agreement with Churchill not to interfere in Greece. Under pressure from the Soviets, in early 1945 King Michael of Romania had established a National Democratic Front government made up of agrarians and Communists. In two years' time the king would be forced to abdicate.

When Churchill and Stalin discussed troop numbers in Greece and Bulgaria, it was revealed that British forces protecting Athens numbered 40,000 while the Soviets claimed to have 30,000 men in Bulgaria. Stalin reassured Churchill that he was demobilising two million men in Europe who would be sent home in the next four months. Churchill complained that Britain and America had been obstructed moving into their allotted occupation zones in Austria and Vienna. Stalin reassured him that there was no problem.

Churchill and Truman on 22 July privately discussed the results of America's atomic bomb tests. They now had the means of shocking Japan into surrender rather than having to conduct a costly invasion of the Japanese mainland. 'It was decided that we must drop an atom bomb on Japan,' noted Anthony Eden, 'if she did not accept unconditional surrender.'[84] The following day Field Marshal Brooke was alarmed by Churchill's enthusiasm for the bomb after he claimed, 'The secret of this explosive, and the power to use it, would completely alter the diplomatic equilibrium which was adrift since the defeat of Germany!'[85] Churchill felt they would not need the Soviet Union's help to defeat Japan and that Moscow would not be in a position to continue getting its own way. Brooke was further aghast when Churchill added, 'We can just blot out Moscow....'[86]

After some discussion it was decided Truman should tell Stalin of the existence of the bomb. Senior Soviet commander Marshal Georgi Zhukov, who was present at Potsdam, recalled, 'Stalin did not betray his feelings and pretended he saw nothing special in what Truman had said.'[87] Later when Molotov was told he remarked, 'They are trying to bid up.'[88] To which Stalin laughed. His secret response was to speed up his own atomic weapons programme. The 'Big Three' subsequently, while smiling for the cameras, drafted a message calling on Japan to surrender or face destruction.

News reached Churchill when he returned to London on 26 July that Attlee and the Labour party had won a landslide victory in the election. 'That evening Churchill resigned and the King sent for Attlee,' said John Colville. 'There was world stupefaction, not least at Potsdam, where Stalin supposed that Churchill would have "fixed" the results.'[89] Stalin and Truman expected Churchill back at the talks within twenty-four hours. Both had not anticipated the British electorate would reject him after leading them to victory over Germany. 'I saw Winston at 7pm and it was a very sad meeting,' recalled the King. 'He was very calm and said that with the majority the Socialists had got over the other parties (153) and with careful management they could remain in power for years.'[90] Attlee would now take the lead for the last few days of the Potsdam conference. 'Roosevelt dead, Germany beaten, Churchill out,' said Elizabeth Layton, 'how swiftly things change.'[91] On 31 July the King wrote to Churchill to thank him for his wartime leadership as both prime minister and minister of defence. 'For myself personally,' he concluded, 'I regret what has happened more than perhaps anyone else. I shall miss your counsel to me more than I can say.'[92]

Despite all the haggling Churchill failed to win any concessions over Poland at Potsdam. Marshal Zhukov wrote in his memoirs, 'I must say that Stalin was extremely scrupulous with regard to the slightest attempt by the US and British delegations to take decisions to the detriment of Poland, Czechoslovakia, Hungary and the German people.'[93] What he really meant was detriment to Soviet interests. Indeed, the crumbs that Churchill, Attlee and Truman got from the table were paltry. Stalin agreed Britain and America could move into their allotted zones in Austria and Vienna. All three allies agreed to withdraw their troops from Iran, which had been protecting Soviet wartime supply lines. It was also agreed to respect Turkey's eastern border after Stalin had started making territorial claims.

Churchill was severely disappointed he was unable to return to the conference and try to influence events. 'After I left Potsdam, Joe [Stalin] did what he liked,' lamented Churchill to Lord Moran. 'The Russians' western frontier was allowed to advance, displacing another eight million people. I'd not have agreed and the Americans would have backed me.'[94] The Soviets though were not happy that they would have to share control of Berlin and Vienna. Each would be divided into four sectors. 'The Potsdam decision was a compromise based on the distribution of power among the Allies at the end of the war,' grumbled Nikita Khrushchev.[95] It was to prove a source of friction.

Chapter 3

Harbinger of Doom

On 6 August 1945 the first American atomic bomb was dropped on the Japanese city of Hiroshima. 'The 9 o'clock news announces that we had split the atom,' noted Harold Nicolson, a former diplomat and Member of Parliament. 'A long statement, drafted by Winston, is read, ... They cannot tell exactly what damage was done.'[1] When the Japanese surrender was not forthcoming three days later a second bomb was dropped on Nagasaki. 'Without any military need whatsoever,' claimed Marshal Zhukov.[2] Field Marshal Montgomery agreed with him, 'In my view it was unnecessary to drop two atomic bombs... The Japanese had already been defeated by conventional weapons.'[3]

Stalin honoured his agreement with the Allies to join the war against Japan on 9 August. The Red Army stormed into Manchuria, parts of Inner Mongolia and northern China and Korea, employing a massive pincer offensive covering an area the size of western Europe.[4] In a case of understatement Field Marshal Brooke noted in his diary, 'A memorable day as regards the war with Japan.'[5] The ill-equipped Japanese and puppet Chinese Manchukuo armies were outclassed and swiftly overrun.[6] Soviet forces in Korea were to stop at the 38th Parallel cutting the country in half.

The Japanese, completely dazed by the atomic bombs and the enormous size of the Soviet assault, initially signalled their intention to accept the terms of the Potsdam Declaration on 10 August. That day Churchill wrote optimistically to Prime Minister Attlee, 'It may well be that events will bring the Japanese War to an early close.'[7] Attlee immediately responded, 'I will let you know as soon as I have news.'[8] He kindly went on to say that this was a crowning moment for Churchill. Five days later Japanese Emperor Hirohito in a radio broadcast announced to his nation acceptance of Potsdam, though he did not actually use the word surrender. King George VI on 15 August opened his first peace-time Parliament since 1938. He also saw Churchill that day. 'I wish he could have been given a proper reception by the people,' wrote the King in his diary with an air of sadness.[9] That evening Churchill and a few of his former colleagues dined at Claridge's in London. 'Dinner was something of an unreality to me,' said Anthony Eden, 'because it seemed so strange that Churchill was not at the centre of the national celebration instead of dining apart, in an hotel.'[10]

The Emperor's statement caused widespread confusion as to whether Japan had capitulated or not, and Japanese forces in China and Korea did not observe the ceasefire until 20 August. Japan formally surrendered on 2 September, finally bringing the Second World War to an end. Six days later American forces landed at Incheon to take control of southern Korea from the Japanese. Victory over Japan had serious ramifications. While Stalin's invasion of Manchuria may have hastened the Japanese surrender, it predictably did not bode well for China's nationalists. When the Red Army eventually withdrew it meant the region would become a base for Mao Zedong's Communists. Furthermore, those troops captured from the Manchukuo army were pressed into the service of Mao. It also meant Mao would have access to Soviet arms for his renewed war against Chiang Kai-shek's Nationalists. China was about to be plunged back into widespread civil war with the prospect of it being taken over by Mao. Such a victory would encourage the Communists in North Korea who would be emboldened to reunite their divided country.

Despite the triumph over Japan, understandably Churchill was upset that he had been cast aside by his country. 'The election result was a body blow to Winston,' wrote Mary his daughter. 'Although on and off in the weeks succeeding Polling Day he envisaged the possibility of defeat, optimism had on the whole prevailed.'[11] Afterwards Churchill told Lord Moran, 'It's no use, Charles, pretending I'm not hard hit.'[12] To recuperate he went on holiday to Italy in September 1945 as a guest of Field Marshal Alexander, and then to Paris as a guest of the British Ambassador to France. Although he was voted out of office, he remained a Member of Parliament and the leader of the Conservative party. This meant he was now head of the Opposition in the House of Commons, which gave him a continued political platform.

However, amongst his own party he was not universally popular. Whilst he was away there was muttering amongst the younger Conservative back benchers that they wanted change. 'They feel that Winston is too old and Anthony [Eden] too weak,' wrote Harold Nicolson in his diary on 16 September. 'They want Harold Macmillan to lead them.'[13] To compound matters Churchill showed little interest in domestic politics as his real passion remained the international arena.[14] He was alert to the growing menace posed by the Soviet Union in both Europe and Asia and planned to be vocal about it. For Prime Minister Attlee's new Labour government trying to build bridges, this would prove highly embarrassing.

Despite his crushing electoral defeat and the end of war Churchill could not resist keeping out of the global limelight for long. Wherever he went he was given a hero's welcome. A prime opportunity to grandstand occurred with the unexpected arrival of an invitation from the president of Westminster College, Fulton, Missouri dated 3 October 1945. It stated, 'This letter is to invite you to deliver the Green Lectures... We should be glad to arrange the date or dates to suit your convenience.' What caught Churchill's eye was a personal handwritten endorsement by President Truman on it. 'This is a wonderful school in my home state,' said Truman. 'Hope you can do it. I'll introduce you.'[15] The pair had not seen each other since Potsdam. Churchill, who loved to travel and be on the public stage, readily accepted. This greatly pleased Mary Churchill. 'Lord Moran had recommended that Winston was better out of England during the bleakest months,' she wrote, 'for the threat of pneumonia always lurked.'[16]

First though he was off to France. Churchill, while in Paris giving a talk at the French Institute, dined with General Charles de Gaulle on 13 November 1945.

He found the former Free French leader was struggling to form a functioning government from the squabbling left- and right-wing political factions. Although Churchill had championed the Free French cause during the war, he and de Gaulle were old sparring partners. De Gaulle had been furious with Churchill for not inviting him to the Yalta and Potsdam conferences. Nonetheless, it was largely thanks to Churchill that France had been granted an occupation zone in Germany as well as a permanent seat, with America, Britain, China and Russia, on the Security Council of the newly-founded United Nations. In light of France's small role in the Allied victory this was not a bad achievement.

Towards the end of the war de Gaulle grandly proposed Britain and France form a European bloc between America and the Soviet Union. Although Churchill had been sympathetic, he was not prepared to do anything that would upset America, especially as Roosevelt detested de Gaulle. By the end of 1945 de Gaulle was still advocating a western European bloc to balance the two new superpowers but without British participation. This struck a cord with Churchill who was formulating a similar idea.

De Gaulle though, like Churchill, was no longer really wanted as a leader now that the war was over. Although the liberator of Paris, many felt that this soldier turned politician was not the man to run their country. In France, as in Britain, there was a swing to the political left. De Gaulle was facing a Communist threat at home and in French Indochina. In the October 1945 French general elections the Left-wing parties swept the country, with the Communists and Socialists gaining the majority of the seats. Although de Gaulle was elected President the day after he met with Churchill, exhausted by the intriguing and political infighting he ended up resigning on 20 January 1946. It would be twelve years before he returned to the presidency. Churchill feared that France's Communist and Socialist parties would continue to obstruct increasing the French defence budget, preferring to spend money on civil reconstruction. If that happened France could not take a leading role in protecting Europe from the Soviet Union.

The reality was that the French armed forces had been in a state of disarray ever since the German invasion. Following the Allied landings in northern and southern France in the summer of 1944, de Gaulle had swiftly recruited the French resistance into his ranks. He did this in part because he knew a large element of the resistance consisted of Communists and he did not want them free to destabilise the state or take power. The Communist press had been swift to denounce him as a Fascist, thereby confirming Roosevelt's suspicions. The result was that his forces were expanded way too quickly and lacked adequate equipment and training. In consequence, apart from a few veteran colonial divisions, French troops struggled to prevail over the battle-hardened Germans. Creating a new metropolitan army proved an enormous and costly task.[17] Furthermore, at the end of the war French resources were to be stretched by the Viet Minh Communist nationalists fighting for independence in Indochina. Under such circumstances it is easy to see why de Gaulle soon gave up trying to make sense of it all without resorting to becoming a dictator.

Churchill, just three days after seeing de Gaulle, was in Brussels addressing a joint session of the Belgian Senate and Chamber. 'Presents of all kinds began to pour into the Embassy long before his arrival,' recalled British Ambassador Sir Hughe

Knatchbull-Hugessen with amusement.[18] Amongst them were models of Snow White and the Seven Dwarfs made of marzipan. Brussels and Louvain universities also awarded him honorary degrees. He was met by cheering crowds as his car drove through the streets, with well-wishers slipping past the motor-cycle escort to throw flowers into the vehicle. Alarmingly others jumped forward to touch or even kiss him. Acknowledging their adoration he stood in the back of the open top limousine waving back with a grin upon his face. 'Teeming crowds thronged the streets of Brussels and Antwerp,' said Mary Churchill, 'and lined the roadside between the cities.'[19] Churchill concluded his speech with a call for a United States of Europe, a concept he would soon return to. Invoking history, he claimed this could unify the continent in a manner unknown since the days of the Roman Empire.

Churchill decided his speech at Fulton would be called 'The Sinews of Peace' and its central theme the spread of Communism and how to deal with it. This would become world famous as the 'Iron Curtain' speech. Beforehand, in January 1946, he and Clementine sailed for New York and then took the train to Miami Beach to stay with a Canadian friend Colonel Frank Clarke, who he had met during the 1943 Quebec conference. After the conference Churchill and Clementine had stayed at Clarke's fishing lodge on the shores of Lac des Neiges in the Laurentian Mountains. In Miami Beach Churchill set about enjoying the weather and painting, though he and Clementine found it a bit too warm after chilly Britain.

Churchill's secretary Jo Sturdee, who accompanied him, noted on the voyage out that he had not started work on his Fulton speech or indeed his extensive war memoirs. Sturdee, once in Miami, despite help from Colonel Clarke's secretary Lorraine Bonar, found herself inundated with Churchill's fan mail. Although he was on holiday and officially had no recourse to public resources, staff were despatched by the British Consul in Miami, the Consul General in New York and the British Embassy in Washington to help with the deluge of correspondence. Sturdee then had Churchill dictating his Fulton speech to her as it took shape in his mind. He was, though, soon distracted by other more relaxing adventures in the Caribbean.

Churchill, along with Clementine, daughter Sarah, Colonel Clarke and Sturdee, flew to the Cuban capital Havana on 1 February in an aircraft generously laid on by Truman. He had last been to the island before it gained independence from Spain as a young officer in 1895. His presence then in an unofficial capacity had caused great controversy, something he excelled at for the rest of his life. Cuba was where he had first experienced coming under fire and he may have had fond memories of the excitement this engendered. Certainly he had been a danger seeker ever since.

This time Churchill was given presidential treatment and mobbed wherever he went. Some Cubans mistakenly thought he had fought for the rebels rather than being embedded with the Spanish army as an observer. As far as his hosts were concerned nothing was too good for him. No expense was spared. The American-owned Hotel Nacional laid on an entire floor with staff and offices. Prominent Cuban businessman and cigar producer Antonio Giraudier loaned them his house which had its own private beach. Churchill was very grateful as the Nacional was not on the shoreline and he preferred to swim in the sea rather than a pool.

Churchill called on Cuban president Ramón Grau San Martin and the pair were photographed seated together. Grau could not hide his delight at meeting Churchill for the first time. He had only been elected the previous autumn, though this was his second term in office; his previous government in the 1930s had lasted just one hundred days.[20] Although Churchill was on holiday he took part in a packed press conference with Grau, at which he thanked his hosts for their kind hospitality and spoke some faltering Spanish. This was met with smiles and applause from the press pack, politicians and military officials alike. When asked about the General Election he was in an impish mood. 'In my country the people can do as they like,' he said with a grin, 'although it often happens that they don't like what they have done.'[21] It was almost as if he was looking to the future. Churchill diplomatically avoided giving his opinion of Attlee's government, remarking, 'I do not discuss the government of my country when I am away from there.'[22] If Attlee heard the radio broadcast he can only have rolled his eyes in amusement; Churchill was not normally so reticent.

Cuban high society turned out in their droves to meet Britain's world-famous wartime leader. Churchill spent the next week sightseeing, socialising and swimming. He enjoyed the island's pleasures, choosing to ignore its corrupt political system and rampant poverty in the interior. This state of affairs would make Cuba fertile ground for Fidel Castro's Communists who would eventually take power. Organised crime had a foothold on the island. In late December 1946 the Hotel Nacional unwittingly or otherwise would host the infamous Havana Conference, attended by leading American mobsters, where they discussed the burgeoning drugs trade.

During his stay Churchill dined with Raymond Norweb, the US Ambassador to Cuba, who was keen to hear about what Churchill planned to say in Fulton. No doubt the gist of their conversation was swiftly relayed back to Washington. Norweb was pleased to have such a distinguished guest, especially as he had only been in post for six months. His previous posting had been Portugal where he successfully negotiated permission for the Allies to use the Azores. When a contented Churchill left Cuba he was well stocked with his favourite Cuban cigars thanks to the generosity of Giraudier.[23]

After returning to Miami, on 10 February Churchill flew to Washington and dined at the White House. He discussed his Fulton speech with Truman and Secretary of State James Byrnes and both were enthusiastic. While in Washington he also met General Eisenhower, the former Allied supreme commander, for lunch at the British Embassy before flying back to Miami. During the war the pair had lunched together at least twice a week and corresponded regularly. Although their working relationship had not always been easy Eisenhower greatly respected Churchill. Eisenhower was currently serving as Chief of Staff of the US Army and overseeing a massive demobilisation. By the end of 1945 some five million American soldiers had been sent home.

Eisenhower was not entirely happy about this, feeling that 'words of caution and counsel by any military authority in early 1946 were overwritten in a mad rush to "get the boys home"'.[24] Churchill was not happy either at such a rapid drawdown of American troops. Furthermore, the US Congress was determined to make drastic budget cuts, to the extent they would not pay for military vehicles to be shipped home. This can only have fuelled Churchill's anxieties about European security. 'We did not openly refer to the Soviets as a potential enemy in those days,' wrote Eisenhower, 'because our political leaders were trying to develop workable arrangements with them. But there was no doubt what we meant when we kept warning.'[25] Churchill's discussions with Eisenhower can only have made him more determined than ever to speak out against the Soviet threat.

In the meantime Attlee's government set about trying to work with the Soviet Union and figure out Stalin's long term goals. Harold Macmillan, now Conservative Member of Parliament for Bromley, because of his wartime experiences often spoke from the Opposition front bench in the House of Commons on international matters. On 20 February 1946, when he led his first Commons debate, he tried to make sense of Soviet policy. He felt that in light of Russia's long history of being invaded, Moscow was now understandably building 'a new cordon sanitaire... of states made satellite and dependent'.[26] Echoing Churchill's sentiments, his hope was that negotiation would temper Stalin's desire to control his neighbours. According to future Soviet premier Nikita Khrushchev, even the senior Soviet leadership were kept in the dark over Stalin's plans. 'He jealously guarded foreign policy in general and our policy towards other Socialist countries in particular as his own special province,' claimed Khrushchev. 'The rest of us were just errand boys.'[27]

After enjoying his holiday in Florida, Churchill's first public appearance in America was to receive an honorary degree from the University of Miami on 26 February in front of a crowd of 17,500 people. Churchill recalled with gratitude how the university had helped train Royal Air Force pilots in 1941. This arrangement, before Lend-Lease and America's entry in the war, had been a clear signal of Roosevelt's determination to assist Britain in its war against Nazi Germany despite deeply entrenched US isolationism.

Churchill then headed for Washington on 3 March where he was hosted by President Truman. He showed his speech to Admiral William Leahy, the President's senior naval advisor, and Secretary of State Byrnes. Churchill noted that Byrnes 'was excited about it and did not suggest any alterations.'[28] It was planned that they would take the Presidential train to Fulton, a journey of eighteen hours which would give them plenty of time to catch up. During the journey he shared his speech with Truman. 'He told me he thought it admirable,' Churchill told Attlee, 'and it would do nothing but good, though it would make a stir.'[29] This was clearly an understatement of a lifetime and one that Truman would regret.

Two days later Truman introduced Churchill at Westminster College, Fulton. Their visit received the full presidential treatment, with Churchill and Truman guarded by out-riders, military vehicles and Secret Service agents hanging from their car. Both men seated on the very back of the open top sedan waved at the well-wishers as they passed through the streets on their way to the college. Some 30,000 people gathered to welcome the pair. Although Churchill was there in a private capacity, in light of the presence of the US President, it was easy to forget that his pronouncements were not official government policy nor necessarily even the views of the Opposition. Nonetheless, he certainly had no plans to avoid a diplomatic furore. First, dressed in a graduation gown, Churchill was awarded another honorary degree.

After Truman's very warm introduction Churchill famously told the gathered audience, 'From Stettin in the Baltic to Trieste in the Adriatic, an iron curtain has descended across the Continent. Behind that line lie all the capitals of the ancient states of Central and Eastern Europe.'[30] He was simply highlighting what he already knew since that fateful meeting with Stalin in October 1944. Churchill understood that he bore some responsibility for failing to prevent this from happening. He had always hoped a swift victory in Italy and a thrust into Austria would forestall Stalin's push into the Balkans as well as Eastern and Central Europe. Instead Churchill had been thwarted by the tenacious German defence in Italy under Field Marshal Albert Kesselring. Lord Moran later wrote, 'Long before Fulton he was alive to the Russian menace; that wanted bringing home to people.' Moran then observed with perhaps an air of cynicism, 'For only one thing mattered now – it was often on his mind – when his record came before posterity they must be fair to him.'[31]

Churchill went on to point out that only Czechoslovakia was lingering as a democracy, everywhere else in the region had become, in his words, 'police states'. 'I do not believe that Soviet Russia desires war,' he said. 'What they desire is the fruits of war and the indefinite expansion of their power and doctrines.'[32] He also warned that from his experience the only thing they respected was strength. Churchill was of the view that the western democracies must stand together to protect the principles of the Atlantic Charter. His audience were left in a sombre mood. Nazi Germany and Imperial Japan had only just been defeated and now Churchill was claiming the Soviet Union was a threat to world peace.

'I wonder if you heard it on the wireless?' wrote Jo Sturdee to her family. 'I feel it was or will be proved in the future to be quite a historic speech.'[33] Although Churchill's oration was filmed and broadcast on the radio, filming did not go as well as hoped. He had soon found himself dazzled by the lighting and called for it to be dimmed. This plunged the cameramen into semi-darkness and made the footage decidedly gloomy.

On 8 March, Churchill, accompanied by General Eisenhower, addressed the General Assembly of Virginia. Once more he spoke in a similar vein. 'We should stand together in malice to none,' he urged, 'in greed for nothing but in defence of those causes which we hold dear'.[34] It was clear Churchill wanted America to continue being the arsenal of democracy when he added, 'Greatheart must have his sword and armour to guard the pilgrims on their way.'[35] The following day Churchill, at Eisenhower's suggestion, met with senior Second World War military commanders. These included Generals Omar Bradley, Jacob Devers, Carl Spaatz and Admiral Chester Nimitz. Bradley and Devers had been army group commanders in Europe. Spaatz had commanded the US Strategic Air Forces in Europe and Nimitz, now chief of naval operations, had led the US Pacific Fleet. This meeting, when it became public knowledge, set further alarm bells ringing in Moscow.

'Churchill roused the world with the eloquent warning he gave in his Iron Curtain speech,' wrote John Colville approvingly.[36] He certainly roused the Soviet Union. Stalin's response in the pages of *Pravda* was predictably to brand Churchill a warmonger who was a danger to international relations. Completely overstepping the mark he then compared Churchill to Hitler. 'In point of fact Mr Churchill and his friends in England and America are presenting those nations who do not speak English with a kind of ultimatum,' wrote Stalin, 'recognize our supremacy over you, voluntarily, and all will be well – otherwise war is inevitable.'[37] If Stalin had ever really considered Churchill a friend, his Fulton speech put an end to it. 'Our relations with England, France, the USA, and the other countries,' wrote Nikita Khrushchev, 'who had cooperated with us in crushing Hitlerite Germany, were, for all intents and purposes, ruined.'[38]

Nor was everyone receptive to his message in the West. Some interpreted it as a call for world domination by Britain and America. In America the reaction was largely hostile; understandably having just got out of one world war no one was in a rush for another one. *The Wall Street Journal* responded with isolationist sentiments declaring, 'The United States wants no alliance, or anything that resembles an alliance, with any other nation.'[39]

Truman came under fire for being associated with 'The Sinews of Peace' when many thought it was the sinews of war that Churchill had been discussing. The President felt obliged publicly to deny he had endorsed Churchill's speech or had seen it in advance. Throughout Churchill's Fulton oration Truman showed no signs of disapproval, nor did he voice any disapproval during the train journey back to Washington. Furthermore on 12 March he wrote to Churchill to say, 'The people of Missouri were highly pleased with your visit and enjoyed what you had to say.'[40] In London Attlee told the House of Commons that Churchill was only speaking for himself and that the Government had no knowledge of the speech. Ninety-three Labour Members of Parliament tabled a motion of censure against Churchill. Amongst the signatories was Jim Callaghan, a future prime minister. Such criticism though chose to ignore Churchill's wider calls for global cooperation in the name of avoiding war.

Churchill then travelled to New York where he was guest of honour at a reception held at the Waldorf Astoria Hotel on 15 March. Angry demonstrators gathered outside the hotel to protest against Churchill's message. 'When I spoke at Fulton ten days ago,' said Churchill in defiant mood, 'I felt it was necessary for someone in an unofficial position to speak in arresting terms about the present plight of the world. I do not wish to withdraw or modify a single word.'[41] However, he moved to take the pressure off Truman by clarifying that he had not called for an Anglo-American military alliance. This though was exactly what he hoped for. He knew that Britain, reliant on American loans, did not have the money or the resources to defend or maintain its Empire, let alone face down the Soviet Union. France was in exactly the same situation.

Churchill's foreign travels continued unabated. On 8 May, along with Clementine and Mary, he visited the Netherlands as a guest of Queen Wilhelmina. A lifelong ardent monarchist, he could not resist the invitation. They were greeted by Prince Bernhard and Princess Juliana and their three young daughters. In the group photograph Churchill was pictured happily puffing away on a cigar next to the eight-year old Princess Beatrix who later became Queen. 'The Dutch had suffered greatly in the war,' recalled Mary, 'particularly as a result of near starvation during the last winter: now they cheered and cheered.'[42] He addressed both Houses of the States-General of the Netherlands at the Hague. His theme was once again European unity. 'I see no reason why, under the guardianship of the world organization,' Churchill told them, 'there should not ultimately arise the United States of Europe'.[43]

The Churchills stayed for five days visiting Amsterdam, Rotterdam and Leyden. Wherever they went they received a rapturous welcome. He was given an honorary degree by Leyden University to add to his collection. 'I shall never forget the seas of upturned joyous faces', said Churchill in his letter of thanks to Queen Wilhelmina.[44] He politely avoided the very problematic issue of the Dutch East Indies. The Dutch were waging a war there to reassert control, with British help, after Indonesian nationalists declared independence following Japan's surrender.[45]

Back in the House of Commons on 5 June Churchill continued to make it clear that he viewed the Soviet Union as a threat rather than dismembered Germany. He stated that Europe was in a worse position than it was at the end of the First World War. He warned that a new Europe could not be created if it contained pariah states. Germany should not be punished indefinitely or it would be impoverished and driven to 'embrace Communism'.[46] At some point Churchill argued Germany and Italy must be forgiven and that Austria and Hungary should be freed. 'It is better to have a world united than a world divided,' he told his fellow parliamentarians, 'but it is also better to have a world divided, than a world destroyed.'[47] Not long after, Churchill was out of the country again visiting the French city of Metz on 14 July for Bastille Day. There he made an appeal for a French revival, for it was vital for Europe to have a strong France.

Churchill's next major speaking engagement was Zurich in Switzerland where he was to hold forth on European unity. He had been offered the use of a villa on the shores of Lake Geneva in August for a three week holiday. There he retired with his family to paint and relax, guarded by Swiss soldiers and police. Out on the lake police speedboats patrolled the waters and the shoreline. When the weather turned bad the former commander-in-chief of the Swiss Army, General Henri Guisan, sent his campaign tent for Churchill to work in. Churchill spent much of his time in seclusion; his few visitors included General Guisan and South African Prime Minister Field Marshal Jan Smuts, who was a wartime friend and confidant. After discussing the Soviet threat Churchill learned, 'The Swiss are most perturbed.'[48]

Although the Churchills had a pleasant time, unfortunately Clementine broke some ribs in a boating accident and had to leave early. Afterwards Churchill visited the cities of Lausanne, Geneva, Berne and Zurich. Although there in a private capacity it was difficult to see his treatment by the Swiss as little more than a state visit. 'In all these cities Winston Churchill was met not only with every conceivable mark of official honour,' said his daughter Mary, 'but also with wildly cheering crowds which thronged the streets and squares.'[49]

On 16 September he and Mary arrived in Berne where they toured in a horse-drawn open carriage attended by uniformed footmen. Churchill raised his trademark victory sign to the crowds lining the streets and those leaning on the surrounding balconies. They stayed the night at the Château du Lohn, the Swiss version of Chequers. The following day he was hosted to lunch by the Swiss Federal Council and on 18 September was the guest of the French Ambassador.

At Zurich University on 19 September, Churchill gave a ground-breaking and highly controversial speech to the students. His intention was to find a way of avoiding yet another war between France and Germany and to safeguard against the Soviet threat. Looking round at all the expectant faces he said, 'I am now going to say something that will astonish you.'[50] Churchill urged the creation of a United States of Europe and called for 'a partnership between France and Germany.'[51]

Churchill then, on a sobering note, pointed out that the inevitable proliferation of the atomic bomb if used by warring nations could lead to the end of civilisation and even the planet. Therefore unifying Europe was now an urgent matter.

He reasoned that the first step to a United States of Europe would be to set up 'a Council of Europe'.[52] Crucially though Churchill saw Britain standing outside this, hoping that it would create a fourth power bloc. 'Great Britain, the British Commonwealth of Nations, mighty America, and I trust Soviet Russia…' he explained, 'must be friends… of the new Europe and must champion its right to live and shine.'[53] The idea of inviting Germany, a divided nation at that, back into the fold so soon was shocking to many. Mary Churchill observed that, 'at the time his words were regarded in many quarters as forging ahead too fast.'[54] Churchill would return to this theme of European unity when he spoke at the Congress of Europe, at The Hague on 7 May 1948. When he had finished speaking there he was reduced to tears by the ovation he received from the enthusiastic delegates.

Soviet intelligence no doubt had full details of Churchill's visit to Switzerland, not only thanks to all the press coverage but also its informants. During the Second World War the country, although neutral, had been a hotbed of foreign espionage. The Soviets had run the Dora and Lucy spy rings in Geneva and Lucerne. Inevitably Stalin could only see Churchill's pronouncements at Fulton and Zurich as a call to arms against the Soviet Union. The birth of a United States of Europe would pose a threat to Soviet interests in Central and Eastern Europe. Marshal Zhukov wrote, 'There were anti-popular forces in the world to whom it was of greater advantage to wield international relations to exacerbate tension and wage the Cold War.'[55] Clearly Moscow felt that Churchill was in the vanguard of this. Behind the scenes in America, whilst not wanting to see another European war, many saw a unified Europe as a potential future threat to American economic interests.

After Fulton Churchill seems to have convinced himself that ultimately war with the Soviet Union was unavoidable. He had told Mackenzie King, the Canadian Prime Minister, in May 1946 that within eight years, by the time the Soviet Union had the atomic bomb, the world would witness, 'The greatest war – the most terrible war which may mean the end of our civilisation.'[56] When Lord Moran asked Churchill in October 1946 if he thought there might be war in two or three years' time his prognosis was worse. 'Perhaps sooner than that,' responded Churchill glumly, 'perhaps this winter.'[57] However, when Moran professed he did not think war was likely, Churchill changed his mind and responded, 'I don't think there will be.'[58] Churchill's fears were fuelled by reports that the Soviets had 225 divisions in occupied Europe, whereas the British and Americans only had about 25.

'The Soviet Union is a peaceful state,' claimed Marshal Zhukov. 'Our people's short- and long-term goals serve the cause of building Communism in our country. We do not need war to attain this.'[59] Churchill desperately wanted to believe such sentiments, but deep down feared the worst. Nikita Khrushchev felt that Churchill only had himself to blame for the mounting international tensions. 'One reason for Stalin's obsession with Eastern Europe was that the Cold War had already set in,' reasoned Khrushchev. 'Churchill had given his famous speech in Fulton urging the imperialist forces of the world to mobilize against the Soviet Union.'[60] He wrote this with the benefit of hindsight, but if Khrushchev, Stalin and the other senior leadership believed this at the time it is easy to see why the Soviet fortress mentality solidified.

Churchill hoped to enlist the support of an old wartime ally with his United States of Europe concept. Duncan Sandys, Churchill's son-in-law married to Diana his eldest daughter, in late November 1946 travelled to visit General de Gaulle who had retired to write his wartime memoirs. Sandys carried with him a letter from Churchill canvassing de Gaulle's views on the current security situation in Europe and calling on France to take a lead with a European union. De Gaulle informed Sandys that Churchill's Zurich speech had not gone down well in France. A divided Germany would keep it weak and no Frenchman was keen to see it revived. 'Germany,' observed de Gaulle, 'as a state, no longer existed.'[61] De Gaulle now felt Britain, with France, should be a founding member of a European union in order to counterbalance Germany.

Churchill's letter went on to say that Attlee's Labour government was anti-Communist and was firmly supported in this by the Conservative party. In London Attlee informed Churchill that he thought the goals of a European union would be better achieved through the United Nations. Churchill felt his warnings about the Soviet Union and the need for European unity were going unheeded. It would be another two years before the world really took notice thanks to Soviet actions in Berlin.

John Colville, who had served diligently as one of Churchill's private secretaries, now found himself without a job. However, he soon gained re-employment with the Foreign Office with the onerous task of dealing with Tito's Yugoslavia. 'In due course,' he wrote, 'I was promoted assistant head of department, which meant that the misdeeds of the new Communist regimes in Hungary, Romania, Bulgaria and Albania were added to my Yugoslav responsibilities.'[62] In the spring of 1947 a new opportunity arose when Sir Alan Lascelles invited him on behalf of the King to fill the post of Private Secretary to Princess Elizabeth, the twenty-one year-old heir apparent. When Colville sought Churchill's advice his response was, 'It is your duty to accept.'[63]

By the end of the year Churchill still remained unpopular with some members of his own party. Senior Conservative peer Lord Butler dined with Harold Nicolson on 18 December 1947 and made his views perfectly clear. 'He says that Winston is a grave liability to the Party,' wrote Nicolson in a letter to his wife the following day. 'He does not consult them and is always making speeches which let them down. But they can't get rid of him.'[64] When Nicolson asked Butler what the Conservatives were going to do, he responded, 'It is a question of which dies first, Winston or the Tory Party.'[65]

PART TWO

A HASTY EXIT

Chapter 4

End of Empire

In India news of Churchill's electoral defeat in 1945 was met with joy in many quarters. 'The Indian people had seen a sign of British weakness which was like hoisting of the white flag,' wrote Nirad Chaudhuri who worked for All India Radio in Delhi during the war. 'The British people had rejected Churchill, the most hated Englishman in India. He was, of course, hated for his opposition to self-government for Indians.'[1] As far as India's nationalists were concerned the last impediment to their independence had been removed. 'The Indian people knew that so far as they were concerned, they had men of straw to deal with,' adds Chaudhuri.[2]

Churchill was a lifelong imperialist but by the end of the Second World War even he had to acknowledge that Indian independence was now inevitable. Britain was bankrupt and did not have the military resources or indeed political willpower to prevent it. 'We are all under the harrow and our position in the East is clattering down,' he lamented, 'in full conformity with our financial situation at home.'[3] Churchill and Attlee knew only too well how the widespread Hindu-led Quit India revolt in the summer of 1942 had challenged British authority. Nobody wanted a repeat of that. At the time the Indian Army, a distinct entity from the British Army, had remained completely loyal but now things were very different.

Churchill greatly respected the Indian Army thanks to its unwavering support during the Second World War. Furthermore, as a young lieutenant he had served on India's North-West Frontier with Punjab and Sikh regiments.[4] They had left a lasting impression on him. 'This is, I believe, the first time a British officer has been attached to a native infantry regiment,' he wrote of his experience. 'After the kindness and courtesy with which I was treated, I can only hope it will not be the last.'[5] He had also witnessed first-hand the brutality of the mountain tribesmen.

In the late 1930s the Indian Army had 205,000 regular Indian troops under arms supported by 84,000 auxiliaries. By the end of the war India had mobilized 2.5 million men. Many of them had loyally fought for Britain in the Far East, Middle East, North Africa and Italy. Indian troops were sent to Greece in December 1944, where they remained for the next two years, and the following year were deployed to Indonesia. In 1946 Indian soldiers were sent to Japan as part of the British occupation force, while Indian forces also remained deployed in Egypt,

36

Palestine, Iran and Iraq. These combat veterans understandably wanted to go home and to independence.

The Royal Indian Navy set alarm bells ringing when it mutinied in Bombay over poor conditions on 18 February 1946. This spread to Karachi and across India.[6] Sailors hoisted the flags of the Indian National Congress, the Muslim League and the Indian Communist party. Amongst their demands were the release of members of the Indian National Army who had fought for the Japanese and the withdrawal of Indian troops from Indonesia. Worryingly some members of the Indian Army and the Royal Indian Air Force were also involved in the mutiny. In support workers took to the streets in Bombay on 22 February, and although the mutineers surrendered the following day, 228 people were killed and over 1,000 injured. Other strikes took place in Karachi, Madras and elsewhere. For the British it signalled they were in danger of losing control. Likewise, India's nationalist politicians did not want a revolution that resulted in India's armed forces losing all discipline, nor did they want a coup. For the rest of the year India endured almost continuous strikes.

Indian independence was not straightforward because of the rift between the Hindu-led Indian National Congress and the Muslim League. The latter demanded the creation of Pakistan or 'Land of the Pure,'[7] as a separate state for fear of becoming a persecuted minority in a Hindu-dominated united states of India.[8] The Sikhs also wanted a separate homeland, Sikhistan or Khalistan. Further complicating matters was the status of the 565 Indian princely states, whose allegiance had always been to Britain.[9] Of the two largest Kashmir was mainly Muslim but with a Hindu prince, while Hyderabad was predominantly Hindu with a Muslim prince.[10] Congress hoped the British Raj would become a united states of India, but it was extremely hard to see how partition could be avoided without the British.

Viscount Wavell, the Viceroy of India, by his own acknowledgement was completely out of his depth when it came to labyrinthine Indian politics. 'I very much doubt,' he wrote in his diary on 1 January 1946, 'whether my brain-power or personality are up to it.'[11] Attlee had not been impressed by Wavell's performance despite his sterling work during the Bengal famine. 'A great man in many ways, you know, but a curiously silent bird,' observed Attlee, 'and I don't think silent people get on very well with Indians who are loquacious.'[12] Wavell was a Churchill appointee during the war, having first served as Commander-in-Chief in India. Churchill may have deliberately chosen Wavell because he did not want to address India's independence and hoped to postpone the inevitable. Certainly he never granted Wavell plenipotentiary powers, which denied him any freedom of independent action. While Wavell supported Indian independence he was hamstrung by this complete lack of political clout. 'If India is not to be ruled by force,' he noted, 'it must be ruled by the heart rather than the head.'[13] However, he never developed a close rapport with nationalist leaders such as Mohandas Gandhi and Jawaharlal Nehru.

Attlee was fully aware that Churchill's previous efforts to buy India's nationalists off with an offer of self-governing dominion status during the war had ended in failure. Churchill sent Sir Stafford Cripps to India in early 1942 to

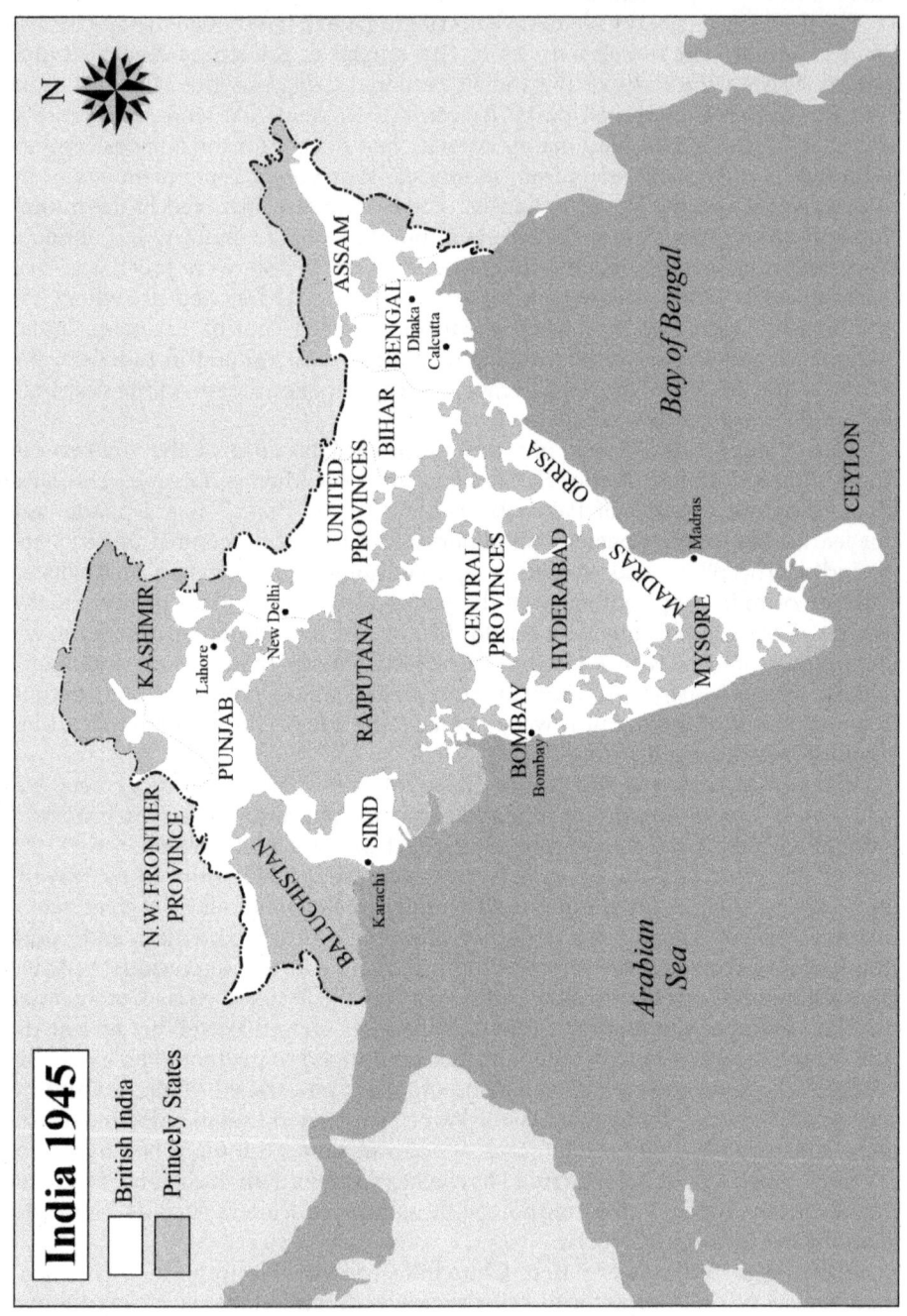

India 1945

British India

Princely States

negotiate this, but his inability to offer independence had simply fuelled the Quit India revolt. Attlee subsequently sent a Cabinet mission to India in late March 1946, which included Cripps. In the name of retaining India's unity they concocted a three-tier Indian union that would be led by a central government. The latter would be responsible for defence, foreign affairs and transport with everything else devolved to the regions. This, it was hoped, could avoid partition.

Churchill was in the House of Commons on 16 May 1946 when Attlee announced that in light of the failure to get agreement over dominion status for India, new proposals would have to be put forward. These were the Cabinet missions plans. 'It will, I hope,' said Churchill, 'be common ground between us that we cannot enforce by British arms a British-made Constitution upon India against the wishes of any of the main elements in Indian life.'[14] Churchill was therefore stung when Muhammad Ali Jinnah, leader of the Muslim League, wrote to him at the end of August accusing him of abandoning India's Muslims. They had provided the bulk of the troops for the Indian Army and had been loyal to Britain during the war. In contrast the Indian National Congress had opposed India's entry into the war and Gandhi and Nehru along with tens of thousands of their followers were thrown in prison. Churchill quickly drafted a reply urging Indians to settle their differences. 'I foresee a period of civil war and anarchy,' he warned, 'not only as a result of a struggle between religions, but also, as in China, between Communists and anti-Communists.'[15] This highlighted Churchill's other major concern. Although the Indian Communist party was not a threat, in China the Communists were on the verge of taking power. He decided, however, not to send it.

Although the Indians initially accepted the Cabinet mission plan, it soon floundered on the intransigence of the Muslim League. Wavell announced on 16 June that Congress and the League could not agree on the composition of a provisional government. Increasingly fearful for the safety of the 100,000 British nationals in India, excluding the military, Wavell even suggested January 1947 as a British departure date. In a debate in the House of Commons on 1 August 1946 Churchill accused the government of putting India's independence 'in hostile and feeble hands, heedless of the dark carnage and confusion which will follow'.[16] He also said that the government was going to consign 400 million Indians to the misery of civil war. Churchill felt that the British Raj had always been the underlying unifying factor.

Wavell asked Nehru to form a provisional government on 12 August. Its task was to create a constitution but the Muslim League still refused to cooperate. Instead four days later it launched a direct action day in Calcutta. This sparked terrible riots resulting in 5,000 dead and 15,000 injured. Nevertheless, Nehru became prime minister in Delhi on 2 September. In response Jinnah declared a day of mourning and told his followers to put out black flags. 'We are not yet in the midst of civil war,' said Gandhi seven days later, 'but we are nearing it.'[17] The failure to agree a constitution meant that a unified independent India was almost an impossibility. Speaking at the Conservative party conference in Blackpool on 5 October 1946 Churchill proceeded to criticise the government's handling of India. He repeated his fears about sectarian violence and warned India could become hostile to Britain.

Churchill began to favour the breakup of India in the hope of avoiding bloodshed. He held the Indian National Congress responsible for the impasse and felt it had been an error to involve Nehru in the provisional government. He met with Jinnah in London in early December and reassured him that if the Muslim League created Pakistan it would not be expelled from the Commonwealth. Then speaking in the House of Commons on 20 December, Churchill objected to India not being given dominion status as an interim step towards full independence. It was clear that he hoped by clinging to this it might buy Britain time to ensure a friendly government was installed in India as well as Pakistan. In the meantime Wavell, fearing a complete breakdown of law and order, recommended to Attlee that Britain relinquish control no later than the end of March 1948.

Since the debates on Indian home rule in the 1930s Churchill and Harold Macmillan had never agreed over India. Churchill's intransigent imperialist views had seen him cast into the political wilderness for almost a decade. Macmillan though now agreed with Churchill and felt that the government was showing a complete 'abdication of duty as well as of power'.[18] In early 1947 he embarked on a fact-finding tour of India. He first stayed in Government House, Bombay and then travelled to Delhi. 'All power is oozing away and only the shell is left,' Macmillan noted sadly. 'And that is made more oppressive because the outward symbols of imperial power remain.'[19]

He met with Wavell on 4 February who he found a rather pathetic figure. That very day Wavell received a letter from Attlee urging him to retire. It was clear he was going to be sacked. Macmillan also met Nehru: 'He is, I should judge, torn between bitter hatred of the British and a desire to be fair and objective.'[20] Jinnah warned Macmillan that India was 'a continent – or sub-continent – not a nation'.[21] He argued as always that partition was the only solution. Macmillan discovered in Calcutta, 'The killings were on a scale quite beyond what we were led to believe at home.'[22] When he returned to London he rapidly briefed Churchill on his depressing findings.

Attlee decided Wavell must go and be replaced with Vice-Admiral Lord Louis Mountbatten. 'He had an extraordinary faculty for getting on with all kinds of people as he'd shown when he was Supremo in South-east Asia,' said Attlee. 'Appointing Mountbatten was one stroke of mine that was entirely successful.'[23] Realising what was at stake Mountbatten initially did not want the job and went to see his cousin King George VI for advice. 'I think you should take it Dickie,' the King told him. 'In fact you are the only one who can pull it off.'[24] The King pointed out that the Indian leaders respected him, also the Indian princes had pledged loyalty to the Crown and only a member of the Royal family could release them.

The King knew that the time for dithering was over and made his feelings known to Attlee. 'Lord Mountbatten,' he wrote, 'must have concrete orders as to what he is to do. Is he to lead the retreat out of India or is he to work for the reconciliation of Hindus and Muslims?'[25] Attlee made it clear it was the former. 'It makes all the difference to me to know that you propose to make a statement in the House,' Mountbatten wrote to Attlee, 'terminating the British "Raj" on a definite and specified date.'[26]

When Mountbatten went to see Attlee to accept the job he made it clear he must have full authority to act completely independently. 'How could I possibly negotiate with the Cabinet breathing down my neck?'[27] he asked the prime minister. The last thing he wanted was to run every single proposal through the Secretary of State for India and his India Office in London. Nor did he want Churchill and the Conservatives constantly criticising his every move in the House of Commons. 'You are asking for plenipotentiary powers,' responded Attlee. 'No one has been given those in this century.'[28] Mountbatten responded firmly, 'Exactly.'[29] Attlee considered the ramifications for a moment then said, 'All right, you have them.'[30] If Churchill had known this he would have been both appalled and furious at the break in diplomatic protocol.

Mountbatten had been given the full backing of the Prime Minister, and the power to negotiate Indian independence without constant authorisation from London. There would be no turning back from this point on. Lord Butler, who had served as Under-Secretary of State for India, was summoned by Attlee. He was asked to see if the Conservative party would support his policy on India. 'I don't speak to Winston on India,' Attlee confessed. 'I don't trust him. I would be grateful if you could take some soundings… and let me know.'[31] The government's new policy towards India and Mountbatten's appointment, with the mission to implement independence by June 1948, was announced on 20 February 1947. The evening before, Attlee personally informed Churchill and Clement Davies the Leader of the Liberal party; Churchill, according to Davies, retorted unkindly that Wavell was 'a bad general and bad statesman'.[32]

Even though Churchill had been forewarned of the change and had not objected, he sought to make political capital out of the situation in the House of Commons. 'Will the Prime Minister lay before the House,' he asked mischievously, 'the reasons for the termination of the appointment of Viscount Wavell at this particular moment?'[33] Attlee, keeping his cool, would not be drawn. 'Mr Churchill knows very well that Lord Wavell was not appointed for a fixed term,' responded the prime minister cooly. 'As has been stated, it was thought that in the changed phase of the Indian problem it was the suitable time to make a change'.[34] Churchill persisted in wanting to know why Wavell had been dismissed, but Attlee stood his ground, refusing to spark a diplomatic incident.

Churchill was disappointed when he heard that his old chum Dickie Mountbatten was to preside, as the last viceroy, over India's transition to independence. 'Everyone knows that the fourteen months' time limit is fatal to any orderly transference of power,' he warned the House of Commons, adding, 'and I am bound to say that the whole thing wears the aspect of an attempt by the Government to make use of brilliant war figures in order to cover up a melancholy and disastrous transaction.'[35] In other words Churchill felt the government was using a war hero to beguile not only the Indians but also the British public. Churchill, who had helped nurture Mountbatten's wartime career, had every confidence in the new Viceroy but not in what he was being sent to achieve.

Churchill understood that by agreeing to a deadline for Indian independence Britain had surrendered any bargaining power. It now had no leverage in trying to shape India's future. Churchill in discussion with Lord Moran let it be known he felt he was being held responsible for this state of affairs. 'But now the war was over, the poor Hindu had got what he wanted,' noted Lord Moran, 'and the Foreign Office complained ungratefully that Mr Churchill had left them nothing to bargain with.'[36] The best that could be hoped for was a federal India constitutionally linking the Hindus, Muslims and princely states. The fate of the country essentially rested with Mountbatten, Gandhi, Nehru and Jinnah. Churchill and Attlee were left on the sidelines.

Although Wavell's relationship with Churchill during the war had been up and down, Wavell seemed to hold no ill-feelings against him. 'I have never loved, nor hated Winston,' he said. 'I have admired him intensely for his indomitable courage, his talents, his wit, his panache.'[37] However, Wavell must have known that Churchill had done nothing to save the Viceroy that he had appointed. Smarting over his dismissal, Wavell wrote to the King on 24 February to highlight the rejected plans he had put before Attlee. As he saw it the options were to re-establish power and rule for at least another fifteen years; make renewed efforts to bring the two main political parties together; support Congress taking power; or admit defeat and leave as soon as possible. Little did he know that Mountbatten would largely opt for the latter option. Wavell, ever the military man, could not help ending his observations by saying, 'the Indian Army... is at the present time perhaps the brightest part of the Indian outlook.'[38]

Churchill on 6 March 1947 continued his anti-Congress stance in the House of Commons, saying the involvement of Nehru was 'a critical mistake'.[39] Looking round at his fellow members of parliament he concluded, 'It is with deep grief that I watch the clattering down of the British Empire... Many have defended Britain against her foes. None can defend her against herself.'[40] The Raj symbolised everything Churchill held sacred and he knew that its dissolution would be a bitter pill to swallow.

Mountbatten and his wife Lady Edwina arrived in Delhi on 22 March 1947 to be met by Wavell with full pomp and ceremony. 'I am sorry for you,' Wavell told Mountbatten. 'You have been given an impossible job.'[41] Mountbatten recalled, 'Wavell was very helpful, but I saw very little of him. He was anxious to quit as soon as possible.'[42] That evening they dined together, but Mountbatten did not find their conversation particularly enlightening and Wavell did not tell him anything he did not already know. The following day the outgoing Viceroy departed.

India's political leaders finally began to believe that change was coming. 'What is different about you from your predecessors?' Nehru asked Mountbatten not long after his arrival, 'Can it be that you have been given plenipotentiary powers? In that case you will succeed where all the others have failed.'[43] Mountbatten observed that Gandhi in India, 'was not compared with some great statesmen like Roosevelt or Churchill. They classified him simply in their minds with Mohammed and with Christ.'[44] Jinnah, who was dying of lung cancer, was adamant about partition, something Gandhi could never reconcile himself to. 'The policy of your predecessors has brought about a situation,' Gandhi told Mountbatten, 'in which there are only two alternatives, either a continuation of British rule to keep law and order, or an Indian blood-bath.'[45] It was very evident to Mountbatten that there was no chance of resurrecting the Cabinet mission plan.

Mountbatten and Edwina showed great courage while touring India. The pair flew to the city of Peshawar in the North-West Frontier, a historically volatile province, on 28 April to see the governor. On arrival they were informed that a crowd of around 75,000 Muslim demonstrators gathered in a local park were intending to march on Government House. They were advised if the crowd stormed the building the police and military would be unable to hold it. Mountbatten and his wife bravely decided to meet the demonstrators face to face. Both were wearing khaki uniforms which immediately marked them out as senior military officials. Holding hands and cheerfully smiling they strode down a railway bank towards the park with their alarmed advisors following reluctantly behind. The noise was such that all they could do was wave. It would only have taken a second for them to have been crushed to death or assassinated. Instead the crowd who had been chanting 'Long live Pakistan', once they learned who the dignitaries were, began chanting 'Long live Mountbatten' and dispersed peacefully after thirty minutes.[46] Mountbatten had been given his first taste of Indian street politics.

When Churchill heard of the Mountbattens' antics he was no doubt impressed. He was after all a lifelong danger seeker himself. Churchill had been to Nowshera to the east of Peshawar in 1897 when he joined the Malakand Field Force. This force was about to embark on a campaign on the North-West Frontier. 'These tribesmen are among the most miserable and brutal creatures on earth,' he later wrote.[47] He had also concluded, 'Military rule is the rule best suited to the character and comprehension of the tribesmen.'[48] Despite his enduring imperial love of India he had not been back since.

Mountbatten's experience helped convince him that he had to do two things. 'The first was that we had to be quick to find a solution,' he observed. 'The second, that it was more important to be quick than to have an undivided India.'[49] Mountbatten was far from happy about the idea of partition but he could see no other way forward. 'The more I look at the problems of India the more I realise that all this partition business is sheer madness,' he wrote to Attlee on 1 May 1947. 'No one would ever induce me to agree to it were it not for this fantastic communal madness that has seized everybody'.[50]

Dividing India though would be no easy task. The creation of Jinnah's Pakistan would require two separate entities separated by an independent India in the shape of West Pakistan and East Pakistan (which would eventually become Bangladesh). The former meant the partition of Punjab, while the latter the partition of Bengal. The princely states would have to decide on an individual basis whether to become independent or join India or Pakistan. Most would lean towards India.

Mountbatten had seen how British rule was in decay and India was sliding towards anarchy. After negotiations with the Indian National Congress and the Muslim League, he recommended partition and brought forward the date for independence to 15 August 1947. This was the anniversary of the Japanese surrender. It was almost a year sooner than originally specified. Mountbatten was of the view that the longer it was left the worse things would become. Gandhi's haunting advice had stuck in his mind, 'You must face the blood-bath and accept it.'[51]

Attlee and Mountbatten convened with Churchill and other senior Conservatives in London on 20 May 1947 to discuss exit plans for India. They were seeking support for their proposals for partition and the accelerated British withdrawal. Both India and Pakistan were to be given dominion status after which they could declare full independence if they so desired. Churchill had always wanted dominion status so supported the government, as he felt this would at least keep India within the British Commonwealth. Regarding partition, he and his fellow Conservatives hoped that a weak and divided India would remain dependent on Britain. Attlee and Mountbatten knew that dominion status was purely a diplomatic nicety to help Britain save face. India's nationalists had always wanted nothing short of full independence and there was no reason to expect that stance to change. Ridiculously Churchill also hoped that the princely states would opt out of an independent India or Pakistan and become British dominions. In particular he pinned his hopes on Kashmir and Hyderabad.

Everything would be divided up amongst the new states including the Indian Army, the police and civil service. Attlee and his government, while happy to use Indian divisions for overseas security duties at the end of the war, did not want to keep them operational. For example the 25th Indian Division, which included Baluch and Punjab regiments deployed to southern Malaya, was disbanded in March 1946. Likewise, the rest of the Indian Army underwent a massive demobilisation and was reduced to 500,000 men by April 1947. This had been done mainly to reduce the enormous cost of maintaining such a large standing force, but also due to the fear of a coup if independence was not forthcoming.

The intention was that what remained of the Indian Army would be split on a three to one basis between India and Pakistan, to reflect the population ratios. Jinnah was adamant about this, 'I must have my own army even if it is one sergeant and one private.'[52] The problem the army faced was that its regiments were so ethnically mixed up that maintaining coherent units post-independence would be almost impossible. Only its traditionally impeccable discipline would ensure the transfer of men was not beset by bloodshed. To further complicate matters there were about a dozen private armies in India, some of which belonged to the princely states and were outside the main chain of command.

Churchill appreciated that Attlee and Mountbatten needed to take action quickly as violence had spread through Punjab, Bengal and Bihar. On 21 May 1947 the Earl of Listowel, the Secretary of State for India and Burma, informed the House of Commons that 4,014 people had been killed in India between 18 November 1946 and 18 May 1947. The majority of them, 3,024, had died in the fighting between Hindus, Muslims and Sikhs in the Punjab. It looked as if a three-way civil war had already started.

Attlee, with Churchill's blessing, presented his plans to the House of Commons on 3 June. 'At 3.30 today Attlee in the House announced the terms of the Indian settlement,' wrote Harold Nicolson in his diary. 'Winston replies and has nice things to say.'[53] 'It is quite true,' Churchill told the assembled members of parliament, 'that the agreement of the various parties in India has only been achieved on the basis of partition.'[54] For him the beacon of hope, as he explained, was that India would remain a collection of self-governing dominions owing allegiance to the

Crown. 'It may, therefore,' he concluded, 'be that through a form of partition, the unity of India may, nonetheless, be preserved.'[55] It was wishful thinking.

Congress and the Muslim League announced the terms on All-India Radio the same day. Mountbatten, now back in India, likewise made a broadcast and tried to clarify his position. 'I am, of course,' he explained, 'just as much opposed to the partition of provinces as I am to the partition of India herself.'[56] Nirad Chaudhuri, a Bengali, was firmly against partition. When he heard the news he said, 'Everyone has cut off his nose to spite his neighbour.'[57] Gandhi was of the same opinion, 'I do not agree with what my closest friends have done or are doing.'[58] He like Churchill had hoped to keep India intact. Many Indians were left in a state of shock; after over two hundred years of British involvement in India they would be gone in two and a half months' time.

When Churchill learned that the necessary legislation was to be called the Indian Independence Bill he immediately protested, pointing out it should be called the Indian Dominion Bill. 'The essence of the Mountbatten proposals,' he wrote to Attlee, 'and the only reason I gave support to them is because they establish the phase of Dominion Status.'[59] Attlee refused to change it and the bill went before the Commons on 4 July with the provision that as of 15 August 1947 India would be self-governing. When the bill went before the Commons for its second reading on 10 July, Churchill was conveniently ill and left the job to Harold Macmillan. He was torn between his loyalty to Churchill, his belief in home rule for India and his sympathy for Attlee's position, though he felt things were being rushed. Macmillan diplomatically confined his comments to praising Britain's contribution to India's illustrious past. Churchill, Macmillan and the rest of the Conservative party knew that holding things up would achieve nothing, other than make them unpopular.

It was explained that after independence Mountbatten would serve as Governor-General of India and Pakistan, whose prime ministers would be Nehru and Jinnah respectively. This was reluctantly agreed to and the independence bill became law on 18 July. This triggered what became a mass exodus in India. As Churchill had so long feared, violence between Hindus, Muslims, Sikhs and other groups escalated. Millions of people were to be displaced and the Indian subcontinent brought to the brink of all-out civil war. The roads and railways became jammed with frightened refugees as they hastened to be on the right side of the as-yet-undefined new frontiers. Communities that had lived side by side peacefully for centuries tore each other apart. The most unspeakable atrocities were committed in the name of religious differences. Massacres and rape became widespread as the Raj unravelled. There had been talk of the North-West Frontier becoming independent but that would have left it at the mercy of Afghanistan. On 20 July 1947 it voted overwhelmingly in favour of union with Baluchistan province, its southern neighbour, and the truncated western half of Punjab to create West Pakistan.

Attlee instructed that from independence day all remaining British units would be withdrawn, subject to the availability of shipping.[60] Nehru was in complete agreement with this, stating, 'I would rather have every village in India go up in flames than keep a single British soldier in India a moment longer than necessary.'[61] Furthermore, it was decided that law and order from that date would be the responsibility of the Indian and Pakistani governments. Therefore British forces would not intervene in internal disorder except to protect British lives. Attlee and Mountbatten did not want to risk being drawn into a war, nor did they want to be seen taking sides. The British having granted independence could hardly then start shooting on Indians and Pakistanis. Across India the once-reliable police quickly fractured along sectarian lines and officers fearful for the safety of their families stopped turning up for duty. To protect themselves people began to take matters into their own hands by forming local militias. Many of these were recruited from demobbed Indian Army soldiers.

In light of the proposed new frontier running somewhere through the Punjab, clearly something had to be done about security. Belatedly on 1 August the Punjab Boundary Force under Major General Thomas 'Pete' Rees, numbering 15,000 men using what had been the 4th Indian Division, was hastily put together to try and keep the peace. This division was a veteran of the battles of Benghazi, Eritrea, El Alamein and Monte Cassino. However, it had been partially demobilised and its remaining Baluchi, Dorga, Gurkha and Rajput recruits wanted to go home. Even when reinforced to 23,000 the Boundary Force did not have the manpower or equipment to be effective. Its area of responsibility covered 37,500 square miles, a region larger than Ireland. This had a population of over fifteen million, more than half of whom were Muslims, and included 17,000 villages. It was assessed that it would take a force of at least 100,000 to police the Punjab.

On 14 August Rees's men discovered the bodies of thirty-five Sikhs stabbed to death at Lahore railway station. This was just a taste of what was to come as the violence intensified across India. The following day India and Pakistan became independent and Churchill's prediction that a fourteen month time limit for an orderly transfer of power would be fatal proved right. Thanks to Mountbatten it had been done much faster than that. Jinnah immediately objected to Mountbatten's new appointment, claiming the role Governor-General of Pakistan for himself. It took messages from the King, Attlee and Churchill to persuade Mountbatten to stay on in his new truncated role as just Governor-General of India.

Major General Rees informed Field Marshal Claude Auchinleck, the former British Commander-in-Chief India, on 17 August that his men were 'standing firm and rock-like as the united Indian Army always has when called on'.[62] The new borders were announced that day but there was no way yet to mark them immediately. Pandemonium reigned in Punjab. Inevitably sectarian tensions began to spill over into the Punjab Boundary Force. Three days later near Gurdaspur, Rees's men opened fire on a Muslim mob and killed eighty-four people. On August 24 Muslim soldiers shot Hindu looters and were confronted by their angry Hindu and Sikh comrades. The following day Rees reported that although there had not been any violence between the Muslim and non-Muslim troops he feared it was only a matter of time.

By the end of the month the remnants of the Indian Army and the police had lost control. The short-lived Punjab Boundary Force was disbanded on 1 September and its men became either Indians or Pakistanis.[63] This was partly due to the wishes of Jinnah and Nehru who understandably did not like troops operating

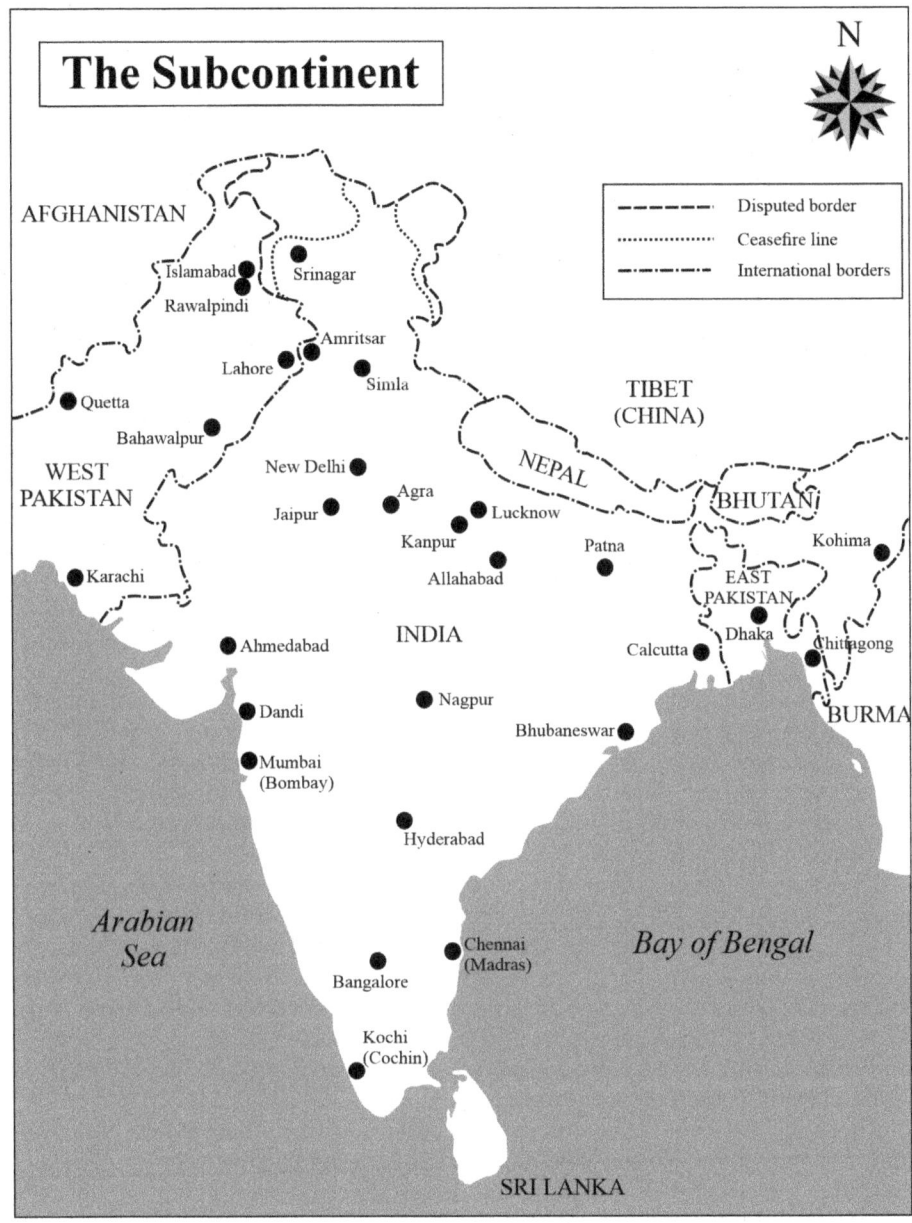

in their countries that were not directly under their authority. Mountbatten was not happy about this but he was powerless. The following day he wrote to King George VI observing that 'it gradually became apparent that the political leaders of both Dominions felt that their hands were tied until this step was taken.'[64] In Punjab law and order collapsed.

Churchill was appalled as was everyone else. Across India around fifteen million people were displaced and about 200,000 massacred in the bloody disorganised chaos of partition.[65] Churchill's Conservative colleagues were equally dismayed if not downright fatalistic. 'My own view is that this course of history was inevitable,' said Lord Butler, 'although some have blamed the Congress for not carrying the Muslims with them.'[66] He also felt, 'Mountbatten, too, should share the responsibility for allowing this to happen.'[67]

The tragedy of partition was not over yet. Violence between Kashmir's Hindus and Muslims forced the ruling maharaja to accede to Indian rule. He had hoped to play for time before deciding his state's fate, instead it ended up a battle ground for its more powerful neighbours. India and Pakistan went to war over control of Kashmir in late October 1947. This conflict saw former Indian Army comrades, veterans of the battles of Imphal and Kohima, fighting each other. By the time the conflict had stopped at the end of the following year, prostrate Kashmir was left divided between the two. India gained around two-thirds of its territory.

Hyderabad's independence was also short-lived. To avoid bloodshed Mountbatten tried to persuade the ruling nizam to join India but to no avail. India had no intention of leaving a large independent Muslim-controlled state in its midst. Nehru was particularly displeased when the nizam loaned two hundred million rupees to Jinnah's new government. 'There can be no solution...,' Nehru warned Mountbatten, 'unless some effective punitive measures are taken... If these measures have to be taken, then there is not much point in indefinitely delaying them.'[68] After enduring an Indian blockade and invasion, which saw the occupation of Hyderabad city, it became part of India in September 1948. Hyderabad received no assistance from Mysore, the very large princely state to the south. Its maharaja wisely opted to become part of India.

The small Hyderabadi armed forces, over half of whom were Muslims, managed to hold out for just five days. There then followed a period of anarchy in which Hindu militias, backed by the Indian Army and local police, massacred up to 40,000 Muslim civilians.[69] Almost 18,000 people were thrown in prison. 'I always regard this as one of the great blots on the history of modern India,' wrote Lord Butler.[70] Churchill was aghast that Attlee stood by and did nothing to uphold the Indian Independence Act that guaranteed Hyderabad's freedom. He protested in the House of Commons but it did no good. Churchill wrote angrily to Anthony Eden saying the British government's acceptance of the situation was 'the most odious of transactions as any in which a British Ministry has ever been implicated.'[71]

A third much smaller princely state likewise found itself being fought over. Junagadh's Muslim ruler favoured Pakistan, though the population was predominantly Hindu. Geographically this was not practical as it was in south-western Gujarat and had no common border with Pakistan. When two of the nawab's principalities declared for India he sent his troops in. India responded by blockading Junagadh and occupying the principalities. The nawab fled to Pakistan following clashes between Junagadhi and Indian soldiers and his state became part of India in early 1948. Churchill's hopes that some of the princely states would choose to be British dominions were dashed. Independent India was to comprise of two countries and no more.

'If India becomes free,' Gandhi told Roosevelt in 1942, 'the rest will follow.'[72] He was right. Its departure heralded the beginning of the end for the imperial dream that Churchill and so many others had held so dear. Burma to the east of India had voted for independence outside the British Commonwealth in June 1947. Churchill and the Conservative party were completely opposed to this as it signalled another blow to the Empire. He spoke with a passion against the Burma Independence Bill on 5 November 1947 which was passing through Parliament. The bill would remove Burma permanently from the Empire and reduce it to a foreign power. Churchill also feared the country's various ethnic groups would set about each other without Britain's steadying hand. Arthur Henderson, for the government, said the Burmese should be able to experience 'the same democratic freedom that we enjoy ourselves'.[73]

In response Churchill highlighted the bloodshed in India, 'What about the deaths of half a million people in India? Enjoying democratic freedom!'[74] When the bill was put to the vote there were 288 for and 114 against. Churchill was annoyed that only half the members of parliament had bothered to turn up. The Burma Independence Act was passed in mid-November and Burma became an independent republic on 4 January 1948. Off India's south-eastern coast the Colony of Ceylon, by Act of Parliament which received Royal Assent on 10 December 1947, became a self-governing dominion within the British Commonwealth from 4 February 1948. Churchill could at least console himself that Ceylon continued to acknowledge the King.

The founders of modern India and Pakistan did not live long after independence. Gandhi was shot dead on 30 April 1948 by a Hindu fanatic in Delhi. Jinnah succumbed to his lung cancer in Karachi on 11 September the same year. Churchill always held Gandhi and Nehru responsible for partition rather than Jinnah. Mountbatten lingered in India as Governor-General until 21 June 1948 when he finally left for good. Many felt that his speedy end to the Raj had consigned India to partition and a wave of terrible sectarian bloodletting. Amongst them was Churchill. When they bumped into each other at Buckingham Palace Churchill made his feelings perfectly clear. 'Dickie, stop,' he ordered when Mountbatten strode towards him. 'What you did in India is as though you had struck me across the face with a riding whip.'[75] After that he refused to speak to Mountbatten over his 'sell-out' of India.[76] They did not properly communicate again until the early 1950s and even then Mountbatten got himself into trouble again. According to Patricia, his eldest daughter, 'I am truly glad to say that my father weathered this storm as he did so many others, and eventually Winston mellowed and forgave him.'[77]

Churchill viewed Indian independence with enormous regret and sorrow. On 28 October 1948 he told the House of Commons, 'Our imperial mission in India is at an end.' He then went on to say, 'It is our duty, whatever part we have taken in the past, to hope and pray for the wellbeing and happiness of all peoples of India.'[78] To date there had been little happiness. Earlier in the month at a Conservative rally in North Wales Churchill stated that 400,000 people had been butchered in Punjab alone. He had turned his ire on Sir Stafford Cripps saying he 'treats this frightful holocaust as a mere incident in the process of oriental self-government.'[79] His prognosis for Burma had also proved true: 'The orgy of anarchy and murder which I predicted to you in Burma has already come to pass.'[80] Churchill knew that India had now set a precedent and that the days of the British Empire were numbered. Few British colonies would settle for anything less than full independence. Churchill told Lord Moran that the Empire had been thrown away 'by a hideous act of self-mutilation, astounding to every nation of the world.'[81]

To Churchill's disappointment India's dominion status did not last long. 'The Prime Ministers of the Dominions plus Attlee plus Nehru go to see the King this afternoon and inform him that India wishes to be both a Republic and a Member of the Commonwealth,' wrote Harold Nicolson with amusement on 27 April 1949. 'They have drawn up a formula in which, ...they make a wholly illogical, meaningless, self-contradictory but admirable statement.'[82] Churchill was delighted though, remarking that 'neither the majesty of the Crown nor the personal dignity of the King had been impaired by the conditions under which India was continuing her membership of the Commonwealth.'[83] However, King George VI only remained India's head of state until January 1950 when it finally became a republic. India's last remaining link to Britain had been severed. It was the end of Empire.

Chapter 5

The Promised Land

Churchill, ever since his days as Colonial Secretary and his visit to the British Mandate of Palestine in 1921, had been impressed by what the Jews achieved in the Holy Land.[1] He always supported the controversial 1917 Balfour Declaration that backed the creation of a Jewish homeland in Palestine, which at the time was still part of the Ottoman Empire. Britain, in the years after the First World War and the collapse of the Ottoman Empire, was assigned responsibility for Palestine by the League of Nations. Although the mandate had been created in 1919 it was not formalised for another four years. It soon transpired that the British government had been extremely foolish in accepting the job.

Around this time the Jewish defence group known as Haganah emerged in Palestine. Initially its role was to protect Jews from their Arab neighbours. Haganah answered to the Jewish Agency, which regarded it as the basis for a future army so ensured that it was reasonably well disciplined. However, in some quarters of the Jewish community Haganah was not considered militant enough in its goals. This led to the emergence of Irgun in the 1930s as the military wing of the New Zionist Organisation.[2] Irgun's stated aim was the overthrow of British rule in preparation for the establishment of a Jewish state. This immediately made it the enemy of Palestine's Muslim Arabs.

When Churchill gave evidence to the Royal Commission in 1937 he made it perfectly clear that he still supported the idea of Zion, a separate Jewish homeland in Palestine. The commission recommended partition as the only way ahead, which the British government accepted in principle but wanted further study of the practicalities. The Arabs opposed partition and certainly did not want a separate Jewish state in their midst. They also wanted a stop to all Jewish immigration and the Jewish acquisition of land for fear that the Jews might one day outnumber them. A second commission was then set up to examine partition; this concluded that it would be all too difficult to achieve. The British government agreed.

Churchill was very well aware of the competing interests of the Jewish and Arab communities. Notably between 1922 and 1939 large numbers of Jews had migrated to Palestine seeking a better life, but had inadvertently made the situation even more volatile. Just before the Second World War the Palestinian Arabs rose up in open revolt against British rule. This necessitated a military campaign to crush them. When Churchill became prime minister in 1940 he refused to implement the recommendations of the 1939 Palestine White Paper that suggested granting an Arab veto on Jewish immigration and proportional representation. It had been hoped that this might help defuse the situation. During the war the question of Palestine's future was put on hold. Churchill, in order to safeguard Britain's position there and in Egypt, had felt it necessary to wage a military campaign against Vichy France's colonial forces in Lebanon and Syria in the summer of 1941. This had secured Palestine's northern borders.

Militant Jews remained just as restive as ever especially after the Arab Revolt. During the war Irgun never ceased its attacks on British army and police facilities in Palestine. In a shocking act of bravado in November 1944 it assassinated Lord Moyne, the British Minister for the Middle East, in Cairo. Moyne was a close friend of Churchill's and he took his murder badly. He angrily told the House of Commons, 'if our dreams for Zionism are to end in the smoke of assassins' pistols and our labours for its future to produce only a new set of gangsters worthy of Nazi Germany, many like myself will have to reconsider the position we have maintained so consistently in the past.'[3] Churchill, since his days as a Liberal Member of Parliament in Manchester, had been friends with Zionist leader and future Israeli President, Chaim Weizmann, who had lived in the city for three decades. Following Moyne's death Churchill refused to meet Weizmann ever again. In December 1944 the Labour party adopted a resolution put forward by Hugh Dalton favouring a shift in Palestine's population in favour of the Jews. It was anticipated by some that Dalton would be Attlee's choice for Foreign Secretary, but it was not to be.

Despite the terror attacks Churchill never forgot that over 30,000 Jews served in the British army during the war compared to just 6,000 Arabs. Moyne's killing was denounced by the Jewish Agency which had been steadily negotiating with the British. In consequence in the closing stages of the Second World War Haganah hunted down Irgun and its equally violent splinter group known as the Stern Gang. Zionist groups in America, to counter the bad publicity caused by the activities of the extremists, waged a publicity campaign highlighting the horrors of the Holocaust. What they wanted from a country where Jews were not universally welcome was support for Jewish immigration to Palestine rather than America.[4] However, William Yale at the US State Department warned President Truman that many of the 1.2 million Jewish refugees in Europe would prefer to emigrate to America. Furthermore, he cautioned that the Arabs would view mass Jewish immigration into Palestine as a move to create a Zionist state. Yale's advice was that America should firmly avoid supporting large-scale immigration into Palestine. Otherwise there would be widespread disorder and troops would be needed.

When the Second World War ended, responsibility for Palestine rested with the newly installed British Prime Minister Clement Attlee and his Foreign Secretary Ernest Bevin. While Bevin proved to be a very fine Foreign Secretary, the fate of Palestine proved to be his one weakness. He showed no inclination to honour Britain's previous pledges. 'The awesome fact is that by his Palestinian policy,' wrote Labour MP Harold Wilson, 'he so far angered the White House, ...that he could have imperilled his grand designs for Europe.'[5] There was a simple reason for this according to Wilson, 'It is not too strong a phrase to say that Ernie was anti-Semitic.' Bevin persuaded the Labour government that a separate Jewish state would not be viable. He was not the only one to hold such views. Hugh Dalton recalled how Attlee freely admitted that he had not offered two Jewish backbencher colleagues ministerial roles 'because they belonged to the Chosen People and he didn't think he wanted any more of them'.[6]

Truman sent Earl Harrison, the US representative on the Inter-Governmental Committee on Refugees, to investigate the situation in Europe in June 1945. He recommended that America should allow Jewish refugees into America within the framework of the existing immigration laws. Truman knew he would not get Congress to relax the stringent immigration quotas.[7] Instead he wrote to Attlee on 31 August 1945 suggesting that the solution lay in evacuating Jews to Palestine. Harrison's recommendation was that 100,000 be let in. In reply Attlee warned Truman that Britain had to consider the reaction of the Arabs. The US War Department estimated that if Palestine was opened to Jewish refugees, up to 400,000 troops would be needed to keep the peace. America might have to provide over 300,000 of them. This was the last thing the US State Department wanted, and in late September it recommended that America accept Attlee's decision that it would be impossible to allow large numbers of refugees into Palestine.

Attlee's government assessed that it was important not to do anything that would alienate Palestine's Arabs as this would upset the Arab states and endanger Britain's imperial interests in the Middle East. In September 1945, after consulting British regional representatives, Bevin produced a memorandum for the Cabinet that advised Britain should move to strengthen its strategic position in the Middle East with the Arab states. They after all represented the Empire's main source of oil and sat astride Britain's lines of communication. Furthermore, Bevin recommended, 'Britain should not make any concession that would assist American commercial penetration into the region which for generations has been an established British market.'[8]

By 1945 Haganah and its offshoots numbered over 10,000, though their training and equipment was mostly poor. At the end of the year the Jewish Agency, frustrated in its hopes for a relaxation of immigration controls to allow in thousands of survivors of the Holocaust, reconciled with Irgun. Attlee and Bevin, newly installed in office, steadfastly refused to permit the Jews to boost their numbers. Churchill during the Second World War had written, 'The systematic cruelties to which the Jewish people – men, women and children – have been exposed under the Nazi regime are amongst the most terrible events of history.'[9] Even he though was hesitant at the idea of allowing around 100,000 Jewish refugees and survivors from the horrific Nazi death camps into Palestine. He worried that there would not be room for them and questioned how they would be integrated. Furthermore, such a massive influx of Jews would almost certainly spark another Arab revolt. The Jews were understandably unhappy about this and launched a co-ordinated guerrilla campaign against the British. Targets were attacked in the cities of Haifa, Jaffa, Jerusalem and Tel Aviv. Irgun, feeling that it had much better shock value, preferred concentrating its attacks against people rather than property. In the early post-war years Britain's evacuation from Egypt led to a massive build-up of British forces in Palestine. Their presence naturally became the focus for both Jewish and Arab attacks.

Churchill had many close Jewish friends in America including influential financier and industrialist Bernard Baruch. They had known each other since the 1919 Paris Peace Conference. A decade later Baruch had helped rescue Churchill's finances after the devastating Wall Street crash. Baruch served Presidents Wilson, Roosevelt and Truman in various capacities. Churchill had even introduced him to King George VI. However, Baruch was not a Zionist. After Churchill met with Baruch and economist Elisha Friedman in New York in March 1946 the latter had written to Churchill. He was a member of the American Economic Committee for Palestine; it worked with the Palestine Economic Corporation which owned land north of Haifa. Friedman noted that he was deeply moved by Churchill's admission that he was a Zionist. He also told Churchill that Baruch 'said you were trying to convert him to Zionism. This is heartening to me for I have not succeeded in doing so, after thirty years of effort.'[10]

Apart from Chaim Weizmann, another man who influenced Churchill's thinking was Liberal politician Sir Herbert Samuel. They had met in Jerusalem in 1921 when Samuel was the British High Commissioner. Samuel was an ardent Zionist and controversially the first Jew to govern the Holy Land for two thousand years. He even told Weizmann that the Zionists needed to think bigger when it came to the future. Understandably Samuel's appointment was not universally popular, nonetheless he proved to be very impartial in his dealings with both sides. In the 1930s he rose to the leadership of the Liberals and served as Home Secretary. He then entered the House of Lords where he led his party. Samuel's aspirations for Palestine left a lasting and favourable impression on Churchill.

Churchill felt that Attlee needed President Truman to help settle the fate of Palestine. He worried that if Britain did not honour its pledge to help build a Jewish homeland then it faced the prospect of being asked to relinquish the mandate by the United Nations before a settlement was achieved. It seemed to Churchill that Bevin was going the right way to achieve this. He wrote to Field Marshal Brooke on 8 May 1946 to express his frustration. 'All idea of America being brought into Palestine to help, on account of their Jewish interests,' he said, 'seems to me to have been destroyed by the Government's policy.'[11] Churchill also worried that if Britain remained in Palestine then America would see it as a deliberate military ploy to counter the rise of Egyptian nationalism.

Britain divested itself of responsibility for part of the Mandate on 25 May 1946 when Transjordan, the large Arab area east of the Jordan River, was granted independence. This became the kingdom of Jordan under King Abdullah. He was backed by a military force known as the Arab Legion, commanded by British officers. This consisted of two brigades of motorised infantry supported by armoured cars and artillery. It was well-trained and disciplined and generously backed by a £10 million a year British subsidy. While this alleviated part of Britain's regional security burden it created a potentially hostile Arab state on the eastern border of Palestine.

There was a rapid upsurge in Jewish terrorism once the various Zionist militant groups agreed that the only way to secure a homeland was to drive the British out. 'Terrorism is no solution to the Palestine problem,' Churchill warned Attlee on 2 July 1946. 'Yielding to terrorism would be a disaster.'[12] He added that they should honour Britain's pledge to establish a Jewish homeland. Furthermore,

Churchill advised Attlee that he thought partition might be the best way ahead. Attlee's response was far from helpful and summed up Britain's dilemma. 'We shall not accept any solution,' he responded, 'which represents abandonment of our pledges to the Jews or our obligations to the Arabs.'[13] It would though be impossible to satisfy both communities, leaving British troops and police caught in the middle. Britain remained trapped by its sense of fair play.

Irgun brazenly bombed the British administrative headquarters in Jerusalem, located at the King David Hotel, on 22 July 1946. The devastation was appalling. Half a dozen bombs killed ninety-one people and wounded another forty-six. The Jewish Agency, realising this act had harmed its cause internationally, withdrew it's forces from the terror campaign, leaving it in the hands of the extremists. Irgun and its supporters could only muster about 1,800 active members, so now concentrated almost exclusively on terrorist attacks rather than larger-scale guerrilla operations.

Churchill always claimed that had he remained in power after the war he would have continued to support Zionism. This cause became more acute as thousands of persecuted and displaced Jews fled war-torn Europe regardless of international restrictions. He spelled out his position when he told the House of Commons on 1 August 1946, 'Palestine was not to be a Jewish National Home, but there was to be set up a Jewish National Home in Palestine.'[14] It was though hard to see how that could be achieved without more bloodshed. 'It is quite clear, however,' he cautioned, 'that this crude idea of letting all the Jews of Europe go into Palestine has no relation either to the problem of Europe or to the problem which arises in Palestine.'[15]

Churchill told the House of Commons that Britain needed to find a solution for Palestine or get out. 'I am convinced that from the moment when we feel ourselves unable to carry out properly and honestly the Zionist policy...,' he said, 'and which is the condition on which we received the Mandate for Palestine, it is our duty at any rate to offer to lay down the Mandate.'[16] He went on to say that as soon as the Second World War ended, Britain should have announced that if America would not help, then the burden should have been given to the United Nations. Churchill added, 'It is perfectly clear that Jewish warfare directed against the British in Palestine will, if protracted, automatically release us from all obligations.'[17] He could not understand why Attlee's government was prepared to 'scuttle' from Egypt and India and yet was prepared to fight on in Palestine.

That summer Field Marshal Montgomery flew out to assess the deteriorating situation. He had been stationed in Haifa as a divisional commander during the Arab Revolt in the late 1930s so knew the country well. Montgomery was not impressed by what he found. The police and the army were poorly co-ordinated and the police, who functioned as armed paramilitaries, had alienated the population. His assessment of General Sir Alan Cunningham, the High Commissioner, was damning. 'The High Commissioner seemed to me to be unable to make up his mind what to do,' remarked Montgomery dismissively. 'Indecision and hesitation were evident all down the line.'[18] He was also perturbed by the unspoken Jewish attitude, 'You dare not touch us.'[19] Jewish terrorists seemed to be regularly operating with impunity.

Montgomery told Lieutenant General Sir Evelyn Barker, the military commander in Palestine, 'All ranks must understand that they were in for a very unpleasant job.' Also they were facing 'a war against a fanatical and cunning enemy... no one would know who was friend and who was foe.'[20] It was, as far as Montgomery was concerned, time to take the gloves off and take firm action. He understood that a security solution was not the same as a political one, but the latter was not his responsibility. Unfortunately his clampdown looked to American eyes as if Britain was now openly declaring war on the Jews. To make matters worse an Anglo-American report was recommending the acceptance of a further 100,000 Jewish refugees into Palestine. Montgomery, on his way back from the Middle East, stopped off in Nicosia. 'The atmosphere in Cyprus was indeed one of peace and quiet,' he wrote in his diary, 'there were no problems (as yet) to disturb the even tenor of the daily round.'[21] Little did he know that the island would soon be the scene of further violent anti-British agitation.

Montgomery was about to be appointed Chief of the Imperial General Staff at exactly the time when he was least suited to the job. Just like Churchill he retained a very Victorian view of empire and Britain's longstanding spheres of influence. Montgomery understandably found it hard to accept that Britain's enormous military power generated during the Second World War was waning rapidly thanks to the unsustainable financial burden. He was foremost a war fighter and a strategist looking to fight the next war, especially in Europe. Instead though his job was now to oversee Britain's painful withdrawal from Empire. This would lead to constant quarrels with Attlee and Bevin.

In the meantime on 5 August 1946 the Jewish Agency proposed partition as the way ahead. Truman agreed that this was probably the best solution and told Attlee on 3 October it would 'command the support of public opinion in the United States'.[22] In addition he called for immediate and substantial immigration into Palestine. At this very point Arthur Creech Jones, a known Zionist sympathiser, was appointed British Colonial Secretary. His department immediately began to work towards partition but this was resisted by Bevin's Foreign Office.

To Churchill and Montgomery's dismay, at the end of October 1946 Creech Jones decided in his wisdom that the best way to ease tensions in Palestine was to release all those arrested for terrorism. His logic was that if this was done then the Jewish Agency would denounce violence and seek a political agreement. The following month detained terrorist leaders were released and British weapons searches suspended. Creech's blind faith was misplaced. The consequence was that with more terrorists on the loose murder and sabotage increased. 'As a result of this concession by the Labour Government, more and more restrictions were placed upon the troops in Palestine,' said Montgomery angrily. 'Meanwhile, British soldiers and British members of the Palestine Police continued to be killed and wounded.' Montgomery immediately confronted Attlee, pointing out all Britain had done was surrender the initiative to the terrorists. He then flew to Palestine to review security measures which he deemed as 'completely gutless'.[23] Montgomery made his recommendations, but the War Office and Colonial Office could not agree on the best approach. Attlee was only finally moved to strengthen security after a British officer and three non-commissioned officers were kidnapped and flogged in retaliation for the whipping of a terrorist.

During the New Year the British government failed to get any semblance of a settlement between the Arabs and the Jews. It then dramatically announced that it was simply giving up. Foreign Secretary Bevin told the House of Commons on 18 February 1947 that Britain was handing the Mandate over to the United Nations sometime in September. He explained the British government did not have the authority to hand Palestine to either of the competing parties or to authorise partition. Bevin, seeking to head off criticism concluded, 'We trust, however, that as the question is now to be referred to the United Nations all concerned will exercise restraint until their judgement is known.'[24]

While this was what Churchill had wanted all along, he was greatly vexed at the government's failure to get an agreement and by the ongoing delay before a British exit. To make matters worse the government was putting Palestine before the United Nations without any British recommendations for a solution. Once Britain had washed its hands, the chances of the United Nations getting a peace settlement were very small. In the meantime before September British forces would still be targeted as the Arabs and Jews manoeuvred for dominance. It was suggested that martial law be declared during the interim but Montgomery opposed it as he felt such a move would be too disruptive. In light of neither the Arabs nor Jews favouring partition it meant both sides would try to take power when the British finally left. The Jews declared they would set up an independent Jewish state regardless of what the United Nations decided. By this point there were over 1.2 million Arabs and 650,000 Jews living in Palestine. The Jews surrounded by Arab neighbours faced a grim future. They would have no choice but to fight or face extermination.

An irate Churchill in early March 1947 continued to castigate the government in the House of Commons. He could not understand why there was a specific time for Britain's withdrawal from India but not one for Palestine. Churchill highlighted in the Commons that the Labour government had spent £82 million in Palestine since coming to power and that 100,000 troops were tied down there keeping the two warring communities apart. In addition he pointed out that there were up to four times the number of troops in Palestine as India. This was rather disingenuous as India was on the brink of independence and Britain had drawn down its forces there.

While all this arguing was going on in the House of Commons, British servicemen and workers were still regularly dying in Palestine. Jewish terrorists' next act was to strike at British commercial interests. The Shell oil refinery at Haifa in northern Palestine was bombed on 30 March 1947 and the railways were constantly sabotaged. Irgun decided to put more pressure on the British government by stepping up attacks on British Army and police personnel. The idea was to increase the casualty rate in order to undermine the British government's resolve even further. For every punishment that the British handed out the terrorists returned in kind.

Violence across Palestine spiralled and the terrorists became ever bolder. Members of Irgun and the Stern Gang attacked Acre prison on 4 May 1947 and liberated forty-one of their members. Two of the attackers were later caught and hanged. In reprisal Irgun hanged two British Army sergeants in late July. The shocked Jewish authorities denounced these murders and called on the Jewish community to report whoever did it. Churchill blamed the sergeants' deaths on the government's indecision. At a Conservative political rally at Blenheim Palace on 4 August he said, 'A year ago I urged the Government to give notice to the U[nited] N[ations] O[rganisation] that we could and would bear the burden of insult and injury no longer. But the Ministers only gaped in shameful indecision.'[25] Still the British government dithered in its decision to go.

At the end of August an exasperated Churchill urged the government to bring the Jewish terrorist campaign to an end as quickly as possible. 'It is quite certain that what is going on now in Palestine,' he said gravely, 'is doing us a great deal of harm in every way.'[26] Churchill went on to reiterate that for eighteen months Britain had been throwing money at the problem and had 100,000 men tied down. 'What are they doing there? he asked. 'What good are we getting out of it?'[27] In his view America should shoulder fifty per cent of the burden otherwise Britain should leave immediately and hand the security problem to the United Nations.

Increasingly it was impossible for the British government to justify Britain's continuing presence in Palestine either at home or abroad. Britain had become a convenient scapegoat while the rest of the world avoided the terrible situation. Attlee, realising it was time to call it a day, on 16 October 1947 declared all British troops would be withdrawn from Palestine by 1 August the following year. This was then brought forward to 15 May 1948 because Attlee and Bevin did not want to upset the Arab states by getting involved in partition. Montgomery was unhappy because abandoning Palestine meant losing Britain's primary military base in the Middle East. Cyprus and Egypt were not as central as Palestine.

The plan was that there would be four timed phases for the withdrawal of British troops and civil servants. The Arabs and Jews would be left to fight over the spoils as best they could. Montgomery warned, 'The fact must be faced that there will be a complete breakdown of civil government, and law and order, as we vacate the [phased withdrawal] areas in turn.'[28] Three main areas were to be held to the very end, Jerusalem, Jaffa and Haifa, with the final evacuation to take place from the latter. In all Montgomery had to safely get 80,000 men out of Palestine, some of whom would be withdrawn to Jordan.

The United Nations still did not ride to the rescue as both Attlee and Churchill vainly hoped. On 29 November 1947 it recommended partition, but crucially would not provide any troops to oversee or enforce the process. 'No one is sleeping,' recalled young Jewish soldier Uri Avnery, 'Everyone is sitting by the radio. …the General Assembly of the United Nations has decided in favour of the founding of a Jewish and an Arab State. Joy explodes like a storm.'[29] Although the Jews accepted the recommendations the Palestinian Arabs and the Arab states backing them refused. The Arabs warned that they would fight if the United Nations' proposal was implemented.

'On 30 November 1947, when the first shots of war sounded,' adds Uri Avnery, 'the national institutions proclaimed the mobilization of everyone between seventeen and twenty-five years of age.'[30] From that point until the following spring the Israelis, appreciating they would need a conventional army to ward off their Arab neighbours, began converting their guerrilla forces. As part of this process Haganah was employed to disarm some of the more extreme and uncooperative Jewish elements. At the end of the year Churchill rather bizarrely blamed the sectarian violence following Indian independence on Attlee's Palestinian policy. In a speech made in Manchester on 6 December 1947 he argued that if half the troops deployed in Palestine had been in India they could have overseen a more orderly transfer of power to the Indians. He was simply making political capital from two terrible situations.

Much to Attlee and Churchill's consternation the United Nations' call for the partition of Palestine sparked unrest in Aden. This British colony and the surrounding protectorates guarded the important approaches to the Red Sea. Aden by the end of the Second World War was home to numerous military and Royal Air Force units, most notably at Khormaksar. In Aden, just like Palestine, there were historic tensions between the Arab and Jewish communities. These were aggravated by gathering Jewish refugees from Yemen hoping to reach Palestine. Refugee Salem Jarufi reassured his wife, 'The British will not let them harm us.'[31] Anti-Jewish riots broke out in December 1947 resulting in almost a hundred casualties, most of whom were Jewish. Tragically amongst them was Jarufi's wife. In an orgy of destruction Jewish homes, shops and schools were smashed. To the embarrassment of the authorities the local British levies sided with the Arabs. To restore order two British infantry battalions had to be airlifted from Egypt. It was clear that despite British efforts the days of the Jews in Yemen were numbered.

Now that Britain's withdrawal was imminent, Palestinian Jews and Arabs moved to secure as much ground as they could. By March 1948 around 5,000 men of the volunteer Arab Liberation Army had infiltrated Palestine from Syria. They began to attack Jewish settlements and tried to hold the key roads. Jewish fighters on 20 April 1948 boldly took control of Haifa despite resistance from local Arab units. The Jews constituted fifty-five percent of the 146,000 population and dominated Mount Carmel as well as the strategic approaches to the city. The British, after warning the Arabs, refused to get involved when the fighting broke out. Major General Hugh Stockwell, the British commander in northern Palestine, brokered a ceasefire and was left occupying only the port area ready for the last of his troops to embark. Outside Haifa at the 3rd Hussars depot two British sergeants, who were sympathetic to the Jewish cause, stole two Cromwell tanks and delivered them to Tel Aviv. These formed the foundation of what was to become the war-winning Israeli armoured corps.

Irgun, under Menachem Begin, five days later in the early hours of 25 April decided to crush the strong Arab enclave at Jaffa. This was the largest Arab town in Palestine, which under the United Nations' partition plan would have been assigned to them. 'This will be one of the most decisive battles in the war for Israel's independence,' Begin told his men.[32] It proved a very international battle with Jaffa defended by Palestinian Arabs, Iraqis, Syrians and Bosnian volunteers. Most of the civilian population had already left in the preceding months, leaving the city an eerie ghost town. Advancing from Tel Aviv the Jews fought their way into the northern suburb of Manshiyyeh. 'They had such firepower and we had strict orders to conserve ammunition,' recalled Irgun commander Yoseph Nachmias. 'That afternoon we withdrew, to lick our wounds.'[33]

When Foreign Secretary Bevin heard what was happening he immediately instructed the British military to 'see to it that the Jews did not manage to occupy Jaffa, or if they did, were immediately turned out.'[34] General Cunningham, the British High Commissioner, ordered Irgun to withdraw from Manshiyyeh otherwise Tel Aviv would be bombed and shelled. Begin ignored his ultimatum. Montgomery and his senior commanders could see no point in losing more British lives, but orders were orders. In the name of fairness and to ensure the Arabs retained a foothold on the

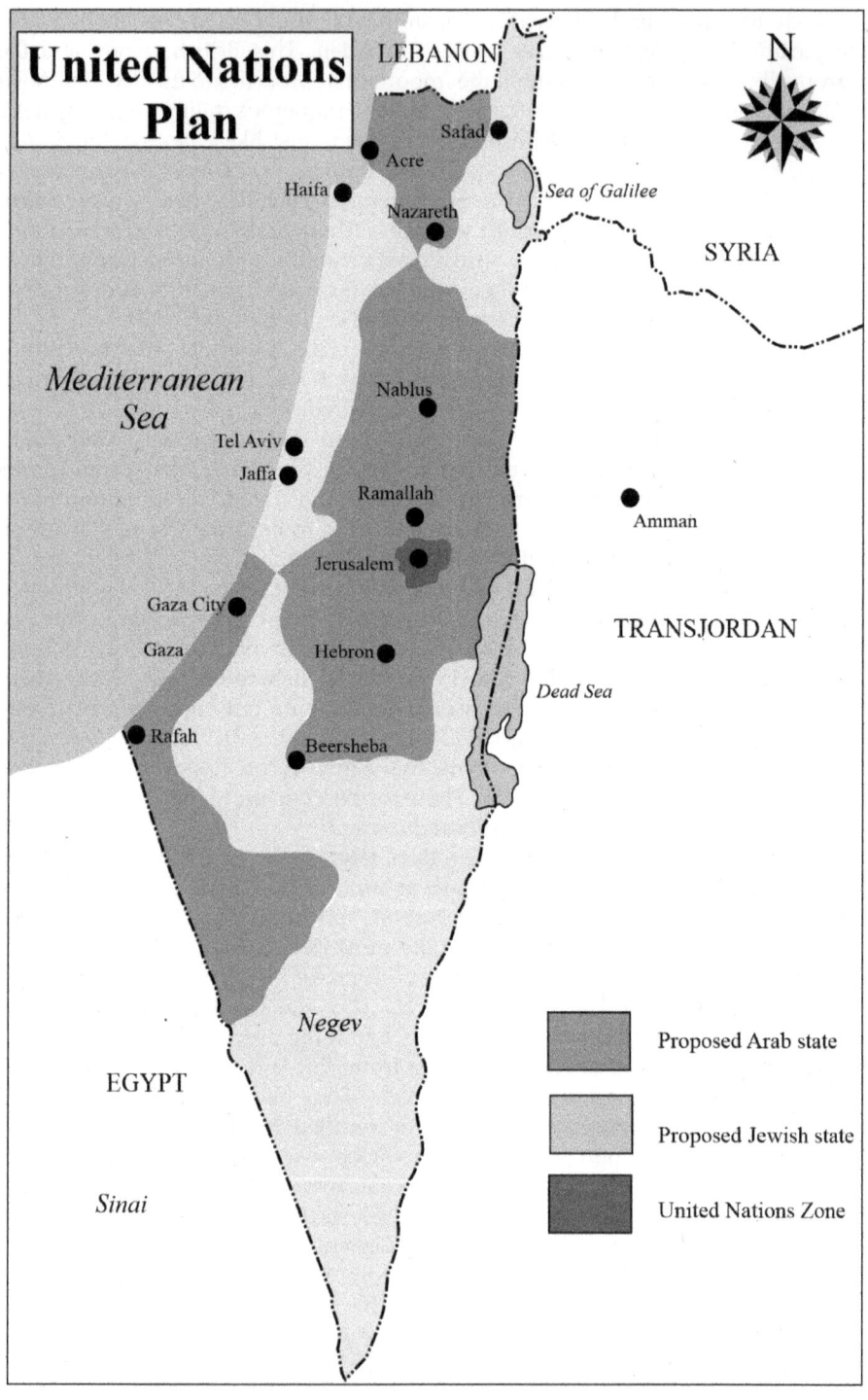

Mediterranean coast he dutifully instructed General Sir Gordon McMillan, the British military commander in Palestine, to forcibly prevent Irgun from taking Jaffa. British infantry, supported by tanks and fighter aircraft, proceeded to drive the Jewish forces off. 'The British gave us hell. We lost forty-one in the fighting for Jaffa, and eighty per cent of those were killed by the British,' said Nachmias. 'They shelled us and shelled us, and when they thought we were exhausted they advanced in tanks.'[35]

This British military intervention proved to be a futile waste of time. 'How can we give Jaffa back to the Arabs when there are hardly any Arabs left to give it back to?' General McMillan asked the British Middle East Commander General Sir John Crocker.[36] The whole affair rapidly became yet another public relations disaster for Britain. Montgomery was angered when confronted by Attlee and Bevin who wanted to know why the army had not prevented the massacre of 23,000 Arabs at Haifa. He pointed out that these were exaggerated press reports and that such numbers had not been verified by the War Office. Jaffa had a peacetime population of 70,000, but less than 5,000 remained in the city during the fighting as General McMillan discovered. Montgomery was further mortified when the government unfairly claimed it had lost confidence in the army. The operation had been pointless because once the British completed their withdrawal Haganah and Irgun units marched into Jaffa anyway.

Just over two weeks later the Jewish state of Israel was declared on 14 May 1948. Harold Nicolson jotted in his diary, 'All the pleasure I might have felt at this realisation of the hopes of Zionism is clouded by the fear of war and the humiliation we have suffered.'[37] In response five neighbouring Arab armies immediately invaded the fledgling country. From the north and northeast came Iraqi, Lebanese and Syrian forces. From the east Jordanian troops attempted to isolate the Israelis in and around Jerusalem; and from the southwest came the Egyptians. British units stationed in the Suez Canal Zone did nothing to prevent the Egyptian army attacking Israel from Sinai.

Attlee and Bevin were in a very tricky diplomatic position. The Egyptian and Jordanian forces were all trained and equipped by Britain. Although the Lebanese and Syrians were armed by the French they had also received British training. Most notably the Jordanian Arab Legion was under the direction of two British officers, Lieutenant General John Glubb and Brigadier Norman Lash. They led the Arab Legion over the River Jordan to occupy the West Bank. Although both were described as soldiers of fortune their actions made Britain complicit in the invasion of Israel. 'The Arab Legion (which is financed and officered by us) have almost captured Jerusalem,' noted Harold Nicolson on 22 May. 'I do not know how the Government can justify this attack on the Holy City under our auspices. It will make a terrible effect abroad.'[38] However, Glubb grumbled to King Abdullah of Jordan, 'The British have not given us any ammunition since they evacuated Palestine.'[39]

Further complicating matters Bevin had approved the formation of the Arab Liberation Army. Before the invasion King Abdullah, against the wishes of Glubb and McMillan, let Arab volunteers cross the Allenby Bridge into Palestine to join it. Bevin had also concluded an agreement with Iraq to supply it with large-scale military assistance. This was swiftly cancelled after riots in Baghdad against British imperialism. Much to Churchill's irritation the British government appeared to think that Israel was doomed and preferred to give tacit support to its Arab neighbours. 'We seem to be behaving badly and malevolently all round,' observed Harold Nicolson despondently.[40]

In the face of such a concerted Arab assault it certainly appeared as if Israel must surely be overwhelmed.[41] Field Marshal Montgomery predicted that the Jews would last less than two weeks; they proved him wrong. In early July they launched a counter-offensive that drove all the Arab armies back except for the Jordanians. The fighting continued into the winter and ended with the Jordanians still holding East Jerusalem and the Egyptians occupying Gaza. Humiliated by their defeat the Arab states reluctantly agreed to separate armistices. Thanks to the war around 750,000 Palestinian Arabs were forced from their homes. Up to 300,000 fled to Gaza, with a similar number crossing to Jordan, Lebanon and Syria. While Jordan attempted to assimilate them by granting citizenship, Egypt refused to do the same. This was to store up terrible trouble for the future, especially after the Egyptians lost control of Gaza to Israel in 1967.

'It seems to me very likely, although I cannot, of course, prove it,' observed Churchill, 'that the Foreign Secretary misjudged the relative power of the two sides, and it certainly looked on paper as if the Syrians, Egyptians and Arabs, invading from so many quarters, would win. That was not my view.'[42] Although Israel had to fight for its very existence, to Churchill's annoyance for six months Britain refused to recognize the new state, despite recognition by America and the Soviet Union. A Jewish homeland had been created but not in the manner that he had hoped for. As far as Churchill and Montgomery were concerned, the Labour government had made a complete and utter mess of Palestine.

The Stern Gang moved to ensure that Churchill's sought-after intervention by the United Nations failed. They wanted no compromise with the Arabs or talk of partition or possible union with Jordan. On 17 September 1948 they murdered Count Bernadotte, the Swedish mediator, on the streets of Jerusalem. 'What harm all this will do to the U[nited] N[ations] O[rganisation] and the cause of Zionism,' lamented Harold Nicolson. 'Poor Weizmann – his life's work sullied by these ghetto thugs.'[43] The only thing achieved was the armistices.

Selwyn Lloyd, who served as Foreign Minister during Churchill's second term as Prime Minister, firmly blamed Ernest Bevin. 'Unfortunately he also deserves a place in history,' wrote Lloyd in his memoirs, 'for the fiasco made by the post-war Government over Palestine.'[44] The Arab world blamed Britain for allowing the Jews to create Israel. The Balfour Declaration had sown the seeds and Britain had been responsible for the Palestine Mandate. As far as the Arabs were concerned, Britain had equipped the Zionists and surrendered Palestine to Haganah. Egypt and the others would not be reconciled with the Jewish state. It closed the approaches to the Suez Canal to Israel in May 1950 in an effort to choke its economy. Tensions continued to mount for the next six years until the Suez Crisis. Churchill agreed with Lloyd when he remarked, 'To say the Opposition might not have done much better is no answer. The blame lay with the Government and its overwhelming majority.'[45] Slowly but surely Israel would align with the West while the Arabs aligned with the Soviet Union. This would bring the Cold War to the Middle East, which was something no one had foreseen or wanted.

PART THREE

THE COLD WAR BEGINS

Chapter 6

Berlin-the First Test

In Europe, as Churchill feared, Stalin soon tested the Western Allies' resolve and opened the Cold War with a vengeance. First though Stalin had unfinished business in Czechoslovakia. In February 1948 a Communist coup in Prague ended the country's brief attempts at democracy. Angrily Churchill declared, 'There will never be a settled peace in Europe, while Asiatic Imperialism and Communist domination rule over the whole of Central and Eastern Europe.'[1] Stalin then upped the ante by sending Finnish President Juho Paasikivi a proposal for a treaty of friendship, similar to the Soviet treaties with Hungary and Romania. This set alarm bells ringing in both London and Washington as it suggested Stalin was intent on absorbing Finland into the Soviet bloc. There were also rumours of a similar proposal to Norway. President Truman on 17 March declared that Soviet pressure on Finland posed a threat to all Scandinavian states.

That same day the Treaty of Brussels was signed creating the Western European Union, a military alliance between Britain, France and the three Benelux countries. Churchill viewed this as a step in the right direction and grudgingly praised the work of Foreign Secretary Ernest Bevin. 'In the Brussels Treaty... he has, albeit somewhat sheepishly,' said Churchill, 'given effect to the theme of United Europe.'[2] However, what it did not do was provide an American security guarantee for Europe. The combined military forces of the Western European Union were hardly capable of stopping the Soviets. Bevin warned Norway not to succumb to Soviet blandishments. He also messaged George Marshall, US Secretary of State, highlighting the threat to Scandinavia, pointing out the defection of Norway would open up the approaches to the Atlantic. 'This would in turn prejudice our chance of calling any halt to the relentless advance of Russia in Western Europe,' warned Bevin.[3]

To the alarm of Churchill, Attlee and Truman, the Finns signed the treaty with the Soviet Union on 6 April 1948. The Finns had already fought two wars against the Soviets that culminated in the loss of about ten percent of their territory. They could not afford another conflict against their vast and well-armed neighbour. President Paasikivi decided prudently that it was better to have Stalin as an ally then an enemy. This development left Norway and Sweden feeling extremely exposed. In response Bevin suggested a regional Atlantic Approaches pact that could include America, Britain, Denmark, Iceland, Norway and Sweden.

In the meantime, Stalin was displeased at the prospect of the establishment of a West German government after the American, British and French combined their occupation zones for administrative and economic purposes. This would formalise the border with the Soviet zone and offered little prospect of a reunified Germany, which Stalin hoped to dominate once the British and Americans were gone. Furthermore, divided Berlin inside the Soviet zone was an open city, which posed a security headache for both sides. The Soviets were not happy that people were crossing from Soviet East Berlin to American, British and French-administered sectors of West Berlin with impunity. In response during April 1948 the Soviets began searching military trains coming into the city, so the Americans started resupplying the garrison by air. Soviet aircraft then began buzzing Allied flights which resulted in a mid-air collision with a British aircraft causing fatalities on both sides.

On 7 April, two days after the incident, Field Marshal Montgomery, Chief of the Imperial General Staff, flew into Berlin to meet with Marshal Vasily Sokolovsky, the Soviet military commander in eastern Germany. When confronted by the waiting media Montgomery responded, referring to Sokolovsky, that he was looking forward to seeing 'a very old friend of mine'.[4] After their two hour meeting Montgomery reported the Soviet commander 'ridiculed the suggestion that the Russians want war'.[5] Ironically Montgomery considered General Lucius Clay, the US commander in Germany, more dangerous than Sokolovsky. 'General Clay considers that World War III will begin in six months' time [i.e. October 1948],' noted Montgomery, 'indeed he might well bring it on himself by shooting his way up the autobahn to Berlin if the Russians were difficult about things.'[6] General Clay informed General Bradley, head of the US Army, that there were only 2,000 American troops in Berlin.[7] Bradley said they might need to consider evacuation as he doubted there was the political will in Washington to fight over the possession of the city. Clay thought this was a bad idea. 'If we mean to hold Europe against Communism,' he told Bradley, 'we must not budge.'[8] Churchill and Truman agreed with such bullish sentiments. However, there were only 60,000 American soldiers in all of Europe, which was nowhere near enough to stop Stalin taking Berlin by force.

Across the Atlantic thought was being given to joint North American and European security. The Canadian Prime Minister Louis St Laurent, who had succeeded Mackenzie King, on 28 April in the Canadian House of Commons advocated a single mutual defence pact that would include and supersede the Brussels Treaty. Ernest Bevin welcomed it in Parliament a week later. The real breakthrough came on 12 May when the Republican Senator Arthur Vandenberg, chairman of the influential Senate Foreign Relations Committee, tabled a motion calling for the United States to enter a collective mutual defence arrangement. The Senate adopted his resolution sixty-four votes to four. This sowed the seeds for the North Atlantic Treaty. Churchill's hope of bonding America with Europe took a step closer.

In early June a conference was held in London that resulted in a six-power pact.[9] Under the terms of this a constituent assembly and a federal government were to be established in western Germany. On 21 June the Allies introduced the Deutsche

Mark to replace the Reichsmark. This showed that the Allies, far from punishing defeated Germany, were determined to help with its economic recovery. Stalin wanted nothing to do with this new currency which was initially suggested for use across the whole of Germany. Furthermore, Stalin considered West Berlin as economically part of the Soviet zone in eastern Germany. The last thing he wanted was a potentially prosperous Western bastion in Berlin far behind Soviet lines. Although the Soviets demanded the Deutsche Mark not be issued in Berlin, it soon became standard currency in all four sectors of the city. The following day the Soviets announced they would introduce the East German Mark in their zone of occupied Germany and in East Berlin.

Stalin, not to be out done, on 23 June called a conference in Warsaw of all the Communist bloc countries. The delegates condemned the London pact and demanded the demilitarization of Germany and the creation of an all-German provisional government. They also called for four-power control of Germany's industrial Ruhr region – the Soviets had been excluded from this under the Potsdam agreement. Churchill, Attlee and Truman saw this as an attempt by Stalin to extend Communist control over the whole of Germany.

Determined to get his own way, Stalin moved to evict the Americans, British and French from West Berlin. He planned, rather than risking force, to make life as unpleasant as possible. On 24 June 1948 the Soviet occupation forces in eastern Germany cut all movement into the city by land and water. 'East and West glared at each other,' wrote Churchill's daughter Mary, 'and the situation was as fraught and potentially deadly as it had been at any time since the end of the war.'[10] West Berlin was left cut off 160 kilometres deep inside Soviet territory without fuel or food. The situation looked grim.

Ernest Bevin immediately voiced the British government's objections to the blockade, which Churchill approved of. Truman also made America's position perfectly clear: 'We stay in Berlin – period.'[11] America, Britain and France sent the Soviet Union a stern message demanding the immediate lifting of the blockade. 'The note was very strongly worded,' noted Montgomery, 'and virtually left no loophole for either side to climb down without serious loss of face.'[12] John Colville, now working as Private Secretary to Princess Elizabeth, was of exactly the same view. 'We have taken a very firm line and cannot go back on it,' he observed. 'The Russians may find it difficult to climb down without losing face.'[13] Montgomery had predicted in April that Stalin would try to squeeze the Allies out of Berlin over a prolonged period. It seemed his assessment was about to come true. What followed was an eleven-month armed standoff with West Berliners enduring siege-like conditions.

If Britain and America were not prepared to fight their way to the city it would require a massive airlift to keep the Allied garrison and the civilian population of West Berlin resupplied. Conducting this would become a symbol of Western defiance to the Soviet threat to Europe. During the Second World War the Allies gained extensive experience of major airlifts. In the Mediterranean and Europe they transported entire divisions by air and in the Far East created an airbridge across the Himalaya Mountains to fly supplies from India to Chiang Kai-shek's Nationalist Chinese forces. Churchill would have been horrified if he had known that Britain's commitment to an airlift hung in the balance thanks to the incompetence of Foreign Office officials. It was a Labour Member of Parliament and President of the Board of Trade, Harold Wilson, who saved the day. 'I was responsible for the Berlin airlift,' he claimed. 'It was done by me on a piece of blotting paper.'[14]

Shortly after the blockade was instigated, Attlee called an emergency Cabinet meeting to consult with his ministers about the feasibility of an airlift. 'Ernie Bevin wanted to do it,' recalled Wilson who was present, 'but the Foreign Office were against it.'[15] Wilson proceeded to point out to Attlee that the Foreign Office's figures were wrong as they had left a nought off. At Attlee's request Wilson recalculated them there and then and said, 'It can be done.'[16] 'Right,' responded Attlee decisively, 'we'll go ahead with it.'[17] According to Wilson no official records were kept of this, presumably to avoid embarrassing Bevin.[18]

The first flights of the Berlin airlift commenced on 26 June. There were three existing air corridors, two from the British-occupied zone of Germany and one from the American zone, that were employed before the blockade. Aircraft either landed at Gatow in the British sector of the city or at Tempelhof in the American sector. In light of the Soviets having closed all ground routes, it seemed only a matter of time before they closed it to air traffic. However, to achieve that would mean shooting down unarmed British or American aircraft.

Four days after the Soviet blockade commenced, Montgomery recommended the best way to show a unified front was to appoint a supreme allied commander of the Western European Union armies. However, he could not get the agreement of the chiefs of the Royal Navy and Royal Air Force. When Montgomery was summoned by Albert Alexander, the Minister of Defence, on 7 July he asked the minister pointedly, 'Is the Government prepared to go to war for Berlin?'[19] Alexander, who had not expected such an ultimatum, passed the matter to Attlee who did not respond. 'I received no answer to my question, neither then nor later,' grumbled Montgomery.[20]

Truman, no doubt with Churchill's Fulton speech on his mind, wrote to Winston on 10 July. '"Communism", so called, is our next great problem,' he said. 'I hope we can solve it without the "blood and tears"'.[21] Although Truman did not want to be driven from West Berlin, he rejected General Clay's proposal to push a convoy with military protection through to the city. Such an act could spark a shooting match along the entire east-west German border. In contrast General Eisenhower, like Churchill, felt a show of force should have been made. 'I believe that had Clay's first advice been accepted at the time…,' he wrote, 'the clear rights of the United States would have been even more effectively demonstrated, and their respect for them underscored.'[22] Nonetheless, Truman did authorise the deployment of B-29 heavy bombers, that could reach targets in the Soviet Union, to bases in Britain. Significantly this type of aircraft had been used to drop the atomic bombs on Japan.

Montgomery met with Attlee on 15 July and gave the prime minister a sobering prognosis. He warned that the British Army was unprepared for war in Europe and the armies of their European allies, Belgium and France 'must be regarded as useless'.[23] The Soviets had over a million men outside their own borders in eastern Europe, that were more than capable of overrunning western Europe.[24] They were backed by up to eighty divisions in the western part of the Soviet Union that could be ready at short notice. Another forty were available in the Soviet Far East. In Europe the British could muster just over four divisions, the Americans two and the French three. These forces were completely uncoordinated, reporting directly to their respective governments. Montgomery urged that it was time once again to appoint a supreme commander if any sort of coherent strategy was going to be put together. He also wanted Albert Alexander, who he viewed as ineffectual, removed. However, after their initial support his service colleagues would not back him in this. Regarding Alexander's fate, Montgomery noted in his diary, 'He still sits tight.'[25]

Montgomery and others felt that the government had brought this situation upon themselves. 'It is so easy to criticise; to blame Winston and Roosevelt for Yalta;' wrote Harold Nicolson on 16 July, 'to blame Bevin for having allowed this untenable Berlin position to consolidate itself.'[26] Nicolson though acknowledged that they were all victims of a 'dreadful chain of circumstance.'[27] Montgomery, who greatly respected Churchill, ensured that the leader of the Opposition was fully briefed. Churchill made it clear he was worried that the government might lose its nerve and seek to appease Stalin. 'The gravity of events makes me anxious,' he told Montgomery on 18 July; 'I trust we are not approaching another "Munich". For such a crime by the British Government there would be no forgiveness.'[28] Montgomery no doubt complained to Churchill about Alexander, though there was nothing Churchill could do. It was not good that the Defence Minister and the Chief of the Imperial General Staff did not get on. 'I am sure he disliked me intensely,' said Montgomery.[29]

Three days after their meeting Churchill wrote to Attlee to express his alarm at the state of Britain's defences. He was also vexed that Attlee had allowed Harold Wilson, in his role as President of the Board of Trade, to negotiate the 1947 Anglo-Soviet Trade Agreement. This essentially agreed to barter Soviet grain and timber for British engineering equipment. Churchill was concerned that such machinery could be used to make weapons. Furthermore, the agreement had scaled back the Soviet wartime debt to Britain. As far as Churchill was concerned the government had been treating the Soviet Union much too leniently.

Air Chief Marshal Arthur Tedder, who was the Chief of the Air Staff and a former Second World War commander, may also have briefed Churchill. Tedder had served as Deputy Supreme Commander, under Eisenhower, for the Allied Expeditionary Force in North-West Europe during the Second World War. He knew all about the use of strategic air power and it was his role to oversee the Royal Air Force's contribution to the Berlin airlift. Ironically he had been responsible for the Transportation Plan designed to cut German lines of communication, now he was trying to throw a lifeline to the German capital. Thanks to Tedder a number of Royal Air Force airfields had been lengthened and widened to accommodate the massive B-29 bomber. As a result two American bomber groups were able to deploy to Britain in mid-July.[30] None of these though were capable of delivering atomic bombs. The modified B-29 variants were initially held back at Roswell Air Force Base in New Mexico.

Although Stalin was aware of the bombers arriving in Britain, it is unclear if he knew what type they were. Despite this, their presence had one meaning. In a deliberate piece of well-staged propaganda, five B-29s were photographed flying over the white cliffs of Dover. Stalin was probably not threatened by this. 'I do not believe the atomic bomb to be as serious a force as certain politicians are inclined to regard it,' he wrote. 'Atomic bombs are intended to intimidate the weak-nerved, but they cannot decide the outcome of a war, since atomic bombs are by no means sufficient for this purpose.'[31]

Despite the continuing tensions over the blockade, Churchill and Clementine went on vacation to France that summer. 'I remember a particularly pleasant and harmonious holiday in August 1948,' said their daughter Mary, 'when my parents installed themselves for nearly a month at the Hôtel du Roi René in Aix-en-Provence.'[32] Mary and her husband Christopher Soames went with them. The night before they departed she jotted in her diary, 'The news from Berlin and Moscow is frightening... I wonder if I shall live to set out on a holiday which is not overshadowed by some impending world disaster.'[33]

At the beginning of August British civilian contractors began to supplement the Berlin airlift using a variant of the Handley Page Halifax bomber. The Soviets did everything short of shooting down the aircraft involved in the airlift. This included radio interference, dazzling the pilots with search lights and releasing balloons into the air corridors. Even more dangerously, Soviet fighter pilots buzzed approaching aircraft and fired their guns in the general vicinity. A total of 733 harassment incidents were logged between 10 August 1948 and 15 August 1949. Crashes were not uncommon. On 25 July a US aircraft hit an apartment block in the Friedenau district of the American sector with the loss of its crew. Nineteen days later a US aircraft overshot the runway at Tempelhof, struck a fence and caught fire; luckily the crew escaped unscathed.

Some senior Conservatives were unhappy about Churchill being absent at such a critical time. Although he was supposed to be working on his memoirs, Berlin was never far from his mind. He felt standing up to Soviet bullying was the only way. 'I would have it out with them now,' he informed a visitor in France. 'If we do not, war might come.'[34] He also told Anthony Eden that they should hold fire for a year to give America time to build more atomic bombs. Unbeknown to him Attlee was already developing Britain's own bomb. Churchill did though find time to relax and indulged in his passion for painting. One particular picture he gifted to Mary and Christopher to hang in Chartwell Farm.

Although the Soviet Army was on full alert along the East German border and around Berlin, it seems Stalin had little intention of opening hostilities.[35] At the end of August his most likely successor Andrei Zhdanov died of heart failure. After attending the funeral, Stalin on 8 September left Moscow, embarking on a three month holiday commencing in Sukhumi on the eastern shores of the Black Sea. This was hardly the action of a man about to take his nation to war. Nonetheless, he showed little sign of ending his blockade of Berlin. Two days later General Clay requested the commitment of additional aircraft to the airlift to increase the daily delivery rate. Stalin, to show he would not be threatened, ordered a partial mobilization doubling the Soviet armed forces to almost six million men. Furthermore, General Sergey Biryuzov's Soviet 37th Army in Bulgaria was posing a threat to Greece, while in Asia General Chistyakov's Soviet 25th Army in North Korea had sealed it off, creating the conditions for an invasion of South Korea.

While still in France the Churchills stayed with the Duke and Duchess of Windsor at La Cröe, Cap d'Antibes for their fortieth wedding anniversary. Although Churchill and the exiled Duke, former King Edward VIII, were old friends, during the war the Duke had proved a diplomatic headache wherever he went. His links to the Nazis had been particularly worrying and there were concerns he might end up a Nazi quisling. Despite this Churchill still seemed to hold him in high regard and did all he could to protect his reputation.[36] Churchill on 12 September, while at La Cröe, wrote Clementine a touching note thanking her 'for giving me so much happiness in a world of accident and storm'.[37] Although he was referring to the past forty years Berlin was foremost in his mind.

Later that month Harold Nicolson flew via Hamburg to Berlin on a fact finding tour and to give four talks. He noted in his diary, 'It is far, far worse than I expected.'[38] He met with the British and America commanders, General Brian Robertson and General Clay. Nicolson found Robertson very taciturn. However, he was slightly reassured when Clay told him, 'the chances of war are only one in ten.'[39] Clay was also confident that the Soviets would not risk cutting the air routes into the city. Likewise Sir Cecil Weir, responsible for western Germany's economy, assessed that the Soviets would stop short at provoking war. Stalin's absence from Moscow seemed to confirm this. 'All night the aeroplanes roared overhead bringing food to Berlin,' said Nicolson in a letter to his wife.[40]

In hindsight Churchill lamented that the Allies had not beaten the Red Army to Berlin in 1945. 'It would... have been wiser and more prudent to have allowed the British Army to enter Berlin,' he told a Conservative party rally in north Wales on 9 October, 'as it could have done, and as many good judges thought would be done'.[41] He conveniently forgot that the western Allies did not have the stomach for the bloodletting required to take Berlin. Furthermore, the Americans had been closest but did not want to pay the price. In the event, after the German surrender it had taken the Allies almost two months to finally move into Berlin, during which time the Soviets had declared martial law over the entire city.

At the end of the month Churchill challenged the government in the House of Commons over what he considered its poor political and military response to the blockade. The people of Berlin had to endure the siege through the winter. Despite the bad weather the airlift continued relentlessly. Although the inhabitants did not run out of food, there was never sufficient fuel, especially coal. In West Berlin the electricity supply was reduced to four hours a day and there was no lighting or public transport after 1800 hours. Fuel was so scarce that coal dust was compressed into briquettes. A counter-blockade was imposed stopping supplies going from western Germany into eastern Germany. This deprived the East Germans of vital coal and steel. In the west the American Marshall Plan boosted the German economy while in the east it stagnated.

Churchill was back in Europe at the end of the year. This time, along with Clementine and Sarah, he was at the Hôtel de Paris in Monte Carlo, in the principality of Monaco, to see in the New Year. Beforehand he had dined with the Duke and Duchess of Windsor in Paris. By this stage 100,000 flights had been conducted by the aircraft participating in the Berlin airlift. Tension continued to mount. Slowly the city began to be physically partitioned. In mid-February 1949 the Soviet-controlled East Berlin police started to block the streets leading into West Berlin. Up to that point there had been only officious checkpoints, but now the Soviets began to obstruct the streets with barriers. Equally worrying, the East Berlin Police began firing on blockade runners who failed to stop.

At the beginning of 1949 Churchill was to embark on a speaking tour of America. Beforehand he was invited to stay with media mogul Lord Beaverbrook at his house near Montego Bay in Jamaica. Beaverbrook, who had served as minister of aircraft production during the war, was held responsible for the Conservatives' electoral defeat in 1945 because he put Churchill centre stage rather than offering coherent policies to challenge Labour. Clementine warned her husband that to stay with Beaverbrook could harm his reputation. 'It would seem cynical and an insult to the Party,' she said to him in a note written on 5 March.[42] He took her advice and did not go to Jamaica. In Washington that month Churchill met with President Truman and urged him to issue a statement that America would use the atomic bomb to protect democracy. Nobody though in their right mind wanted the bomb deployed in Europe.

Both Churchill and Macmillan felt that Attlee's Labour government had not taken a strong enough stance against the Soviet Union. They argued it would have been better to threaten Stalin with military force and an economic boycott of the Soviet zone. Macmillan accused the government of succumbing to a 'semi-religious Socialist fervour' and attacked the ongoing airlift as 'an act of political appeasement'.[43] In Britain, where rationing was still a fact of life, in some quarters it was seen as an insult that precious resources were being sent to a defeated enemy. Nonetheless, Macmillan told the House of Commons on 23 March 1949, 'Step by step the Cold War must be won. ...It is, perhaps, the last Crusade.'[44] Such words were appropriately very Churchillian.

The North Atlantic Treaty was signed in Washington on 4 April 1949, committing America and Canada to the defence of western Europe. Conservative peer Lord Butler was moved to write, 'The Atlantic Treaty showed that British foreign policy was not only active but effective.' He then added, 'It was the culmination of Bevin's career and his most striking achievement.'[45] This led to the creation of the North Atlantic Treaty Organisation or NATO. Its twelve original members came together for mutual military assistance in the event of aggression against any of its members. Even after two world wars Germany was no longer seen as the potential aggressor, but rather the Soviet Union. 'Churchill was the great wartime figure who led the nation to victory but it was Bevin who enabled his orations to be turned into action,' said Butler. 'He was one of the greatest Foreign Secretaries.'[46]

Churchill spoke in the House of Commons on 12 May 1949 in support of the government's conclusion of the treaty, the very day that Stalin finally ended the Berlin blockade. Having failed to impede the emergence of democracy in western Germany or drive the Allies from the city, Stalin decided there was little point in maintaining it if he was not going to war. That morning the Soviets opened the Helmstedt-Marienborn border crossing, the spot where the blockade had first been imposed the previous June. Just to make life complicated they insisted that all trains crossing the border use Soviet-supplied locomotives and crews. Churchill warned Stalin he was not in a position to take the moral high ground.

'I am glad that the lifting by the Soviet Government of the blockade of Berlin,' he informed the House of Commons, 'has not been taken by him as an occasion for proclaiming that an important peace gesture has been made.' Churchill then added that, 'mere manoeuvres will be watched with utmost vigilance.'[47]

Stalin naturally tried to make the ending of the Berlin blockade look like a victory. The Soviet authorities organised a massed rally involving 75,000 people in front of Berlin University on the Unter Den Linden in the Soviet sector. A banner was unfurled calling 'For Understanding and Peace.'[48] American aircrews in West Berlin were less subtle, producing a placard that read, 'Blockade Ends "Airlift" Wins!'[49] The following day supply convoys began to roll over the Helmstedt-Marienborn crossing, though the airlift did not officially come to an end until the close of September.[50]

Marshal Sokolovsky, commander of Soviet forces in Germany, was sent home and appointed First Deputy War Minister. His replacement, signalling Stalin still meant business, was none other than General Vasily Chuikov, hero of Stalingrad and conqueror of Berlin. The following year Stalin summoned his trusted righthand man Khrushchev from Ukraine to head the Moscow Communist party. Many members of the senior Soviet leadership were unclear what Stalin's intentions had been, nor what he had hoped to achieve with the blockade. Andrei Gromyko, the former Soviet ambassador to the United Nations, observed, 'Of course nobody ever asked him directly what those motives were.'[51] Khrushchev felt the crisis had done the Soviet Union's interests in Germany more harm than good. 'The West had managed to exploit the tension generated by the blockade,' he wrote, 'and to impose conditions on East Germany which were even more constraining... than the ones set by the Potsdam agreement.'[52]

Churchill understandably felt the views he had expressed about the threat of Communism and the need for European unity were vindicated by the Berlin blockade. Although a hot war had been avoided there was now an unmistakable Cold War between NATO and the Soviet Union. The Federal Republic of Germany or West Germany came into being on 23 May 1949 with Bonn as the capital city. The rival Communist state known as the German Democratic Republic or East Germany was created that October with East Berlin as its capital. Germany at that point was politically partitioned between the capitalist west and the Communist east. These were no longer just two occupation zones but rather separate states with separate ideologies.

In early August Churchill and Clementine went on holiday to Italy. While there he had a speech to prepare for the first meeting of the Council of Europe in Strasbourg which he gave on 17 August. 'Ten ancient capitals of Europe are behind the Iron Curtain,' he told the delegates. 'A large part of this continent is held in bondage. They have escaped from Nazism only to fall into the other extreme of Communism.'[53] The previous day the last of the British civilian aircraft supporting the airlift were withdrawn from West Berlin.

Leaving Harold Macmillan and Duncan Sandys in charge of the Conservative contingent, Churchill headed south to Monte Carlo to resume his holiday. Clementine pointedly flew home. He stayed at Lord Beaverbrook's villa La Capponcina. 'Perched on the rocks above the sea, below the railway and the road and protected by trees,' recalled Mary, 'La Capponcina was an oasis of privacy.'[54] This visit caused some consternation amongst senior Conservatives including Anthony Eden and Lord Salisbury. The latter was so incensed by Churchill's presence at La Capponcina with Beaverbrook that he branded it a 'criminal error.'[55]

Churchill seemed in very good form, teasing one of the other house guests that they were a disgrace to the British Empire because of their puny body. However, for a man of 74 Churchill's regime was punishing and he was pushing himself too hard. Unfortunately on the night of 23/24 August he suffered the first of a series of strokes that were to afflict his later years. During the early hours, whilst playing cards with Lord Beaverbrook and Brigadier Michael Wardell, he began to suffer cramp in his right arm and leg. By daybreak it had not gone away. A local British doctor was summoned and he called Lord Moran, Churchill's trusted physician, to inform him he thought Churchill had had a stroke. Churchill's two secretaries Elizabeth Gilliat and Lettice Marston who had accompanied him were equally worried about his condition. The latter recalled that 'it was pretty obvious something had happened, because his face was slightly collapsed'.[56]

Moran immediately flew out to attend Churchill who enquired plaintively, 'Have I had a stroke?'[57] Finding no loss of grip, speech or memory Moran declared reassuringly, 'You've not had that. A very small clot has blocked a very small artery.'[58] It was though clearly a stroke and Churchill experienced a very narrow escape.[59] 'He had had the great good fortune...,' admitted Moran, 'that there was no paralysis'.[60] Churchill was worried that he might have another one and complained of a tightening in his shoulder blade. Again Moran reassured him that all was fine. 'The dagger struck,' Churchill said to Wardell, 'but this time it was not plunged in to the hilt. At least I think not.'[61] He was intending to return to Strasbourg that day to dine with his fellow Conservatives, but wisely he did not go.

With the prospect of an election looming, Harold Macmillan was alarmed when he heard Churchill had been taken ill. 'We got the most exaggerated stories,' Macmillan noted in his diary, 'he had pneumonia, he had had a stroke, he was gravely ill.'[62] Luckily Duncan Sandys was able to talk to him on the telephone and reassured Macmillan that he was fine. The stroke was hushed up and it was announced that Churchill caught a chill while on holiday. Lord Moran had even taken his golf clubs to avoid his presence arousing suspicion. A few days later when Churchill lunched at the Hôtel du Paris no one noticed any difference. Although he seemed to make a full recovery those closest to him felt he had lost some of his zest. Mary noted, 'The stroke did leave its mark, however imperceptible, and somewhat undermined his self-confidence.'[63] The thought of retiring though was simply not in Churchill's character.

Seeking some winter sunshine and hoping to paint, he sailed with Clementine and Diana to Madeira in late December. Churchill had been to the island once before in October 1899 on his way to war in South Africa. His latest visit was short-lived. They had been there for nine days when Attlee announced the dissolution of Parliament and scheduled a General Election for 23 February 1950. Churchill immediately boarded a flying boat and flew home to start campaigning. Clementine decided to remain in the sun a bit longer and returned later by sea.

Chapter 7

Mao Triumphant

While Churchill worried about Communism's grip on Central and Eastern Europe, a new threat was emerging in the Far East that would dramatically change the balance of power there. During the 1930s Churchill's focus had been the rise of the Nazis and he had taken little notice of the civil war between China's Nationalists and Communists. To his shame, he felt Japan's opportunist military intervention in Manchuria was a welcome stabilising influence amidst the chaos that reigned in China. Ironically he was right in that Chiang Kai-shek's Nationalists and Mao Zedong's Communists buried their differences to fight the Japanese. In the event the Nationalists conducted most of the fighting, losing their best officers in the process. Mao simply bided his time.

Churchill's strategy in the Far East during the Second World War had been to defend India from the Japanese, then restore Burma, Malaya, Singapore and Hong Kong to British control. In particular he saw the restoration of Singapore as key to British prestige in the region. Churchill also wanted to help the French reassert control over Indochina. In 1942, following the humiliating surrender of Singapore, and desperate for allies, he had been full of praise for the Chinese Nationalists. 'We can now measure the wonderful strength of the Chinese people,' he said in a broadcast to the nation, 'who under Generalissimo Chiang Kai-shek have single-handed fought this hideous Japanese aggressor for four and a half years.'[1] Churchill also noted approvingly in his wartime memoirs, 'He was a strong anti-Communist.'[2]

Churchill and Roosevelt, prior to their meeting with Stalin in Tehran in late 1943, met with Chiang Kai-shek in Cairo to formulate their plans. Churchill did not find this productive. 'The talks of the British and American Staff were sadly distracted by the Chinese story, which was lengthy, complicated and minor,' he wrote in his wartime memoirs.[3] Harold Macmillan recalled, 'The Chinese were glamorously represented by General and Mme Chiang Kai-shek, supported by a large entourage.'[4] Churchill was completely enchanted by Madame Chiang who over dinner acted as interpreter for her husband. In a letter to Clementine he said, 'I got on excellently with Madame Chiang Kai-shek and I withdraw all unfavourable remarks which I may have made about her.'[5] Even Sarah Churchill, who was with her father's delegation, was moved to tell her mother, 'Papa was impressed by her – and there is no doubt that she is far and away the best interpreter!'[6]

Earlier in the year though, while in America, she had made herself unpopular with President Roosevelt, his wife Eleanor and Churchill. 'Harold Butler [working at the British Embassy in Washington]..., told me,' said Sir Alan Lascelles, 'that Madame Chiang Kai-shek's visit had been disastrous from the Chinese point of view. By her capriciousness and exigencies she offended all the big-wigs, beginning with the Roosevelts.'[7] Eleanor, ever the diplomat, observed that it had been 'very interesting to have Madame Chiang Kai-shek at the White House.'[8] She was perplexed when Madame Chiang, who was in New York, refused to have lunch with her husband and Churchill in Washington. Instead Madame Chiang said Churchill could come to her. 'He wouldn't go and I could see Franklin thought they might fight if left alone,' wrote Eleanor of the incident.[9] In the end the meeting never took place. Churchill perhaps understandably felt slighted by being summoned by Madame Chiang. Eleanor also noted in her memoirs that Madame Chiang had a 'certain casualness about cruelty'.[10] When on one occasion President Roosevelt had asked her how China dealt with difficult labour leaders she had silently and chillingly run her hand across her throat.

For the Cairo press conference it was notable that both Chiang and his wife were included in the line-up. They were seated flanking either side of Churchill and Roosevelt as if to emphasis China's role in the proceedings. 'This was the first time I had met Chiang Kai-shek,' recalled Churchill. 'I was impressed by his calm, reserved, and efficient personality.'[11] Anthony Eden, who was in attendance, likewise noted, 'I was much impressed by Chiang.'[12] However, Churchill by this stage did not hold Chiang in very high regard and viewed him as ineffectual. 'The accepted belief in American circles,' said Churchill, 'was that he would be the head of the great Fourth Power in the world after the victory had been won.'[13] He certainly did not agree with that view. Lord Moran recalled Churchill 'is sceptical of China as a great power and grudges all the time that Roosevelt has given to her affairs.'[14] Chiang certainly did little to endear himself to people. 'I had seen Chiang Kai-shek many times during the height of his power,' observed Dr Li Zhisui who became Mao's physician, 'and he had always been aloof, demanding subservience from everyone around him. The effect was invariably alienating.'[15]

General Joe Stilwell, the US military advisor to Chiang during part of the Second World War, held a similar opinion to Churchill. He was greatly vexed that the Nationalists deliberately held back a large proportion of the American equipment supplied to fight the Japanese. Instead it was stored away ready for a resumption of operations against the Communists or issued to provincial warlords supporting Chiang. As a result the pair did not get on and Chiang urged Roosevelt to sack Stilwell, which is what happened. Clark Kerr, the British Ambassador even went as far as telling Chiang that in the event of civil war, regardless of who started it, Britain would not back him. Such a sentiment could only have come from Churchill.

Roosevelt had pressed Churchill to recognise China as an equal ally in 1943. Although Churchill acquiesced he thought it was a pointless exercise. Furthermore, it annoyed him greatly that Chiang Kai-shek had been talking to India's nationalists, particularly Gandhi. 'It is an affection to pretend that China is a power in any way comparable to the other three...' he told Anthony Eden. 'China might fall again into a state of great confusion and possibly civil war.'[16] He was to be proved right. Churchill also confessed to Eden, 'I have told the President I would be reasonably polite about this American obsession, but I cannot agree that we should take a positive attitude on the matter.'[17] In the summer of 1944 Churchill vented his displeasure over American strategy in the Far East to his wife. He felt the British Army was fighting in Burma, 'to guard the American air line over the Himalayas into their very over-rated China.'[18] He chose to ignore the fact that Chiang's troops had been fighting the Japanese in Burma and suffered significant losses.

Churchill was right about China in that it was neither the Chinese nor Japanese that ended the stalemate in the Sino-Japanese war, but American air power. In return for Chiang's participation in the Burma campaign America poured supplies into Nationalist-held China. The Americans also deployed an air task force to China that included B-29 bombers. Chiang made sure this support only benefited him. He blocked American aid to Mao and deployed 200,000 of his best troops to contain the Communist area in Yenan.

Churchill not only considered China weak, he did not want it in a post war position where it could meddle with Britain's colonial interests in India or the Far East. Nor did he want China siding with America on this issue. Roosevelt always made it clear that America would not help Britain and France restore their empires at the end of the war. Roosevelt wanted the United Nations to assume responsibility for the old League of Nations mandated territories created after the First World War. Furthermore, he had wanted the mandates to have the right to eventual self-determination. Churchill saw this as American interference in both British and French interests.

Roosevelt raised this issue at Yalta in 1945, when he specifically suggested Hong Kong should be granted to China once the Japanese occupation came to an end. He also suggested that Korea should be placed in trusteeship without British involvement and that Indochina should be given independence rather than restored to France. Stalin enjoyed watching Britain and America at loggerheads. 'One can almost see the grim old gentleman from the Kremlin rubbing his hands with glee...' said Lord Moran. 'He purrs when anything like this happens.'[19] At the time Stalin was cautious about Hong Kong because of the deal he had cut with Churchill in October 1944 regarding Eastern Europe and the Far East.

Churchill was furious and declared he would not agree 'to forty or fifty nations thrusting interfering fingers into the life's existence of the British Empire'.[20] After losing Hong Kong to the Japanese in 1941 he had no intention of losing it again once it was liberated. He felt Roosevelt was simply trying to gain favour with Chiang Kai-shek. Churchill told Roosevelt that there was no question of the British government being compelled 'to give Hong Kong back to China if they did not think that this was the right step for them to take'.[21] Then trying to sound conciliatory he had added, 'On the other hand they felt it would be wrong that China should not have a chance of stating her case fully.'[22]

Anthony Eden thought that it was wrong that China's leaders had not been invited to Yalta. 'It was unjust to take decisions affecting the future of China,' he said, 'without consulting her and in absence of her representatives.'[23] As far as Churchill was concerned he did not favour Chiang or Mao. A victory by either would be detrimental to British interests; arguably though Mao represented a far greater ideological threat. Despite him not considering China an equal, on 26 July 1945 Churchill, Truman and Chiang issued a joint statement to Japan warning that if the country did not surrender, its cities would be completely destroyed. This threat of course was backed by America's atomic bomb.

Following the Japanese surrender in September 1945 the two Chinese factions were once again at each other's throats. Mao's forces swiftly infiltrated Soviet-liberated Manchuria which provided him with a safe haven. 'If we have Manchuria,' he had told his comrades earlier in the year, 'our victory will be guaranteed.'[24]

Mao welcomed the presence of the Soviets as he knew they were his ticket to power. Back in 1923 he said that Communism 'had to be brought into China from the north by the Russian army'.[25] Some twenty-two years later his dream was coming true. Soviet troops responded to the presence of the Chinese Communists by transferring large quantities of Japanese weapons to them. The Soviets had captured in the region of 300,000 rifles, 4,836 machine guns, 2,300 vehicles, 1,226 pieces of artillery, 925 aircraft and 369 tanks. They also prevented the landing of Nationalist troops in the southern Manchurian ports, which gave Mao a breathing space to build up his strength.

Stalin, to facilitate a smooth transition of power to Mao, delayed the withdrawal of the Soviet army until early 1946. Liu Shao-chi, Mao's second in command, knew they did not have the ability to stop Chiang marching into Manchuria when the time came. 'Do not deploy the main forces at the gate to Manchuria to try to keep Chiang out,' he ordered on 2 October 1945, 'but at the borders with the USSR, Mongolia and Korea, and dig our heels in.'[26] He also instructed their forces in Manchuria to be ready to abandon the big cities and to occupy the surrounding countryside and towns.

In northern China, south of the Great Wall, the Communists moved to take control there when the Japanese laid down their weapons. In Yenan, south west of Peking, the New China News Agency announced in early September 1945, 'We hold the entire region stretching from Kalgan [Zhangjiakou] to the Yangtze, and from Shensi to the China Sea, except for the largest cities and some fortified points along the railroads.'[27] Mao's forces though did not have it all their own way. Chiang, in the wake of Japan's surrender, quickly moved into previously Japanese-occupied Peking without a shot. He did this even though there were the large areas south of the Great Wall now held by Mao. Truman helped Chiang assert control by organising an enormous sea-and-air lift of half a million Nationalist troops into the seaports and cities of eastern and northern China. He also deployed 50,000 US Marines. They were greeted by civilians as liberators and raised hopes that stability might be restored. The Marines though were not to stay for long as Truman did not want to be dragged into the civil war.

Chiang tried to counter the Communists' infiltration of Manchuria by sending 30,000 soldiers in ships of the US 7th Fleet to Dalian on the Liaodong peninsula in October 1945. The Soviets would not let them ashore on the grounds this was against the conditions of the Sino-Soviet friendship treaty. This had recognised the Nationalists' sovereignty over Manchuria in return for recognition of the Mongolian People's Republic once the Soviets withdrew. Now under Soviet protection, Outer Mongolia had freed itself from Chinese control in 1911, but failed to gain recognition of its independence from China. When the Nationalists tried to land at Huludao and Yingkou, cities on the Bohai Sea, they found they were held by the Communists. Vice Admiral Daniel Barbey commanding the fleet did not have the authority to force a landing so sailed to Qinhuanghao, which was controlled by the US Marines. Chiang's troops would eventually have to be transported north by railway and air. All this meant that crucial time was lost.

Churchill, Roosevelt, Stalin and Chiang had agreed that to punish Japan for its campaigns of conquest in China, Southeast Asia and the Pacific, its empire would be dissolved, the country disarmed and occupied. The only problem with this in strategic terms was that it would neutralise a regional counterweight to China and the Soviet Union. This was especially the case once the Soviets moved into Manchuria, southern Sakhalin and northern Korea. The granting of southern Sakhalin to the Soviets placed them perilously close to the northern Japanese island of Hokkaido. It also meant they could dominate the northern approaches to the Sea of Japan.

Churchill was unhappy that the Foreign Office was reluctant to lobby the US State Department for joint Anglo-American control of occupied Japan. After the Japanese surrender he informed Attlee that the issue of sole American control of Japan without the involvement of an Allied control commission had never been discussed by him and Truman. Although China and the Soviet Union were not invited to take part in the occupation, Stalin had been bought off with full control of Sakhalin. The problem the British government faced was that it did not have the military resources to spare. In the Far East, reasserting control of Burma, Malaya, Singapore and Hong Kong was already a drain on British funds and manpower. Likewise, in Europe it had its military commitments in occupied western Germany and West Berlin.

General MacArthur's US army of occupation arrived in Japan in the autumn of 1945 and encountered no overt resistance. MacArthur rather optimistically announced, 'Let us pray that peace be now restored to the world and that God will preserve it always.'[28] After almost nine years of war and the firebombing of their cities the Japanese were resigned to their fate. Many of the Americans who were veterans of the Pacific campaigns were surprised by this passivity after the suicidal resistance they had encountered previously. One of the first tasks of the occupation forces was to ensure the Japanese army was completely disarmed. The Japanese had massed about twenty-five divisions of varying quality in Japan to fend off an American seaborne assault. These included at least two intact armoured divisions, one of which had been formed the previous year specifically to help ward off invasion.[29]

Before the atomic bombs were dropped the Japanese correctly assessed that Truman would first attack in the south, and had massed 400,000 men on the island of Kyushu. Their headquarters was in Hiroshima on the neighbouring main island of Honshu. Kyushu, defended by fourteen divisions, had been turned into a fortress. There were concerns that Japanese diehards might take to the mountains of Japan's four main islands and continue the fight. Fortunately the Japanese army followed orders and laid down its weapons as instructed.

There was little danger of Japanese troops returning home from Manchuria or North Korea to cause trouble. Stalin shipped over half a million Japanese prisoners to Soviet labour camps in Siberia, the Russian Far East and Mongolia. Two entire Japanese armies comprising twenty-five divisions simply vanished.[30] Many members of the collaborationist Chinese Manchukuo Imperial Army, numbering fifteen divisions, suffered the same fate or were handed over to Mao. At its height it had numbered 200,000 men but many of them had been deployed elsewhere by the Japanese and those who remained largely melted away. The fate of the Japanese in Manchuria reminded Churchill of the dark days of 1940 when Stalin massacred over 20,000 members of the Polish military and imprisoned thousands more to ensure his control of eastern Poland. More recently there had been the Allies' forced repatriation to an unknown fate of Soviet citizens who had fought for the Nazis.

Churchill in November 1945 wrote to Foreign Secretary Bevin urging that when it came to Japan, 'in principle there is no doubt that the Joint occupation greatly strengthens the power of the United States and the safety of Britain.'[31] Nor did he agree with the suggestion by Lord Halifax, the British Ambassador in Washington, that Japan be placed under United Nations Trusteeship. Churchill felt that Britain and America were now in a unique position and should make the most of it. He added in his letter to Bevin, 'we must always insist upon coming in on equal terms.'[32] Bevin agreed with Churchill. The previous year, in a Foreign Office memo written shortly after the Japanese surrender, he had stated it was 'important that we should not play a lesser part in the control of Japan than Russia and China, as otherwise our prestige and standing as one of the Big Four Powers might suffer damage.'[33] When Truman agreed to share responsibility for Japan, Attlee was obliged to look to Australia for assistance.

During the winter of 1945-46 Truman completed equipping almost forty of Chiang's divisions.[34] Although American Lend-Lease equipment flooded into Nationalist China, Chiang's forces struggled to assimilate it. By early 1946 over 240,000 Nationalist troops of varying quality had been gathered in northern China. General Albert Wedemeyer, senior US advisor to Chiang who had replaced Stilwell, cautioned against sending the better divisions into Manchuria. He reasoned it would be prudent to first concentrate Nationalist units south of the Great Wall before entering Manchuria in force. Truman, fearful that China was about to slip back into civil war, sent General George Marshall, the former US Army Chief of Staff, to seek unification of the country by democratic means. Marshall negotiated a truce between the two sides that became effective on 13 January 1946. It proved short lived as the protagonists fought to secure ground.

Communism also made itself felt in Southeast Asia. Britain and France hoped that it would be business as usual after the Japanese capitulation, but this was not to be the case. In Indochina the Communist forces of Ho Ch Minh had received guerrilla warfare training from Mao in Yenan during the Second World War. They fought the Japanese until Japan's surrender and then liberated northern Indochina sparking the first Indochina War with France in 1946. After eight years of fighting this would lead to humiliating defeat for France, independence for Cambodia and Laos and partition for Vietnam, with the Communists controlling the north.

The British Commonwealth Occupation Force, comprising Australian, British, Indian and New Zealander troops arrived in Japan in February 1946 to support the American units there. Britain's commitment to this was minimal. Although a British brigade was involved, the bulk of the manpower was provided by Australia and the task force was commanded by an Australian general. An Indian brigade also came under British control until India's independence when its soldiers were sent home. While America was responsible for the military government of Japan, the Commonwealth forces were tasked with overseeing the country's demilitarisation.

In southern and eastern China, Chiang was not entirely happy about the return of foreign businesses, most notably in Hong Kong and Shanghai. To Attlee and Churchill's displeasure, Chiang made it clear that he did not want his wartime ally reimposing its economic grip on China. This had been loosened in 1943 by the Anglo-Sino Treaty which banned foreign shipping on the Yangtze. In 1946 the Nationalists moved to restrict foreign imports in an effort to stimulate Chinese commerce and industry. This made life challenging for British businesses when they returned to Hong Kong. It confirmed Churchill's concerns that Chiang was not at all sympathetic to British strategic or economic interests. Ironically Mao was of a completely different opinion. He knew that when he triumphed he would need western investment if Communist China was to survive.

Churchill on 7 March 1946, just two days after he had given his Fulton speech, wrote to Attlee to highlight American attitudes toward Soviet foreign policy in China. 'I have no doubt that the Executive forces here are deeply distressed at the way they are being treated by Russia,' he explained, 'and that they did not intend to put up with treaty breaches... or encroachments in Manchuria and Korea.'[35] Churchill was clearly conscious that Stalin was looking to replicate his plans in Europe by creating Communist satellite states in China and Korea. The People's Republic of Mongolia was already providing the Soviet Far East a massive security buffer with China. Churchill did not though take into account the independent-minded characters of the Chinese and Korean Communist party leaders when it came to dealing with Stalin.

Stalin finally withdrew all his troops from Manchuria by early May, but not before they handed most of it over to the Communists in violation of the treaty of friendship signed with Chiang Kai-shek. During the evacuation the Soviets supplied Mao with further military equipment that was vastly superior to that taken from the Japanese Army. 'Mao, though, could not admit,' noted Dr Zhisui, 'that the Soviets had helped at all.'[36] Mao lied, claiming, 'Stalin offered no help, refusing to give the Communist forces a single gun or bullet, "not even a fart"'.[37] Mao had sent 60,000 troops into Manchuria, but this force swelled to 300,000 thanks in part to recruits from the disbanded Manchukuo Imperial Army and other local militia armies.

Chiang took no heed of Wedemeyer's advice and began to deploy his best troops into Manchuria occupying its capital Changchun and the city of Mukden

(Shenyang). The Nationalists secured a massive salient anchored on Mukden. In the south this bordered the Bohai Sea, which in theory made it relatively easy to supply and reinforce. In practice though the troops in the salient were reliant on a 1,600km railway running from Peking through the Great Wall to Chinchow, Mukden, and over the Sungari River on to Harbin in the far north. Defending this supply line would tie down most of Chiang's forces obliging them to fight a static war. This immediately passed the initiative over to the more mobile Communists. General Marshall arranged a second truce that lasted from 6 June until the end of the month. This derailed Nationalist plans to take Harbin. The latter had been surrendered to the Communists by the Soviets when they withdrew. After that, fighting spread across China, marking the beginning of widespread civil war.

Initially it seemed as if Chiang could not lose. His Nationalist armies had three million men under arms whereas the Communists only had about one million. Although the Nationalists were able to secure many of the provincial capitals, the Communists were deeply entrenched in northern China and Manchuria. Also, holding the cities, like the railways, meant tying down large numbers of Nationalist troops. The civil war would become a contest of Nationalist manpower and firepower against Communist discipline, morale and mobility. Furthermore, many of the Nationalist soldiers were recruited from southern China and were viewed as foreigners by the people of Manchuria.

Chiang sought to conduct a south-north strategy designed to fragment the Communist armies. In turn Mao pursued a west-east strategy pushing eastwards from Shensi province to the China Sea, thereby cutting the country in two. By the summer of 1946 Churchill was beginning to worry about what would happen in China, especially as America seemed to be losing interest. Truman became concerned that he might be backing a losing side. Behind the scenes Mao had let it be known to American diplomats that he was prepared to do business with America as long as it stopped supporting the Nationalists. General Marshall, having failed to prevent civil war, was summoned back to Washington in January 1947, by which time most of the US Marines had been withdrawn.

In late December 1947 the Communists cut the rail links into Mukden, and the Nationalist forces in northern China and Manchuria were encircled in the cities. Without the railways, their poorly-led troops lacked initiative and mobility. In the New Year Chiang appointed General Wei Li-huang as his commander in Manchuria. The only problem was that Wei was a covert Communist sympathiser who would do all he could to undermine the Nationalist cause. On his orders, in March 1948 the Nationalists abandoned their outer defences in Manchuria when they evacuated Kirin and Szeping to the northeast of Mukden. This allowed the Communists to take control of ninety percent of Manchuria without a fight. Wei also ignored Chiang's orders to move his forces into southern Manchuria ready to withdraw into northern China. Foolishly Chiang did not sack him for this insubordination. Two campaigns were now to settle China's fate. In September 1948 the Communists opened their Manchurian offensive that would lead to the capture of Mukden and Changchun.

In the meantime Churchill, having expended so much blood to defend Burma from the Japanese, was far from pleased to see this country descend into civil war.

The Burmese Communist party had two competing factions known as the Red Flags and the White Flags. When Burma became independent on 4 January 1948 under the leadership of U Nu, the Red Flags were already in open revolt, and the White flags launched their own rising two months later on 27 March. Alarmingly their area of control soon expanded from the Irrawaddy Delta in the south all the way north to Mandalay. Churchill lamented to his fellow conservatives, declaring that he had warned them this would happen.[38]

The fighting developed into a five-way war when part of the Burmese military revolted, as did the Karen people in the southeast who lived along the border with China and Thailand. The Burmese army lost its Karen regiments as they sided with the rebels. The latter declared an independent Karen state with Toungoo as its capital. Further complicating the country's myriad of problems, Chinese Nationalist forces moved back into Burma once Mao began to win in China. Although Britain had signed a Treaty of Alliance with Burma in October 1947, and upon its declaration of independence signed a defence agreement with the Burmese, there was little Attlee could do to help. Burma, once the bulwark of India, was lost to years of chaos and infighting.

Attlee, with Churchill's backing, had conducted Operation Zipper after Japan's defeat to take back control of Malaya. It was soon split by the competing interests of its Malay and ethnic Chinese population. Malaya's Chinese were opposed to the Federation of Malaya which occurred in February 1948. Cheng Ping the Communist leader, after visiting Mao, employed his revolutionary methods of guerrilla warfare against the British. The attacks by predominantly Chinese insurgents commenced in June 1948, and continued for many years until British and Commonwealth forces eventually managed to contain them.

Churchill watched these developments with dismay. He held Stalin and the Soviet Union responsible for the spread of Communism in the Far East. He made this clear when he attended a Conservative party rally in north Wales on 9 October 1948. 'Let them cease to distract Malaya and Indonesia,' he told the audience. 'Let them liberate the Communist-held portion of Korea. Let them cease to foment the hideous protracted civil war in China.'[39] That day General Wei Li-huang broke out of Mukden with the aim of relieving Chinchow to the southwest. General Cheng Tung-kao, the commander at Changchun, was also ordered to breakout towards Chinchow. They were too late and the city fell to the Communists on 15 October along with a huge quantity of stores. Four days later the Nationalists lost Changchun.

General Wei's forces were defeated west of Mukden on 27 October. The Communists marched into the city on 2 November taking 200,000 prisoners and its massive supply dumps. The entire Nationalist salient in Manchuria had collapsed. That day the *Daily Herald* reported, 'Only one Nationalist Army stands between North China and the Communists are now in complete control of Manchuria. Commanded by General Fu Tso-yi [Fu Zuoyi], the "Montgomery of North China" and one of Chiang Kai-shek's most able commanders, it is the Nationalists only hope if the Communists turn south.'[40] Chiang placed Wei under house arrest, but he was not court-martialled, imprisoned or executed. Instead he was allowed to seek exile in Hong Kong.

The second campaign that sealed the Nationalists' fate was fought for the vital rail junction at Hsuchow on the north China plain. Here Chiang gathered fifty divisions, the bulk of his remaining armies. If the Communists captured Hsuchow and its railway network then they would gain control of all of China as far as the Yangtze river. From there they could threaten Chiang Kai-shek's wartime capital at Chungking. The Communist offensive opened in November 1948 and was initially stopped, but by the end of the month their forces were both to the east and west of the city. In early December the demoralised Nationalist forces abandoned Hsuchow. After a two month battle the Nationalist armies to the south of the city surrendered on 10 January 1949 having lost 500,000 men.

At the end of the month Mao entered Peking and Chiang Kai-shek resigned the Nationalist presidency. General Fu Zuoyi and much of his army of 250,000 men, who were supposed to have defended Peking, simply defected. Mao, rather than execute Fu, told him, 'I see you still have great ability.'[41] He and his men were then pressed into service against their old masters. According to Dr Zhisui, 'Stalin had urged them to stop their campaign north of the Yangtze River and allow the Guomindang [Nationalists] control over the south.'[42] It would have meant partition for China. Mao's response to this was, 'We didn't pay attention to him.' Korean Communist leader Kim Il Sung suggested to Stalin that Korea be forcibly reunified in March 1949. Stalin was occupied by the Berlin Blockade so told Kim to wait.

Li Tsung-jen, Chiang's successor, hoped he might be able to negotiate a ceasefire but in April the Communists crossed the Yangtze. Mao instructed, 'All warships which get in the way of our crossing may be bombarded. Treat them as Nationalist ships.'[43] Two British warships, HMS Amethyst and HMS Consort, were caught on the river between Shanghai and Nanking. Consort escaped but Amethyst was grounded and thirty-two British sailors were killed. This was more than all the other Western military deaths in the entire civil war. Churchill was outraged and demanded to know why the British government did not have aircraft carriers in Chinese waters 'capable of... effective power of retaliation.'[44] The reality was that Attlee did not have the resources to force Mao to desist.

Stalin was alarmed by this incident, fearing it might spark Western intervention in China that would then involve the Soviet Union. He placed Soviet forces in the Far East on full alert, which was the only time this occurred during the Chinese civil war. 'We do not think now is the right moment to publicise the friendship between the USSR and Democratic China,' Stalin warned Mao.[45] The latter was forced to issue orders to avoid firing on foreign vessels. Mao on 27 April, realising that Shanghai with its considerable Western interests and military presence could become a flashpoint, delayed his advance on the city. In the meantime Churchill wrote to Lord Salisbury on 7 May 1949 to say 'I told you so' about Burma. 'Perhaps you will remember the difficulty I had to get the party to vote against the Burma Independence Bill,' he said. 'But now, in their tragedy and misery, many Burmese must be turning their minds back to the palmy days of Queen Victoria.'[46] The fate of Burma though was the least of Britain's concerns.

In China Nationalist-held Nanking surrendered at the end of April and Shanghai was lost in late May. Everywhere the Nationalist armies fell back in disarray. HMS Amethyst, having got free, sailed away under the cover of darkness at the end of July, though a nearby civilian passenger ship was not so fortunate and was sunk by Communist guns. For Mao it was now just a case of mopping up the Nationalists' numerous pockets of resistance. The Communist People's Republic of China was proclaimed on 1 October 1949.

Chiang and the remains of his armies, after abandoning Chungking, fled to the island of Taiwan at the end of the year. He left General Hu Zongnan to hold Xichang but his resistance only lasted until the end of March 1950. Two months after that the Communists took Hainan. Churchill observed, perhaps with a little smugness, 'Both the Generalissimo and his wife are now regarded as wicked and corrupt reactionaries by many of their former admirers.'[47] Eleanor Roosevelt summed up American feelings when she wrote, 'I felt that Chiang Kai-shek had had his chance and had not used the right methods to unify the country, and I did not believe that he any longer had any chance to do so.'[48]

The defeat of the Nationalists caused concern in London; would Mao now attempt to take Hong Kong which lay to the northeast of Hainan? The British government was nervous about his intentions towards the colony, which was full of Nationalist refugees who had fled the mainland. Governor Alexander Grantham, when Communist forces began to approach the border with Hong Kong's mainland New Territories, became worried about the colony's security. Although the New Territories provided some protection, the Japanese had easily overwhelmed the 11,000 strong British, Canadian and Indian garrison. It seemed quite possible that the Communists might try to achieve the same feat. Grantham, a colonial service veteran who had worked in Hong Kong in the early 1930s, was not easily flappable. He had taken up post as governor at the end of July 1947 and kept a close watch on events in China so Mao's victory had come as no real surprise.

To show resolve Attlee deployed the newly-raised British 40th Infantry Division, comprising three infantry brigades supported by a tank regiment, to Hong Kong in 1949. The divisional commander Major General Geoffrey Evans was a highly experienced veteran of the fighting in North and East Africa and Burma during the Second World War. This signalled to Mao that the British government meant business. New Zealand obligingly also sent troops to reinforce the garrison, which showed Mao any military action would be met by members of the British Commonwealth.

Mao, luckily for Attlee and Churchill, had much bigger problems than the future of Hong Kong. He had to clear the last of the Nationalist strongholds in China, and then there was Taiwan. He did not really have the amphibious forces with which to take the latter. In addition any assault might spark American intervention. 'If Chiang Kai-shek and the reactionaries form an alliance with the United States, the CCP [Chinese Communist party] must align itself with the Soviet Union,' said Mao. 'It is a fond dream of the United States to split China from the Soviet Union. However, the CCP cannot afford to make enemies on both sides.'[49] Mao knew that only the Soviet Union could supply the necessary equipment for an amphibious operation against Taiwan. Such a move though would escalate tension between America and the Soviet Union.

Ultimately Mao's triumph did not greatly affect British strategic interests apart from Hong Kong. By this stage the British Commonwealth occupation force in Japan only consisted of Australians. Britain, India and New Zealand had withdrawn their forces. India and Burma, with their vast borders with China, were by this stage independent so it was up to their governments to establish relations with the new People's Republic of China. For America, with forces stationed in South Korea, Japan and the Philippines, it presented a much more immediate strategic challenge.

The world was now confronted by two enormous Communist blocs in the shape of the Soviet Union and the People's Republic of China. However, they were so culturally different it was hardly a marriage made in heaven. 'I can't think that there is anything on an ideological basis to link the Chinese with the Russians,' wrote Field Marshal Montgomery astutely. 'Chinese life and everything they do is based on family life... That is entirely against the Communist idea.' He concluded they were 'not ideologically on the same wave length'.[50] His observations proved right. 'After Mao came to power,' said Khrushchev, 'his relations with Stalin soon became strained.'[51]

When Churchill's American financier friend Bernard Baruch advocated withholding diplomatic recognition of Mao's new government, Churchill was more cautious. 'Diplomatic relations are not a compliment, but a convenience,' he told Baruch in a telegram sent on 15 November 1949. 'If we recognise the bear why should we not recognise the cub?'[52] The following day Baruch made his views on the Soviet Union and China perfectly clear in his response to Churchill. 'I would not recognise the bear if we had to do it over again,' he said, 'nor would I recognise the cub who may grow up to be an even greater bear.'[53] As far as Churchill was concerned the Soviet Union remained the greater threat. It would after all take China decades to recover from the ravages of the civil war and Mao would remain distracted by the Nationalist stronghold in Taiwan. However, there were the unresolved issues of the British outpost in Hong Kong and Communist North Korea. On 16 December 1949 Mao met with Stalin in Moscow. A treaty of friendship and alliance was signed the following year.

While Attlee's government chose to open diplomatic relations with Communist China, Truman continued to recognise the Nationalist regime in Taiwan as the legitimate Chinese government. Britain formally recognised the People's Republic of China on 6 January 1950, which was to prove a source of friction with America. The worry was that once tensions started to ramp up over the future of partitioned Korea, Truman would contemplate an all-out offensive against Communist China. Some feared such a course of action would force Stalin to side with Mao and result in a Third World War. Mao in turn also began to court Japanese Communists. The Far East now looked as fraught as Europe.

Chapter 8

Troublesome Neighbour

While the Cold War was gathering pace in Europe, Britain was facing ongoing diplomatic and security problems with Ireland (or Eire). Its government was determined not to be drawn into the confrontation with the Soviet Union. This was especially the case if it meant a military alliance involving Britain. Churchill throughout the Second World War was exasperated by Ireland's insistence on neutrality. Although Irish Prime Minister Éamon de Valera adhered to the External Relations Act of 1936, which maintained a tenuous link with Britain and the Crown, he refused to go to war with Germany. To compound matters, in 1938 the Royal Navy had relinquished its three naval bases in Ireland at the very point they were needed the most. Luckily for de Valera this prevented Britain from violating Ireland's neutrality by using them for operations against German U-boats. Churchill appealed to de Valera on a number of occasions to join the Allies, but he steadfastly declined.

Friction over the historic Irish north-south divide always loomed large when it came to relations between Britain and Ireland. 'Apparently de Valera is contemplating introducing conscription! at any rate after the war,' Field Marshal Brooke noted in his diary in the summer of 1944, 'Must discuss effect of this on Northern Ireland.'[1] The latter had remained under British control following Irish independence in 1921 because predominantly Protestant Northern Ireland or Ulster did not want to be ruled by the largely Catholic south.

Churchill had no real option but to respect Ireland's neutrality during the war even though he strongly suspected that it was pro-Nazi. The final insult occurred when de Valera visited the German Legation to sign the book of sympathy marking Hitler's death. 'De Valera, according to the *Times*,' wrote Sir Alan Lascelles, King George VI's Private Secretary, on 3 May 1945, 'called yesterday on the German Minister in Dublin, to offer his condolences on Hitler's death; this will not easily be forgiven him.'[2] *The New Statesman* castigated de Valera's actions as a 'degradation of civilized beliefs and standards which made Hitler and his Nazi regime possible.'[3] Certainly Lascelles felt that the Irish leader hated the English: 'de Valera prefaces every conversation with a lengthy tirade against Oliver Cromwell.'[4] Churchill rightly or wrongly felt vindicated with his suspicions about Ireland's political leanings.

Foremost, Ireland's neutrality hampered the Allies conduct of the decisive Battle of the Atlantic, although bases in Northern Ireland, particularly Belfast, helped maintain the lines of communication into the Clyde and Mersey. Nonetheless, Churchill on 8 May 1945, the very day of the German surrender, in a letter to Field Marshal Brooke, did not mince his words, claiming the loss of Ireland's ports had 'brought us to within an ace of destruction'.[5] Afterwards Churchill made a point of very publicly castigating Ireland for not joining the Allied war effort. On 13 May in a broadcast made from Downing Street he said, 'Owing to the action of the Dublin Government, so much at variance with the temper and instinct of thousands of Southern Irishmen who hasted to the battle-front…, the approaches which the southern Irish ports and airfields could so easily have guarded were closed by the hostile aircraft and U-boats.'[6] Even though the war with Germany was over it almost felt as if he bore Dublin a lasting grudge.

Churchill in his broadcast then went on to praise the Northern Irish who had stood shoulder to shoulder with Britain in her hour of need. They had been led by Unionist party Prime Minister John Miller Andrews, followed by Sir Basil Brooke. Churchill also praised his own coalition government for showing restraint by not taking military action against Ireland to pre-empt Hitler. Churchill noted instead, 'We left the Dublin Government to frolic with the Germans and later with the Japanese representatives to their hearts' content.'[7] 'It was a fine speech,' observed Lascelles, '…the trouncing of de Valera scathing but not immoderate.'[8]

Churchill had considered occupying Ireland, but such a course of action would have been impossible to justify unless the Germans invaded first. A pre-emptive operation would have done irreparable harm to the close relationship he was developing with America. Nor did he have the troops for such an operation. Had he tried to use the Canadian forces deployed to Britain it is doubtful Canada's Prime Minister Mackenzie King would have given permission. Field Marshal Brooke discussed plans as late as 1942 for troops to move into Ireland from Ulster. However, as he clarified this was only 'in the event of invasion'.[9] Two years later Brooke recalled, 'Winston had asked us to consider the advisability of pressing de Valera to sack the German Ambassador in Dublin for security's sake.'[10] It was in the run up to D-Day, the Allied invasion of France, and Churchill was concerned the Irish were passing intelligence to the Germans. This idea though was abandoned as pointless. Britain was reading all the German embassy's cable messages so closing it would have lost an avenue of intelligence.

Churchill also contemplated imposing severe sanctions on Ireland, but it was felt these would be counterproductive. At the time John Colville noted, 'The Irish are an explosive race and economic coercion might mean trouble.'[11] Despite this Churchill refused to let the pressure off. 'It seems to me that so far from allaying alarm in de Valera's circles,' he told Roosevelt on 19 March 1944, 'we should let fear work its healthy process.'[12] He even proposed banning Irish ships from sailing to foreign ports. Churchill tried to reassure Roosevelt, 'The object of these measures is not spite against the Irish, but preservation of British and American soldiers' lives.'[13] It did though seem that at times he had an unhealthy obsession with Ireland.

Part of the problem Churchill had with Ireland was that he could never forgive it for becoming fully independent with the creation of the Irish Free State. He felt that when it refused to accept dominion status this set a dangerous precedent that had undermined the British Empire and Commonwealth. In particular it had shown India the way to independence. Churchill hoped rather naively that one day the Irish might come to their senses. 'He thought if he had gone on he would have been able to bring her back into the fold,' noted Lord Moran on 10 September 1945. 'Anyway, as far as he was concerned, there would always be a candle burning in the window for the wandering daughter.'[14]

Despite the end of the war Churchill seemed unable to let the Irish ports issue rest. In the House of Commons on 24 May 1946 he warned the government not to abandon the 1936 Anglo-Egyptian Treaty. He said that to withdraw British troops from the Suez Canal would be the same as surrendering the Irish naval bases. That decision he said, 'nearly brought us to our ruin'.[15] His comparison was met by laughter from Labour Members of Parliament. Unperturbed Churchill retorted, 'I would hardly believe it possible that such things could happen twice in a lifetime.'[16] He was right about Suez as the British withdrawal would spark a major international crisis.

Although de Valera had always paid lip service to the External Relations Act, he made it clear to his fellow countrymen that he had little regard for such outdated diplomatic niceties. As far as he was concerned Ireland was independent and that was the end of it. 'I did not say that we are in the Commonwealth,' he told the Irish Parliament on 24 June 1947. 'I carefully pointed out that if being in the Commonwealth implied in any way allegiance, or acceptance of the British King as King here, we are not in the Commonwealth.'[17] Nonetheless, when Prince George, the Duke of Kent was killed in an air crash in 1942 Sir Alan Lascelles noted, 'Even de Valera sent a message of sympathy.'[18] It was an unexpected move for someone so vehemently republican.

In another bizarre twist involving the royal family, in late 1945 the Duke of Windsor wrote to Irishman Sir Shane Leslie asking if he could stay with him at Castle Leslie in Ireland. The castle, also known as Glaslough House, is not far from the border with Northern Ireland. The Duke claimed he wanted 'to study the Irish background of Anglo-American relations'.[19] Leslie was a first cousin of Churchill's on his mother's side. When Sir Alan Lascelles learned of this from Sir John Maffey, the British representative to Ireland, he was horrified. He branded it 'a crazy idea' and noted 'besides infuriating the Ulstermen – and, if he had any contact with de Valera, many people in this country.'[20] The presence of the Duke in Ireland would have caused a storm of outrage from the Republicans. Lascelles immediately wrote to Churchill who responded he had heard nothing of this from Sir Leslie or the Duke. Lascelles noted, 'He considers it a most dangerous plan, which ought to be stopped at all costs.'[21]

Lascelles knew just how unreliable the Duke of Windsor was. He had worked for him when the Duke was still the Prince of Wales. Constantly avoiding his duties, the Prince had proved impossible and Lascelles finally resigned. 'He was without a soul,' concluded Lascelles.[22] Churchill and Lascelles knew that the press would be all over the Duke's intention to visit Ireland if it became public knowledge. The Dominions Office was warned and Maffey made discreet enquires in Dublin, but fortunately nothing more was heard of the matter.

However, the Duke of Windsor did not give up on his Irish adventure. In early 1948 he sent Irishman Kenneth de Courcy to sound out de Valera about moving to Ireland.[23] The Duke and Duchess of Windsor were living in exile in France but were increasingly nervous about its radical left-wing government. Wealthy businessman de Courcy had made himself unpopular with the British government during the war because he supported appeasement with Hitler and had been highly critical of the Soviet Union. Quite what possessed the Duke to think that this was a good idea is anyone's guess. De Valera might have said yes just to inconvenience the British government, but in the event the Windsors stayed in France.[24]

If Churchill had been made aware of the Duke's latest idea he would certainly have cautioned against such a politically-embarrassing course of action. It is doubtful that Attlee would have welcomed such a development either. Likewise, Churchill may not have been too pleased to learn that one of the Duke's golfing companions in Paris was Hardit Singh Malik, the Indian Ambassador to France. The Duke's conversations with 'H.S.' as he was popularly known went unrecorded.[25] They were though no doubt reported back in detail to the Indian government by Malik. In light of the Duke's reputation there is a good chance that his remarks were ill-advised.

After the Second World War opposition to the division of Ireland manifested itself with the creation of the Irish Anti-Partition League. This organisation gained some support from sympathetic members of the British Labour party, but the leaguers suspected their Socialist credentials and their motives. The Anti-Partition League held a rally in Dublin on 25 January 1948 calling on de Valera to tackle the British government over the issue. He did not get the chance to act. To Churchill's glee, de Valera's sixteen years in office came to an end following the Irish General Election in early February 1948. The country was tired of his administration and wanted change. The new coalition government was led by the Fine Gael party that had pledged during the election to maintain the status quo in relation to membership of the British Commonwealth. Churchill naturally assumed that things would remain unchanged. However, Sean MacBride, leader of the Republican party, who became the government's Minister of External Affairs, made it perfectly clear during the election campaign he would repeal the External Relations Act given the opportunity.

At the end of February western Europe was alarmed by the Communist seizure of power in Czechoslovakia and mounting pressure from the Soviet Union on Scandinavia. The Irish though had little interest in Communism. The Communist party of Ireland was formed in the early 1930s, but when the Soviet Union entered the Second World War it disbanded, with its members joining the Irish Labour party. It re-emerged as the Irish Worker League in 1948 under Michael O'Riordan, a Spanish Civil War veteran. Thanks to his links to the banned Irish Republican Army he spent part of the war interned at Curragh. The camp was also used to hold thousands of members of the Irish Republican Army who de Valera saw as a threat to his government. It was soon apparent that the re-emergence of Communism in Ireland posed no risk. The Irish Worker League was so poorly supported that it never had any electoral success nor did it pose a security threat in terms of terror attacks.

In the meantime Ernest Bevin, the British Foreign Secretary, tried to enlist Ireland in presenting a united front against the Soviet Union. Bevin sent Washington his telegram on 10 March outlining the need for a regional Atlantic approaches pact; in his list of potential members he rather hopefully included Ireland. It was also hoped that Ireland would join the Western European Union. By the summer of 1948 Stalin had imposed the Berlin Blockade, ramping up tensions even further in Europe. Ireland, though, seemed more preoccupied with redefining its relationship with Britain than the prospect of conflict between the emerging postwar western and eastern blocs.

The new Irish Prime Minister John Costello, during a visit to America and Canada, announced on 7 September his intention to repeal the External Relations Act. 'Friendship with Britain,' said Costello, 'did not depend on archaic forms, but on principles of association unrelated to outworn formulae.'[26] This remark caught everyone by surprise. It has been speculated that it was in response to Field Marshal Alexander, Governor General of Canada, causing offense at an official reception. However, Costello later denied this was the case and claimed he had already made his mind up. He was intent on completing the Anglo-Irish divorce, which was something even de Valera had never managed.

De Valera, now leader of the Irish Opposition, had no intention of retiring and was spoiling for a fight with the British and the new Irish government. Much to Churchill's chagrin, de Valera on 10 October 1948 started a political campaign to end partition. 'Southern Ireland, or Eire, is about to cast off the last tenuous association with the Crown,' Churchill said in response, 'and is apparently expecting Ulster... to be driven out against her will from the British Empire.'[27] When he went before the House of Commons eighteen days later he made his feelings about the situation perfectly clear. His first loyalty was to the people of Northern Ireland. While he supported the idea of a united Ireland, he argued it should not be achieved at the cost of forcing predominantly Protestant Ulster to join the largely Catholic south. It was this very sectarianism that had driven them apart in the first place.

Sir Richard Pim, the Inspector-General of the Royal Ulster Constabulary, braced himself for trouble. He knew that he could count on Churchill as an ally. Pim, as a naval reserve captain during the war, had been first in charge of the Upper War Room at the Admiralty when Churchill was First Lord of the Admiralty and then the Map Room at 10 Downing Street when Churchill was Prime Minister. Churchill was very impressed when Pim had requested leave so that he could take part in the Dunkirk evacuation.[28] It was Pim who informed Churchill of Germany's surrender. The Prime Minister thanked him and his staff in the Map Room by presenting them with a bottle of Champagne and a large Gruyère cheese. Pim had been at his side as the fatal election results came in. Afterwards such was Churchill's regard for the man that he recommended him for a knighthood. Pim then returned to Northern Ireland and in the summer of 1945 was appointed to head Ulster's police. It was a thankless task but he excelled at it. He certainly needed a great deal of tact and diplomacy when it came to dealing with some of the more extreme members of the Northern Ireland government.

Churchill, after his highly dangerous visit to Belfast in 1912 when serving for the first time as the First Lord of the Admiralty, had taken it upon himself to champion Ulster's Protestants and to try to defuse the historic tensions with Ireland's Catholics.[29] While in the city he had appealed to Ulster to accept Home Rule, but found things were not that simple. Sectarian and political tensions were so high that the authorities, fearing for Churchill and Clementine's safety, had advised them not to go. Some 3,500 troops were sent into Belfast just in case there was a riot. On arrival they were greeted by a crowd of 10,000 angry Protestant Unionists singing the National Anthem and 'Rule Britannia'. Their car was rocked so violently the police feared it would be overturned. It was only after the demonstrators spotted Clementine that they let go of the car. At the Home Rule rally the pair were met by a much warmer crowd of 5,000 Catholic Republicans who were very receptive to his message.

Clementine later confided that she was not so much afraid of being killed, but rather disfigured by flying glass had the windows of their vehicle been smashed. She was pregnant during the Belfast trip and miscarried shortly after returning home. Although Churchill had lived in Dublin for four years as a child when his grandfather was Viceroy of Ireland, he pointedly never returned to either city. Churchill realised that Home Rule would only work if Ulster was given an exemption from government by the Catholic south, such was the animosity between the two communities. Ultimately though Ulster preferred to remain under British rule, much to the annoyance of de Valera and his supporters.

David Lloyd George, who as Prime Minister negotiated Irish independence along with Churchill, in his role as Secretary of State for the Colonies, had found de Valera a difficult character to deal with. Lloyd George had failed to achieve his aim of 'ascertaining how the association of Ireland with the community of nations known as the British Empire may best be reconciled with Irish national aspirations'.[30] As far as Ireland's nationalists were concerned it was all or nothing. De Valera had resisted Ireland becoming 'a helpless dependency' with dominion status and had insisted on 'absolute separation'.[31] Churchill's stance in protecting Northern Ireland's Protestants had gained him great respect there not only from Sir Basil Brooke and Sir Richard Pim, but also from Field Marshals Alexander and Montgomery, both of whom had Ulster ancestry.

Churchill once more during his speech on 28 October 1948 returned to the matter of Ireland's neutrality and the loss of the Irish ports during the war. He explained that he had pledged not to take the ports by force unless Britain's very survival was at stake. 'In the end we got through without this step,' he said. Furthermore, reflecting Bevin's optimism, he felt the threat of Communism and Soviet aggression 'have made new ties of unity… between the Irish and the British peoples'.[32] Churchill concluded by saying he would view Irish unification as a blessing to the British Empire, but Ulster should be 'wooed and won of her own free will and consent'.[33] Such sentiments were little more than wishful thinking.

Sir Basil Brooke and his ruling Ulster Unionist party wanted nothing to do with Dublin. The war had heralded an economic and industrial boom in Northern Ireland; in particular Belfast's shipyard and weapons factories had thrived. Harold Wilson was in the city looking into this very issue when it was bombed by the Luftwaffe. During the immediate post-war years there was a substantial improvement in the standard of living so there was initially no incentive to end partition. In contrast Ireland struggled to recover from the economic dislocation and shortages caused by the war. Its imports had come via the same shipping routes under attack by the U-boats. This was the primary reason why de Valera had lost the election; his government simply failed to deliver any discernible economic recovery. Northern Ireland would only start to struggle in the mid-1950s when industrial demand began to decline.

By coincidence Harold Nicolson met Ireland's leaders just after Churchill's appearance in the House of Commons. He jotted in his diary on 29 October, 'When de Valera makes speeches threatening force against Ulster he adds two thousand votes to the Tories every time.'[34] Nicolson dined at the Kildare Street Club in Dublin with Prime Minister Costello, External Affairs Minister MacBride, Sir John Maffey, Britain's representative and Scottish Member of Parliament Walter Elliot. Nicolson had previously been hosted by Maffey during the war when he had given a lecture at Powerscourt House outside Dublin. Maffey, who had become Lord Rugby the previous year, was clearly in a mischievous mood when he chose the venue for their latest meeting. The place was traditionally a Protestant Anglo-Irish members-only club, in other words an old Unionist stronghold.[35] Not surprisingly neither Costello nor MacBride had been there before. Nicolson was amused that the members comprised 'broken-down peers and landlords dressed in tweeds'.[36]

Inevitably the conversation turned to de Valera and Churchill. Costello and MacBride were pleased that Churchill supported a united Ireland. 'Make no mistake about it,' Elliot warned them, 'what Winston meant was an Ireland united under the crown.'[37] Nicolson was unconvinced that Costello and MacBride were being entirely sincere. 'They pretend that the threat of force,' he observed, 'was one of the gravest errors that de Valera ever committed.'[38] Elliot thought that if Ireland tried to take Ulster the British government would send two divisions of troops to stop them. Nicholson also noted in his diary, 'What Eire does not realise is that she has lost the sympathy of the United States.'[39] Costello and MacBride knew that any attacks on Ulster would not go down well with their friends in Washington, and few Irishmen wanted a return to the dark days of the civil war. 'I do not think we leave them happy,' concluded Nicolson at the end of the meal.[40]

The military option was not really on the table for Dublin. The Irish Army hardly constituted a threat to Northern Ireland and would have struggled to fend off a single British armoured division. Throughout the war Churchill refused to supply de Valera with heavy equipment apart from some tracked carriers. It was only in later years that Britain grudgingly transferred to Ireland a handful of surplus Churchill and Comet tanks and 25-pounder field guns of Second World War vintage. It was rather ironic that three tanks named after de Valera's nemesis were delivered in 1948 with a fourth the following year. Even then they were only rented and eventually all the spares ran out. If Churchill was aware of the deal negotiated by the British War Office he would probably have been highly amused. Costello's government simply did not have the firepower to take Ulster in a conventional war. The only other option was a protracted guerrilla campaign, but even that could not guarantee victory.

While achieving an end to Irish partition was an impossibility without terrible bloodshed, Ireland's severing of its last ties to Britain was much easier. The Irish government finally moved to make the country officially a republic. The Republic of Ireland Act went before the Irish Parliament on 17 November 1948. Its implementation was formally announced on 18 April 1949 at the General Post Office in Dublin. This building was chosen because it was where the failed Easter Rising against British rule had started in 1916. From that point on, Ireland stopped all cooperation with the Commonwealth and ended its acknowledgement of the British crown.

King George VI sent Ireland's new President Sean O'Kelly a message offering his sincere good wishes. He also offered thanks for 'the services and sacrifices of the men and women of your country who rendered gallant assistance to our cause in the recent war'.[41] This was reference to the thousands of southern Irish who, in defiance of their country's neutrality, had volunteered for the British armed forces. The Conference of Commonwealth Prime Ministers, that opened three days after the declaration, was notable as the first to meet without representation from Ireland and was also the first to be attended by the premiers from Ceylon, India and Pakistan.

Although Ireland had formally seceded from the Commonwealth, London and Dublin struggled on with a strange refusal to acknowledge this change. It was agreed that citizens of Ireland and the Commonwealth would not be viewed as foreigners. Furthermore, Anglo-Irish relations would still be handled in Britain by the Commonwealth Relations Office. When George VI received Sean MacBride, Irish Minister of External Affairs, on 3 May 1949 he quipped, 'Tell me, Mr MacBride, what does this new legislation of yours make me in Ireland, an undesirable alien?'[42] MacBride's reply was not recorded. Churchill had to concede that Ireland was now lost forever.

Nine days later western Europe heaved a collective sigh of relief as Stalin ended his Berlin Blockade. To Churchill's great displeasure Ireland refused to play a role in defending western Europe from the threat of Communism. It was invited by both America and Britain to sign up to the North Atlantic Treaty, but the Irish government's response was that it would only join once Britain returned Ulster to Dublin's control. Ireland wanted a separate defence treaty with the United States, but the Americans saw little point in this and would have preferred it to join NATO. The Irish also suspected if they joined the alliance they would be expected to host permanent US air force bases, which was now the case in Britain.

After the war the US air force stationed in Britain had begun to rapidly drawdown. By 1948 most of its facilities had been handed back to the British government. However, with the Berlin airlift and the arrival of B-29 bombers this process was reversed. From that point on aircraft from the US Strategic Air Command were regularly deployed to Britain. Churchill knew it would not be long before the Soviet Union developed its own atomic bomb. He took solace from the presence of the Americans. On 12 September 1948 he wrote to Anthony Eden saying, 'The United States will have a third more atomic bombs and better, and far more effective, means of delivery both by airplanes and the bases they are developing, the largest of which is in East Anglia.'[43]

In the summer of 1949 America detected a cloud of radiation over the north Pacific, indicating the Soviet Union had tested an atomic bomb at Semipalatinsk in Kazakhstan. Churchill was alarmed that such a weapon had fallen into the hands of a country 'where there is no customary, traditional, moral or religious restraint'.[44] Shortly after, America's nuclear-capable B-50 Superfortress bombers deployed to Britain, putting the country firmly on the frontline of the Cold War. The Irish decided they wanted no part of becoming embroiled in a potential nuclear conflict. Nor were they keen on embarking on an expensive rearmament programme. Dublin watched as Washington increased its defence spending to almost eighteen percent of American gross national product in the early 1950s. Washington also leant on its NATO allies, and Britain's spending on defence rose to nearly ten percent of gross national product. This was at a time when it could ill-afford to do so. Ireland felt it prudent to remain on the sidelines.

Churchill inevitably saw this as history repeating itself; NATO's western flank would be left exposed just as Britain's had in the 1940s. Irish neutrality would make protecting the western approaches to the British Isles and Europe that much harder. If the republic was not vigilant, foreign submarines could lurk in the Bays of Donegal and Galway. Neutrality would leave the western shoreline of St George's Channel leading into the Irish Sea and the Welsh coast potentially open. On the other hand having Northern Ireland, along with Scotland, in NATO created a valuable choke point at the mouth of the North Channel that also led into the Irish Sea. This though was little consolation and Churchill saw Ireland's refusal to join the alliance as yet another betrayal by the recalcitrant southern Irish.

Churchill held de Valera personally responsible for all this. Ironically when he became Prime Minister for a second time, he lunched with de Valera. Such a meeting was likely to be explosive, but surprisingly it proved not to be the case. 'A very agreeable occasion,' Churchill informed Lord Moran. 'I like the man.'[45] The nationalist Irish Republican Army, though frustrated by the lack of progress over unification, would slowly step up its attacks north of the border in the hope of making Ulster ungovernable.

After Churchill stepped down in the mid-1950s, the Irish Republican Army's strategy was to force the British from Ulster, leaving it ripe for unification with the republic. It was partly emboldened by Britain's humiliation over the Suez Crisis. They used flying columns operating from the republic to attack army depots, customs posts and police stations in Ulster on or near the border. This forced the British Army to back up Pim's Royal Ulster Constabulary. The Irish Republican Army's campaign in Ulster during 1956-62 failed largely because of the increasing prosperity there. In the republic, the Irish government once again feared the Irish Republican Army would become a threat to stability, and arrested many of its members.

For a time the terror attacks declined. Instead the Republican movement in Northern Ireland opted for a campaign of large-scale social agitation. The idea of this was to highlight the disadvantages suffered by the Catholic population imposed on it by the Protestant Unionist government. Nonetheless, violence would re-occur, culminating in The Troubles in the late 1960s that lasted for almost thirty years. Fortunately for Britain and America, Ireland would become a strategic irrelevance when it came to the truly global nature of the fast-spreading Cold War. Churchill though never really forgive it for its insistence on standing alone. Ireland remained a troublesome neighbour.

PART FOUR

BACK IN
DOWNING STREET

Chapter 9

Return of the Bulldog

By 1950 Prime Minister Attlee felt his government could not muddle on any longer. It was simply not delivering. In a break from protocol, rather than see the King in person, Attlee wrote to him on 5 January requesting that he dissolve Parliament. Attlee tried to put a brave face on things. 'We had now been in power for more than four years,' he said, 'and had carried out the programme which we had put forward at the last General Election. We had no reason to think that we had lost the confidence of the country, for we had created a record in having never lost a by-election.'[1] Although the King wrote back, he delivered his reply in person at Chequers two days later.

Churchill and Clementine were on holiday in Madeira when the announcement of the dissolution of Parliament prior to the election was made on 11 January. He immediately returned to Britain by flying-boat leaving Clementine behind. His first task was to write the Conservative Manifesto. 'I am much depressed about the country,' he wrote to Clementine on 19 January, 'because for whoever wins there will be nothing but bitterness and strife'.[2] The ailing economy and Britain's waning status would challenge whoever ended up in power.

Despite Churchill's advancing years, ill-health and electoral defeat in 1945 he still had the urge to lead. Perhaps not so much his fellow Conservatives, but certainly the country. He looked forward to the challenge of the General Election scheduled for 23 February 1950. His daughter Mary observed, 'He felt he still had work to do – and the strength to do it.'[3] His continual foreign travel showed that he still enjoyed the global limelight. However, Churchill knew that he could not fight an election solely on international issues. To appeal to the electorate he would have to focus on Labour's failure to improve the standard of living in the post-war years. The Conservatives felt that ending rationing which had dragged on since the Second World War was a very key issue for voters.

Nonetheless, Churchill took full advantage of the Cold War and the fear of Left-wing governments and their very rigid way of doing things. On 21 January in a party Political broadcast he warned the country that it faced a choice over 'whether we should take another plunge into Socialist regimentation, or by a strong effort regain the freedom, initiative and opportunity of British life'.[4] Did the country, he asked listeners, want greater state control and ownership or greater freedom of choice? Churchill went on to explain that in alliance with the National Liberal party he wanted to establish a basic standard of living below which no one should fall. 'Everyone,' Churchill told his audience, 'will be allowed to make the best of himself'.[5]

Three days later Churchill felt unwell and sent for Lord Moran. 'About an hour ago everything went misty,' he told his doctor. Churchill understandably was concerned that he was going to have another stroke. 'I am more frightened than Winston,' noted Moran. 'This is a grim start to the racket of a General Election.'[6] After their meeting he continued to worry about Churchill's health. 'An election like this might well flatten a younger man,' he noted in his diary on 5 February, 'and I keep wondering how Winston is wearing under the strain.'[7] He tried to get Churchill to take on fewer public speaking engagements, suggesting radio broadcasts were just as effective. Predictably Churchill took no heed of such wise advice. 'After all,' observed Moran sagely, 'if anything does happen he would prefer to go out fighting a General Election, with plenty of cheering and booing and heckling.'[8] Political campaigning was in Churchill's blood and he was not going to stop now.

Churchill stuck with his theme of the perils of Socialism. At a rally in Cardiff three days later he invoked the words of Lloyd George, who had warned nearly a quarter of a century ago, 'You cannot trust the battle of freedom to Socialism. Socialism has no interest in liberty. Socialism is the very negation of liberty.'[9] Churchill in the back of his mind no doubt felt that this was equally applicable to Communism, which favoured a one-party state. There were lots of those now lurking behind the Iron Curtain. He then went to Devonport to speak in support of his son Randolph, who was contesting the seat against the Labour candidate Michael Foot.

Inevitably Churchill could not resist criticising Labour's track record with foreign policy. When campaigning in Edinburgh on 14 February he said that Bevin had committed 'many pitiful blunders' overseas. However, he had to acknowledge that Bevin had 'followed with steadfastness the line I marked out at Fulton of fraternal association with the United States... In the Atlantic Pact we have a great instrument making for world peace.'[10] He also warned that 'we must not forget the gravity of our position or indeed that of the whole world.'[11] He went on to highlight how the Soviet Union was facing down the Western democracies from an array of compliant satellite states. Likewise, he warned that China, once a wartime ally, had fallen to Communism. He did though add, 'I do not regard China as having finally accepted Soviet servitude.'[12] Such sentiments made little difference to South Korea and Japan who were now on the frontline of the so-called Bamboo Curtain.

It was the Soviet Union that remained his constant preoccupation. 'The Soviet Communist world has by far the greatest military force,' he told the crowd, 'but the United States have the atom bomb; and now, we are told that they have a thousandfold more terrible manifestation.'[13] Even in the rapidly changing Cold War era Churchill hoped he could mould events as he had done in the past by sheer will-power. Thinking of his wartime meetings with Stalin he suggested that the way ahead was a high level conference with the Soviets. He obviously hoped that his track record of being a world-class statesman would appeal to voters. This was Churchill the peacemaker not the warmonger.

His comments swiftly drew criticism and provided ammunition for his opponents. 'I do not think that Winston was right in raising the atom bomb question in that way at this moment,' said Harold Nicolson disapprovingly. 'To suggest talks with Stalin on the highest level inevitably makes people think "Winston could talk to Stalin on more or less the same level. But if Attlee goes, it would be like a mouse addressing a tiger. Therefore vote for Winston." No – I agree with Bevin, it was a stunt, and unworthy of him.'[14] Nicolson was right in that most voters did not want to be reminded that a nuclear war with the Soviet Union was a very real possibility.

To the dismay of the Churchill family it was widely and very erroneously reported on 16 February that Churchill had died. He suspected this was the work of the Labour party and issued a rebuttal, 'I am informed from many quarters that a rumour has been put about that I died this morning. This is quite untrue.' He then pointed the finger at Labour and the Left-wing press by adding, 'It would have been more artistic to keep this one for Polling Day.'[15]

Although Labour won the election its victory was a humiliating one. Attlee's overall majority was cut from 146 to just six. Harold Wilson, who was defending his Huyton constituency, noted gloomily, 'I scraped in by 834 votes.'[16] Labour remained in government but was even more powerless than before. The Conservatives gained 90 seats with a 2.8 percent national swing in their favour. Churchill won his seat but his son did not. Both his sons-in-law, Duncan Sandys and Christopher Soames were elected. One unsuccessful Conservative candidate Anthony Barber wrote to Churchill, 'I hope you will not consider it either impertinent or commonplace when I say your leadership since the end of the war has been one of the most vital factors which has brought our Party back to its present position.'[17] He was right but many younger Conservatives felt that Anthony Eden or Harold Macmillan should be leading them.

'Whatever happens,' said Churchill to Sir Alan Lascelles, 'I think that another General Election in the next few months is inevitable.'[18] Harold Macmillan, after looking at Conservative strategy, was not optimistic about their chances. He cautioned, 'Unless there is a dramatic change in either the economic or the political situation, another election will not produce a substantially different result.'[19] The sudden outbreak of the Korean War and its economic fallout would provide just such a catalyst. First though the Labour government would limp on for an agonising eighteen months.

Attlee, with such a tiny majority, was simply unable to get anything done in Parliament. Rumours began to circulate in London of a possible coalition. Churchill was not interested and knew that Attlee would not consider power sharing again either. He told Sir Alan Lascelles, 'The principle that a new House of Commons has the right to live if it can and should not be destroyed until some fresh issue or situation has arisen to place before the electors, is I believe sound.'[20] In other words he was prepared to bide his time until such point as Attlee capitulated and went to the King again.

International events soon added to the woes of Attlee's beleaguered government. Communist North Korean troops supported by Soviet-supplied tanks swept across the 38th Parallel and invaded South Korea in June 1950. They swiftly overran the city of Seoul and by the end of the summer had driven the South Koreans and the Americans into the Pusan pocket in the southeast. For a moment it looked as if the North Koreans might triumph. Truman was forced to pour reinforcements into Korea from Japan to try to stem the tide. Britain was asked to help and Churchill supported the government's decision to send troops as part of a United Nations force.

Attlee though did not really have the men to spare. The 27th British Commonwealth Brigade, which included Australian and Canadian soldiers, began to arrive at Pusan in August. This was later joined by two further brigades to form the 1st Commonwealth Division. Only just over half of this was British. In stark contrast Britain had deployed an entire army with thirteen divisions in Burma to fight the Japanese.[21] America would commit nine divisions to Korea. Besides America, Britain and the Commonwealth, ten other countries sent armed forces and four contributed medical units.[22]

Churchill in his speech to Parliament on 31 October reasoned that Attlee must call an election. 'The House of Commons is not at its best,' he told them, 'when Parties are so evenly balanced.' He held Attlee personally responsible for the inertia. 'All I can say is that I am quite satisfied that the right hon. Gentleman is indulging his personal power in these matters,' said Churchill, 'in a manner most costly to the community and harmful to all large enduring interests of State.'[23] Attlee chose to ignore his appeal.

Macmillan felt that Labour's foreign policy under Ernest Bevin was coming home to roost. Nowhere was Bevin standing up for Britain's national interests, and the country's response to the Korean War could at best be seen as feeble. 'What is strange is that he (and his friends) still seem quite unable to grasp the complete and utter failure of the policy,' wrote Macmillan in November 1950, 'for which he has been responsible during five years.'[24] By this stage American forces had reached the Yalu River in North Korea on the border with China. This escalated the conflict because the Chinese responded by entering the war on the side of the North Koreans. Hundreds of thousands of Chinese troops poured south, driving the United Nations forces out of liberated Seoul and beyond the 38th Parallel. The intervention of China meant that outright victory was unachievable for either side. It also threatened to spark a much wider war.

By the end of the year the Conservatives had taken a big lead in the opinion polls. This was thanks to the economic crisis caused by the Korean War and the growing cost of British rearmament. After the Second World War Britain's armed forces had been progressively run down as had its weapons factories. Resuscitating both would be costly and unwelcome. Churchill explicitly linked the government's plans for the nationalisation of the iron and steel industry with the war in Korea. Labour had already nationalised the coal industry four years earlier. State ownership was the last thing Churchill wanted. The Iron and Steel Act which was passed in 1949 was due to see nationalisation implemented in 1951. All this, he argued, made industry less flexible.

In January 1951 Churchill was heartened by a Gallup Poll which gave the Conservatives an eleven percent lead over Labour, with forty-four percent of the predicted poll compared to thirty-three percent for Labour. Churchill continued with his gruelling political schedule, with his party doing all it could to prevent iron and steel nationalisation. In the House of Commons the Conservatives launched a campaign in March using parliamentary procedure to draw out sittings to try and wear out the government. After four days they gave up, but this was just a taste of things to come.

The war in Korea dragged on. Seoul was once again liberated by the United Nations' forces in mid-March. In April and the following month the Communists launched two massive offensives, each of which gained some ground before being contained by superior firepower. British forces, thanks to their defence of Hill 235, narrowly avoided being overwhelmed on the Imjin River and helped save Seoul. Yakov Malik, the Soviet Ambassador to the United Nations, proposed a ceasefire on 23 June. Talks opened at Kaesong in 'No Man's Land' just north of Seoul on 10 July. These broke down at the end of the following month and the fighting resumed with the United Nations lacking a clear strategic goal. Field Marshal Montgomery, when later describing the conduct of the war in Korea, said, 'It is absolutely nonsense.'[25]

By now Attlee's government was really failing having lost a series of highly experienced politicians. Sir Stafford Cripps, his Chancellor of the Exchequer, had stepped down in October 1950 due to ill-health. His replacement Hugh Gaitskell was struggling with rearmament and proposing the unpopular measure of prescription charges thanks to overspending. 'The Treasury in Gaitskell's time had thrown money at the armourers,' noted Harold Wilson.[26] Foreign Secretary Bevin's health was failing and he resigned in early March. His successor Herbert Morrison had not lived up to expectations especially over his handling of Iran. Both the Health Minister Nye Bevan, the architect of the National Health Service, and Harold Wilson, the President of the Board of Trade, resigned over the health charges issue and defence spending. Bevan though made a lasting impression. Senior civil servant Sir William Douglas at the Ministry of Health had said, 'I would never work with a man like that, who attacked Churchill in the war.'[27] Later Douglas completely changed his mind stating, 'He is the best minister we ever had.'[28]

'During the summer of 1951 the Conservatives forced several all-night sittings with constant divisions upon the House;' recalled Churchill's daughter Mary, 'Winston took his part in these marathons, and in every way demonstrated his vitality and capacity to continue to lead his party.'[29] This forced Labour Ministers and Members of Parliament to be in constant attendance and on the defensive. 'The advantage of this tactic was that it was far harder on the government MPs than the opposition ones,' recalled Labour MP Roy Jenkins. 'I remember 1951 as the most burdensome summer of all my thirty-four years in the House of Commons.'[30] Churchill effectively waged a guerrilla campaign to exhaust his opponents. 'Churchill was in a happier position,' adds Jenkins. 'He could blow in when he liked and leave when he wanted to.'[31]

Once more Churchill exhibited quite remarkable resilience. On 7 June he spent twenty-one hours leading the Opposition in the House of Commons. 'His object,' noted Jenkins, 'was to show vigour to his followers.'[32] Macmillan remained impressed as ever by Churchill's stamina. At the age of seventy-six he voted in every division in Parliament. Macmillan recalled that Churchill made 'brilliant little speeches... and crowned all by a remarkable breakfast at 7.30 a.m. of eggs, bacon, sausages and coffee, followed by a large whisky and soda and a huge cigar.'[33] He adds with some humour, 'This latter feat commanded general admiration.'[34]

'Whether this campaign of attrition, in which Churchill's participation was more symbolic than regular,' adds Roy Jenkins, 'was a major factor in forcing Attlee into an October election is open to argument.'[35] Regardless, Churchill kept the pressure up. He set about Labour's foreign policy track record on 30 July in the House of Commons. In particular Churchill criticised it for failing to address Egypt banning shipping bound for Israel from travelling through the Suez Canal. Likewise he thought it had been weak over giving in to pressure from Iran to withdraw British workers from Abadan's oilfields. He poured scorn on Labour's decision to withdraw from the Palestine Mandate in the face of mounting terrorism.

That September Churchill was greatly saddened by news of King George VI's lung cancer diagnosis. Ever since the Second World War he had been a close friend and ally of Churchill's. 'To comfort Winston,' recalled Lord Moran, 'I explained that if the King's doctors could do nothing, they would at least concentrate on making him comfortable.'[36] Churchill replied, 'Under the Constitution, the duty of the King's doctors is to prolong his life as long as possible.'[37] Shortly after their conversation Sir Alan Lascelles wrote to Churchill confirming the King had a growth in his lung and needed surgery.

During Parliament's summer recess Churchill and Clementine travelled to Venice, staying at the Excelsior Hotel on the Lido. On the way he managed to have one of his habitual close brushes with death. When the train neared Venice he decided to lean out of the window to enjoy the view. He seemed oblivious to the concrete pole bearing cables racing toward his head. In the nick of time Edmund Murray, Churchill's personal detective, pulled him back into the train. A shaken Churchill turned and rather sheepishly said, 'Anthony Eden nearly got a new job then, didn't he?'[38] Churchill spent his time in Italy bathing in the sea and painting. He also had to work on the fifth volume of his wartime memoirs.

They came back via Paris and while there Churchill dined with his old comrade-in-arms General Eisenhower, who had been appointed the Supreme Allied Commander Europe in April that year. This meant that Eisenhower was in charge of NATO's forces that were facing off with the Soviet Union. Montgomery had been selected as his deputy at the same time. Churchill was very pleased that the security of western Europe was in the hands of such competent commanders. Truman had come round to the idea of having an American supreme commander in Europe once the Korean crisis escalated. However, as far as Truman was concerned if America was to reinforce the defence of Europe, then the Europeans had to accept German involvement with up to ten divisions. Churchill appreciated that this would not only be seen as a controversial move by the Europeans, it would also be seen as provocative by Stalin.

Montgomery was to embrace his latest role wholeheartedly and used it to indulge a passion. 'My brother very much enjoyed his time at NATO,' wrote

Brian Montgomery, 'largely because he travelled so extensively, visiting all fifteen NATO countries and inspecting their armies and defence establishments.'[39] This conveniently meant he was regularly absent from his headquarters and all the political wrangling. Brian adds with some amusement, 'So he was not often in Paris.'[40] Churchill though would almost certainly have approved of Montgomery's field trips.

Attlee finally succumbed to political pressure and called a snap election for 25 October 1951. 'This news was received with relief,' recalled Mary Soames, 'for the Parliamentary situation had become increasingly fraught.'[41] This seems to have caught some members of the Labour party by surprise. 'Attlee never told me why he suddenly called his second election...' said Harold Wilson, 'but he was himself tired and felt that he could only carry on with some sort of improved majority.'[42] There were concerns in many quarters that the election would be a rerun of the previous one. Sir Alan Lascelles advised the King that if Attlee was returned with a similar majority then he should recommend a coalition. Lascelles cautioned though that neither Attlee nor Churchill were likely to agree to this. For Churchill it was his fourteenth General Election and his seventeenth individual parliamentary challenge, as he had also fought three by-elections during his long political career.

Once more Lord Moran was concerned that Churchill was incapable of facing the exhausting challenge of fighting a General Election. By this stage Churchill was increasingly deaf, but disliked using a hearing aid. Moran noted gloomily, 'If he wins this election and goes back to No.10 I doubt whether he is up to the job.'[43] It seems that Churchill's desire to be in charge and recapture his glory days was undiminished. He told Lord Moran that if he won he would also take on the role of Minister of Defence as he had done during the war. 'He had never felt any desire to share with anyone the burden that he carried in the war,' observed Moran. 'But now things were changed; he was an old man.'[44]

When Moran said he was opposed to Churchill taking on two roles, Churchill said he had approached Air Chief Marshal Charles Portal about being Defence Minister. Portal had served as Chief of the Air Staff during the war so was an ideal candidate, however he did not want to get involved in politics. Portal's response may have also been influenced by the government's subsequent treatment of Bomber Command and its distancing from the strategic bomber campaign against Germany's cities. Churchill's other candidate was Field Marshal Alexander, but he was serving as the Governor-General of Canada and was unavailable.

Churchill was portrayed as a warmonger thanks to his references to the atom bomb during the previous election. 'The *Daily Mirror* ran an odious campaign,' said Mary, 'on the theme: "Whose finger do you want on the trigger?..." – inferring that war was more likely under Churchill's leadership.'[45] Churchill responded to this in a speech to his Woodford parliamentary constituency on 6 October. 'I am sure we do not want any fingers upon any trigger,' he told his audience. 'Least of all do we want a fumbling finger.'[46] Churchill felt that Britain's problems with Iran were a direct result of Indian independence. That day he highlighted 'the great decline of British prestige and authority in the Middle East following the inevitable loss of our military power in India'.[47]

Churchill made his first Conservative political broadcast two days later. Once more he campaigned on domestic issues, warning Britain was at risk 'if we go on consuming our strength in bitter party or class conflicts.'[48] He then added, 'The difference between our outlook and the Socialist outlook is the difference between the ladder and the queue.'[49] Churchill spoke almost every day. International affairs also dominated the agenda, especially the Middle East. On 17 October Egyptian nationalists threatened Britain's bases in the Suez Canal Zone. In response Attlee deployed the 16th Parachute Brigade from Cyprus to the Canal. Despite this the *Daily Mirror's* 'Trigger' headline may have accounted for a swing in the opinion polls in favour of Labour during the final days of the election.

Harold Wilson felt that Labour candidates branding Churchill 'the warmonger' was unwarranted. 'A fairer assessment would have been based on his long experience of defence matters, in peace as well as in war,' said Wilson, 'and his clear perception of the overstraining of the economy in general and the productive potentialities of the munitions industries.'[50] When in Plymouth, three days before the country voted, Churchill told an audience that he hoped to make 'an important contribution to the prevention of a third world war'. Looking round at the expectant faces he added, 'It is the last prize I seek to win.'[51]

On the morning of polling day the *Daily Mirror* repeated its 'Whose finger on the trigger?' caption accompanying a silhouette of Churchill. 'Labour leads during the night,' noted Harold Nicolson, 'as always happens since the industrial seats are counted first.'[52] Things though began to change. 'As the day goes on,' observed Nicolson, 'the Tories catch up and by 12.45 it is clear that they will have a majority.'[53] This time the Conservatives ended up with a majority of 17 seats and Churchill was back in Downing Street. Churchill himself kept his seat with a slightly larger majority than in 1950, with 18,579 votes compared to 18,499 previously. Once again Randolph Churchill lost to Michael Foot. Churchill's sons-in-law Duncan Sandys at Streatham and Christopher Soames at Bedford were both re-elected.

The *Evening Standard* proclaimed, 'Winston in Power: Working majority but a small one.'[54] On the afternoon of 26 October Attlee tendered his resignation to the King. He was always grateful that the King had not made life difficult while he slowly dismembered the British Empire. 'During his reign there were developments in the Commonwealth,' said Attlee, 'some of which entailed the abandonment of outward forms which a lesser man might have felt it difficult to surrender.'[55] The King, like Churchill, had little option but to accept independence for Burma, Ceylon, India and Pakistan.

Shortly after, Churchill, at the age of seventy-six, arrived to accept the King's invitation to form a government. Field Marshal Montgomery was amongst the first of Churchill's well-wishers. 'Thank God,' he wrote. 'At last we have you back again and in charge of the ship.' Then rather prophetically he added, 'May you stay there for five years and more.'[56] When Lord Moran asked one of Churchill's secretaries if Winston was disappointed that his majority was not bigger, she responded, 'Oh, I don't think so; he's relieved he is in.'[57] A proud Clementine wrote to a friend saying, 'I do hope Winston will be able to help the country. It will be up-hill work, but he has a willing eager heart.'[58]

Aside from Britain's domestic issues such as its shaky economy, Churchill inherited two live wars, the one in Korea and one in Malaya. While the insurgency in Malaya was regional in nature and containable, tensions over Korea risked breaking out again and spreading. Trouble was also brewing in Cyprus, Egypt, Kenya and Sudan. Churchill could not resist the call of the drums and as promised immediately combined the office of Prime Minister with that of Defence Minister. He chose to ignore Lord Moran's advice and the recommendations of a 1946 government White Paper which had called for the creation of a separate Minister of Defence.

'There is no doubt that the arrangements adopted in war-time by Mr. Churchill worked well,' said Field Marshal Montgomery, 'and that high-level matters of strategy and operational policy were dealt with expeditiously.'[59] The question was would Churchill's combined role work well in what was essentially peacetime and when he was no longer at the height of his powers? Churchill would not relinquish the Defence Minister post until March 1952 when Field Marshal Alexander was free to fill the role. However, Alexander had been made a member of the House of Lords in 1946, which meant Churchill still took the lead on defence matters in the Commons. Furthermore, as John Colville observed, Churchill was 'oblivious to the fact that Alexander, while a soldier of indisputable gallantry and an excellent emollient as Supreme Allied Commander in Italy, had no experience of Whitehall or Parliament.'[60] The result of this, adds Colville, was that Alexander was 'to become an unhappy and unsuccessful Minister of Defence'.[61]

Clementine was alarmed when it was suggested that Duncan Sandys be appointed Secretary of State for War. 'Do you think it wise to have him working immediately under your orders as Minister of Defence,' she cautioned in a letter to her husband on 29 October 1951. 'If anything were to go wrong it would be delicate and tricky – first of all having to defend your son-in-law, and later if by chance he made a mistake having to dismiss him.'[62] Churchill listened to his wife's sage advice. 'Winston esteemed and liked Duncan very much,' wrote Mary, 'and their family bond was reinforced by their mutual concern for the cause of European unity.'[63] Instead Sandys was appointed Minister of Supply, a much junior post to that of Secretary of State for War.[64] Antony Head was sent to the War Office and survived his dealings with the Defence Minister, eventually assuming that role himself in the mid-1950s.

At the War Office Churchill inherited one of his veteran Second World War commanders as head of the army. Attlee appointed Field Marshal Sir William Slim to succeed Field Marshal Montgomery in1948 as Chief of the Imperial General Staff. At the time Slim was a very controversial choice as he was a former Indian Army general, and no career soldier from the Indian Army had ever been Chief of the Imperial General Staff before. During Churchill's wartime premiership Slim had led the Fourteenth Army to victory in Burma. The naysayers in the British Army were proved wrong as Slim turned out to be a highly capable CIGS, if not even better than Montgomery. Slim would continue in the role under Churchill until November 1952 when he was succeeded by Sir John Harding.

Duncan Sandys had been the least of Churchill's worries. When Lord Moran met with him on 8 November 1951 he found Churchill exhausted, having had to fill seventy-five ministerial posts. 'The last fortnight has been more tiring than anything in the war,' Churchill confessed to Moran. 'There were great decisions then, of course,' he added, 'but I was swept along by events.'[65] Amongst the numerous appointments was Anthony Eden who Churchill made Foreign Secretary. Not long afterwards Churchill approached Conservative Member of Parliament Robert Boothby to head a British delegation for discussions on a United Europe. He was qualified for such a role as he had served as a delegate to the Consultative Assembly of the Council of Europe. During the 1920s Boothby had been Parliamentary Private Secretary to Churchill when he was the Chancellor of the Exchequer. When they met on 15 November Churchill told Boothby, 'I would have you know what a deep concern I take in your career.'[66] Boothby was unconvinced and did not believe that this job would lead to something better. After his meeting he uncharitably told Harold Nicolson that Winston was looking 'very, very old; tragically old'.[67] The elderly British bulldog did not care, he was back in Downing Street and was delighted about it. He had proved a political point. The British public had voted him into power unlike in 1940 when he replaced Neville Chamberlain to head a wartime coalition government and five years later when they refused to keep him in office.

'There were many, including his wife,' noted John Colville, 'who did not think Churchill should return to office a month short of his seventy-seventh birthday.'[68] Churchill privately agreed with this, but he knew he was the Conservatives' best chance of getting back into power. 'At first he himself,' adds Colville, 'as he told me when I rejoined him, intended to remain Prime Minister for one year only, and then hand over to... Anthony Eden'.[69] Churchill claimed he had two goals; he told Colville he wanted 'to have time to re-establish the intimate relationship with the United States' he had developed during the war and to restore 'liberties... eroded by wartime restrictions and post-war socialist measures'.[70]

Chapter 10

Seeing Old Friends

One of the first things Churchill did after being voted back into Downing Street was to see President Truman. He had a plethora of international issues he wished to discuss, none of which Britain was capable of dealing with on its own. Key amongst them was the future of NATO and European defence, Britain's ongoing problems in the Middle East and the wars in the Far East. Churchill was desperate for the country to play its part as a world player, but the reality was it simply did not have the resources to do so. The war had impoverished Britain and Indian independence had denied its armed forces a massive pool of manpower, that had traditionally helped British power-projection. The governments of Australia, Canada and New Zealand, although they had committed forces to the Korean War, were tired of conflict. 'In Washington they will feel we are down and out,' Churchill lamented to Lord Moran.[1]

Interestingly, when Churchill announced his visit to America to his Cabinet he was at pains to point out that he would not be going armed with a begging bowl. 'He said he was going to America to re-establish relations,' said John Colville, 'not to transact business.'[2] Nonetheless, Britain's dollar reserves were running perilously low and Churchill was fretting that by mid-year the country would run out of funds. This would severely impact on the Conservatives' efforts to end rationing. 'The British were not very popular in America at this time,' observed Sarah Churchill who was acting in the States, 'as it seemed we were always asking for money.'[3] Although Truman would be pleased to see Churchill, he fully appreciated that Britain and France were struggling to meet their defence responsibilities in Europe because of their reluctance to relinquish their empires. He was also conscious that America was doing most of the fighting in Korea. The French were so stretched by the war in Indochina that they had only sent a single infantry battalion. As far as Truman was concerned both countries needed to get their priorities right.

Churchill on 31 December 1951 headed to Southampton to board the Queen Mary for the voyage to New York. Churchill liked to travel in luxury and he particularly enjoyed the fine dining to be had in the ship's 'Verandah Grill'.[4] This was an exclusive restaurant and night club high up on part of the sun deck that offered the most amazing ocean views from the stern. It was considered far more

106

select than the first-class restaurants. His dining room at Chartwell may have been partly inspired by this with the Weald replacing the sea. Amongst Churchill's thirty-strong delegation was Anthony Eden, Foreign Secretary, Hastings 'Pug' Ismay, Commonwealth Relations Secretary, Field Marshal Slim, Chief of the Imperial General Staff, Admiral Sir Rhoderick McGrigor, First Sea Lord, Churchill's doctor Lord Moran and his Private Secretary John Colville. Inauspiciously their departure was delayed when it was found that the ship's anchor was fouled.

That night on New Year's Eve, rather surprisingly Churchill invited Lord Mountbatten to dinner. He still held him responsible for giving away India, even though ultimate responsibility lay with Attlee. Churchill did not want to acknowledge that Mountbatten had done the best he could under the circumstances. Churchill was perhaps hoping to end their differences and may have been intending to capitalise on Mountbatten's extensive wartime experience. Mountbatten in turn may have thought an audience with the new Prime Minister might be a good idea. He had been serving as the Fourth Sea Lord in charge of naval supplies and transport at the Admiralty. This was hardly a career progression for the last viceroy of India. Mountbatten felt he should be First Sea Lord, the military head of the Royal Navy. Despite his royal connections, Mountbatten, since his latest appointment, had initially kept a low profile. 'He didn't attempt to interfere with anything outside his own department,' observed Sir John Lang, Secretary of the Admiralty. 'He just got up and spoke his part on his subject and no more.'[5]

In contrast his efforts to make an impression on the Queen Mary quickly made him unpopular with the others. Mountbatten, having served as the Supreme Allied Commander South East Asia and then Viceroy of India, had got used to people treating his views with deference. He therefore found it hard to hold his tongue. 'Lord Mountbatten came from Broadlands to dine and talked arrant political nonsense,' John Colville recorded crossly in his diary. 'He caused much irritation to the Chiefs of Staff.'[6] Mountbatten's reunion with Churchill did not go well either when he argued against tying Britain too closely to America. This was a foolish line to take when Churchill was poised to sail to America to strengthen the Anglo-American relationship. Nonetheless, he persisted with his view that America was going to drag Britain into war.

Churchill did not appreciate Mountbatten's advice. He scolded him for expressing Left-wing views when as a sailor he should be non-political. 'The PM laughed at him,' noted John Colville who sat listening to their exchange, 'but did not, so Pug Ismay thought, snub him sufficiently.'[7] After dinner Colville had the task of escorting Mountbatten off the ship. He was irritated by Mountbatten's over-familiarity as they parted, especially when Mountbatten intimated he could put in a good word for him with Churchill.

Mountbatten was clearly not very captivated by Churchill. 'My impressions of this grand old man are that he is really past his prime,' Mountbatten confided in his diary. 'He is very sentimental and full of good will towards me. He kept telling me what a friend he was of mine and of my family.'[8] In light of their heated words over India it is doubtful that Mountbatten completely believed him. Luckily for Mountbatten he had an ally in James Thomas, Churchill's new First Lord of the Admiralty. Thomas would support Mountbatten's appointment as the NATO commander-in-chief in the Mediterranean in June 1952.[9] However, it would be another three years before Mountbatten got the coveted role of First Sea Lord by which time Churchill was stepping down.

During the voyage Churchill had to prepare speeches for the US Congress and Canadian Parliament. It was not a task that he readily relished. 'I am not so good mentally as I used to be,' he told Lord Moran. 'A speech has become a burden and an anxiety.'[10] The others were not spared. Colville recalled, 'During the crossing we worked on our briefs: oh, the amount of paper that even a small conference evokes!'[11] He found it a challenge to get Churchill to concentrate, noting, 'It was very difficult to get the PM to read any of it.'[12] Churchill also confided in Moran that he was worried that if the cost of rearmament was not spread out over a longer period then 'Western Europe will be rushing to bankruptcy and starvation.'[13] Moran pointed out that it was in America's interests to help, otherwise if Britain's economy failed there would be a swing to the left which might be detrimental to rearmament. Churchill remained unconvinced.

Upon arrival in New York on 5 January 1952 they flew to Washington in the Presidential plane. President Truman was waiting for Churchill as he exited the aircraft onto the runway. There were smiles all round and a firm handshake. The pair were later photographed smiling in the Oval Office. They dined on the Presidential yacht Williamsburg where discussions were held on European defence and the threat from the Soviet Union. 'There were twelve of us round the table,' recounted Churchill, 'the guidance of the world was in our hands, not for domination but to work for the good of mankind.'[14] Amongst those in attendance were Dean Acheson, US Secretary of State, Robert Lovett, US Secretary of Defence and Walter Gifford, US Ambassador to London.

Churchill informed Truman that he did not anticipate a Soviet attack in 1952, after all he noted, 'they had gained half Europe and all China without loss.'[15] The Americans made it clear that they were unhappy Britain was continuing to trade with Communist China through Hong Kong. Churchill was looking for American support for British policy in Egypt, Iran and Iraq. In particular he was keen on the idea of an international supervisory force being sent to the Suez Canal. To that end he suggested America send a brigade as it might deter the Egyptians from causing more trouble. Truman had no intention of propping up British imperial interests in Egypt. Colville jotted in his diary, 'President Truman was affable but not impressive and I did not think Acheson or Lovett anything out of the way.'[16]

For the next two days the talks were taken up with how best to organise NATO and its commands. Churchill was at pains to highlight that Britain was pressing on with its costly rearmament programme to help defend against Communism. This, he explained, was causing Britain difficulties, but he was not seeking American aid. He told Truman, 'The great burden which the United States was bearing on behalf of the free world was a matter of universal admiration.'[17] When it came to putting the case for a British naval commander for the Atlantic, Admiral McGrigor suddenly lost his nerve. 'He went red in the face,' recalled John Colville, 'large drops of perspiration appeared on his brow and he was too overawed to do more than stutter a few disjointed words.'[18] Somewhat embarrassingly Field Marshal Slim had to take over his presentation. 'It was a magnificent tour de force by the representative of another service,' adds Colville.[19] The Americans did not agree and stuck to their demand that an American commander should be appointed.

On 8 January Churchill returned to the issue of Egypt. He tried to explain that Britain was clinging on out of a sense of international duty to protect the Suez Canal. Churchill said that if America helped, 'The trouble in Egypt would soon be brought to an end and the British would be able to make more forces available to Europe or to the United Kingdom itself, which was without adequate defences.'[20] He supported the US proposal for a four-power pact in the Middle East consisting of America, Britain, France and Turkey. His hope was that the others would also send troops to Suez thereby alleviating the burden on Britain. This would also serve to intimidate the Egyptians.

Turning to Asia, Churchill praised Truman's stance over Korea and felt it signalled a turning point in standing up to Communist aggression. In response Truman wanted a more sympathetic attitude from Britain toward the Chinese Nationalists in Taiwan. Churchill agreed that, 'in spite of the weakness and corruption of Chiang Kai-shek's regime, it would be wrong to leave his three- to four-hundred thousand followers in Formosa to be murdered by the Communists.' In other words as far as Churchill was concerned Chiang and his island fiefdom were no longer political players in the future of China. Turning to the French war in Indochina, Churchill highlighted that this was an unwelcome drain on the French armed forces, which was leaving France weakened in Europe and anxious about the prospect of rearming Germany.

Churchill, after his meetings with Truman, went to address the staff of the British Embassy on 9 January and was very surprised to be greeted by almost a thousand people. After speaking to them Churchill instructed John Colville to find out why the embassy contingent was so enormous. 'Evidently nobody had given thought to reducing the vast staffs established in a war which had ended six and a half years previously,' noted Colville. 'The Prime Minister then issued a peremptory order, in his capacity as Minister of Defence, and a drastic reduction was effected.'[21] That day Churchill travelled to New York to briefly stay with his friend Bernard Baruch. While there John Colville bumped into the Duke and Duchess of Windsor at the Metropolitan Opera.

When Anthony Eden addressed New York's Columbia University on 11 January he reflected Churchill's more cautious views on European unity. When talking about the possibility of Britain joining a European federation Eden cautioned, 'This is something which we know in our bones we cannot do.'[22] Such a viewpoint was not in accordance with those of Harold Macmillan and Duncan Sandys. However, Churchill saw Britain supporting Europe from the outside with America beside it. He felt that integration with Europe would alienate the Americans. Furthermore, Britain had been working on its own atomic bomb since 1948 and he saw no reason for the Europeans to join the nuclear club.

Afterwards Churchill headed for Ottawa where he met with Governor-General Field Marshal Alexander and General Sir Gerald Templer. In a pique of temper he almost did not go after he was informed that the Canadian air force and navy were no longer to play 'Rule Britannia' on the instructions of the Canadian government. Clementine had made him see the error of his ways and he was delighted as the train pulled into Ottawa to be greeted by a Royal Canadian Air Force band playing 'Rule Britannia.' Churchill later grumbled to Lord Moran, 'Canada is quite touchy about being called a Dominion, but look what happened when the Princess went there.'[23] Princess Elizabeth and her husband Prince Philip, Duke of Edinburgh, had visited Canada, including Ottawa, at the end of 1951 and been largely warmly welcomed.[24]

General Templer had flown out to Canada at short notice to be appointed the High Commissioner of the Malayan Federation. 'Alex was quite sure he was the man for the job of rooting out the Communist guerrillas from the jungle,' noted Lord Moran, 'and Monty, too, had sent a letter, so we are hopeful that all will go well.'[25] Churchill first offered Montgomery the job, but he had declined saying, 'I understand Germans, and know how to deal with them. I would be no good whatsoever at dealing with scorpions and snakes!'[26] Montgomery knew that his real strength lay with NATO.

When Templer arrived at his hotel in Ottawa he retired for the night only to be roused in the early hours. He was then taken to the Prime Minister's hotel. In light of the previous high commissioner being assassinated Churchill acknowledged, 'I may be sending you to your death.'[27] This was hardly a good way to encourage Templer, but Churchill assured him he would have complete authority. 'I must warn you that you have probably heard that Lord Acton said that absolute power corrupts absolutely,' said Churchill. 'You will have absolute power in Malaya. See that you do not get corrupted by it. Good night.'[28] Templer was slightly bemused by all this for although he knew why he was in Ottawa, he had not been officially offered the job and his appointment was taken for granted. Nevertheless, he soon found himself on a flight to Malaya and Alexander and Montgomery were to be proved right.

On 14 January Churchill spoke at a banquet held in his honour by the Canadian Prime Minister. 'The fervour of his reception was a tribute, not to anything he had to say,' said Lord Moran, 'but to his own corner in the hearts of the Canadian people.'[29] The following day he returned to Washington ready to address Congress on 17 January. Churchill was particularly anxious about this despite having addressed Congress twice before in 1941 and again in 1943. The international situation was not the same and nor was Congress. 'This speech has become an obsession,' noted Lord Moran, 'it has hung over him, like a dark cloud, since the day we left England.'[30] Churchill planned to put the fear of God into Congress in the hope that they might help Britain. Most notably he was to compare the dangers facing the Middle East to what had happened in Korea. Nonetheless, his overarching theme was the hope of achieving a greater harmony in the world.

When Churchill arrived his welcome by Congress was initially very lukewarm. 'We were dismayed at his entry as there was no applause or recognition,' recalled Sarah Churchill, 'as is generally politely accorded, and the little old man stumped his way through in dead silence.'[31] John Colville described it as a decidedly 'chilly reception'.[32] Churchill, having cleared his throat and put on his spectacles, opened by saying, 'I have not come here to ask for money to make life more comfortable or easier for us in Britain.'[33] The audience stirred, thinking "Wait for it". 'I have not come here to ask for money!' He paused then added, 'For myself!'[34] It broke the ice. 'This remark received roars of laughter and a standing ovation,' said Sarah Churchill, 'before he was able to continue with his important speech.'[35]

Churchill then spoke of China and the Korean War and said if they all worked together they should 'avert the danger of a Third World War'.[36] Turning to the Middle East Churchill acknowledged that Britain was no longer able 'to bear the whole burden of maintaining the freedom of the famous waterway of the Suez Canal'.[37] Britain by this stage had 80,000 troops tied down in the Canal Zone. Churchill called for the Four-Powers to work to 'bring an end to the widespread disorders of the Middle East in which, let me assure you, there lurk dangers no less great than those which the United States has stemmed in Korea'.[38] He sought to justify Britain's continuing presence in Egypt by saying, 'We do not seek to be masters of Egypt. We are there only as the servants and guardians of the commerce of the world.'[39] It is doubtful that many Americans in the audience saw it that way.

Churchill also praised Israel, but warned with great foresight, 'They must strive to renew and preserve their friendly relations with the Arab world without which widespread misery might follow for all.'[40] He felt that in Europe peace should be maintained by strong armed forces as much as by the deterrence of the atomic bomb. Churchill argued that the bomb should only be used as a last resort. Lord Moran observed, 'Only now, when he spoke of the atomic bomb, was there any real warmth in the applause.'[41]

He ended as planned on an optimistic note, 'It may be that presently a new mood will reign behind the Iron Curtain. If so it will be easy for them to show it, but the democracies must be on their guard against being deceived by a false dawn.'[42] Churchill was alluding to Stalin dying, which many hoped might lead to a softening of east-west relations. He may have been drawing on intelligence that indicated that the Red Czar's days were numbered. Certainly all was not well in the Kremlin. Stalin was approaching 74 and suffering from poor health. He was regularly away from Moscow and in 1950 and 1951 had stayed at his dacha on the Abkhazian coast for a total of almost five months. He was suffering from cardiac problems and a host of other ailments. However, his distrust of doctors made it increasingly difficult and dangerous to treat him. He convinced himself that the medical profession was plotting to kill him. After Stalin's personal physician Vladimir Vinogradov in January 1952 suggested the Soviet leader retire, the unfortunate doctor ended up in Lubyanka prison. Inevitably there would be regime change for better or worse at some stage in the Soviet Union.

Churchill concluded by calling on the fraternal friendship that existed between Britain and America. 'Bismarck once said that the supreme fact of the nineteenth century was that Britain and the United States spoke the same language,' he said. 'Let us make sure that the supreme fact of the twentieth century is that they tread the same path.'[43] As Churchill sat down he was rewarded with great applause. 'When it was done the PM, flushed and happy, was like a man who had been granted a reprieve,' recounted Lord Moran.[44]

Afterwards he met with former US Defense Secretary General Marshall who congratulated him on his speech at the British Embassy. Marshall, after a long and distinguished military career, had recently retired. He reminisced that one of the best Churchill speeches he had heard was at Carthage following the liberation of North Africa during the Second World War. That had been a particularly euphoric moment which Churchill recalled with pride. The press coverage proved favourable. *The Times'* Washington correspondent observed that Churchill was still 'well informed, and as full of ideas, vivid language, and wit as ever'.[45]

On the agenda at the final meeting between Churchill and Truman was a possible gathering of Western and Soviet leaders. Rather surprisingly Churchill stated that he was not currently amenable to such an idea. He was worried that if such a summit broke down people might think that war was inevitable. In Churchill's defence it is very doubtful that Stalin would have personally accepted an invitation. Dean Acheson, who had held talks with both Churchill and Eden, noted in both he saw, 'evidence of six years in opposition and the absence of familiarity with frustrating detail and of intuition instilled by the daily pain of decision and action'.[46]

On 19 January Churchill returned to New York to stay with Bernard Baruch for forty-eight hours to recover before heading home. 'This visit to America has been a gamble,' he told Lord Moran on the train to New York. 'But it has come off, I think. It will do a lot of good. We have taken up old friendships and made new ones. I like Truman fearfully.'[47] The problem Churchill and his government now faced was that America was due a presidential election at the end of the year. A change of administration would mean that he would have to start all over again. 'Congress reacted slowly, but the subsequent praise was generous,' wrote John Colville in his diary, 'except at home where the Labour party asserted that the PM had committed us to a more active part against China.'[48] This accusation was to cause a massive row in the House of Commons that would result in a political trouncing for Labour.

Churchill on 20 January cabled Clementine sounding rather dispirited, 'I never had such a whirl of people and problems, and the two speeches were very hard and exacting ordeals.'[49] That day he received a telegram from Sir Alan Lascelles bearing bad news about King George VI's deteriorating health. It was evident that he was very ill. Churchill cabled Clementine on 21 January to say that when he got home, 'I have only one piece of urgent business… This may settle itself beforehand.'[50] He then sailed home on the Queen Mary intent on seeing his monarch, which he did at the end of the month.

The ailing King, along with Churchill, waved goodbye to Princess Elizabeth and Prince Philip, Duke of Edinburgh when they departed for their Commonwealth tour from London airport on 31 January. Despite it being a cold, blustery winter's day the King had insisted on seeing them off personally. 'He was gay and even jaunty, and drank a glass of champagne,' recalled Churchill.[51] However the King, turning to Margaret MacDonald, Princess Elizabeth's dresser, said sadly, 'Look after the princess for me.'[52] It was almost as if he knew it would be the last time he would see her. It was a very selfless act seeing her off and against the advice of his doctors. 'He is like that,' his daughter later recalled. 'He never thinks of himself.'[53]

A week later the King lost his battle with ill-health in the early hours of 6 February 1952, dying of coronary thrombosis. A blood clot fatally impeded his heart. He was just fifty-six. Edward Ford, the King's assistant private secretary, was sent to Downing Street that morning. Ford was ushered into the Prime

Minister's bedroom where he found him surrounded by documents. 'I've got bad news, Prime Minister,' said Ford falteringly. 'The King died last night.'[54] For a second Churchill was slack-jawed. 'Bad news?' he cried. 'The worst!'[55] Although not unexpected Churchill took the King's death badly. John Colville arrived just after Ford had left to find him highly distressed. 'When I went to the Prime Minister's bedroom he was sitting alone with tears in his eyes,' recalled Colville, 'looking straight in front of him and reading neither his official papers nor the newspapers.'[56] For Churchill it was the end of an era, another valued friend and ally was gone.

Recovering from the shock Churchill summoned his Cabinet that morning and informed them. He then spent all day preparing a radio broadcast. When he read through his draft at lunchtime he burst into tears. Mary felt that her father 'was genuinely personally devoted to the King'.[57] John Colville confided, 'I had not realised how much the King meant to him.' America was very sympathetic to Britain's loss. 'American friends seemed to grieve as if he were their friend and King;' Sarah Churchill wrote to her mother, 'it really was remarkable.'[58] The US House of Representatives passed a resolution and adjourned for the day.

Princess Elizabeth, who automatically became Queen, was in Kenya when she received word. She and Prince Philip were then immediately on their way home. 'She became Queen while perched in a tree in Africa, watching the rhinoceros come down to the pool to drink,' noted Harold Nicolson in his diary.[59] On 7 February Churchill drove to London airport to greet them along with Prince Henry, Duke of Gloucester, the late King's brother, and Lord Mountbatten, who was a second cousin of the King's and a maternal uncle of Prince Philip's. During the drive Churchill prepared his speech announcing the King's death with his secretary Jane Portal who accompanied him.

Portal recalled, 'As he was sitting in the car dictating, the tears were pouring down his face and he was heaving with sobs... he was weeping at his own words and his own thoughts.'[60] Churchill no doubt cast his mind back to the fond memories he had of the King during the Second World War. Most famously the pair had concocted a plan to attend the D-Day landings aboard a warship until Sir Alan Lascelles put a stop to things. Subsequently by way of compensation Churchill had pressured Montgomery to host the King just after the landings had taken place. On another occasion Churchill had been offended on the King's behalf when Stalin proposed a toast at Yalta to George VI, with the Communist proviso that as a man of the people he was against kings. Lord Moran found the Prime Minister in a maudlin mood. Churchill reminisced how he had seen the King when the Princess left. 'I think he knew he had not long to live,' Churchill told Moran. 'It was a perfect ending.'[61] That evening Churchill told the nation that the King's death had 'struck a deep and solemn note in our lives which, as it resounded far and wide, stilled the clatter and traffic of the twentieth century in many lands'.[62] He welcomed the 'Second Queen Elizabeth' and ended with 'God Save the Queen.'[63]

The following day the Queen told her Privy Councillors, 'My heart is too full for me to say more to you today than that I shall always work as my father did.'[64] When Churchill first heard of Elizabeth's accession he felt that she was too young. In a state of distress he had remarked to John Colville 'that he did not know her and that she was only a child'. However, Churchill was to watch with admiration as she rose magnificently to the role of monarch. Over 300,000 people paid their respects to her father's coffin in Westminster Hall. 'For a week all normal business came to a standstill,' noted John Colville.[65] Churchill had his first official audience as Prime Minister with the young Queen on 12 February; they buried the King at Windsor Castle three days later. 'Now the accession of the young Queen Elizabeth II aroused in him every instinct of chivalry,' wrote Mary Churchill.[66]

Behind the scenes there was a slight kerfuffle when Prince Philip objected to the Royal family still being known as the House of Windsor. He perhaps understandably favoured the House of Edinburgh. Lord Mountbatten, in an act of even greater insensitivity to royal continuity, told friends that the House of Mountbatten now ruled. This got back to Churchill via John Colville much to his displeasure. On the grounds that Windsor had been adopted by royal decree by George V in 1917, Churchill, the Cabinet and royal household agreed no change was to be made. Prince Philip, who knew that his naval career was now ruined, grumbled to his friends, 'I am the only man in the country not allowed to give his name to his own children.'[67]

By the end of February, Mountbatten was alarmed by rumours that he was to be posted abroad so he could not sway Queen Elizabeth and Prince Philip. He wrote to Edwina his wife reporting, 'My own influence was viewed with apprehension, and there was also the view that I would be passing on extreme left-wing views from you!'[68] Privately he may have suspected Churchill of spreading such rumours, but his politics were well known. Queen Mary, Elizabeth's grandmother, had been greatly upset by Mountbatten's remarks over the family name and had lobbied Churchill to intercede. She may have also suggested that Mountbatten be given a role abroad, which is certainly what happened when he was appointed commander-in-chief in the Mediterranean. His headquarters were in Malta. This conveniently kept him away from Queen Elizabeth II and the Duke of Edinburgh until their Commonwealth tour took them to the island in 1954.

The King's sudden death had given Churchill a stay of execution in the House of Commons. Labour had been planning a vote of censure against the Prime Minister on 6 February 1952 over his foreign policy toward China. Former Labour Foreign Secretary Herbert Morrison accused him of advocating attacking China to end the deadlock in Korea. Churchill intended a riposte by revealing that Labour while in power had already proposed bombing China, the very thing they were now accusing him of. Regardless of the consequences he was going to leak the gist of a classified Labour Cabinet document. This would cause what Conservative MP Nigel Nicolson later called 'a volcanic flash'.[69]

Churchill finally addressed the delayed foreign affairs debate on 26 February. 'Herbert Morrison spoke for an hour so badly that people shuffled and groaned,' Nigel Nicolson later told his father Harold. 'It made a deplorable effect, and Winston's case was won before he got up.'[70] Churchill was spoiling for a fight and he still planned to drop his bombshell to lay bare Labour's hypocrisy. 'He started off pugnaciously and then pretended to go dull on us,' recalled Nicolson with amusement.[71] Churchill explained he wanted to look at the last Government's track record at which point everyone relaxed assuming they had heard it all before.

'It was agreed,' said Churchill with a glint in his eye, 'between the United States Government and the late Socialist Administration that in certain circumstances and contingencies action would be taken not confined to Korea.'[72] At this point his fellow MPs sat up and took note of what he was saying. He then recounted how Attlee had consented, in the event of Chinese air attacks launched from China against United Nations forces, British aircraft would take part in retaliatory raids in Manchuria. This agreement, said Churchill, had first been made by Labour in May 1950 and renewed in September that year. The Labour front benches went mad with fury, but they could do nothing to refute what he was saying as it was true.

'There was pandemonium,' observed Nigel Nicolson. 'I was sitting directly opposite Attlee. He was sitting hunched up... and stared at Winston, turning slowly white.'[73] Nye Bevan tried unsuccessfully to defend the indefensible. 'We had won,' concluded Nicolson.[74] Labour MP Richard Crossman demanded to see the document that Churchill was citing. He responded that he was stating fact and not quoting. Afterwards Churchill was delighted with his performance and celebrated with a glass of brandy and a cigar. 'It was a great day,' he said, 'a great triumph'. He also told Lord Moran, 'I feel it has gone well. Morrison was really very feeble.'[75] John Colville agreed with him. 'The PM made a good but much interrupted speech,' he noted, 'discrediting Attlee and Morrison and dumbfounding his attackers.'[76] It was clear that there was still fire in Churchill's belly when it came to the House of Commons.

Although politically Churchill may have felt on top of the world, militarily was another matter. While the warlord in Churchill might have revelled at the opportunity to direct conflicts again, Britain was in no position to fight them. Churchill was facing growing insurgencies against British rule in Malaya and Kenya. He was also under mounting pressure to withdraw from the Suez Canal. The Egyptian monarchy and government were corrupt and in some places considered too soft on the British. This meant the country was ripe for a coup and when that happened Egyptian nationalists would back Sudanese independence from Britain. Churchill clinging to the imperial dream would ensure that the conflicts in Malaya and Kenya would become long drawn out affairs. Trouble was also brewing in British-controlled Aden and Cyprus. Churchill was going back to war whether he liked it or not. One thing was certain: he would get no help from America which viewed these as imperial conflicts, that did not honour the Atlantic Charter and the right to self-determination. Churchill though was of the view that stability must be restored before independence could ever be contemplated.

PART FIVE

ONCE MORE
TO WAR

Chapter 11

Emergency in Malaya

As far as Churchill was concerned he inherited a foreign policy mess thanks to Labour. He made this evidently clear when he told an audience at the Lord Mayor of London's Banquet on 9 November 1951 that he was facing 'a tangled web of commitments and shortages, the like of which I have never seen before'.[1] Two days earlier he had informed his Cabinet that he was alarmed by the growing expense of British military efforts to contain the Malayan Communist guerrilla campaign. This ongoing conflict had resulted in a countrywide state of emergency.

Churchill insisted that Oliver Lyttelton, his new Secretary of State for the Colonies, must get to grips with the situation which had been rumbling on since the end of the Second World War. Lyttelton had served in Churchill's wartime coalition government and was extremely anti-Communist. He had been worried by Labour's election victory in 1945 and wrote that he 'began to fear for my country'.[2] Churchill had wanted to make Lyttelton the Chancellor of the Exchequer, but was deterred by the Conservative Whip who warned that Lyttelton did not have sufficient support in the House of Commons because of his business links. Instead he was given responsibility for Britain's colonies and facing down Communism in Malaya.

When Churchill addressed the House of Commons on 6 December 1951 on British defence interests he again touched on that issue. He told his fellow MPs that, 'Dull tragedy rolls forward in Malaya.'[3] Churchill explained that there were over 25,000 British soldiers deployed there, as well as 10,000 Gurkhas and some 7,000 other colonial soldiers. On top of this there were 60,000 local police. 'Thus the whole amounts to over 100,000 men employed in the most costly manner,' grumbled Churchill.[4] This amounted to almost £50 million a year not including the Malayan government's substantial contribution. Churchill was particularly concerned that all of Britain's active service units were overseas; half of them were in Malaya, the Middle East and Korea.

Luckily for Churchill the Malayan Communists, unless Indochina fell to Communism, were a long way from external help. All the time that the French held on in Indochina there was no easy way for Mao to get aid to them. This essentially meant that they were on their own. Furthermore, an upside to the Korean War was that tin and rubber prices had shot up, both of which were Malaya's two main exports. America also helped push prices up by stockpiling raw materials in case of a war with the Soviet Union. The result was that the Malayan government was able to finance all its expenditure during the emergency. Fortunately this meant that Churchill's government only had to cover the cost of British forces deployed there.

The Malayan Communist party had originally been armed towards the end of the Second World War to fight the Japanese occupation. It drew its strength from the Chinese in Malaya who had moved there over the years to work in the rubber plantations and the mines. They constituted roughly forty per cent of the total population of about six million people. The Japanese had sowed the seeds of enmity between the Malay and Chinese communities by treating the Malays more leniently. Japan and China were at war at the time so the Japanese distrusted and hated the Chinese settlers. Whereas thousands of Chinese were massacred at the beginning of the occupation, thousands of Malays were recruited into pro-Japanese militia units. The Japanese had also indulged in a divide and rule policy by rewarding Thailand's collaboration with the sultanates of Kedah, Kelantan, Perlis and Trengannu in northern Malaya.

Churchill and his wartime Cabinet had agreed to cooperate with the Malayan People's Anti-Japanese Army on 11 May 1945, on the grounds their activities would distract the Japanese prior to the liberation of Malaya. When the British returned, they angered many Malay Chinese by relying on Japanese and pro-Japanese Malay paramilitaries to help keep the peace until sufficient troops had arrived. After the war the Communists surrendered some of their weapons but others were hidden away. The return of British rule was soon met by regular demonstrations and strikes. This was part of a Communist strategy to destabilise Malaya in order to make it ripe for a popular revolution. In 1947 they organised over 300 strikes in an effort to disrupt the economy, much to the displeasure of the British business community.

In the summer of 1948, when both Chinese and Greek Civil Wars were at their height, an international Communist youth conference was held in India. Afterwards the Communists in Burma, Malaya and the Philippines launched armed struggles to take power. Attlee and Truman naturally saw them as proxies of the Soviet Union and Mao's China. 'Soviet Communism,' observed Attlee, 'pursues a policy of imperialism in a new form – ideological, economic and strategic – which threatens the welfare and way of life of other nations of the world.'[5] The Communists in the Far East foremost considered themselves as patriots who were fighting for the political future of their countries. Malayan Communist leader Chin Peng and his central executive committee, though, agreed to a campaign of political agitation and escalating terrorism in Malaya as part of this concerted effort throughout Southeast Asia. Chin was a war hero who Britain had awarded the Burma Star and the 1939-1945 War medals. He had also been appointed to the Order of the British Empire for his wartime services. Now he turned on his old masters.

Malaya's Communists took to the vast tropical jungles and formed the Malayan Races Liberation Army to fight the British and Malay authorities. Despite its inclusive title this organisation was almost entirely composed of ethnic Chinese

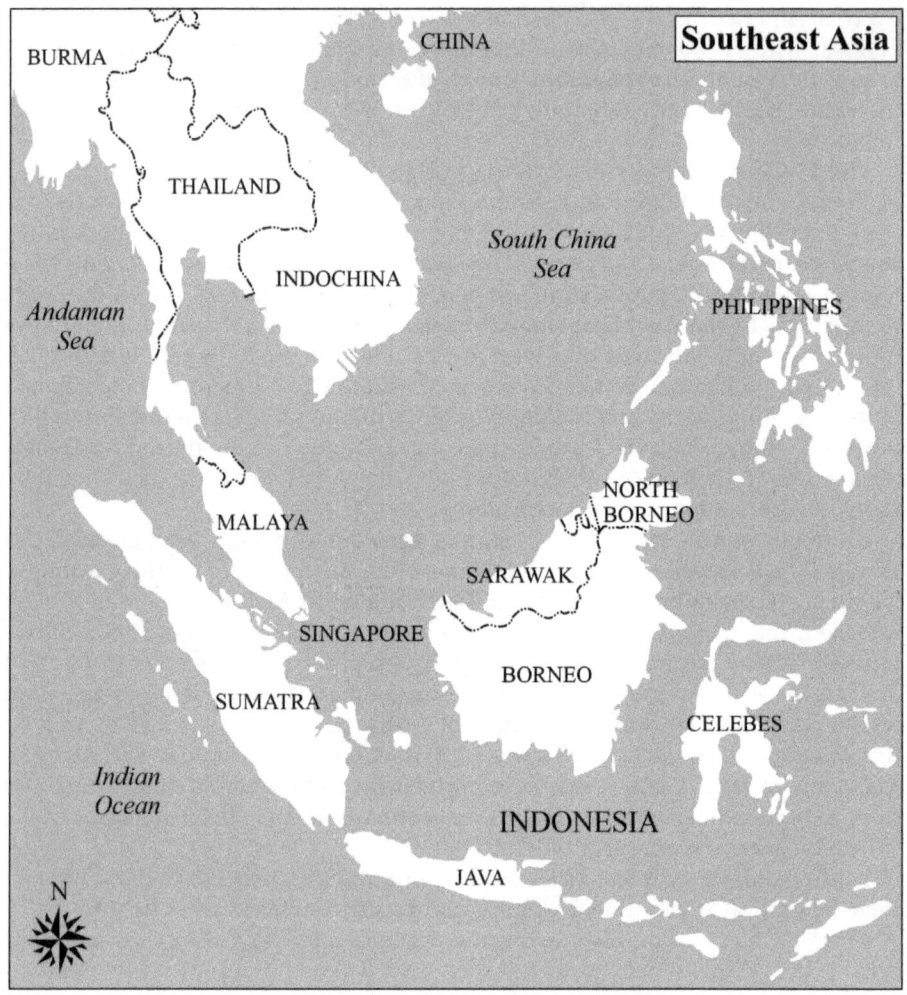

recruits. This meant it did not appeal to the majority of the Malay and Indian population, plus Britain had already promised independence. In light of Burma, India and Pakistan gaining theirs, there was little reason not to believe this undertaking. Furthermore, the Communists were not universally supported by the Chinese community either.

'There is no immediate threat to internal security in Malaya although the position is constantly changing and is potentially dangerous,' the Malayan Security Service reported to London on 14 June 1948.[6] Just two days later Communist violence broke out in the western province of Perak. Three assailants calmly walked into the office of plantation manager Arthur Walker and shot him dead. That same day two other managers were murdered. This heralded a guerrilla campaign specialising in killing plantation staff and Malay officials, though they also attacked police and military patrols within the plantations. This resulted in the declaration of a state of emergency which was soon extended to the entire country. The Malayan Union, which Britain had formed in 1946, was disbanded that year and replaced by the Federation of Malaya after protests from Malay nationalists. However, neither included Singapore, Malacca and Penang, which remained firmly British colonies.

Sir Henry Gurney, the new High Commissioner, with the support of Attlee's government quickly moved to enhance security. Gurney requested Attlee send out a veteran officer to serve as his Director of Operations to shake things up. The man selected for the job was General Sir Harold Briggs, a former commander of the 5th Indian Division and general officer commanding in Burma. 'I know of few commanders who made as many immediate and critical decisions on every step of the ladder of promotion,' observed Field Marshal Slim approvingly, 'and I know none who made so few mistakes.'[7] Slim also described Briggs as 'quietly efficient'.[8]

Malaya was not an easy country to police. Over 80 per cent of it was jungle, with a central mountain range running its length. This provided the guerrillas with an ideal haven and a great deal of freedom of movement. General Briggs' solution to the problem was simple; deny the Communists all support from the civilian population. He achieved this by moving half a million Chinese, many of whom had been squatting in the jungle after the war, into 500 new purpose-built villages. These had fresh water, schools, shops and healthcare. Each family was given the title to their new property. However, they were fenced in, access was controlled and there were curfews. Inhabitants were warned that they faced prosecution if they took food from their village. This made it extremely difficult to supply the guerrillas, though sympathisers found ingenious ways and means to smuggle food out. It was hoped that as a result of the 'Briggs Plan' the guerrilla units hiding in the jungle would wither away.

Attlee and his government, understandably after the horrors of Nazi Germany, certainly did not want the term concentration camp employed in Malaya. This would have been an unmitigated public relations disaster, especially in America. Instead the relocation compounds were dubbed 'New Villages'. These comprised of two types. There was the agricultural village for farmers who depended on the land for their living and the dormitory village for those who were wage earners. Many such settlements were built in Johore in the vicinity of the railway running north from Singapore. Despite their name these were essentially humane concentration camps. Churchill was only too familiar with the use of the latter after his experiences in South Africa during the Boer War. To deny the Boer commandos support, Britain had imprisoned tens of thousands of Boer families with catastrophic results. Attlee chose to ignore the fact that the deportation of Chinese civilians and the destruction of their homes was against the Geneva Convention.

In the meantime the violence escalated. Men of the King's Own Yorkshire Light Infantry were ambushed near Ampang on 10 June 1950. Six soldiers were killed and four wounded, one of whom died several days later. Attlee was conscious that

Britain must not be perceived as trying to prevent Malayan independence. James Griffiths, his Colonial Secretary, eleven days later told the House of Commons, 'British troops serving in Malaya, their relatives, and the nation as a whole may rest assured that we are in no sense attempting to stop a national movement of the Malayan people seeking independence.'[9] He added that Britain was simply trying to stop 'a small, but well organised, minority from seizing power'.[10] What was not clear was how much external help this 'minority' was receiving. The outbreak of the Korean War that month led Harold Macmillan to ponder in his diary towards the end of the year, 'If Indochina goes, Siam [Thailand] follows. Then Malaya falls.'[11] He was espousing what later became widely known as the domino theory.

Attlee and Churchill were not altogether pleased when the Americans began to take a much closer interest in the conflict in Malaya. Thomas Dewey, the New York State Governor, arrived in Singapore in the summer of 1951 as part of an unofficial fact-finding tour of Southeast Asia and the Pacific.[12] Dewey was an influential Republican politician who had run against Truman in 1948 and now supported Eisenhower. He claimed, 'I will not engage on any diplomatic forays.'[13] However, his trip was approved by President Truman and organised through the US State Department. Furthermore, he was hosted at the highest levels wherever he went, so his presence could hardly be viewed as unofficial.

Although Dewey's visit to Malaya was greenlit by Attlee's government, there were concerns he might be critical of Britain's actions. Churchill though was encouraged that Dewey, when campaigning in opposition to Truman, had called for a tougher stance towards the Soviet Union. If Dewey could be persuaded that what was going on in Malaya was part of the wider war against Communism and not a colonial war, then he might report back more favourably. In Singapore he met with Malcolm MacDonald, the British Commissioner-General for Southeast Asia. His responsibilities included co-ordinating British defence policy in the region and intelligence gathering. Top of their agenda were the conflicts in Indochina and Malaya. One of Dewey's interests was whether a NATO-type defence pact could be replicated in Southeast Asia to counter the spread of Communism.

Afterwards Dewey travelled north to Kajang in Selangor to visit Lieutenant Colonel Philip Morcombe and the young men of the Suffolk Regiment. There he was briefed in greater detail about the counter-insurgency war. Dewey was impressed by what he saw, as the Suffolks were the most successful Communist-hunter unit in Malaya. During their three year tour they killed 181 enemy guerrillas and captured 15. Dewey also learned that two thirds of the battalion-strength regiment were conscripted 18-year-olds doing their National Service. Dewey was photographed inspecting some of them on their dusty parade ground.

To Attlee and Churchill's relief, Dewey, far from criticising Britain and France's colonial policies in Southeast Asia, proved to be supportive. *The West Australian* newspaper reported on 20 August, 'The Governor of New York State (Mr. Thomas Dewey) paid tribute yesterday to the courage of British and French troops fighting Communist rebels in Malaya and Indochina.'[14] Dewey seemed to accept the status quo there as he warned, 'The United States should stop telling others to be like us. The free world must survive pretty much as it is or it will not survive at all.'[15] A few years later Churchill met Dewey in New York where the pair unfortunately fell out over Commonwealth economic talks. It was a poor thank you for Dewey's public relations exercise in Malaya.

General Briggs ordered the army to operate in the jungle and isolated rubber plantations while the police operated in the populated areas. To curtail Communist operations the army adopted the ambush as the most suitable tactic. These were often conducted on jungle trails leading to villages known to be helping the enemy. The Special Air Service specialised in parachuting into the jungle canopy to lay ambushes. Much closer to the villages the police also laid traps. The security forces though did not have it all their own way.

On 6 October 1951, just before Churchill became Prime Minister, Gurney was killed in an ambush on the open road about forty miles north of Kuala Lumpur. 'He was one of Britain's "strong men" in that troubled land,' reported the *Northern Daily Mail*.[16] Just over two weeks later a patrol from the 1st Battalion, Royal West Kent Regiment was ambushed in Selangor. They suffered eleven dead and a dozen wounded. That month Chin Peng met with officers sent by Mao. By this stage the Malayan Communist forces had grown to about 10,000 strong. However, Mao's representatives were not impressed by what they saw and did not remain in Malaya.

The murder of Gurney sent a shock wave through Malaya and Churchill's new government. It was very clear that the war against the guerrillas was being lost if after four years they still had the capability to kill the High Commissioner in broad daylight. The authorities at the time were unaware that the Communists caught Gurney purely by chance and had not specifically targeted him. Churchill sent Oliver Lyttelton, the Colonial Secretary, out to Malaya to assess the situation and boost morale. Lyttelton was the man for the job as he had the ability to get on with people. Churchill noted approvingly, 'He's an agreeable personality.'[17]

Lyttelton arrived in Singapore on 29 November and toured Malaya's trouble spots by aeroplane and armoured car. He gave off an air of confidence and efficiency as he met with both British and Malay officials. His every move was filmed by a Pathé news team and photographed by newspaper cameramen. He was pictured in a Daimler armoured car named *Avenger* while visiting a resettlement area in Johore. The use of armoured vehicles did not say much for the security situation and gave the impression of an administration that had lost the initiative. Although the authorities were taking no chances with his safety, at Penang aerodrome his twin-engine transport aircraft crash-landed due to a puncture on the left landing wheel. Luckily he was unharmed. Lyttelton was not encouraged by what he found. After Gurney's death British and Malay morale was extremely low. The administration was in denial that it was fighting a war and that the security forces were poorly co-ordinated.

Lyttelton, on his return to London, met to brief Churchill and Montgomery on 23 December 1951. He warned them that they could not win the war without the assistance of the population, especially the Chinese. Lyttelton made six key recommendations that included centralised control of the security effort, the reorganisation of the police and the integration of the Chinese in the Home Guard units. He also insisted on the resignation of Colonel William Gray, the British Police Commissioner. Gray had drawn criticism not only for the High Commissioner's

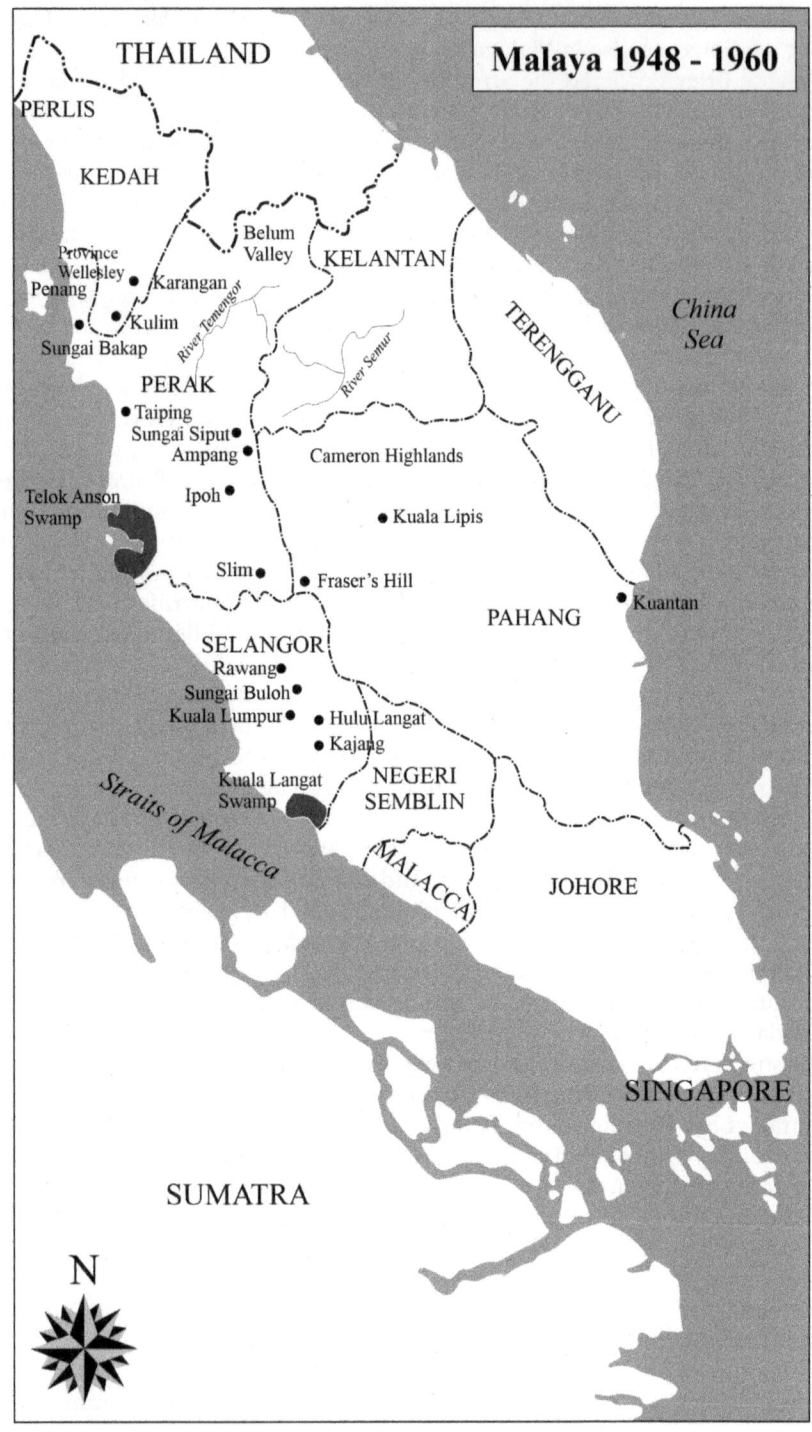

Malaya 1948 - 1960

death but also for not permitting the police to patrol in armoured vehicles. The police had been continually suffering as a result. Afterwards Montgomery wrote to Lyttelton saying they needed a plan and a man for the job. In response Lyttelton recommended General Templer, who was a Second World War divisional commander and had served as the director of the military government of the British occupied zone of Germany. This meant that he was experienced in combat and handling civil-military relations.

Churchill duly appointed General Templer joint High Commissioner and Director of Operations. While in Ottawa in January 1952 Templer astutely told Lord Moran, 'What we have to do is to get the Malay and the Chinaman, with their different languages and religions... to say: "This is our country"'.[18] It was a sound assessment; both groups needed to bury their differences in order to work together for a common future. Templer understood a solely military approach would not be enough. He had confessed to Churchill, 'I know nothing of this job. I will do my best because I recognize its importance.'[19] Government forces in Malaya went over to the offensive against the Communists on 7 February 1952. These operations consisted of long-range search and destroy missions. Chin Peng responded by moving headquarters from Malaya to the safety of southern Thailand.

Churchill's move to shake things up came under pressure in the House of Lords on 27 February 1952. Labour peer Lord Ogmore motioned a debate on the situation in Malaya. He questioned the government's intentions now that General Templer had been appointed to his dual role. Ogmore claimed that the directive issued to Templer was far from clear and wanted to know if the government was going for a military or political solution. Furthermore, he urged the government to ensure that Malaya spoke through one political leader and not multiple federal leaders. The latter was a potential recipe for partition. He also called on the government to concentrate on rural development to increase food production and the provision of rural schools and clinics. The Marquess of Salisbury, the Leader of the House, speaking for the government said Templer's key aim 'must be the crushing of terrorism'.[20] He then added, 'The primary duty, therefore, of the High Commissioner at the present moment is the restoration of law and order.'[21] In other words Churchill was going for the military solution.

Churchill appreciated that the cost of trying to contain the situation in Malaya would escalate vastly should the French be defeated in Indochina. He did not want to contemplate the possibility of an external Communist threat to Malaya, but he understood that he had to. The fear was that if Indochina fell to Communism it would be swiftly followed by Thailand and Malaya. Nonetheless, there was no way of knowing how things might go in the Far East and Southeast Asia if America leant on the Soviet Union to desist from supporting international Communist groups. 'It would, therefore be wrong,' Churchill told the Cabinet's Defence Committee on 19 March 1952, 'to commit ourselves at this stage to preparations for the defence of Malaya against a possible [foreign] threat in the future. It would, however, be prudent to make plans without expenditure of money or resources.'[22] In the event of an external threat the intention was to seek Australian and New Zealander assistance and to support Thailand.

When Templer arrived in Malaya he made three tasks a priority. The first was Lyttelton's recommendation that the police be reorganised from an overtly paramilitary organisation to something more akin to the British Police. Part of the problem was that policing had not been confined to urban areas. Their jungle companies actively took part in offensive operations. These units looked more like soldiers as they wore military uniforms and webbing rather than the standard Malay police uniform. It was felt there should now be a distinct difference between the military and the police. This it was hoped would improve police-civilian relations particularly with the rural population.

Templer's second task was to create a centralised intelligence organisation so he could get a better understanding of the enemy. His third was to try to win the hearts and minds of the people in order to present a unified front against Communism. Having assessed the political situation, Templer confirmed to himself that the only way lasting peace could be achieved was through reconciliation between the Malay, Chinese and Indian populations. They all had to work together. Otherwise partition seemed unavoidable when Malaya finally became independent, and the country would go the same way as India. To this end Templer supported the formation of the Alliance party under Tunku Abdul Rahman. Significantly this consisted of the Malayan National Organisation, the Malayan Indian Congress and the Malayan Chinese Association. It was hoped that this would politically unify Malaya and firmly cast the Communists and their supporters into the political wilderness. Templer also promised early elections to the legislature followed by independence.

Churchill's government soon found itself facing allegations of atrocities in Malaya. Oliver Lyttelton, the Colonial Secretary, was obliged to address the practice of severing the heads of 'bandits' with the House of Commons on 7 May 1952. He clarified that an incident had occurred in April the previous year. It had come to light when incriminating photographs were recently published in the *Daily Worker*. 'After the bandits had retired, a tribesman, not a Royal Marine, who had acted as a tracker, decapitated the body,' clarified Lyttelton. 'The head was brought in for identification.'[23] Trying to put an end to the matter he then added, 'Instructions are being given by the High Commissioner that bodies should not be decapitated for identification, which should be secured by photographs and fingerprints.'[24] When pressed to confirm whether the images were genuine, he acknowledged they were. It was a humiliating and embarrassing admission for Churchill's government.

The *Daily Worker* responded by publishing more photographs. Two weeks later the issue was revisited in the House of Commons when it was confirmed that no disciplinary action had been taken against those responsible. The British military only had themselves to blame as they employed Iban or Dayak from Borneo as trackers in Malaya. These people excelled at their job but they had a long tradition of headhunting and keeping other body parts as grisly trophies. The authorities had made no move to prevent such practices in Malaya. This may have been on the grounds it would put fear into the Communists. The Colonial Office warned a public relations disaster was looming; 'Other practices may have grown up, particularly in units which employ Dayak, which would provide ugly photographs.'[25] Churchill immediately banned all tribal practices for fear it would give the Communists a propaganda coup and expose British soldiers to similar treatment if captured.

To make it clear that what was happening in Malaya was part of the wider Cold War, the guerrillas of the Malayan Races Liberation Army, who had previously been referred to by the authorities as 'bandits', were redesignated Communist Terrorists or 'CTs' in early 1952. This was in part designed to reassure America that Britain was not fighting a colonial war, but rather fighting to prevent a Communist takeover prior to independence. This was true, though substantial British business interests remained keen to cling on in Malaya and Singapore as long as possible.

In reality Malaya's Communists were largely isolated from the outside world. While Mao was actively supporting Communist parties throughout Southeast Asia, after his experiences with the Korean War and the Chinese occupation of Tibet he was opposed to further direct intervention. Mao in the summer of 1952 sent Zhou Enlai the Chinese Foreign Minister to Moscow to hold discussions with Stalin. On 3 September the minutes of their meeting note that Zhou 'says that in their relations with Southeast Asian countries they are maintaining a strategy of exerting peaceful influence without sending armed forces.'[26] Backing the Communists in Burma and Indochina was relatively easy because of their long mutual borders with China. Mao's 'peaceful influence' consisted of the provision of weapons and instructors. In the case of Indochina it included artillery. Getting weapons to the Malayan Communists was much harder as it meant shipping them through the South China Sea and running the gauntlet of the British and French navies. That month Templer, in a further effort to help create a united Malayan state, granted citizenship to all aliens born in Malaya. By this stage the Communists had been driven from the urban areas and were hiding in small groups in the jungle.

In January 1953, much to Churchill's delight, Eisenhower succeeded Truman as president. Eisenhower had firmly campaigned against Truman over his handling of Communism and the Korean War during the American election. Churchill knew that Eisenhower was most definitely a man he could do business with and saw no reason for any change in Anglo-American relations. Eisenhower though, like his predecessor, had no interest in propping up British colonial interests. However, when need be he was prepared to play extremely tough with China especially over Indochina and Korea.

Churchill returned to the issue of how best to defend Malaya from an external threat on 26 April 1953. He discussed this with Lord Alexander, General Sir John Harding, Chief of the Imperial General Staff, Air Chief Marshal Sir William Dickson, Chief of the Air Staff and Sir William Strang, the Foreign Office's Permanent Under-Secretary of State. Harding suggested that British forces would have to move into southern Thailand in the event of Communist attack. Churchill agreed to this, but he knew full well that when it had been attempted to forestall the Japanese invasion in 1941 it failed spectacularly.

Ironically in Burma, Thailand's western neighbour, the presence of Nationalist Chinese troops was more of a problem than Chinese-backed Communist forces. They had fled there after the Chinese Civil War. Up to 12,000 troops were engaged in a war against the Burmese in eastern Burma. 'We have been conscious of the problem of Chinese Nationalist troops in Burma for a long time,' Churchill told the Commonwealth Prime Ministers' Conference on 4 June 1953. 'We would be very glad to see them leave Burma and we should do all we could to get them out.'[27] However, these troops were a very long way from sanctuary in Taiwan. Their presence would continue to consign Burma to war.

The authorities in Malaya now decided to try to prevent the guerrillas from growing their own food in the jungle. Amongst their arsenal was the herbicide Trioxene, a precursor to Agent Orange later used by the Americans in Vietnam. This began to be sprayed onto Communist crops in Johore by helicopters in August 1953.[28] Unfortunately it was carcinogenic. Churchill had no way of knowing this at the time and like everyone else was led to believe it was just a high-powered weedkiller. By the end of the year eighty-eight guerrilla farms had been sprayed and operations continued into 1954. Helicopters though were always in short supply so its effectiveness was limited. The conventional bombing of Communist bases and farms was much more widespread.

Way to the north of Malaya in Indochina the war against the Communist Viet Minh was not going well. The French suffered a series of defeats and kept losing ground. At the end of 1952 they had ventured beyond their defensive perimeter around Hanoi with Operation Lorraine, only to be driven back again. The Viet Minh in April 1953 expanded the war by invading French Laos. This was a significant turning point as the French did not have the troops to counter this. When Field Marshal Montgomery dined with Churchill on 5 July 1953 they discussed what might happen in the event of a French defeat. Surprisingly Churchill felt that Indochina did not really matter. 'We gave up India,' he reasoned. 'Why shouldn't France give up Indochina?'[29] Montgomery did not agree. Instead he echoed Harold Macmillan's concerns. 'If Indochina goes, Siam [Thailand] goes too,' he warned. 'And then Malaya would be in danger.'[30] In Malaya progress was being made against the guerrillas. The first region considered to be free of terrorist activity was declared in Malacca in early September 1953. This was designated a 'White Area'.

At the end of the year the French solution in Indochina was to dig in at a place called Dien Bien Phu and then draw the Viet Minh to them to be destroyed. A sound plan in principle, but they did not have sufficient transport aircraft to keep their troops supplied nor to provide overwhelming air to ground support. Chinese-supplied artillery also proved a nasty surprise. Eisenhower and US Secretary of State John Foster Dulles by April 1954 were seriously considering intervening in Indochina to save the French. The garrison at Dien Bien Phu had been under siege since mid-March and was facing imminent and decisive defeat. No one though in Washington was keen on a repeat of the Korean War. 'I don't see why we should fight for France in Indochina when we have given away India,' Churchill grumbled to Lord Moran on 28 April. 'We think we can hold Malaya even if Indochina falls.' Just over a week later the Viet Minh overran Dien Bien Phu.

France was humiliated and its position in Indochina was rendered untenable, forcing withdrawal. At the time the British Embassy in Paris was holding a dinner party for the Duke of Edinburgh, Field Marshal Montgomery and the French

Defence Minister René Pleven. The news had just broken and Pleven and his wife were late. 'Well Mister Pleven, what does it feel like to be the most unpopular man in France?' asked Montgomery with a complete lack of tact.[31] Pleven held his tongue, but quietly fumed, knowing full well that Churchill and Eisenhower had refused to help France in her hour of need. French Indochina was subsequently broken up, with the partition of Vietnam between the communist north and the democratic south formally recognised, while Cambodia and Laos were granted independence. All French troops were withdrawn from South Vietnam by the spring of 1956. Elections intended to reunite the two halves were not held for fear the Communists would win in South Vietnam. This sowed the seeds for the subsequent Vietnam War.

Trouble was also brewing to the south of Malaya in newly-independent Indonesia. Following the withdrawal of the Dutch, the three key islands had fallen into a state of civil war thanks to a series of revolts. Controversially the Dutch had chosen to retain Western New Guinea on the grounds that it was ethnically and culturally different from Indonesia. In April 1950 they had to evacuate 12,000 Christian Ambonese to the Netherlands from the Moluccas islands between Sulawesi and Western New Guinea. The Ambonese had supported Dutch rule and faced death when the Indonesians took control of the islands.

For Churchill and Eisenhower, unlike the situation in Indochina, Indonesia was not considered to be on the frontline of the Cold War. The Indonesian Communist party actively supported President Koesno Sukarno's plans for democracy so did not constitute a threat. This also meant that Malaya's Communists got little if any support from them. Although around three million overseas Chinese lived in Indonesia, very few were members of the party, which was dominated by the indigenous Indonesians. As a consequence Indonesia's Chinese population did not support their Malayan cousins either. While this helped Churchill's war effort in Malaya it was of little consolation to Sukarno.

By 1954 the rebel Islamic group Darul Islam controlled parts of Sumatra, western Java, central and southern Sulawesi and Borneo. Dissident army officers also started a rebellion in Sumatra. America, because the insurgencies were not driven by Communism, stated it would not intervene. President Eisenhower claimed, 'Our policy is one of careful neutrality... so as not to be taking sides where it is none of our business.'[32] Nevertheless, the rebels in the Celebes and Sumatra persuaded America that Sukarno was anti-Western. Secretly the Central Intelligence Agency began shipping weapons to them and in some cases provided covert air support. In turn Sukarno set about strengthening his armed forces ready to reclaim the lost territories and drive the Dutch from Western New Guinea. Indonesia was plagued by conflict well into the 1960s and it was not until then that the influence of the country's Communists became an issue.

General Templer departed Malaya in June 1954 when his tour of duty ended. Thanks to him Chin Peng and his liberation army had failed to spark a popular revolution. Although Churchill was pleased with Templer's efforts, along with the authorities in Malaya he was keen that Malayan Communists were not inspired by the Viet Minh's victory to renew their efforts. To keep Chin Peng's forces off balance a whole series of military operations were conducted the length and breadth of Malaya. Between July and November 1954, the British launched their largest operation to date with Operation Termite in the jungle east of Ipoh in the north west region of Perak. This involved the bombing of suspected Communist bases by the Royal Air Force, parachute drops by the Special Air Service and infantry airlifted by helicopter. From mid-1954 until mid-1955 Operation Apollo was conducted in the Kuala Lipis region of Pahang. In December 1954 Operation Nassau combed the swamps in southern Selangor. Wherever possible the battle was taken to the 'CTs'. The tempo of all this military activity put a great burden on Britain's armed forces.

In the meantime the nations of Southeast Asia, shaken by the loss of Indochina, agreed that they needed to do something to prevent further Communist gains. To that end America, Australia, Britain, France, New Zealand, Pakistan, the Philippines and Thailand all signed up to the Southeast Asia Treaty Organisation on 8 September 1954. By the end of the year Churchill was seeking the help of the Australian and New Zealand governments with security in Malaya. Both countries made it known that they might be prepared to deploy modest ground or air forces. This was a topic of conversation during the Commonwealth Prime Ministers' Conference in London in January 1955. That April a New Zealand Special Air Service squadron and units from the Royal New Zealand Air Force began to operate in Malaya. The Royal Australian Air Force already had units in Malaya and they were joined by an infantry battalion. Australia sent artillery and engineering units as well to support their ground operations. Fijian, Kenyan and Rhodesian troops also fought in Malaya. By the spring parts of Pahang and Terengganu had been declared 'White Areas' free of Communist forces.

Tunku Abdul Rahman's Alliance party won the elections in Malaya in the summer of 1955. At the end of the year his new Malayan government held two-day talks at Baling, near the Thai border, with Chin Peng whose forces still numbered about 3,500. The Communists offered to lay down their arms if the government took complete control of internal security from Britain. This though was not on the table. Tunku would only offer amnesty following a loyalty test. Chin felt this amounted to surrender. Tunku's only alternative to the test was repatriation to China. Chin refused and returned to the jungle saying, 'We will never accept surrender at any time and will continue our struggle to the last man.'[33] His forces though were too weak to constitute a real threat.

Malaya, thanks to Attlee and Churchill, had been saved from Communism, civil war and partition though at considerable expense. Chin and his remaining followers continued to resist for another five years from the depths of the jungle. Independence was granted in 1957 but it would be three years before the state of emergency was lifted. By this stage the Communists had lost 10,684 killed or captured. Chin Peng spent the rest of his life in exile in Thailand. Churchill convinced himself that by standing up to Communism in Malaya he had also saved Burma and Thailand. This to his mind had stopped a domino effect following the Communist victories in China and Indochina. However, the partition of Vietnam would consign the region to yet more terrible bloodletting in the name of containing Communism. This ultimately would lead to the loss of Vietnam, Laos and Cambodia and humiliation for America. Malaya though was not Churchill's only active war; he still had Kenya and Korea to contend with.

Chapter 12

Korean Impasse

Churchill had firmly supported Attlee's response to the North Korean invasion of South Korea in the summer of 1950. Ever since the end of the Second World War he had fretted about Soviet intentions in Manchuria and Korea. The assault on South Korea also heightened his concerns about security in Europe where twelve Western divisions, of which only two were armoured, were facing 80 Soviet divisions of which up to a third were armoured. This disparity was important in light of the ease with which North Korea's tanks sliced through South Korea's weak defences. Seven years earlier at the Cairo Conference the future of Korea had seemed such a minor issue in the grand scheme of things. Then Churchill, Roosevelt and Stalin, with Chiang Kai-shek on the side lines, had agreed to the eventual restoration of Korean independence, though immediate self-government had been viewed as unrealistic. The partition of the country by the Americans and Soviets meant it inevitably became embroiled in the Cold War.

Behind the scenes Attlee's government had tried to stand up for the fate of Korea. Foreign Secretary Ernest Bevin on 2 December 1947 firmly told his Soviet counterpart Vyacheslav Molotov, 'Do you want Korea? You can't have that. You are putting your neck out too far, and one day you will have it chopped off.'[1] Two years later Kim Il Sung, the North Korean Communist leader, arrived in Moscow seeking Stalin's approval for an invasion of the south. Stalin was concerned America would intervene, but Kim reassured him that a swift victory would easily pre-empt this. When Stalin consulted Mao, the Chinese leader was of the view America would not intervene as re-unification was an internal Korean matter. 'Unfortunately,' wrote Nikita Khrushchev in his memoirs, 'the war wasn't ended quickly at all.'[2] To avoid all accusations of complicity Stalin, just before the invasion, withdrew all his military advisors which greatly hampered the North Korean army. Nobody though was fooled. Sir David Kelly, the British Ambassador to Moscow, assessed, 'Attack was certainly launched with Soviet knowledge and almost certainly at Soviet instigation.'[3]

To some the Opposition's support for Labour in the House of Commons came as a surprise, but it simply echoed the close cooperation of the Conservative-Labour-Liberal coalition during the Second World War. Furthermore, both the government and the Conservatives had a shared fear of Communist fifth columnists causing trouble in Britain. Attlee tasked the nation to 'guard against the enemy within'.[4] In certain Left-wing circles Churchill and the Conservatives' behaviour was perceived as overt anti-Communist sabre rattling. Labour MP Tom Driberg expressed such sentiments when he commented on the 'substantial number of back-bench Tories, who true to their jungle philosophy, cannot help baying at the smell of blood in the air.'[5]

In response to the invasion the United Nations called on its members to assist in the defence of South Korea, and America immediately sent reinforcements, initially using its garrison forces in Japan. Attlee authorised the deployment of the Royal Navy's Far East fleet, consisting of a light carrier, two cruisers and five escorts, to join American naval operations.[6] 'The old man [God] is very good to me,' remarked Churchill to a Conservative colleague. 'I could not have managed this situation had I been in Attlee's place. I should have been called a "war-monger"'.[7] Truman felt that it was vital to save the South otherwise the Japanese would be facing a hostile Communist state directly across the Korea Strait. It was bad enough that the northern part of the Sea of Japan was bordered by the Soviet Union. Worryingly, if China and the Soviet Union got involved then Korea had all the makings of a world war. However, Attlee was reassured by Ambassador Kelly's prognosis, 'I would judge that the Soviet Government are extremely anxious not to find themselves engaged directly with the United States.'[8]

Churchill though was disappointed by the painfully slow response of the British government in actually getting boots on the ground. He went to see Attlee on 2 August 1950 to discuss Britain's preparedness for war. Attlee informed him that it would take two months to put together an infantry brigade and all its equipment to send to Korea. Anti-aircraft guns were in such short supply that those protecting America's B-29 bombers based in Lincolnshire would have to be redeployed. Churchill suggested that a token force be sent from Hong Kong as an initial show of solidarity. He was told that this was impossible. In the meantime the fierce fighting in Korea continued.

Amongst the wounded was Churchill's son Randolph, who was in Korea covering the war as a reporter for the *Daily Telegraph*. Randolph was not new to conflict having seen military service in North Africa and the Balkans during the Second World War. He was sent out to replace Christopher Buckley who had been killed by a landmine within an hour of arriving. The unfortunate Buckley was just 45 years old. Churchill had provided Randolph with a letter of recommendation to give General Douglas MacArthur, the United Nations commander in Korea. 'His outlook is broadly mine,' wrote Churchill, 'and I therefore feel I may trespass upon you in these days of growing stress by commending him to you as a comprehending admirer of all the work you have done and are doing.'[9]

Randolph, an enthusiastic drinker, was not universally liked in the bars of Hong Kong, Korea and Japan. Fellow correspondent Alan Whicker recalled, 'The nearest to a compliment you could get was to say that he was as rude to ambassadors as he was to waiters.'[10] Randolph was shot in the leg while accompanying a patrol near the Naktong River on 23 August. After treatment in Tokyo he returned to the front, reporting on Korea until February 1951. 'I can never win,' he lamented to Alan Whicker. 'If I achieve anything they all say it's only because of Father, and when I do something badly they say, "What a tragedy for the old man"'.[11] For Randolph there was no escaping his father's shadow. Their relationship would remain fractious, though he ended up appointed his father's initial official biographer.

Churchill on 26 August 1950 made a party political broadcast in which he was scathing about the government's performance. 'It took the Socialist Government a month to make up their minds whether or not to send an expeditionary force to comply with this request of the United Nations Organization,' he told listeners.[12] Churchill then highlighted another month had elapsed since the decision had been announced to send troops and that over a month would pass before they undertook the six week voyage. In other words it would be almost four months before any troops arrived. This was not true, as Attlee managed to get troops to Korea within two months by sending them from Hong Kong. Churchill was fully aware of this development as he had discussed the matter with journalist Malcolm Muggeridge several days before his broadcast.

Two British infantry battalions from Hong Kong arrived in Pusan, the United Nations' last foothold in the southeast, on 29 August and were committed to the defence of the perimeter. The force, numbering about 2,000 men, comprised 27th Brigade Headquarters, the 1st Battalion Argyll and Sutherland Highlanders and the 1st Battalion Middlesex Regiment. These forces though were far from battle ready. When Malcolm Muggeridge met with Churchill he recalled, 'I told him that the troops going from Hong Kong were going naked, with no proper equipment and, to all intents and purposes unarmed except for ammunition.'[13] It would take until December to complete the brigade using Australian and New Zealand troops. A second brigade would reach Pusan in November. A Canadian brigade arrived the following year to help form the composite 1st Commonwealth Division.

On 12 September Churchill laid into the government in the House of Commons, again not allowing the facts to get in the way of a good story. 'The Prime Minister has appealed to us,' he said, 'for national unity on Defence. This does not mean national unity on mismanagement of Defence.'[14] He then again criticised the government's delay in getting British forces to Korea. 'The campaign in Korea is being run by the Americans,' responded Attlee defensively. 'We respond to their requests. If the request changes from what it was before it is not the fault of His Majesty's Government.'[15] Churchill's critics saw his actions as him reverting to his old warmongering, but he felt it was foremost vital to stand up to the spread of Communism in Korea and show solidarity with America.

Three days later General MacArthur launched his masterstroke with Operation Chromite, the daring amphibious assault on Inchon. It was an all or nothing plan to turn the North Koreans' western flank and retake Seoul. MacArthur had overridden his commanders' serious concerns at taking such a risk. They feared the North Koreans might prove as tenacious as the Japanese and easily contain the bridgehead. Churchill shared such misgivings with good reason. He was haunted by the disastrous Anzio landings in 1944, which had attempted a similar feat against the Germans in Italy. 'I had hoped that we were hurling a wild cat at the shore,' Churchill famously wrote at the time, 'but all we got was a stranded whale.'[16] He and the others need not have worried as Chromite proved a decisive success. Churchill once described the Battle of El Alamein in 1942 as 'the end of the beginning' and so this proved to be the case at Inchon.[17] The landings were timed to coincide with a push north from the Pusan perimeter. The two forces linked up south of Inchon at Osan on 26 September.

Brigadier Basil Coad, the commander of the 27th British Commonwealth Brigade, noted with wry amusement, 'Although very little is known about the enemy's order of battle, it is believed that elements of 27 North Korean Brigade are in our area. ...If contact is made, it is hoped that the Brigade will no longer have any rivals in the North Korean Army bearing the same number.'[18] Attlee sent British reinforcements to Korea from Britain on 11 October when the 1st Battalion Royal Northumberland Fusiliers sailed from Southampton. Including supporting units they numbered about 1,400 men. They were to form part of the 29th British Infantry Brigade. Normally soldiers were required to remove their boots during a voyage, but they were given permission to keep them on. 'The object is to prevent the men's feet becoming soft,' explained their commanding officer Lieutenant Colonel Kingsley Foster. 'It is certainly most unusual for a troopship, but I am determined that the men will arrive with hard feet.'[19]

By now there was growing cause for optimism in Korea as the tide had dramatically turned against the Communists. The combined American, Commonwealth and South Korean counteroffensive rolled the North Koreans right back out of the South. Seoul was liberated and the 38th Parallel, the former border between North and South Korea, crossed. The United Nations forces were soon driving the North Koreans towards the Chinese border. This though unfortunately rapidly sparked massive Chinese intervention. Churchill completely underestimated how Mao would react and the capabilities of his enormous forces. 'Four million pigtails don't make an army,' he told a friend glibly.[20] In a matter of weeks the United Nations forces were driven back 200km in the most appalling winter conditions. 'Everybody is terribly distressed by the Korean situation,' Harold Nicolson wrote in his diary on 28 November. 'Only a few days ago MacArthur was saying, "Home by Christmas", and now he is saying, "This is a new war"'.[21] The *Liverpool Echo* reported ominously, 'General MacArthur estimates that 200,000 Chinese troops are in North Korea.'[22]

Truman, alarmed at the prospects of losing all the hard won gains, announced at a press conference two days later that America was prepared to use the atomic bomb in Korea if necessary. Somewhat alarmingly General MacArthur requested permission to use 'between thirty and fifty atomic bombs'.[23] He had even grander plans and wanted to widen the war. Labour MP Harold Wilson noted, 'MacArthur determined to resolve the conflict by bombing mainland China itself, together with a blockade of the entire coast and the employment of President Chiang Kai-shek's forces in Taiwan in an almost unlimited offensive.'[24] Truman, sensing this had the makings of a world war, refused to give him authorisation. Churchill was equally concerned that Mao's intervention had much wider strategic motives. On 30 November he told the House of Commons, 'I think this could be a plan to get the US and UN to commit forces to China and weaken our forces here in Europe.' Surveying his colleagues' faces, he added, 'I am sure that all MPs agree that the sooner we can establish a settlement in the Far East the better. For it's in Europe that the Cold War will be won or lost.'[25]

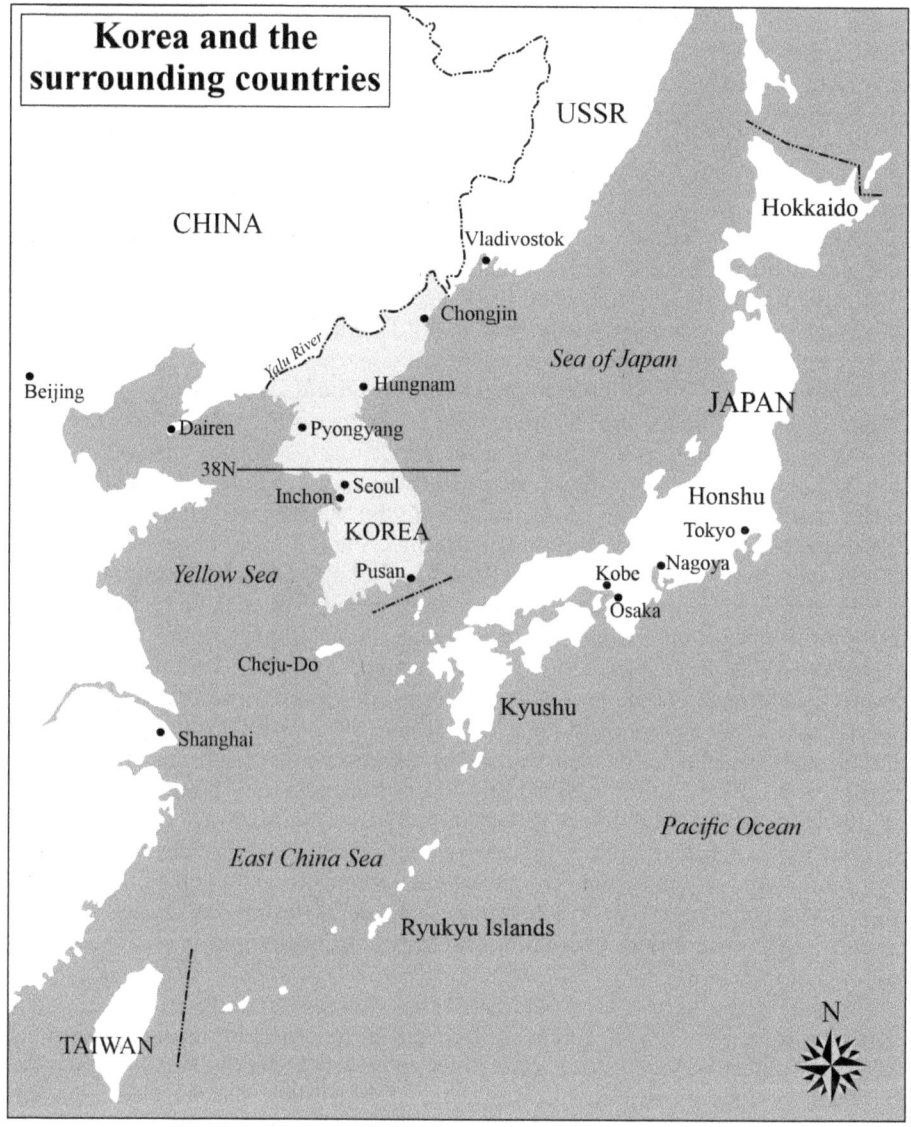

Korea and the surrounding countries

USSR

CHINA

Vladivostok

Hokkaido

Chongjin

Yalu River

Sea of Japan

Beijing

Hungnam

JAPAN

Dairen

Pyongyang

38N

Inchon

Seoul

Honshu

KOREA

Tokyo

Yellow Sea

Pusan

Kobe

Nagoya

Osaka

Cheju-Do

Kyushu

Shanghai

Pacific Ocean

East China Sea

Ryukyu Islands

TAIWAN

N

Despite the paucity of British troops the Americans were grateful for Attlee's meagre contribution. 'When I took over the US Eighth Army in Korea in late December 1950,' recalled American Second World War veteran General Matthew Ridgway, 'I was particularly gratified to find included the British 27th Brigade.'[26] He made a point of visiting its commander as soon as he could. 'If you are coming by light plane General,' Brigadier Coad told him, 'you'll have no trouble spotting the empty tin cans scattered around my area.'[27] This provided Ridgway with some welcome amusement at a time when the situation in Korea was dire. Coad recalled after reporting to Major General John Coulter, his American Corps commander, one of his own staff asked for orders. 'All they said was to, er, haul ass,' replied the bemused brigadier.[28]

Truman on 15 December took the extreme measure of announcing a State of National Emergency on the radio. This had never happened during the Second World War and it felt as if the world was on the brink of global conflict. 'Our homes, our Nation... are in great danger,' Truman warned the American people.[29] Churchill wrote to his wife on Christmas Day hoping that the United Nations forces had dug in. 'They have had three weeks to do this and if they have behaved in a sensible way they should be able to teach the Chinese,' he noted with optimism, 'the sort of lessons we learned upon the Somme and at Passchendaele.'[30] Churchill anticipated that they would suffer 'heavy slaughter'.[31] When he heard this had not happened he wrote to Anthony Eden to express his frustration, 'I do not understand why the Americans could not form a defensive line in Korea after nearly three weeks' breathing space'.[32] Eden responded he had heard that the American divisions, apart from the Marines, were not up to the job. 'So ends a horrible year with worse to come,' noted Harold Nicolson gloomily. 'I fear that the discomfiture of the U[nited] N[ations] O[rganisation] in Korea is a bad portent.' He then echoed the anxiety of many, 'We shall be lucky if we get through 1951 without a war.'[33] There was war, but fought by proxy.

Harold Wilson was alarmed when he learned, 'President Truman had said in Washington that General MacArthur possessed delegated authority to use nuclear weapons without reference to the White House.'[34] Churchill though was still not greatly concerned with the Korean conflict because he saw the bigger Communist threat much closer to home in Europe. He expressed such sentiments when he wrote to President Truman on 12 February 1951. 'I have always hoped that the United States, while maintaining her necessary rights in the Far East,' explained Churchill, 'would not become too heavily involved there, for it is in Europe that the mortal challenge to world freedom must be confronted.'[35] Truman was in complete agreement with Churchill. The last thing he wanted was an escalation of the war in Korea.

Truman, deciding that General MacArthur was far too gung-ho after publicly lobbying to bomb Chinese air bases, sacked him in April and replaced him with Matthew Ridgway. MacArthur's fall from grace was brutal and spectacular. Not only was he fired as Supreme Commander of the United Nations forces, he was also sacked from his jobs as Supreme Commander for Allied Powers in Japan, Commander-in-Chief Far East and Commanding General US Army Far East. There was immediate uproar in the American press and amongst the public over his treatment. 'We do not want to see the conflict in Korea extended,' said Truman justifying his actions. 'We are trying to prevent a world war – not to start one.'[36] Attlee, Churchill and the United Nations agreed with him.

Churchill's electoral win at the end of the year meant that he became directly responsible for Britain's involvement in Korea. Knowing that the country's other global commitments were a massive strain, he remained resistant to extending the Korean War beyond its borders or expanding Britain's role. 'On his return as Prime Minister in 1951,' Churchill biographer Clive Ponting wrote scathingly, 'Churchill showed an almost pathetic determination to recreate the world he had known in Whitehall during the Second World War.'[37] This was a little harsh as Britain was no longer the same place and Churchill knew it. By the time he got back into power and assumed the mantle of Defence Minister the Korean War was almost over, as armistice talks had commenced on 10 July 1951.

Churchill inherited an enormous rearmament programme from Attlee's government which it had implemented in the wake of the outbreak of the Korean War. This would cost the country just short of £5 billion which was well beyond its capabilities to fund. Churchill had no option but to make drastic reductions. Despite these he still faced spending up to ten per cent of the country's wealth on defence. Churchill had to continue to maintain Britain's worldwide commitments which needed military manpower numbering 900,000 men. To ensure such numbers meant continuing peacetime conscription that Labour had implemented in 1948 with the National Service Act. This understandably remained unpopular at a time when Britain was supposed to be at peace.

In Churchill's first Defence Debate in the House of Commons he tried to rein in Labour's extravagant defence budget. This was hardly the act of a warmonger. 'Now Churchill was announcing that it could not be spent,' recalled Harold Wilson, 'and rubbed this in by saying that the lag in production "will of course be helpful to the Chancellor of the Exchequer in his fiscal problems" – the very issue on which Nye [Bevan] resigned.'[38] Churchill told the House of Commons, 'We shall not, however, succeed in spending the £1,250 million programme and some of the late Government's programme must necessarily roll forward into the future year.'[39] This brought outrage from the Labour front benches. 'Did this mean that the whole three-year programme would be rolled forward?' demanded Bevan. 'Over how many years was it to be spread?'[40] Churchill refused to be drawn and said he had only mentioned Bevan's spending because he had 'been right by accident'.[41]

Churchill knew that in light of Britain's changing place in the world it was vital he conduct a strategic defence review. Although he was helped by Field Marshal Alexander as his Defence Minister from March 1952, Churchill largely oversaw the task himself. It was he who ordered the Chiefs of Staff to get their heads together to reassess British defence requirements. This resulted in a global strategy paper that emphasised deterrence underpinned by the atomic bomb. Therefore, argued the paper, less importance needed to be attached to conventional forces. In Britain the requirement was for bombers capable of delivering atomic bombs and Churchill's Cabinet agreed to build the new V-bombers in quantity.

Churchill now faced an internal challenge to his authority over British policy towards Korea. On 19 June 1952 he gathered his Cabinet to discuss Field Marshal Alexander's report. Alexander and Foreign Minister Selwyn Lloyd had just returned from South Korea, where they met the new United Nations Commander, General Mark Clark who had succeeded Ridgway, to discuss the situation. Clark suggested appointing a British Deputy Chief of Staff to his headquarters. Clark who had met Churchill a number of times during the Second World War presumably thought he would be delighted by this. He certainly held Churchill in very high regard calling him 'the greatest man I ever knew'.[42]

Field Marshal Slim, the Chief of the Imperial General Staff, who was at the Cabinet meeting, supported Clark's offer. Churchill though was against it, pointing out, 'the United Nations had entrusted the conduct of the Korean campaign to the United States; and we should be well-advised to avoid a position in which we shared the responsibility without the means of making our influence effective.'[43] He then added that Britain would be better trying to influence events through the office of the Foreign Secretary and Washington. However, he was outvoted by the Cabinet who felt it unwise to say no as this would be seen as a snub to America and the United Nations.

Notably war correspondent Alan Whicker did not have a very high opinion of General Clark. Their paths had first crossed when Clark was commanding the US 5th Army in Italy during the Second World War. Clark's decisions during the Italian campaign had proved divisive, especially his controversial liberation of Rome. Whicker considered him as a shameless glory hunter especially after the advance on Rome failed to trap the retreating German divisions. 'Churchill had called him, admiringly, "The American Eagle" – until he tumbled him,' wrote Whicker in his wartime memoirs. 'His vanity was remarkable – he could have given lessons to any Hollywood prima donna.'[44]

Some of this may have clouded Churchill's judgement when it came to sending Clark assistance in Korea. He discussed the provision of a senior officer with the Defence Committee on 16 July. Churchill remained adamantly opposed to the appointment of a British Deputy Chief of Staff and argued that if his colleagues proceeded to make an announcement then they should include a caveat that the appointee would only answer to the United Nations Commander. Otherwise he worried that the appointment would signal Britain was assuming a greater role in the war. Churchill argued they would be better directing strategic comments to the President or the US Chiefs of Staff. The Defence Committee though would not be swayed either. Anthony Eden reasoned 'that it would be a mistake to abandon the proposal, which had first been put forward by the United Nations Commander himself'.[45] To keep Churchill happy it was agreed that the announcement would make it clear that the British government was taking no further responsibility for Korea. Major General Stephen Shoosmith was duly appointed Deputy Chief of Staff, United Nations Forces, Korea.

During the Second World War Churchill would have expected to get his own way, but times had changed. This incident seemed to indicate that his authority was waning and his judgement no longer respected. Ironically Labour immediately started asking difficult questions in the House of Commons about the nature of Shoosmith's role, whether he would have direct access to the British government and where his allegiance lay. This obliged Nigel Birch, the Parliamentary Secretary to the Ministry of Defence, on 28 July 1952 to clarify, 'As General Clark is the Supreme Commander, clearly he must have the right of access to his own Government. Major General Shoosmith will be a staff officer at General Clark's headquarters, and therefore he is in a quite different position.'[46] In other words Shoosmith was not acting as the official representative of the British government. This did not satisfy the critics on the Labour benches who took the absent Churchill to task for not making the statement himself.

Despite the armistice talks hostilities continued, with both sides launching regular attacks. Birch informed the House of Commons, 'Since the armistice talks began a year ago, the United Nations forces have suffered over 80,000 casualties, including about 48,000 South Koreans and 16,000 of these have been killed. The Commonwealth casualties during this period total about 2,500, including over 400 killed. During the first three weeks of this month when no major operations were in progress, the United Nations casualties amounted to nearly 4,000.'[47] He went on to praise the performance of the Commonwealth Division.[48]

In the early days of the North Korean assault the Americans had used every means at their disposal to stop them. This included napalm. Despite having been a keen advocate of chemical weapons in the past, Churchill was concerned about its use in Korea. Napalm is a highly flammable mixture of petrochemicals and a gelling agent. It was found to be effective against North Korean tanks, troop concentrations and factories and was employed in support of the Inchon landings and the liberation of Seoul. Inevitably civilians were killed or left hideously burned by it.

In early July Churchill wrote to General Bradley, Chairman of the US Joint Chiefs of Staff, to express his hope that the use of this weapon would not cause needless suffering or loss of life. Then towards the end of the following month he informed Field Marshal Alexander that the government should take no responsibility for the deployment of napalm against urban areas. 'No one ever thought of splashing napalm about all over the civilian population,' lamented Churchill.[49] Pyongyang, the North Korean capital, was bombed in July and August, during which napalm was employed. Kim Il Sung informed Stalin that 6,000 civilians were killed in the raids. There was international outrage.

In August 1952 the Royal Fusiliers were deployed to Korea. Amongst their ranks was Maurice Micklewhite, better known as future Hollywood star Michael Caine. His experiences were typical of many national servicemen. 'I was only nineteen when I was sent off to Korea... I'd never heard of the place,' he noted in his memoirs.[50] Micklewhite and his comrades soon found themselves fending off Chinese troops, 'No training could have prepared me for... the first time I saw hordes of the enemy charging towards me.'[51] He later recalled how no one seemed to care that they were there, 'Whenever I've mentioned it to American friends, they are completely taken aback. "The British were in Korea?"'[52] Nor did they know that Australians, New Zealanders and South Africans fought in Korea. This was though simply a reflection of the enormous American commitment.

Ironically the Korean War came to the rescue of the beleaguered British economy. Following the outbreak of the war America had embarked on a massive rearmament, which drove up the world's commodity prices. This had hurt Britain which was left with a massive external deficit of around £700 million a year. Britain's own rearmament did not help either. However, by the end of 1952, fortunately for Churchill, the haemorrhaging of Britain's reserves was reversed as the commodity boom levelled out and there was an improvement in the terms of trade.

In the meantime General Clark began to press for an escalation of American military operations. He felt that this was the only way to force the Communists to agree to a ceasefire. Clark's ideas echoed those of MacArthur's in that he wanted to expand the war in order to hurt China. He suggested blockading China, bombing targets in north China and Manchuria as well as a ground offensive towards the Yalu River. He wanted the latter supported by nuclear weapons, but no one in Washington was keen on his plan.

After Eisenhower succeeded Truman as President in late 1952, he immediately faced the quandary of how best to resolve the Korean War. Harold Nicolson observed in his diary, 'What can he do in Korea? The electors will expect him to end the war, but he cannot do that without abandoning the prisoners or bringing in new divisions from Formosa [Taiwan]. In fact he is out on a limb.'[53] Eisenhower appreciated that he would get little help from Churchill who had his hands full elsewhere. Churchill felt that Eisenhower would stand up to the Soviet Union in Europe, but Korea was a diplomatic minefield because of the involvement of China and the Soviet Union. Soviet jet pilots were now operating over North Korea south of the Yalu in an area that became dubbed 'MiG Alley', in support of the North Koreans. Although Moscow denied it, their presence was a poorly kept secret.

In early December 1952 Eisenhower visited Korea to assess the situation for himself. General Clark pressed him to authorise the expansion of the war. Eisenhower said no. However, he resorted to strong arm tactics when, in his State of the Union address on 2 February 1953, he suggested that America might use the atomic bomb against China. Eisenhower recognised that the war, now in a static phase, could not continue to be fought without any visible results. He decided that the best way ahead would be through a combination of sabre rattling and diplomacy. As part of that process the air war over North Korea was intensified. Chinese and North Korean jets were to be hunted down and North Korean dams bombed in order to flood the rice fields.

In response to Eisenhower's threat Mao asked Stalin if he could have nuclear weapons. This was the last thing Stalin wanted as it could only lead to an escalation of the war and atomic rivalry with the Soviet Union. He feared that Mao's China might follow Tito's Yugoslavia and break from the Communist camp. At the end of February Stalin decided the best course of action was to end the war, but promptly suffered a life-threatening stroke before he could take any action. Some might argue it had been brought on by the strain of dealing with Mao and Kim Il Sung. Stalin died on 5 March 1953 and was succeeded by Georgy Malenkov. Churchill hoped that this might lead to an easing of Cold War tensions in Europe and Asia. Certainly Malenkov was determined to lower the risk of conflict with America. However, in the case of Korea it was Mao's China not the Soviet Union that was driving Communist foreign policy there. Fortunately though an end to the Korean War was in sight.

Churchill was in an optimistic mood when on 1 April 1953 he informed the Cabinet of China's acceptance of an exchange of sick and wounded prisoners. He added that 'their apparent readiness to consider thereafter arrangements for the disposal of other prisoners of war, was a welcome step towards breaking the present deadlock.'[54] Harold Nicolson, after dining in the House of Commons that day reported, 'I think there is a good chance now of ending this Korean War.'[55] Churchill four days later sent President Eisenhower a telegram saying, 'There

Above: 1. The Big Three, Churchill, Roosevelt and Stalin at Yalta in early 1945.

Below: 2. In the summer of 1945 the Big Three got together at Potsdam, this time with Truman replacing Roosevelt.

Above left: 3. After the defeat of Germany the British people did not want to go forward with Churchill.

Above right: 4. Britain in July 1945 rejected Churchill and voted in Clement Attlee and his Labour government.

5. Churchill took his electoral defeat badly but refused to retire from politics.

Above: 6. In 1946 Truman encouraged Churchill to make his now famous Sinews of Peace speech at Fulton, Missouri.

Right: 7. Churchill's only post-war trip to Latin America was in 1946 when he visited Cuba.

Above: 8. Attlee oversaw the hasty British withdrawal from India and Palestine.

Below: 9. It was always doubtful that India's Hindus, Muslims and Sikhs could live peacefully together post-independence.

Above left: 10. Churchill
supported Muhammad
Ali Jinnah's desire for a
separate Pakistan.

Above right: 11.
Churchill blamed
Lord Mountbatten
for Britain's rapid
scramble from India.

Right: 12. Ultimately
Churchill held
Jawaharlal Nehru
responsible for India's
bloody partition.

13. Churchill at the Congress of Europe in 1948. He wanted unity in the face of the Soviet threat.

14. The Berlin Blockade and the subsequent airlift heralded the Cold War.

Right: 15. In the late 1940s President Truman pledged America would help to protect democracy from Communism.

Below: 16. Mao Zedong with Jospeh Stalin in Moscow in December 1949.

Above: 17. The outbreak of the Korean War announced the Cold War going hot in Asia.

Below: 18. The commitment of British forces to Korea was very small due to limited resources.

Above: 19. General Douglas MacArthur wanted to use the atomic bomb in Korea to stop the Chinese.

Right: 20. The Bulldog is back. Churchill weakened Attlee's government in 1950 and defeated it the following year.

Left: 21. The handsome Anthony Eden served as Foreign Secretary twice under Churchill.

Below: 22. Churchill with Eden, Dean Acheson and Harry Truman in January 1952.

Above: 23. During his second premiership Churchill had to contend with guerrilla wars in Malaya and Kenya.

Right: 24. Kenyan nationalist leader Jomo Kenyatta was arrested in 1952.

Above: 25. Churchill did not want to relinquish control of the vital Suez Canal to Egypt.

Left: 26. Dwight D. Eisenhower became US President in January 1953.

Above left: 27. Georgy Malenkov succeeded Stalin in 1953.

Above right: 28. In 1953 Churchill had British Guiana's left-wing Chief Minister Cheddi Jagan arrested.

29. Churchill and Eisenhower at the unsuccessful three Power Summit in Bermuda in December 1953.

Left: 30. After the use of the Atomic Bomb against Japan Churchill did not want it ever deployed again.

Below: 31. Eisenhower in South Korea. He threatened China with nuclear weapons if it did not end hostilities.

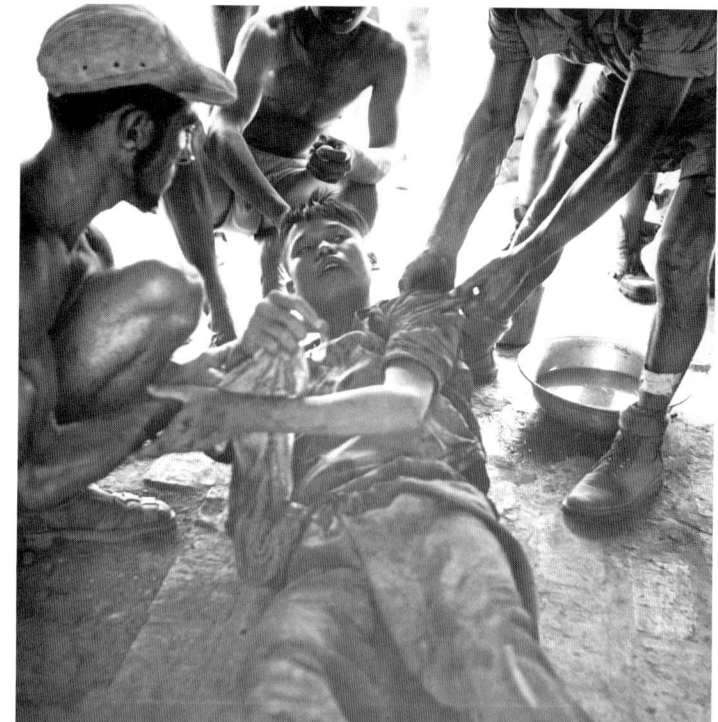

Right: 32. The defeat of the French at Dien Bien Phu meant partition for Vietnam.

Below: 33. Anthony Eden at the Geneva Conference trying to defuse Cold War tensions.

Above left: 34. After the Suez Crisis in 1956 Harold Macmillan replaced Eden as prime minister.

Above right: 35. Nikita Khrushchev visited America in September 1959. Three years later he and President Kennedy were embroiled in the Cuban Missile crisis.

36. Churchill as he is best remembered – the elder statesman.

seem certainly to be great possibilities in Korea and we are very glad of the steps you have taken to resume Truce negotiations.'[56]

The first prisoner exchanges took place that April. A follow-up prisoner agreement was signed in early June at Panmunjom. This was seen as a possible prelude to an armistice. The only sticking point for Eisenhower was that the South Korean President Syngman Rhee wanted to continue fighting. Churchill responded, 'I would vote for Rhee going to hell and taking Korea with him and would talk to Russia directly on a heavily armed basis.'[57] He increasingly saw the stalemate in Korea as a strategic irrelevance.

Kim Il Sung, after witnessing the devastating American bombing campaign against North Korea, had long wanted out of the war. Mao though had continually refused. Now that Stalin had gone Moscow was refusing to supply him with the atomic bomb and insisting on a ceasefire. For good measure Moscow withdrew its air divisions and the Chinese air force suffered heavy losses at the hands of the United Nations' air forces. On the night of 11 May after seeing the new Soviet ambassador, who spelt out the Soviet position in no uncertain terms, Mao relented and gave orders to end the war. In return Moscow agreed to sell China over ninety weapons factories to help build up its armed forces. According to Li Zhisui, 'Almost 90 percent of the munitions used by China during the Korean War were bought from the Soviet Union.'[58] Stalin had loaned Mao $1.3 billion to pay for them.

The butcher's bill for China had been enormous. Mao committed over three million Chinese troops to Korea, half of whom had become casualties with at least 400,000 dead. For all this sacrifice Korea remained divided just as it had at the start of the conflict. However, Mao's decision to stop the war had serious ramifications elsewhere. It sealed the fate of the French in Indochina. He immediately sent Chinese officers from Korea to help the Viet Minh, plus a copy of the French strategic plan obtained by Chinese intelligence. This and massive Chinese military aid gave the Viet Minh the ability to give battle at Dien Bien Phu.

The South Koreans continued to be difficult over the terms of the armistice. On 18 June 1953 Syngman Rhee unilaterally ordered the release of 25,000 Chinese and North Korean prisoners of war. These men did not want to be repatriated so the South Koreans simply released them. To facilitate this in some cases American camp guards were locked up and even fired on. Two days later Churchill sent Eisenhower a rather terse message via the British ambassador. 'The following is only a thought of my own,' he wrote. 'Syngman Rhee arrested or dismissed from office. British send an extra brigade from Egypt to Korea. Winston.'[59] The extra troops were presumably to help maintain control in Seoul. This though was not a route that Eisenhower or indeed the United Nations wanted to go.

After Field Marshal Montgomery quizzed Churchill on government policy in early July 1953, Churchill explained that if it was up to him he would abandon South Korea to the Chinese. 'Korea does not really matter now,' he told Montgomery. 'I'd never heard of the bloody place till I was seventy.' Churchill felt that the only positive thing to come out of the war was that it had forced America to rearm, which for the rest of the world was a good thing. 'It's Germany, not Korea, that matters,' concluded Churchill.[60] Much to everyone's relief, on

27 July 1953 the Korean War came to an end when an armistice agreement was finally signed at Panmunjom. John Colville noted, 'Today the Korean War ended – after months of infuriating haggling over the terms of the armistice.'[61] Reflecting Britain's diminished status the armistice was only signed by America and North Korea.

Despite the close Anglo-American relationship that Churchill always worked so hard to foster, Britain had essentially stood on the side-lines during the Korean War. Furthermore, Britain's ongoing relationship with China had brought criticism from America – Attlee had officially recognised Mao's China in early 1950. After the armistice Churchill was cross that the *Daily Mirror* had printed quotes from the US media about friction between Britain and America. 'The Americans are angry with us,' he told Lord Moran. 'They have lost more than a hundred thousand men in Korea, and all they hear is the Socialists bleating about China.'[62]

As far as Churchill was concerned America had become the world's policeman thanks to the Korean War. 'The fighting in Korea has shifted from the trenches to the tables,' he told the House of Commons on 3 November 1953. 'But whatever else comes, or may come as a result of the Korean War, one major world fact is outstanding. The United States have become again a heavily armed nation.'[63] During the conflict the US army had expanded from 1.5 million to 3.5 million and the military budget had grown from $15 billion a year to $50 billion. Churchill felt only this would keep Communism in check.

Chapter 13

Clinging to Suez

One of the reasons that Britain was so short of troops after the Second World War was its insistence on retaining control of the Suez Canal. Access to this ensured British lines of communication through the Mediterranean, down the Red Sea to Aden and then across the Indian Ocean to India, Ceylon and Malaya. Essentially it was the lynchpin of the British Empire. As far as Churchill was concerned Britain should never surrender control of Suez to the Egyptians. In light of the mounting Cold War this was not an altogether selfish viewpoint. In the event of hostilities with the Soviet Union, the Soviets could strike from the Transcaucasus south through the Levant to block the canal, severing international trade and oil supplies. If Egypt took control it would be able to use the canal as an economic lever against Israel or any other country it had a dispute with.

Churchill always considered Egypt part of the British Empire though technically it was not. He had opposed Egyptian nationalism since the 1920s when the Egyptians unilaterally declared independence and the British Protectorate came to an end. However, Britain had maintained its security interests in the country. Under the Anglo-Egyptian Treaty of 1936 Britain had agreed to withdraw its troops apart from those guarding the Suez Canal. This had been completely derailed by the Second World War and the attempted invasions by the Italians and the Germans. After the war the Egyptian authorities wanted all British troops withdrawn and the annexation of Anglo-Egyptian Sudan. With India demanding independence, it was understandable that Egyptians should want to see the British finally gone. After all the British presence had almost brought Field Marshal Rommel to the very gates of Cairo in 1942. As a half measure Attlee agreed in 1946 to withdraw all British forces into the Suez Canal Zone, which was done the following year.

Churchill was alarmed by Attlee's policies towards Egypt, India and Palestine. He wrote to Attlee on 1 May 1946 to highlight his concerns especially regarding Egypt. 'I could not myself support the evacuation of British troops and air forces from the country,' he said. 'I consider that even if we consent, as may be necessary, to withdraw from Cairo, we must hold the Canal Zone with British troops.'[1] A week later Churchill echoed similar sentiments in a letter to Field Marshal Brooke his former wartime Chief of the Imperial General Staff. He was disappointed that Brooke supported withdrawal from Egypt. 'There is no way whatever of guarding the Canal,' wrote Churchill, 'in the sense of keeping it open, except by the permanent presence of British personnel in the Nile Valley.'[2]

Field Marshal Montgomery, the victor of El Alamein, shared Churchill's concerns when he wrote to him on 12 May. 'You must be upset,' said Montgomery, 'at what is happening in Egypt and the way it has been handled. We lack your strong hand on the helm at these times.'[3] Churchill made his feelings on the future of Egypt known on 1 August 1946 in the House of Commons. 'We scuttle from Egypt which we twice successfully defended from foreign massacre and pillage,' he said. 'We scuttle from it, we abandon the Canal Zone... having been driven out of Egypt'.[4] This was not entirely true, but Churchill saw the withdrawal to the Canal Zone as the thin end of the wedge.

The Egyptian nationalist Wafd party won the election in 1950 and began agitating for the British to go completely. In April that year Churchill questioned the wisdom of the British government's decision to sell 110 jet aircraft to Egypt if there was a danger they could be used against British forces or Israel. Following the 1948 Arab-Israeli War the Israelis had signed separate armistice agreements with Egypt, Lebanon, Transjordan and Syria. While these brought the hostilities to an end, they were not peace treaties. Meaning all the Arab states still remained in a state of war with Israel.

The Suez Canal inevitably became a pawn in the Arab-Israeli confrontation. The new Egyptian government refused to let ships heading for Israel use it. Churchill castigated Attlee's government in the House of Lords on 30 July 1951 for not doing anything about this. In October, just as Churchill was coming to power, the Egyptian government renounced the Anglo-Egyptian Treaty, though they did not have the strength to force the issue. Churchill at his first Cabinet meeting as Prime Minister made sure Egypt was on the agenda. He said that British foreign policy should be 'based on the principle that it was the duty of the United Kingdom Government to keep the Suez Canal open to the shipping of the world, using such force as might be necessary for that purpose'.[5] Churchill wanted to help Israel, but Foreign Secretary Anthony Eden urged caution for fear of rousing the neighbouring Arab states. In the event the blockade of ships destined for Israel continued. Nonetheless, Churchill also told the House of Commons on 1 November, 'We are resolved to maintain our rightful position in the Canal Zone in spite of the illegal and one-sided Egyptian action over the 1936 Treaty.'[6] It was clear he had no intention of quitting Egypt.

Churchill then discussed Britain's extensive defence interests in the House of Commons on 6 December 1951. He talked about Labour's establishment of National Service, the Atlantic Pact and the creation of NATO. He also discussed Egypt and Malaya. In particular he called upon the Egyptian government to do more to prevent mob violence and lawlessness. The following day Anthony Eden said that Britain would introduce Military Government in the Canal Zone if the Egyptian government did not curtail the growing terrorist attacks on British troops. Shortly after Eden suggested to Churchill that if the Egyptian King Farouk did not get a grip on things then there ought to be a joint British, American and French operation against Cairo and Alexandria. This was wishful thinking as America would certainly never countenance such action. Churchill, when he saw President Truman in the New Year, insisted that Britain was in Egypt out of 'a sense of international duty and for no other reason'.[7] He wanted America's help but Truman sensibly had no intention of getting involved in what he saw as British imperial strategic interests. Churchill vainly hoped that responsibility for the canal could be shared with America, France and Turkey, but there was absolutely no incentive for them to prop up Britain's position.

Tensions were ramped up on 25 January 1952 in the Egyptian city of Ismailia, which sits on the west bank of the Suez Canal. The British Army instructed the police barracks, held by 800 armed local police and auxiliaries, to lay down their weapons. Under orders from the Egyptian Ministry of the Interior they refused to surrender. A firefight followed. The police held out for a whole day and did not give up until forty-six of their number were dead and one hundred wounded. The Lancashire Fusiliers, supported by a tank, lost four dead and ten wounded. The incident sparked riots in Cairo where foreign-owned property was set on fire and twenty people were killed including eleven Britons. The Egyptian police and army made no attempt to intervene. Churchill was furious and wrote to Anthony Eden, 'I doubt whether any relationship is possible with them. They cannot be classed as a civilised power until they purge themselves.'[8] For the British military in Egypt the level of resistance came as a nasty surprise.

Churchill did not want the Canal Zone handed over to the Egyptians. He still hoped that a new international defence pact would assume responsibility, but Truman was not prepared to send American troops. Anthony Eden felt the only way to make progress was to offer the Egyptians concessions. When he suggested to Churchill in February 1952 that an agreement should be sought to reduce the number of British troops in the Canal Zone, the Prime Minister was not receptive. Nor was he receptive when Eden proposed handing the military installations in the Canal Zone over to the Egyptians on the condition that they were made available to Britain in an emergency. Field Marshal Slim, Chief of the Imperial General Staff, supported Churchill's stance, reasoning that if Britain was to conduct military operations in the Middle East then it needed a permanent base in Egypt. The only other options were to station troops in British Cyprus or Gaza, but the latter was administered by Egypt. Churchill clung to the delusion that America could be persuaded to help out in Egypt in order to ease the burden.

In Egypt the political situation became increasingly hostile to British interests. The Free Officer's Movement, founded by General Mohamed Naguib and Colonel Gamal Abdul Nasser, overthrew King Farouk on 23 July 1952. Farouk's government was seen as corrupt and incompetent, especially after its failure to remove British influence or defeat Israel. Naguib became president with Nasser as his deputy. All political parties were banned. Naguib and his supporters made it clear that they would resist any attempts by Britain to interfere in Egyptian domestic affairs. Churchill could do nothing but stand by. Furthermore, Naguib and Nasser called on Britain to grant Sudan independence. To strengthen their hand they began to build up the Egyptian army.

Churchill though took a surprisingly conciliatory stance toward Egypt when he spoke at the Lord Mayor's Banquet at the Guildhall on 10 November. 'I am bound to say that I felt much sympathy with the hope aroused by General Naguib,' he said, 'that the shocking conditions of the Egyptian peasantry under the corrupt rule of former Egyptian Governments would be definitely removed.'[9] Nonetheless, Churchill did preface this by calling Naguib 'virtually a military dictator'. Sure enough four days later Naguib was granted absolute power for the next six months. Churchill definitely had no intention of handing the Suez Canal over to a military dictatorship. By the end of 1952 Britain was maintaining about 80,000 troops in the Canal Zone. This was in direct violation of the Anglo-Egyptian Treaty which only permitted the presence of 10,000. Churchill was getting desperate about the situation and told a meeting of the Defence Committee on 11 December, 'Other countries must be made to share this burden.'[10]

It greatly irked Churchill that Britain was being pressured by Egypt to relinquish control of Sudan. Under British rule Sudan had been administered jointly as part of Egypt. When Britain ended its occupation of Egypt in 1936, apart from Suez, British forces had remained deployed in Sudan. Many Egyptian nationalists wanted an independent unified Egyptian-Sudanese state. Churchill had been to Sudan as a young man in 1898 when he had fought at the Battle of Omdurman with the 21st Lancers. He had no desire to see an Anglo-Egyptian agreement on the future of Sudan. He felt that its loss would be yet another blow to British prestige in the Middle East. Furthermore, he suspected that Naguib would seek to annex Sudan once Britain had withdrawn.

When Churchill returned home from holiday in January 1953 he was angry to discover that Eden had held talks with the Egyptians about Sudan. He told John Colville that he 'positively desired the talks on the Sudan to fail, just as he positively hoped we should not succeed in getting into conversations with the Egyptians on defence which might lead to our abandonment of the Canal Zone'.[11] Churchill wanted to break with Egypt over Sudan and was even prepared to take over the Foreign Office himself if Eden resigned. When the issue was discussed by the Cabinet on 11 February 1953 Churchill found his viewpoint was in the minority. Britain had already promised Sudan self-determination and this could not be put off any longer. The following day Harold Nicolson noted in his diary, 'Eden announced in the House today that we have signed an agreement with Naguib abandoning Sudan. I know this was inevitable, but it is sad for me to see the fruit of that great work picked before it was even ripe.'[12] This recognised Sudan's independence which would come into effect from January 1956.

The same day as the Cabinet meeting Churchill instructed the Defence Committee, 'The least sign of military activity, whether by the Egyptian Army or by guerrilla forces against us, would be sufficient justification for rounding up and disarming that part of the Egyptian Army which is located in the Sinai Peninsula.'[13] This force amounted to a division or about 15,000 men. On 18 February Churchill sent Eisenhower a message saying he might have to enter Alexandria and Cairo to prevent a massacre and that he was prepared to cut off the Egyptian forces in the Sinai. Eisenhower must have been aghast as such action could only result in war between Britain and the Arab states.

When Eden was taken ill with gall bladder problems Churchill took over the Foreign Office. He made it known to the British embassy in Cairo that he

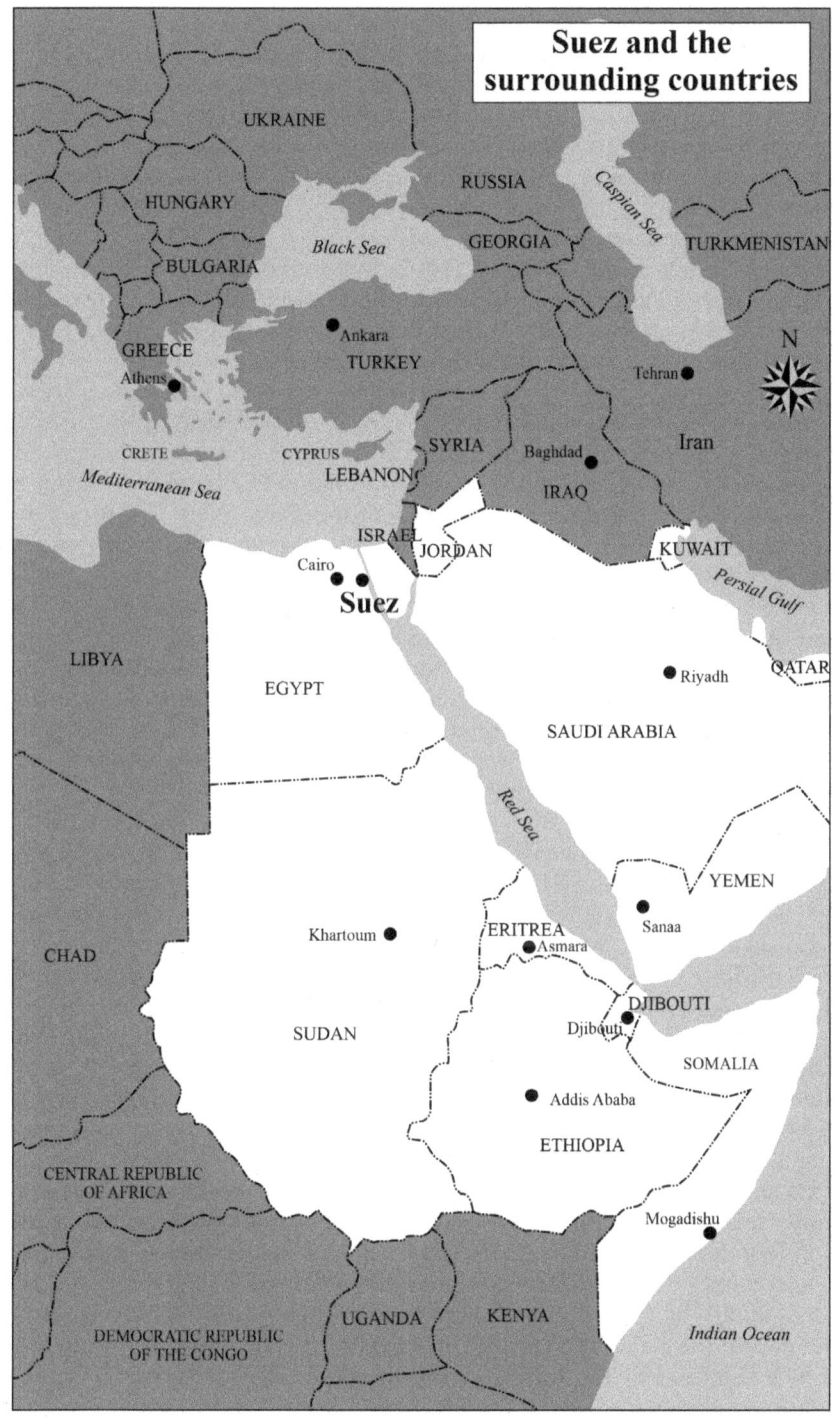

Suez and the surrounding countries

wanted a deal with the Egyptians that would allow British forces to remain in Egypt for twenty years. In the summer of 1953 Churchill and his Cabinet held discussions about what to do should the Egyptians try to forcibly remove British troops from the Canal Zone. On the table were economic sanctions that included blocking Egypt's sterling balances and oil supplies to Cairo. In light of Egypt's growing hostility to Britain, Churchill was all in favour of the former, however without military action by the Egyptians it would make Britain in breach of an international agreement. Churchill's powers though were declining and in June he suffered a serious stroke. Remarkably he bounced back.

In December 1953 Churchill agreed to the transfer of British Middle Eastern command headquarters from the Canal Zone to Cyprus. This was met by outrage by some Conservative backbenchers who saw this as further evidence of Britain's steady retreat from Empire. By mid-December forty-one Conservative Members of Parliament had formed the Suez Group. It was headed by Julian Amery, the son of a cabinet minister in Churchill's wartime government, and Captain Charles Waterhouse, a backbencher who had once held a minor ministerial post. They continually lobbied for the retention of the Canal Zone. The group found a sympathetic ear with Churchill and Zionists who valued Britain's steadying presence in Egypt.

Field Marshal Montgomery knew that Britain could not continue holding the Suez Canal on its own. In his role as deputy commander of NATO he suggested to Churchill and Eden that the canal should be taken under its security umbrella. 'I intend to press upon Eisenhower the active and complete co-operation of Britain and the United States,' responded Churchill, 'in winding up the Egyptian entanglement.'[14] This message was also copied to the Chiefs of Staff and the Defence Minister. Nothing though was to come of it.

In January 1954 the Egyptian government announced it was intensifying the blockade of Israel. This once again included banning Israeli ships and any ships bound for Israel from the Suez Canal. Churchill called on his Cabinet to support the Israeli government which was raising the matter with the United Nations Security Council. Churchill, at a meeting on 21 January, urged the Cabinet that everything should be done to help Israel. Anthony Eden pointed out that legally Egypt still had every right to do so because its war with Israel had not been terminated. Five days later Churchill returned to the matter, highlighting 'the importance of upholding the right of international passage through the Suez Canal'.[15]

He knew that the Egyptians could ill afford a war against Britain. Their army was assessed to be short of ammunition, which meant that they could not fight for long. Furthermore, they were struggling to assimilate their new weapons. By this stage though Churchill was in a very tricky position as the Anglo-Egyptian defence treaty was coming to an end. If a new one was not negotiated then Britain would be required to withdraw from the Canal Zone as soon as possible. Time was not on his side, whereas the Egyptians could afford to wait things out. At the end of January he consulted the Cabinet over whether 10,000 troops could hold either end of the canal by force. The answer from Field Marshal Alexander was that such manpower was insufficient to hold off the Egyptian army. The best they could do was hold Suez itself.

'It was evident,' Churchill informed the Cabinet on 3 February 1954, 'from the record of a conversation between Gamal Abdul Nasser and a member of Her Majesty's Embassy that the Egyptians felt that time was on their side and that it was of no advantage to them to conclude an agreement.'[16] In the meantime the Egyptians turned their attentions to Sudan. When General Naguib visited Khartoum, the Sudanese capital, his presence sparked riots. The Sudanese were not prepared to swap British rule for Egyptian. The country was also split over historic tensions between the Muslim and Christian populations. British Foreign Minister Selwyn Lloyd, who was in the city, recalled, 'The police were shooting and using tear gas. Dead and wounded were being carried through the west gate, and some bodies were being fished out of the Nile.'[17] Lloyd and Tony Duff his Private Secretary began to fear they might suffer the same fate as Gordon of Khartoum who had been killed during the Mahdi revolt.

Churchill was concerned Naguib's presence might indicate that the Egyptians were considering invading before Sudan gained independence. In light of Sudan being divided between the Muslim north and the Christian south this was not as far-fetched as it sounded. Churchill suggested two infantry battalions and two squadrons of aircraft be sent to the city from the Canal Zone. In the event of an Egyptian invasion it could be thwarted by cutting the main railway. Anthony Eden urged caution as the arrival of British troops might inflame the Sudanese even more. Privately he wished Churchill would retire to make his life easier. 'If I went, Anthony would succeed,' Churchill told Lord Moran, 'and he is passionately for our getting out of Sudan.'[18]

Sir Robert Howe, the British Governor-General of Sudan, had on call in Khartoum the 1st Battalion the York and Lancaster Regiment and a battalion of Egyptian troops. Keeping a very cool head Howe refrained from deploying them on the streets. Just before Selwyn Lloyd flew back to London he held a press conference and he wished self-governing Sudan well. 'Churchill saw me on my return and said that he had not liked that at all,' said Lloyd, 'but I think that he had read a garbled report.'[19] Churchill cannot have been that cross as he presented Lloyd with a signed copy of his book *The River War*. The Egyptians though had greater immediate concerns than the future of Sudan. Naguib was arrested by Nasser on 26 February 1954, though the latter waited until June 1956 to become president. Churchill welcomed this change, remarking, 'I have been afraid they might agree.'[20] His hope was that the Anglo-Egyptian talks would now be completely derailed, allowing Britain to take military action.

Churchill continued to view the problems with Egypt and Sudan largely in military terms. In mid-March he suggested to the Cabinet that if negotiations did not go well Britain should send an armoured brigade to the Canal Zone from Libya. Another brigade should be sent to Khartoum to safeguard Sudanese independence. Eden immediately vetoed the idea. Churchill then tried to wring concessions from the Egyptians. Amongst these was that 1,200 civilian technicians would continue to maintain the base area and that British troops would be allowed to re-enter it if Egypt or its neighbours were attacked. The Treasury pointed out that the Canal Zone was costing £56 million a year just to maintain and that defence cuts had to be made. Churchill's government knew that something had to be done.

Eden then informed the Cabinet that Nasser had accepted a seven-year agreement giving Britain the right to reactivate its facilities if Turkey or any Arab country was attacked. Britain in turn agreed that its remaining technicians would not wear uniforms. Whether of course Nasser intended to honour this deal was another matter. On 22 June 1954 Churchill cautioned the Cabinet of 'the political disadvantages of abandoning the position we had held in Egypt since 1882'.[21]

Despite Churchill's ongoing protests, Britain's occupation of the Canal Zone finally ended with the signing of a new Anglo-Egyptian Treaty on 28 July 1954, which replaced the 1936 Treaty. Under its terms all British troops were to be withdrawn by the summer of 1956. The twenty-month evacuation period though did not allow Churchill to save face. He was stung by the *Daily Express* which ran a leader proclaiming, 'Under our very eyes, by the hand of a Tory Government, the greatest surrender is taking place since the Socialists and Mountbatten engineered the scuttle from India.'[22] Labour also attacked the government. Selwyn Lloyd observed, 'Attlee, in a debate on 29 July 1954, accused us of having sold the Sudanese down the river and prophesised that there was very great danger of the Sudanese falling into the hands of the Egyptians.'[23] At the age of eighty-one the pressure was simply too much for Churchill. In April 1955 he finally resigned due to ill-health and was replaced by Anthony Eden. Churchill suffered another stroke in June, but he soldiered on.

Nasser, just as Churchill was stepping down in favour of Eden, sought to court the Communist states further. Whilst on the way to a conference of non-aligned states, he stopped off in Rangoon in April 1955 and met with Communist China's Foreign Minister Chou Enlai. Nasser complained about problems he was having with Soviet arms supplies and Chou promised to intervene on his behalf with Moscow. It had greatly alarmed Churchill when Nasser turned to the Soviet Union seeking weapons. 'Soon after the coup,' recalled Nikita Khrushchev, 'Nasser's representatives came to us with a request for military aid.'[24] Moscow saw Egypt as a potential recruit for the Communist camp, which would be a major strategic gain. 'We agreed,' adds Khrushchev. 'We gave them weapons ranging from rifles to regular artillery.'[25] This was not all, as Soviet supplies included tanks and naval equipment.

Moscow generously arranged for Czechoslovakia to supply Egypt with 530 tanks, armoured personnel carriers and self-propelled guns. The Soviet Union also sent 120 of its latest tanks. Jet fighters and bombers were to follow. Khrushchev though was not convinced of Nasser's Socialist credentials, noting that he may have had 'some ulterior motive for espousing the Socialist cause'.[26] Nasser was prepared to say anything if it meant the Egyptian armed forces would be equipped with vast quantities of discounted Soviet weapons. 'This dramatically changed the balance of power in the Middle East,' observed Foreign Minister Selwyn Lloyd.[27] Much to Israel's alarm the bulk of this new military equipment was deployed in Sinai facing its southern border.

Churchill had inadvertently sown the seeds for more trouble in the Mediterranean. Just before he stepped down, Greek Cypriots of the National Organisation of Cypriot Fighters known as EOKA declared an armed struggle against British rule. In the wake of the Egyptian treaty the British government announced that Cyprus would never gain independence. After the loss of the Canal Zone, the island was simply a much too important base for operations in the eastern Mediterranean and the Middle East to relinquish. Not everyone was convinced by such arguments. Harold Nicolson noted in his diary, 'Nothing shows up the Tories so badly as situations which they know to be false.'[28]

Churchill had visited Cyprus in early 1943 after a meeting with the Turkish President at Adana. While there he stayed with the governor and had inspected his old regiment the 4th Hussars. Most of the population were Greek and although it had never formed part of modern Greece, the Greek government wanted it. The Turkish minority naturally looked to Turkey, who had ruled Cyprus until 1925 when it became a British colony. Turkey wanted it returned or partitioned. Eisenhower, after the Greek Cypriot call for union with Greece began to gather momentum, on 20 August 1954 wrote to Churchill suggesting that the matter be referred to the United Nations. Churchill's response was an emphatic no.

For the Greek Cypriots, with no political solution in sight, the only option seemed to be to take up arms. They first started to cause trouble in late 1954 when British troops evacuated from Egypt began to arrive. Then in late March and early April 1955 there were a series of bomb attacks carried out by EOKA. Alan Lennox-Boyd, Secretary of State for the Colonies, tried to play down the situation in the House of Commons on 6 April. He reassured parliament that the police, special constabulary and the military had been deployed. 'I am sure that the House will join with me in expressing the strongest condemnation of these wicked and malicious activities,' he said, 'by a group of criminals who have attempted to disrupt in this way public order in Cyprus. It is indeed fortunate that no loss of life has occurred.'[29] He also told the Commons that twenty-one arrests had been made. Lennox-Boyd added, 'The Turkish community of Cyprus has condemned these acts of violence; so too have Communist leaders.'[30]

'Although I do not say that this is a decisive argument,' Churchill explained in a letter to Clementine on 20 August 1955, 'we have embarked upon a clearance plan from Egypt which is based upon our base in Cyprus, and we are not likely to choose this moment (above all others) to compromise it.'[31] He was very irritated by American criticism of Britain's treatment of Cyprus. 'We saved Greece from being inside the Iron Curtain by our personal exertions,' he told Clementine irritably. 'Cyprus has never had any pledges from us that she should be handed over to the Greeks, who have never had her.'[32]

Escalating violence forced Eden to declare a State of Emergency in Cyprus on 27 November 1955. Egypt was complicit in this. 'Nasser was actively assisting EOKA in Cyprus,' reported Selwyn Lloyd.[33] Intelligence showed that he was also fomenting trouble elsewhere. 'France has every reason to resent Nasser's attitude and action in regard to Algeria,' noted Churchill.[34] Greek Cypriot nationalists then tried to kill Governor Lord Harding on 21 March 1956. Fortunately for him the bomb they had placed under his bed failed to go off. Eden's government did everything it could to cut EOKA off from Greece. This included secretly jamming Athens' anti-British broadcasts to Cyprus. When this leaked out the government was forced to confess in the House of Commons. Churchill felt that this course of action was rather hypocritical as Britain was always criticising the Soviet Union for jamming British broadcasts. Another security measure was to exile Archbishop Makarios to the Seychelles because of his links to EOKA.

Eden was struggling to keep the Conservative party, and indeed the country, alongside. Churchill cast a long shadow and in many ways it would have been better for Eden if he had stepped down much sooner. On the Conservative back benches there were mutterings that Eden was a poor substitute for Churchill. His job had not been made any easier by the Suez Group. In the six months up to March 1956 a Gallup poll showed that Eden's approval rating had dropped from seventy to forty percent. In mid-June the last British forces departed the Canal Zone. Shortly after, Eden faced a crisis in Egypt that would break his political career.

Nasser, on 26 July 1956, nationalised the Suez Canal, precipitating the ill-advised and short-lived Anglo-French re-occupation of the waterway. Anthony Eden and Harold Macmillan had concocted plans to safeguard the canal in the event of this happening. Four days later Churchill met with Eden to discuss the situation. Churchill was in favour of military action. 'Personally,' he told his wife afterwards, 'I think France and England ought to act together with vigour, and if necessary with arms.'[35] Macmillan briefed Churchill at Chartwell on 5 August with his ideas. 'I said that unless we brought in Israel it couldn't be done,' Macmillan recalled in his diary. 'Surely if we landed, we must seek out the Egyptian forces, destroy them and bring Nasser's government down.'[36] Churchill became quite excited and got his maps out. Such overt regime change though could hardly be seen as simply safeguarding the canal. Churchill immediately lobbied Eden to involve the Israelis and when pressed he confessed that this was Macmillan's idea.

Over the next few days Churchill offered feedback. He worried about the speed of the operation, for if they did not act quickly he feared that the Soviets would pour instructors and volunteers into Egypt to man the Egyptians' aircraft and tanks. Churchill did not like taking the Suez Canal on the grounds that if it was blocked there would be an international outcry. He thought perhaps that Cairo would be a better target. 'I think it is doubtful whether the purpose of the plan is the right one,' Macmillan wrote back on 7 August. 'The object of the exercise, if we have to embark upon it, is surely to bring about the fall of Nasser and create a government in Egypt which will work satisfactorily with us.'[37] Rather than grabbing the Suez Canal, Macmillan preferred invading Egypt from Libya, where Britain maintained a military presence, with an armoured division which could link up with a landing to the west of Alexandria. A drive on Cairo could then be mounted. These ideas he prepared as a memorandum.

Eden though did not like Churchill and Macmillan confusing matters with their alternate plans. 'As I expected the P.M. was in a very bad mood,' noted Macmillan when they got together with the Egypt Committee. 'He refused to allow my paper to be circulated to the Committee or to the Chiefs of Staff,' recorded Macmillan in his diary. 'I discovered later that the source of the trouble was the Churchill visit. Eden no doubt thought that I was conspiring with Churchill against him.'[38] In the face of conflicting advice from Macmillan, Churchill and the Chiefs of Staff Eden found it difficult to make a decision. This was especially the case when the latter were pointing out the limitations of their military options.

Lord Moran noted in his diary, 'Winston is very angry about Nasser's seizure of the Suez Canal.'[39] Churchill's response was, 'We can't have that malicious swine sitting across our communications.'[40] However, Nasser felt obliged to do this when Britain and America withdrew funding for the Aswan Dam after the Soviet Union tried to get involved. He wanted the canal revenues to finance the dam. Churchill held Eden responsible for the situation. 'It serves Anthony right,' he told Moran. 'He has inherited what he let me in for.'[41]

Field Marshal Montgomery met with General Paul Ely, the Chairman of the French Chiefs of Staff, on 3 September 1956 to discuss potential British and French plans should the need arise to invade Egypt. Ely unhelpfully informed Montgomery that France was short of suitable generals to lead the French contingent. In mid-September Churchill and Montgomery discussed their latest ideas with Eden. Montgomery proposed a landing on the beaches near Mersa Matruh to the west of El Alamein and Alexandria. Antony Head, Secretary of State for War, had already dismissed Montgomery's plan as impractical. Britain and France did not have sufficient landing craft for such a operation. Furthermore it was much too far from the Suez Canal. 'We have always thought, rightly in my opinion,' Head cautioned Eden, 'that we should avoid entangling ourselves by fighting in, and the subsequent occupation of, Cairo.'[42] Unfortunately the strain on Churchill was beginning to show again. Whilst on holiday in the south of France he suffered a further stroke on 20 October. To everyone's amazement though he quickly recovered yet again.

Just nine days later Israeli forces, having been re-equipped by the French, rolled into the Sinai and thrust as far as the Suez Canal and Sharm el-Sheik, way to the south on the Red Sea. In the north they took Gaza. The newly-armed Egyptian army was swiftly routed. Britain immediately demanded that Egypt and Israel keep 16km from the Suez Canal in order to prevent the disruption of international trade. Neither side took any notice. Rather suspiciously, that morning the American Embassy in Cairo issued a warning to their nationals working in Egypt. They then began to evacuate them by car to Alexandria from where they shipped out on American naval transports from the US 6th Fleet.

Nasser and Humphrey Trevelyan, the British ambassador in Cairo, were caught by surprise. Neither was anticipating military action over the Egyptian seizure of the Suez Canal. Trevelyan had learned through his contacts that Nasser thought the chances of a direct Anglo-French attack on the canal was only about forty per cent, and that the chances of one following an Israeli attack was nil. Nor did Trevelyan get any advance warning. 'It was not surprising that even as late as 30 October,' he wrote, 'we in Cairo had not expected a British and French attack.'[43] Trevelyan also thought 'it was inconceivable that we should intervene as a result of an Israeli attack except to stop the Israelis through the United Nations or on the basis of a tripartite declaration.'[44] Yet shortly after, the Royal Air Force began to bomb Egyptian targets.

Israel's timing could not have been worse. A week earlier in Budapest the Hungarians had risen up against Soviet rule. In response Moscow poured troops into the city and fighting had broken out. The Soviets agreed to a ceasefire with the insurgents on 28 October, but threatened to use further force to end the uprising.

'Eden and Selwyn Lloyd... made revolting unctuous statements in the House about Hungary,' observed Harold Nicolson. 'When people rise up against foreign oppression, they are hailed as patriots and heroes; but the Greeks whom we are shooting and hanging in Cyprus are dismissed as terrorists.'[45] Seven days later overwhelming Soviet forces attacked the Hungarian insurgents, who resisted until 11 November. Some 3,000 Hungarians were killed and almost 200,000 fled their country. NATO stood by powerless to help.

'The Russians were trying to divert attention from Hungary,' said Humphrey Trevelyan, 'to cause us as much trouble as possible and to increase their influence in Egypt and the rest of the Arab world by giving Egypt all possible support.'[46] Just after the fighting was renewed in Budapest, on 5 November British and French airborne troops secured Port Said at the entrance to the Suez Canal. The *Evening Standard*'s headlines read 'Firmly in After Tough Fighting' and 'The House of Commons Begins with a Storm.'[47] Churchill issued a press release saying that he supported the government and Israel. He also said he was confident that America would understand that Britain and France had acted for the common good. Eden was very grateful and hoped his statement might smooth the inevitable ruffled feathers with the Americans who had not been consulted. To make matters worse America was distracted by the presidential election.

The following day on 6 November British and French amphibious forces came ashore at Port Said. This operation was run from the British military headquarters in Cyprus. Although British and French options had included landing at Alexandria with an advance on Cairo, in the end it was decided to take Port Said with a view to securing just the northern part of the Suez Canal. The Anglo-French invasion force made no attempt to fight its way to the city of Suez and the southern entrance to the canal. This was the very day that Eisenhower was re-elected as President. The Anglo-French and Israeli invasions sparked immediate international outrage. Nasser angrily responded by sinking blockships in the canal to obstruct all international commerce. 'Eden's policy was not only morally wrong but a costly failure as well,' Harold Nicolson told his wife. 'People will talk less about keeping the Canal open and safeguarding our oil supplies when they have to have petrol coupons.'[48]

In Paris there was also political outrage at the French government's military adventurism. France like Britain could not afford a lengthy war against Egypt. In March 1956 the French had ended their North African protectorates and granted Morocco and Tunisia independence. This meant that Algerian nationalists, who had been fighting French rule in Algeria for the past fourteen months, now had safe sanctuaries from which to operate both to the west and east. By this stage the French had 200,000 troops tied down in Algeria with the figure doubling by the end of the year. They were trying to contain 30,000 Algerian guerrillas plus a further 15,000 operating from Morocco and Tunisia. Amongst their ranks were former French colonial veterans who, after indoctrination by the Viet Minh, had been sent home to fight their former masters. In mid-1956 they had started a terror campaign in Algiers. The French were obliged to deploy an entire parachute division into the city. In the long term the paras' brutality simply made things even worse. It would be six years though before Algeria gained independence. For the French, Suez was an unwanted commitment.

Britain's role in the ill-judged attack on Suez did serious harm to Anglo-American relations and resulted in censure by the United Nations. It also enabled the Soviet Union to take the moral high ground over Hungary. Moscow argued it had sought to help a legitimate government, whereas Britain and France had sought to unseat one. Churchill wrote rather pleadingly to Eisenhower on 22 November 1956 saying, 'It will now be an act of folly, on which our whole civilisation many founder, to let events in the Middle East come between us.'[49] Behind the scenes Churchill confessed to John Colville that he thought 'the whole operation the most ill-conceived and ill-executed imaginable'.[50] This was completely unfair as Eden and Macmillan had made him privy to the government's plans from the start. When Colville asked Churchill whether if he was still Prime Minister he would have done the same thing, he replied, 'I would never have dared; and if I had dared, I would certainly never have dared stop.'[51]

Field Marshal Montgomery agreed with Churchill's prognosis in a letter he sent him on 6 December. 'In all my military experience I have never known anything to have been so "bungled"', he wrote, 'as the Suez affair. You would not have handled it that way.'[52] A disgraced Eden told the House of Commons on 20 December that he had no foreknowledge of the Israeli attack. Few people believed him. Three days later the last of the British and French forces were withdrawn from Port Said. 'Thus ends a squalid and most humiliating episode,' said Harold Nicolson.[53] The Israelis remained in Sinai until March 1957; the Suez Canal did not reopen until early the following month. A humiliated Anthony Eden resigned and was replaced by Harold Macmillan. The invasion had achieved nothing except incur the wrath of the international community. Churchill had got his own way and Britain had belatedly stood up to Nasser, only to fail spectacularly. The Suez Crisis as it became known signalled an end to Britain's global standing as a military power.

Chapter 14

East African Revolution

When Churchill took up office for the second time, he and his Conservative government decided that they wanted to bring a halt to Labour's policy that had resulted in swift independence for Burma, Ceylon, India, Israel and Pakistan. From now on a brake would be put on home rule for British colonies. He agreed with Oliver Lyttelton, his Colonial Secretary, that the last thing they wanted was hostile left-wing nationalist governments being established in the British Commonwealth. Shamefully, to head this off meant ensuring white minority rule for Britain's numerous African colonial territories. Churchill had always considered the compromise reached with Jan Smuts and the Boers over white minority rule in South Africa a political success. This was for the simple reason that it had ensured a viable and functioning state that had remained loyal to Britain especially during the Second World War. This view was reinforced when Churchill and Smuts became very close friends. The fate of South Africa's black population at the time was seen as completely irrelevant.

Lyttelton in the early 1950s hoped to replicate the Central African Federation with Britain's East African possessions. This was created to give power to the white minorities in Northern and Southern Rhodesia, with the aim of eventually granting them dominion status. If something similar could be achieved in East Africa it could be run from Nairobi by the white settlers in Kenya. A stable Kenya would not only safeguard the future of the white population, but also guarantee British access to the port of Mombasa, as well as Kenyan tea and coffee.

Churchill was very familiar with Kenya. As a young man, working for the Colonial Office, he had travelled through the colony by train in 1907 visiting Mombasa and Nairobi. The expansion of the railway had brought more and more of the interior under British control. In a letter home to his mother he had noted, 'Thus the Empire grows under radical Administration!'[1] Such was his optimism that he had naively estimated that the increased population could be policed by about a hundred soldiers. Churchill also visited neighbouring Uganda and Sudan during his trip. After his time in Kenya he concluded, 'There are already in miniature all the elements of keen political and racial discord, all the materials for hot and acrimonious debate.'[2] This proved an accurate forecast over forty years later.

Churchill, when he was Colonial Secretary, helped sow the seeds of trouble by supporting the reservation of parts of Kenya for white farmers. This was typified by the White Highlands, comprising the central uplands, which excluded indigenous Africans and Indian immigrants. This inevitably caused a land shortage. Nor was he keen on the idea of treating Indians as equals to the European settlers. Africans were held in such low regard that they were not considered a factor in the political future of the territory. Segregation was achieved through Part Thirteen of Kenya's Public Health Act in the 1920s. After the Second World War Churchill imagined Kenya peacefully moving to white minority rule on the same lines as South Africa. This meant that while the Indians were treated as second class citizens, the Africans were relegated to third class in their own land.

Churchill was well aware of the hedonistic and selfish reputation of some of the wealthier European settlers who treated Kenya as their personal playground. This was typified by the behaviour of the inhabitants of Happy Valley north of Nairobi in the decades leading up to the Second World War. This culminated in the murder of the Earl of Erroll after one affair too many in 1941. During the war Kenya briefly came under threat from Italian-controlled Ethiopia and Somaliland but soon returned to being a British backwater. Harold Macmillan, who was then Parliamentary Under Secretary of State for the Colonies warned, 'The whites cannot afford economically to abandon their supremacy. ...the land hunger and the pressure of the natives will not be relieved.'[3] His radical solution was to nationalise the white farms and redistribute the land. This was pointedly ignored by Prime Minister Churchill who did not want to alienate Rhodesia and South Africa at a point when their support was vital for the British war effort. When the conflict ended the whites had no real interest in politics other than maintaining the status quo. They wanted to return undisturbed to their segregated country clubs, hotels, restaurants and theatres.

British ex-service men who settled in Kenya following the war saw the Labour government's foreign policy towards the Empire and its wide-ranging social reforms as tantamount to Communism. Britain's lurch to the political left was not welcomed by the ruling elites in Kenya. Its economy relied on two types of farming, the cash crops of the white farmers and the subsistence crops of the black population who also worked on the white farms. In the wake of the war food and commodity prices rose dramatically. The white farmers in order to increase production began to reduce African smallholdings and increase African labour obligations. The standard of living for the black population began to fall drastically. The latter were understandably concerned at the prospect of the white settlers achieving some level of self-government, that would remove Britain's influence.

The economic situation and the post-war influx of white settlers began to fuel a sense of grievance amongst Kenya's tribes, in particular the Kikuyu. Their proximity to Nairobi left them the most discriminated against. Some of the 75,000 demobilized Kenyan soldiers who returned home and were frustrated by the lack of change formed the Forty Group. Its leaders included Dedan Kimathi who was to become a prominent commander of the secret organisation known as the Mau Mau.[4] However, most of Kenya's tribes were divided over how best to proceed and many had a vestige interest in maintaining the status quo. Only the Embu and Meru sided with the Kikuyu, and even these three groups were divided in their goals and how best to achieve them. Although the Kikuyu were Kenya's largest tribe they constituted a minority of the African population.[5] This meant that a revolt by them would be more a tribal insurrection than a nationalist uprising. This lack of unity would result in a terrible civil war.

Sir Philip Mitchell, who had been appointed Governor of Kenya in December 1944, largely ignored growing African nationalism and the emergence of armed resistance to British rule by the Mau Mau. Although he had served as the Governor of Uganda in the late 1930s his last posting had been in sleepy Fiji. During the late 1940s there was increasing civil unrest in Kenya. In January 1947 around 15,000 workers went on general strike in Mombasa, which the authorities branded illegal. The disruption to the docks and railway led to questions in the House of Commons. At Kahura in the Fort Hall district that August, tribal police opened fire on demonstrators trying to rescue two arrested ringleaders and one person was shot dead. It is thought that the Mau Mau were established around this period.

The following year, with spreading lawlessness, members of the Kenya Police Reserve began helping to conduct patrols. Fort Hall was placed under curfew in the hope of deterring further trouble. At the same time white farmers and settlers were calling for their way of life to be protected. The Electors' Union, which represented their political interests, in September 1949 published its Kenya Plan. This called for further white settlement and financial support from Britain, Rhodesia and South Africa. There was to be no talk of handing power over to the Africans or land redistribution. The next year its members made themselves clear when they stated, 'We are here to stay and the other races must accept that premise with all it implies.'[6]

British intelligence in August 1951 made its first official confirmation of the existence of the Mau Mau, even though it had undoubtedly been around for a number of years already. Against this background Governor Mitchell in February 1952 had the responsibility of hosting Princess Elizabeth just before she became Queen. The Kenyan colonial government had given the Princess and the Duke of Edinburgh a farm, Sagana Lodge, as a wedding gift in 1947 and had been seeking a royal visit ever since. Such an event would help reassure the white settlers that they had not been forgotten by London in increasingly troubled times. Officially the royal tour was only to be for recreational purposes. As far as Mitchell was concerned though it would give Kenya's colonial government the royal seal of approval amidst a blaze of publicity. Mitchell planned for the royal couple to meet over a hundred leaders of the colony.

Mitchell seemed completely blind to any threat to the Princess and the Duke.[7] Sagana Lodge, located in the foothills of Mount Kenya to the north of Nairobi, was in the middle of Mau Mau territory. The only concession to the royal couples' security was the assignment of a Kenya Police Force Special Branch unit to Sagana. This though was a standard precaution. It was commanded by colonial police officer Ian Henderson who had grown up amongst the Kikuyu and could speak their language, so he must have had an inkling of the risk.

Mitchell even sent the couple to the Treetops Hotel in the Aberdare Mountains. He wrote to Lyttelton saying, 'I am sure that H.R.H would enjoy it enormously; it really is something not to be missed and it does require, for its full enjoyment, as much moonlight as possible.'[8] This was to illuminate the big game that came to the water-hole at night. Treetops also just happened to be in the heart of Mau Mau territory so was a potentially highly dangerous place to be, especially at night time. Mitchell's recommendation indicated a shocking lack of intelligence on the part of the authorities in Kenya regarding the intentions of the Forty Group and the Mau Mau. Either that, or deliberate negligence on the part of the colonial government who wanted nothing to deprive Nairobi of its royal visit.

Unfortunately for Churchill and Princess Elizabeth, Mitchell's understanding of the domestic political situation outside white circles was poor. The Kenyan Directorate of Intelligence and Security rarely ventured beyond the confines of Nairobi. Special Branch were completely unprepared for the Mau Mau revolt and assessed the nationalist Kenya African Union not to be a threat. The latter was a political organisation agitating for the return of Kikuyu land and ultimately black majority rule. Some of its membership undoubtedly had links to the Mau Mau. Mombasa during the Second World War had been a centre for British intelligence gathering. Notably Bletchley Park's codebreakers operated an out-station there, eavesdropping on the Japanese fleet. Clearly in the intervening years such efforts had lapsed. Part of the blame for this lay with Lieutenant General Sir Alexander Cameron, who was responsible for East Africa Command based in Nairobi, which encompassed Uganda and Tanganyika. His background was anti-aircraft defence and staff work so hardly suited for counter-insurgency and intelligence.

If Churchill had been made aware of the growing danger he would certainly have put a stop to Princess Elizabeth's trip. Thankfully the royal visit went without incident, though Treetops was later burned down by the Mau Mau. It is a miracle they did not act sooner, but they must have realised the international backlash would have been enormous and detrimental to their cause. Instead of the Mau Mau the Princess was confronted by a herd of forty-seven noisy elephants. Having climbed from her car she showed no fear. Big game hunter Jim Corbett recalled with some alarm 'the small figure which, from her photographs, I recognize as Princess Elizabeth, walking unswervingly toward the elephants'.[9] The Princess led her party past them to Treetops and up the ladder to safety. 'I have seen some courageous acts,' remarked Corbett, 'but few to compare with what I witnessed on that fifth day of February.'[10]

That night Princess Elizabeth was informed that the armed guard deployed beneath Treetops were there to keep the big game at a safe distance, in reality they were protecting her from the Mau Mau. Corbett, armed with a rifle, posted himself at the top of the ladder on the grounds there might be leopards about. If the Mau Mau had attacked, her meagre guard would have been easily overwhelmed. Two days later she was safely back in London as Queen. Although Churchill fretted about her assuming the crown at twenty-five, when Edward Windley the commissioner of Kenya's Central Province was asked how she took the news of her father's death, he said, 'She took it like a queen.'[11]

Shortly after, Mitchell went on holiday before retiring, leaving Henry Potter as acting governor. That summer Potter sent Oliver Lyttelton and the Colonial Office reports about escalating violence by the Mau Mau. Mitchell and Cameron had left Kenya wholly unprepared for what was coming. In return the Colonial Office did Churchill, Potter and Kenya a great disservice. 'For a reason that may have seemed sufficient to the Colonial Office – that two governors cannot be on the payroll at once,' wrote Sydney Fazan, a former colonial official and now a Kenyan farmer,

'- his successor, Sir Evelyn Baring, had to wait until that period of [Mitchell's] leave had expired.'[12] As a result Baring did not take up post until the end of September. When he arrived Fazan recalled, 'A quick tour of the afflicted areas convinced him that he would have to report that a state of emergency existed and must be declared forthwith.'[13]

African violence through the summer of 1952, especially around Nairobi, began to spiral into what became generally known as the Mau Mau Rebellion. To the north of the capital lay the Kikuyu Reserve, northwest of that is the forest-covered Aberdare Mountains and to the northeast the equally forested Mount Kenya. The Reserve, with its land exhausted by over-farming and expanding population, was hemmed in by white farms. All three areas provided the Mau Mau with havens from which to operate and rich recruiting grounds. The revolt only affected the Kikuyu Reserve, the Central Province and the eastern part of the Rift Valley Province which constituted just one-sixteenth of Kenya's land mass. British district officers and their police escorts were ambushed on the open road and murdered. The Mau Mau not only targeted the white authorities and settlers, but they also attacked any Kikuyu who they deemed collaborators. Amongst those murdered was Senior Chief Waruhiu who was a staunch British supporter. The situation rapidly became critical.

Churchill on 20 October 1952 was forced to back Sir Evelyn Baring when he declared his State of Emergency. For Churchill this was not a welcome development particularly when he had so much else going on in the Middle East and Far East. Although Baring had not been in post for very long he was an experienced colonial administrator. Previously he served as the High Commissioner for Southern Africa and prior to that was Governor of Southern Rhodesia. Baring, just like Churchill, was a product of the class system and conservative through and through. 'Sir Evelyn is one of the most aristocratic aristocrats I have ever met...' observed American writer John Gunther, 'They made Government House in Kenya resemble a stately island lost in time, drowned in forces nobody could comprehend.'[14] He proved a controversial figure, not least because he supported the use of torture. Baring, the Colonial Office and other Whitehall departments were convinced that the Mau Mau rebellion was a Communist plot to overthrow British rule. Lyttelton no doubt relayed this to Churchill.

Churchill was so alarmed by events that he immediately sent Lyttelton to assess the situation first-hand. The day after the declaration of the emergency, Lyttelton informed the House of Commons, 'I am leaving for Kenya next week, not to discuss the present measures – which... have my full support, but to see for myself what is happening and to consider, with the Governor, plans for the future development of the Colony.'[15] This seemed to offer the possibility of some sort of political solution. Lyttelton's first priority though was that the emergency should be ended as quickly as possible to avoid a lengthy security clampdown and awkward questions from the Opposition.

One of Baring's initial actions was to implement Operation Jock Scott, which rounded up 100 African nationalist leaders who were deemed troublemakers. Key amongst them was Jomo Kenyatta, head of the Kenya African Union, who was accused of being directly linked to the Mau Mau. 'KAU is not a fighting union that uses fists and weapons,' Kenyatta had declared at a meeting of his followers

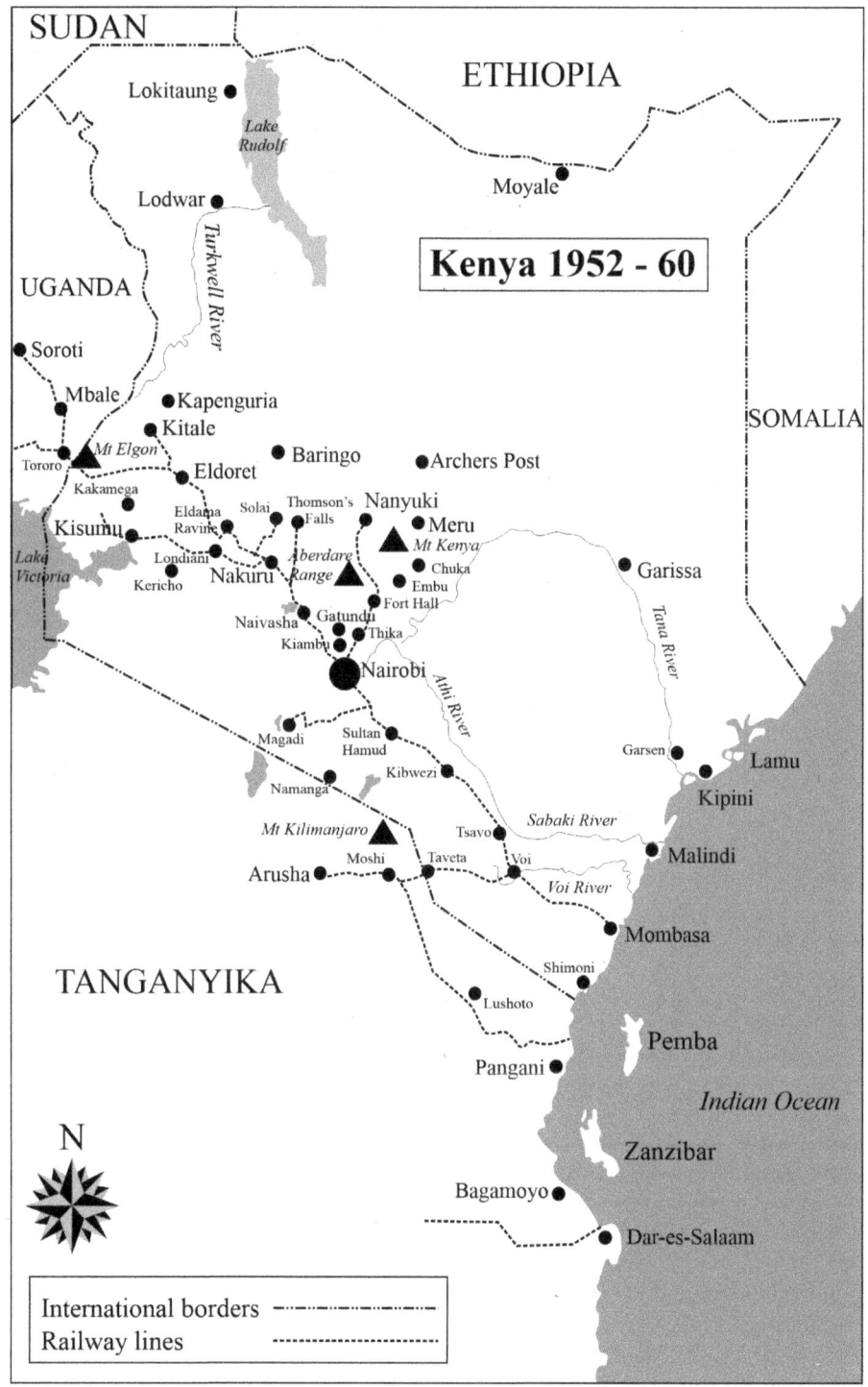

earlier in the year. 'If any of you here think that force is good, I do not agree with you.'[16] After his arrest he was flown out of Nairobi and later claimed he feared he was going to be thrown from the aircraft. Some in Churchill's government and the white Kenyan colonial government sincerely believed that the colony was on the frontlines of the Cold War because Kenyatta was a card-carrying Communist.

When Lyttelton arrived in Nairobi at the end of the month, Baring explained if 'twenty or so leaders could be put out of the way for a long time, Mau Mau would die, but it was vain to hope for quick success'.[17] He also proposed to let the Kikuyu fight the Mau Mau themselves by expanding the local Kenya Police within the African reserves and creating a Home Guard militia. 'Big and bluff Colonial Secretary Oliver Lyttelton toured the colony last week,' reported Alexander Campbell from Nairobi. 'From the Kenya Africa Union... he got a list of Kikuyu demands: 1) more land; 2) higher wages and better education; 3) votes for all Negros who pass literacy and property tests.'[18] They also wanted Kenyatta's immediate release. 'Military action may or may not stamp out Mau Mau terror, only reform can get at the deep roots of black unrest,' concluded Campbell.[19]

During Kenyatta's time in London as a student in the 1930s his activities had been closely monitored by MI5 and the Metropolitan Police's Special Branch. Several visits to Moscow during this period triggered alarm bells and convinced the British authorities that Kenyatta was a Communist agent. This was reported to the Colonial Office and the Commissioner of Police in Nairobi. Robin Page Arnot, a leading British Communist, dubbed Kenyatta 'the future revolutionary leader of Kenya'.[20] In reality Kenyatta soon became disillusioned with the Soviet Union when he found its treatment of Africans to be racist. After Kenyatta returned to Kenya in 1946 there was still no evidence to support suspicions that he was a Communist, but the fear persisted, nonetheless.

Sir Percy Sillitoe, Director General of MI5, reported in January 1953, 'Our sources have produced nothing to indicate that Kenyatta, or his associates in the UK, are directly implicated in Mau Mau activities, or that Kenyatta is essential to Mau Mau as a leader, or that he is in a position to direct its activities.'[21] During his trial Kenyatta told his accusers, 'I have denounced Mau Mau in the most strong terms I could use.'[22] Then looking the prosecutor in the eye he added, 'The Government is not handling Mau Mau in the proper way, and you blame it to me.'[23] No one listened to Sillitoe or Kenyatta.

Although MI5's assessment was relayed to Churchill and Baring, the governor and certain Colonial Office officials remained convinced that Kenyatta was a Communist and that he was vital to the rebellion. In light of the Mau Mau revolt being tribal and so poorly supported, it is hard to believe that anyone seriously thought that Moscow was behind it. Nonetheless, Kenyatta was found guilty even though the evidence was far from conclusive, and sentenced to seven years in prison. Later it was alleged that witnesses had been coached and rewarded for taking the stand. Baring clearly treated Kenyatta as a scapegoat in order to reassure the white settlers that he was taking firm action against the rebellion. Journalist Alexander Campbell noted, 'A major difficulty will be the white Kenyans, who now fear to concede anything lest they lose everything.'[24]

Baring, like his predecessor, chose to ignore the dangers to visiting dignitaries. Since the late 1940s Kenya had been an enormously popular destination for Hollywood film studios seeking exotic locations with a steady supply of wildlife. Baring wanted to do nothing to put them off as their presence helped to glamorize Kenya and attract new settlers and tourists. At the end of 1952 he found himself hosting Hollywood royalty including Clark Gable, Ava Gardner and Grace Kelly along with director John Houston. 'Arriving in Kenya last week to make a big-game move, US cine actor Clark Gable boldly announced that he wasn't going to worry about Mau Mau terrorism,' reported *Time* magazine on 10 November. 'But Kenya's 30,000 whites, who have been around a little longer, are frankly worried.'[25] There was a rumour that the Mau Mau planned to kill Gable so he had to be given an armed guard round the clock. Houston was forced on one occasion to move to another location because of the threat. Embarrassingly two of the locally-employed film crew were discovered to be Mau Mau members. Despite this the film makers and the stars kept coming, with, on a number of occasions, the Mau Mau revolt worked into the plot.

To coordinate the security effort Baring decided to request the appointment of a major general as director of operations, similar to that in Malaya. The British service chiefs, backed by the Colonial Secretary, argued that the problem was not the same and that Baring would have to make do with a colonel as his personal staff officer. This was true but no help whatsoever, as a colonel wielded no authority with the senior commanders. Baring personally took the matter up with Churchill, and Major General Robert Hinde was appointed as his chief staff officer in January 1953. Hinde rather alarmingly had gained the nickname 'Looney' thanks to his antics on the battlefield in Normandy. However, his appointment proved popular. 'I had no idea as to precisely what General Hinde was supposed to do,' recalled Major Frank Kitson, 'but it always seemed that he would turn up just when things were going badly and he exerted a steadying influence on affairs.'[26]

Baring also requested MI5's assistance, and Sir Percy Sillitoe and a team arrived in Nairobi to shake up Kenya's Special Branch. Amongst them was highly competent MI5 officer A.M. MacDonald who was appointed Baring's security advisor. His prognosis of Special Branch was not good, 'The officers were largely untrained, equipment was lacking and intelligence funds were meagre.'[27] He also found they were swamped in paperwork and their offices were inadequate with poor security. MacDonald immediately swung into action to improve things. Special Branch's manpower was boosted by sergeants from the Kenya Regiment. He was so successful that he was later seconded to become Lyttelton's security intelligence advisor with responsibility for Special Branch in every colony. No doubt Lyttelton and Sillitoe briefed Churchill on all these developments.

Fortunately for Churchill, Lyttelton and Baring, the Mau Mau were nowhere near as well-organised or equipped as the Communist insurgents in Malaya. In light of Britain controlling Sudan, Uganda and Tanganyika, and with a friendly government in Ethiopia, it was almost impossible for the Mau Mau to receive outside help. The Royal East African Navy based in Mombasa patrolled the waters off Kenya's coast, further helping to isolate the rebels. British intelligence assessed that of an estimated 12,500 Mau Mau recruits less than 12 per cent were actually armed. They were backed by around 30,000 unarmed supporters who provided basic supplies including food. The lack of weapons meant that the Mau Mau had to resort to the most basic terror tactics rather than an orchestrated guerrilla campaign. Often equipped with just simple clubs and pangas, the insurgents inflicted the most horrific injuries on their victims. People and livestock were regularly mutilated and whole communities terrorised. The Mau Mau stole firearms when they could and even resorted to making their own, though these were usually of a greater danger to the user than the intended target.

Kenyan security became the responsibility of General Sir George Erskine when he was appointed to East Africa Command in 1953. Erskine was a veteran of both the First and Second World Wars; during the latter he had led the 7th Armoured Division. In recent years he had commanded British troops stationed in the Suez Canal Zone. 'It is doubtful whether any other officer had such a wide field of operational experience as General Erskine,' observed Major Kitson.[28] The lacklustre Lieutenant General Cameron was demoted, becoming Erskine's deputy. In practice though Erskine functioned as Director of Operations with Hinde as his Deputy Director. Erskine was instructed to answer directly to the War Office in London and not to Middle East Command in Egypt which was the normal chain of command. Reorganising and reinforcing the security effort to counter the insurgency would take time.

Erskine acted quickly to assess things. 'In these internal security situations you must develop your intelligence service to meet your needs,' he noted, 'and you must not be content with a general picture and trends.'[29] It soon became obvious that the army and police needed to be better coordinated. They also needed to be reinforced. The Home Guard, drawn from Embu, Kikuyu and Meru militias, was expanded to 15,000 men and inevitably became targets for the Mau Mau. In response the Home Guard would kill more insurgents than the army and police combined. The Kenyan colonial government, fearful this force might become a fifth column, largely armed them with just spears and bows. This stopped them defecting or passing firearms to the insurgents. Erskine, who saw the rebels as products of a system that marginalised them and not simply as bloodthirsty cultists, ordered an immediate end to the keeping of kill scorecards and the £5 kill bonus.

Alarmed by what was happening, the European settlers took to the streets of Nairobi in January 1953 demanding a firmer response to the Mau Mau. Governor Baring and General Erskine took heed. That month they conducted Operation Longstop in an effort to clear 100 square miles of the Aberdares. Nonetheless, by February the Mau Mau had killed 190 people, though most of them were fellow Africans. As a result there was no shortage of recruits for the locally-raised Kenya Regiment.

Churchill during his briefings took a tactical interest in operations in Kenya. In a Defence Committee meeting on 6 March 1953 he asked about the use of helicopters. He 'stressed the importance of making a display of air power over the heads of the Mau Mau'. Churchill reasoned, 'The more often they saw an aircraft overhead, the more they would feel that all their movements were under observation.'[30] His interest may have been sparked by the imminent entry into service of the Sycamore helicopter with the British Army for search and rescue and casualty evacuation. Despite Churchill's interest in helicopters supporting Erskine, they did not become operational in Kenya until December 1954. They were so few in number that they made no discernible impact.

While the security forces got their act together the insurgents stepped up their activities. On March 26 they conducted a successful raid on the Naivasha police station and seized forty-seven weapons. They also killed two police officers and released about 180 prisoners. While this setback was embarrassing to the police, such quantities of guns were hardly going to make much impact on the course of the fighting. That same day at Lari almost 100 anti-Mau Mau Kikuyu were brutally hacked to death. Most of them were women and children. Both these towns lay on the railway running north from Nairobi and the attacks sent shock waves of alarm through the white population. Baring feared that there would be a steady exodus of whites to Rhodesia and South Africa if the security situation did not improve.

Although Churchill and the authorities in Kenya did not condone the mistreatment of prisoners, regular torture and human rights violations nonetheless took place. General Erskine in April 1953 was moved to issue orders that the army and the police were not to tolerate the abuse of civilians or prisoners. The problem he faced was that Mau Mau atrocities, such as at Lari, often sparked bloody reprisals by the Home Guard. Churchill was concerned by a briefing given by Oliver Lyttelton on 21 May in which he explained that roving emergency courts were now operating in Kenya. Churchill cautioned against conducting multiple hangings, warning that British public opinion 'would be critical of anything resembling mass executions'.[31] Initially General Erskine's approach to the insurgency produced largely limited results. However, on 15 June 1953 an operation in the Aberdares ended with the deaths of 125 insurgents.

Churchill's health took a turn for the worse when on the evening on 23 June, while at 10 Downing Street, he suffered another stroke. At the time he was entertaining the Italian Prime Minister and other guests. No one noticed and afterwards he was escorted upstairs to bed and Lord Moran his doctor was summoned. Churchill withdrew to Chartwell to recuperate and he did not attend a Cabinet meeting again until 18 August. At the age of 79 and with failing health he should have retired, instead he soldiered on. He was not really capable of overseeing the ongoing conflicts in Malaya and Kenya effectively.

The tactics and strategies developed to deal with the Malayan Emergency were to be repeated in Kenya. These included physically and psychologically isolating the Mau Mau fighters from the rest of the population. Baring sent Thomas Askwith to Malaya in June 1953 to examine the use of detention camps and new villages. When Askwith returned two months later he was appointed Permanent Secretary in the Ministry of African Affairs, charged with implementing something similar. His strategy was to include three types of camps, one for hard core Mau Mau, an intermediate one for those who could be rehabilitated and one for those to be repatriated to the tribal reserves. Askwith was later to lose his job for suggesting those held in the camps should be treated more humanely.

It was not until September 1953, almost a year after the emergency commenced, that British reinforcements began to arrive. The campaign would tie up five British and six King's African Rifles infantry battalions, supported by Royal Air Force bombers, the Kenya Regiment, the police and Home Guard. It would not be until the following year that the military effort against the Mau Mau really began to get underway. The security forces scored a major coup on 15 January 1954 when they captured Waruhiu Itote, also known as 'General China', who had been one of the most effective Mau Mau leaders in the Mount Kenya area. Itote, tired of the struggle, cooperated with his captors and provided a wealth of intelligence. Initially he was sentenced to death, but this was commuted to life imprisonment. Churchill requested that Itote be asked to send surrender terms to his comrades still hiding in the forests. This was done but no one thought to clarify the situation with a unit of the King's African Rifles who promptly ambushed a group hoping to surrender, killing twenty-five of them.

The Mau Mau thoroughly alienated their cause domestically and internationally thanks to their brutal practices. The insurgent groups were held together through a mixture of respect and terror. Members were expected to swear lengthy oaths of loyalty to their leaders and take part in macabre initiation ceremonies involving witch doctors. This included self-mutilation using razors. Bizarrely the oath was called on to kill the oath-taker if they failed in their allotted tasks. 'Clearly the value of the oath,' observed Major Kitson, 'depended on the intensity with which the taker believed that the oath would kill him should he fail to do as he had sworn.'[32] When Churchill was shown the typical wording of such an oath he said, 'It was certainly calculated to impress the recipient.'[33]

Sydney Fazan noted, 'As the Mau Mau campaign proceeded, several types [of oath] were employed – probably seven – becoming progressively more bestial and nauseating at each successive stage.'[34] Churchill in February 1954 considered publishing the oath to show what monsters the Mau Mau were. 'It is very long,' he remarked to Lord Moran. 'No one could have made it up if he had tried. It is incredibly filthy.'[35] In the end he decided that it was not suitable for public consumption, so instead a copy was placed in the House of Commons as reference for the members. The power of the witch doctors though seemed to be waning. 'By the beginning of 1954 the binding power of the oath had been greatly reduced,' reported Major Kitson. 'By August the mystical effects had gone and the Mau Mau looked on it as little more than a racket.'[36] He got the impression that the oaths had 'little effect'.[37]

General Erskine moved to clear the Mau Mau from the capital and surrounding towns in April 1954 with Operation Anvil. This involved 20,000 British and African soldiers. It also served to cut the Mau Mau's supply lines from Nairobi to the insurgent groups operating in the Aberdares and on Mount Kenya. The Kikuyu made up three quarters of the African population in the city so needed to be screened on a regular basis. 'The headquarters and principal committee of the Mau Mau organisation were known to be in Nairobi,' recalled Sydney Fazan, 'and something like a reign of terror among Africans not actively supporting them prevailed. Hold-ups were a commonplace and murders very frequent.'[38] North and northeast of the capital the military moved to secure Kiambu, Thika and Fort Hall. Kiambu, which was closest to Nairobi, proved the most problematic because its large population meant relocating all the people to new villages was difficult. The Kikuyu Reserve was also cleared of Mau Mau sympathisers who were rounded up and replaced by loyalists. 'This dealt a shattering blow to the Mau Mau organisation,' said Fazan.[39]

At the end of July 1954 Lyttelton was succeeded as Colonial Secretary by Alan Lennox-Boyd. Previously he had served as Minister of Transport so did not seem an immediately obvious candidate to grapple with Britain's colonial problems. However, prior to that in late 1951 and early 1952 Lennox-Boyd had done six months as Minister for the Colonies, during which time he had flown to Kenya and, accompanied by Erskine, met senior Kikuyu leaders. Also in 1954 Kenyan farmer and politician Michael Blundell informed Churchill that any settlement for the future could only be achieved once the Mau Mau were defeated. Blundell was the leader of the moderate whites who supported multi-racialism. However, they were opposed to opening up the White Highlands. Churchill was fully aware that the intransigence of the white settlers was part of the problem. General Erskine agreed with him, 'I hate the guts of all of them... They are not prepared to do anything to help themselves.'[40] Such was his complete distaste for the settlers he dubbed them 'middle class sluts'.[41]

Churchill was alarmed to learn that his wife Clementine and Oliver Lyttelton's wife Moira had received death threats as a result of the Kenyan emergency. A Mau Mau, calling himself General Stalin, claiming to be in London wrote to Clementine in 1954, 'I as well as most of my ruthless gang will be out to shoot you dead... I am demanding the withdrawal of all troops from Kenya within two months' time. ...We are also sure that Mrs Lyttelton's life is at present not safe too.'[42] For Churchill over the years regular death threats came with the job, but it must have been distressing that Clementine was in danger. The idea of Mau Mau lurking in the streets of London seemed ridiculous but the letter had to be taken seriously. Although nothing happened when the deadline passed all such correspondence was handed over to MI5. Invoking Stalin's name may have been designed to fuel paranoia that the Soviet Union was somehow involved with the Mau Mau. Such notions though were complete nonsense.

The British authorities' other solution to the Mau Mau Rebellion was largescale incarceration. By the end of 1954 the Kenyan government had around 17,000 convicts and 50,000 detainees held in prison camps. Most of them were Kikuyu. They also instigated a campaign of counter-terror. This was on the basis that because experts concluded the Kikuyu were very afraid of Mau Mau witchcraft, they needed to be made more afraid of the Kenyan government. By the time Churchill stepped down to be replaced by Anthony Eden in April 1955, conditions in many of the overcrowded camps had become intolerable. Just as he resigned those located at Gilgil and Langata had to be closed due to outbreaks of disease, which should have been preventable.

The security forces now attempted to completely clear the forests to the north of Nairobi. Around the Aberdares and Mount Kenya engineers built defensive barriers as stop lines to prevent the Mau Mau from escaping a major military sweep. In June 1955 around 10,000 troops backed by the Royal Air Force launched an operation to kill or capture the last concentration of around 4,000 insurgents. The survivors were driven from their remaining safe havens and forced to go on the run. By this stage although Churchill had resigned, his legacy was that the Mau Mau were defeated as a fighting force.

Even though the Kenyan emergency dragged on until January 1960 it effectively came to an end in October 1956 when the last senior insurgent commander, Dedan Kimathi, was captured and hanged. He had led the resistance in the Aberdares until his forces were scattered. From that point on British battalion-sized operations ceased. Nonetheless, General Erskine still urged caution, 'It would be the worst possible service to the people of Africa to give independence against a background of confusion.'[43]

The casualty figures show just what a wholly one-sided struggle the emergency really was. It resulted in the deaths of 11,500 Mau Mau compared to just under 600 members of the security forces, of whom only twelve were from the British army. In total just 32 European civilians were killed; in contrast several thousand African civilians lost their lives. Around 50,000 were held for varying lengths of time in the prison camps and over a thousand executions were carried out by April 1956. Over a million civilians were moved to over 800 new villages or concentration camps.[44] There many inhabitants were brutalised and raped by members of the Home Guard who were supposed to be protecting them. The campaign cost Britain £55 million.

Despite the colonial government's victory, Kenya could not be denied independence for much longer. This was especially the case when on 6 March 1957, the British colony of the Gold Coast became the independent state of Ghana. By this stage Harold Macmillan had taken over from an ailing Eden. It was felt that more trouble was brewing in Africa. 'There may be civil war in South Africa,' observed Harold Nicolson in alarm, 'and that will spread to Nyasaland and Kenya.'[45]

Britain's policies in Kenya were once again put under the international spotlight when on 3 March 1959 eleven Mau Mau prisoners were beaten to death by guards at the Hola prison camp for refusing to work. In response prominent Conservative Lord Butler 'felt that a much more radical approach to problems in Africa was essential'.[46] Lennox-Boyd, the Secretary of State for the Colonies, facing censure over the killings, found himself having to answer some very tough questions in the House of Commons. Macmillan, recalling his school days to Lord Moran quipped, 'You know, Alan Lennox-Boyd couldn't have endured the last fortnight without that training.'[47] Nonetheless, Lennox-Boyd, who knew all about the use of torture in Kenya, quietly stepped down. Hola helped finally convince Macmillan that the British government must give Africans majority rule in Kenya as soon as possible. 'We cannot suppress the darkies by shooting them,' acknowledged Harold Nicolson reflecting attitudes of the time. 'In fact the rule of Empire is over, and I fear that the Tories will not face the fact.'[48]

Jomo Kenyatta was released from prison in 1961 and three years later he became the first president of an independent Kenya. Nyasaland also gained independence becoming Malawi. 'I do not think that any of us at the time,' recalled Lord Butler, 'realised how happily Kenya would develop under Kenyatta and how quietly the whites would accept the new position.'[49] In contrast, to head off black majority rule, the white population in Rhodesia unilaterally declared independence in 1965. In the years to come Churchill would unfairly be held personally to account for what happened in Kenya, not Baring, Lyttelton, Lennox-Boyd and Erskine. 'In operations of this kind you can take it for granted that you will be under constant criticism from certain sections of the Press and public,' acknowledged General Erskine. 'There is not much you can do about it except to stick to the rules and not to lose your temper with your critics.'[50] In Kenya though, the rules were biased and racist as Churchill well knew.

PART SIX

FADING GLORY

Chapter 15

Rendezvous in Bermuda

After Eisenhower's presidential victory in early 1953 Churchill desperately wanted to hold a 'Big Three' summit. He felt that this was vitally important following Stalin's death on 5 March. Churchill optimistically hoped that a change in Soviet leadership might provide the opportunity for a rapprochement with the Soviet Union and ease mounting Cold War tensions. Ongoing international intervention in Indochina and Korea had highlighted how easy it could be for regional wars to escalate into all-out global conflict between Communist China and the Soviet Union on the one hand and the western democracies on the other. Churchill aimed to replicate his wartime friendship with Stalin with the new leader and thereby influence Soviet foreign policy. Beforehand he hoped that by sheer willpower he could sway Eisenhower to his way of thinking as he had done so many times before during the war.

Although Churchill had got on with Eisenhower and been pleased by his appointment as NATO supreme commander in April 1951, he did not welcome his election as president. As far as Churchill was concerned Eisenhower was a soldier and not a politician. He told John Colville, 'I am greatly disturbed. I think this makes war much more probable.'[1] Ironically in the Second World War Eisenhower had proved a master diplomat as much as a strategist. When Churchill met with Eisenhower and his Secretary of State John Dulles in New York in January 1953 he took an instant disliking to Dulles. Churchill was later to rudely remark, 'It seems that everything is left to Dulles. It appears that the President is no more than a ventriloquist doll.'[2] Colville did not have high hopes for Eisenhower. He noted in his diary, 'Ike in particular I suspect of being a genial and dynamic mediocrity.'[3]

The problem Churchill faced was that Eisenhower's new government saw the Soviet Union as an ongoing threat despite Stalin's demise. This meant that it was not prepared to make the slightest concession to Soviet interests. Churchill put pressure on Eisenhower on 5 May when he informed him that he was prepared to go to Moscow on his own if necessary. Six days later Churchill informed the House of Commons of his intentions. Foreign Secretary Anthony Eden thought this was a really bad idea as it might undermine European unity. In contrast Foreign Minister Selwyn Lloyd felt that it was a good idea. Secret approaches were made to both the Soviet Embassy in London and Moscow.

The French Prime Minister, René Mayer, was determined not to miss out on a meeting between the new American president and Churchill so approached Eisenhower. He pointed out that as France was a leading ally in facing down Communism in Europe and Indochina it should be included. On 20 May Eisenhower called Churchill and suggested this. Churchill agreed and recommended they get together in the British colony of Bermuda in the north Atlantic. The islands were host to a number of American bases, which were a hangover from the Second World War. Eisenhower had visited Bermuda in 1945 when he was Allied Supreme Commander. Churchill hoped that this conference would lead to a senior meeting with the Soviets. He did not want the French there but acquiesced just to please Eisenhower.

In the meantime the problem of defending Europe from the Soviet menace rumbled on. Efforts to form a pan-European defence force that would include West German manpower resulted in the European Defence Community treaty on 27 May. This comprised Belgium, the Netherlands, Luxembourg, France, Italy and West Germany. Britain, thanks to Churchill's aversion to closer integration into Europe, was not party to the treaty. This inevitably showed a lack of solidarity. The idea was its members should create a European army that would be put at the disposal of NATO. 'Each unit of division strength would be homogenous as to nationality while larger units, corps and armies,' noted Eisenhower, 'could logically contain within themselves units of different nationalities.'[4] However, the French and Italians failed to ratify the treaty meaning it did not come into force.

Eisenhower found this rather ironic as 'the plan, largely designed by the French, soon ran into opposition – from the French.'[5] For many in the French National Assembly the idea of West Germany's rearmament was intolerable. They were in no hurry to be at risk from a resurgent Germany once more. The French were also rightly worried that closer European integration might herald America's departure from the continent. Once France dropped out of the community Italy followed suit. The only solution would be to allow West Germany directly into NATO, this though would take time to secure agreement from its existing members. Meanwhile western European leaders agreed there would be no talks with Moscow until such time as the treaty was ratified and elections held in West Germany.

Preparations for Bermuda were distracted by Queen Elizabeth II's coronation on 2 June 1953. In addition a political crisis in Paris meant that the French were unable to commit for three weeks. Churchill attended the coronation at Westminster Abbey but was against the idea of televising the event. He was though overruled by the Queen. In deference to the historical occasion Churchill was keen that the coronation was not portrayed 'as if it were a theatrical performance'.[6] The weather was suitably British, it poured with rain. Almost 45,000 British and Commonwealth troops were involved, which was quite a feat considering Britain's global military commitments. Harold Nicolson witnessed the pomp and ceremony. 'After a short wait the troops appear,' he recalled. 'There is a long pause …and eventually comes Winston in his Garter robes waving his plumed hat and making the V sign.'[7] Around 27 million people reportedly watched on just three million televisions.

British troops overseas also celebrated the Queen's coronation. Chinese positions in Korea were deluged in red, white and blue smoke. They had no way of knowing what was going on and probably assumed that this was some new British tactic. The men of A Company, 1st Battalion, Durham Light Infantry got in on the act by sneaking out under the cover of darkness to place a large 'E II R' sign made from aircraft panels in front of enemy lines. British prisoners of war, to the fury of their Chinese captors, made merry with a parade and home-made rice wine. The guards responded by reducing their rations.

'We have had a day which the oldest are proud to have lived to see,' said Churchill in his broadcast to the nation, 'and the younger will remember all their lives.'[8] Later that evening John Colville noted, 'We joined the Prime Minister in a room in the Ministry of Materials from which to see the great fireworks display on the Thames.'[9] The newspapers attributed the lavishness of the coronation to Churchill. According to Colville though, 'He has had little or nothing to do with the preparations.'[10]

The day after, Churchill found himself chairing the opening meeting of eight Commonwealth Prime Ministers at Downing Street.[11] He explained that there seemed to be no change in Soviet foreign policy since Stalin's death and warned, 'We should do all we could to avoid a drift into war.'[12] Churchill added it was important for the members of the Commonwealth to remain united, which would help them influence American foreign policy. He felt that only the atomic bomb was keeping the Soviet Union in check. 'Though they had the power to overrun much of Western Europe they must know that their central government machinery,' explained Churchill, 'their communications and their war potential would be shattered by atomic attack.'[13] Furthermore, he thought such an attack would break the Communist hold over the Soviet Union and lead to rebellion. Churchill reasoned that the way ahead was to open dialogue with Moscow as soon as possible through formal high-level talks.

The Commonwealth Prime Ministers were supportive of this reasonable approach. Louis St Laurent the Canadian leader agreed that the Bermuda conference should be a stepping stone to a meeting with the Soviet Union. Churchill pointed out the challenge would be to persuade Eisenhower that this was desirable. He was back in the chair on 4 June and warned that if the Korean truce broke down 'there would probably be a demand by the United States for a vigorous impulse to active operations'.[14] Sir Robert Menzies the Australian Prime Minister aired his concerns that America might step up its operations in Korea. Churchill reassured him that he was sure Eisenhower would not act before consulting the other United Nations members.

Although Foreign Secretary Anthony Eden was unwell, Churchill could see no reason not to press on with the gathering in Bermuda involving America, Britain and France. This though meant that Churchill assumed direct responsibility for the Foreign Office, which he characterised as 'very hard work'.[15] On 19 June he wrote to Eisenhower to complain about French delays and suggested they meet during the second week of July with or without them. Churchill seemed invigorated by the proposed summit and perhaps recalled the glory days of the Second World War. The following day in the Cabinet Room, Pierson Dixon from the Foreign Office observed, 'Mentally he is more alert than he was towards the end of the war.'[16]

Unfortunately there were soon signs that Churchill was overdoing it. A few days later Lord Moran said, 'I thought his speech was slurred and a little indistinct. Twice I had to ask him to repeat what he had said.'[17] Not long after, Churchill suffered a serious stroke. This meant that he was unable to travel to Bermuda. His closest friends were sworn to secrecy about just how bad he was. 'You will see from the attached medical report the reasons why I cannot come to Bermuda,' Churchill explained in an apologetic telegram to Eisenhower on 26 June. 'I am as bad as the French, thinking that the conference should be postponed.'[18] Eisenhower kindly responded with, 'I look upon this as a temporary deferment to our meeting.'[19] Privately though he hoped that Churchill would retire and he could deal with Anthony Eden who had a much closer mindset. As far as Eisenhower was concerned it was seven long years since the Second World War and he felt that Churchill was too old and set in his ways. Churchill spent much of the summer lamenting not being able to meet the president.

In the Soviet Union after Stalin's death the senior leadership were in a state of flux. Stalin's brutal lackey Lavrentiy Beria initially formed a ruling troika with Georgy Malenkov and Vyacheslav Molotov. Beria though had few friends, and on 26 June Nikita Khrushchev, assisted by Marshal Zhukov, had him arrested for treason and later executed. Beria was made a convenient scapegoat for Stalin's reign of terror. 'There were shocking revelations about the secret machinery which had been hidden from us,' claimed Khrushchev disingenuously, 'and which had caused the deaths of so many people.'[20] Molotov, who had made his name as the Soviet foreign minister during the Second World War, had no ambition to succeed Stalin. Nor was Malenkov the man to rule the Soviet Union. 'I knew that Malenkov had never really had a position or a role of his own and that he was just an errand boy,' said Khrushchev dismissively.[21]

Churchill was convinced, 'When I meet Malenkov we can build for peace.'[22] This was put in jeopardy when Khrushchev took over as head of the Soviet Communist party in mid-September, which gave him executive control of the government. Churchill and Eisenhower were unaware of the implications of this at the time. Khrushchev knew that the Soviet Union was facing numerous challenges, the latest of which was the uprising in East Germany in mid-June. The fact that Soviet tanks had to be deployed on the streets showed just how tenuous Soviet fraternal friendship was in the satellite states. There had also been civil unrest in Czechoslovakia and Poland earlier in the year. Churchill refused to make political capital out of this. Instead he castigated the Foreign Office when it protested about Soviet actions. 'Is it suggested that the Soviets should have allowed the Eastern Zone to fall into anarchy and riot?' he asked sternly. 'I have the impression that they acted with considerable restraint in the face of mounting disorder.'[23] Churchill clearly tried to play down the situation for fear of America's reaction.

Konrad Adenauer the West German leader was alarmed by Churchill's wish for a summit with the Soviet Union. He feared that the fate of Germany was about to be settled without involving it. Adenauer was facing an election in the autumn so needed to shore up his position domestically. To do this he gained American support and got a resolution through the West German parliament that a united Germany should be protected by NATO. Furthermore, he got it to agree that it would not recognise the Oder-Neisse line. When Churchill heard of this he was very vexed that West Germany was trying to shape its own future. 'But we won the War did we not?' he exclaimed crossly.[24]

Following the clamp down in East Germany, Khrushchev recognised the need to denounce Stalin's policies and herald change or the Soviet Union might likewise be facing internal unrest. Both during and after the war, on Stalin's instructions Beria had conducted widespread ethnic cleansing across the western Soviet Union, which resulted in hundreds of thousands of people being deported, imprisoned or executed. Embarrassingly for Moscow, lingering resistance from nationalist partisans in Chechnya, Lithuania and Ukraine, who had fought the Germans and the Red Army during the Second World War, continued well into the 1950s.[25] Furthermore, there was the danger that Mao's foreign policy might drag the Soviet Union into war. While Mao made it clear he would honour the armistice in Korea, he was still determined to help Ho Chi Minh defeat the French in Indochina, which risked Eisenhower's intervention.

On 3 November Churchill addressed the House of Commons with an air of optimism. 'Have there been far-reaching changes in the temper and outlook of all the Russians?' he asked. 'I do not find it unreasonable or dangerous to conclude that internal prosperity rather than external conquest is not only the deep desire of the Russian people but also the long-term interest of their rulers.'[26] Afterwards he told Lord Moran, 'I must see Malenkov. Then I can depart in peace.'[27] Beforehand Churchill toyed with the idea of meeting Eisenhower in the Azores but then reverted to Bermuda, suggesting 4 December for four days.

While Eisenhower was immediately amenable to Churchill's proposal, he was not keen to offer the hand of friendship to Moscow. 'It would be necessary of course,' he said in his reply, 'to avoid creating a false impression that our purpose in meeting is to issue another invitation to the Soviets.'[28] Churchill was completely undeterred. 'There is a feeling that I am the only person who could do anything with Russia,' he told Lord Moran. 'I believe in Moscow they think that too.'[29] Unfortunately Eisenhower and Anthony Eden did not agree with him. 'What an asset his optimism is!' noted Lord Moran. 'It keeps out the facts.'[30] On 24 November William Hayter, the British Ambassador in Moscow, assessed that Malenkov 'seems to have concluded that Stalin's methods were too rough. Other and more subtle methods of weakening the West are henceforth to be adopted.'[31] Just two days later the Soviets accepted the idea of a four-power meeting, including the French, in Berlin at foreign secretary level. This convinced Churchill that it gave the Bermuda conference even greater impetus.

Churchill, the day after his seventy-ninth birthday, flew to Bermuda on 1 December with a sizeable entourage that included Eden, Moran and Colville. He also took two secretaries, Elizabeth Gilliatt and Jane Portal. 'It was a wonderful experience for me,' recalled Portal, 'For the prime minister it was a journey to see an old friend.'[32] She claimed that Churchill 'was absolutely devoted' to Eisenhower.[33] The flight took seventeen hours with landings at Shannon in Ireland due to unwelcome headwinds and Gander in Newfoundland. It was clear from the discussions that Churchill and Eden did not have much faith in the French. During the journey Churchill pointedly read C.S. Forester's novel set during the Napoleonic Wars called *Death to the French*. Eden was annoyed not only by Churchill's provocative reading, but also by his refusal to examine any of the briefings or prepare an agenda. This was very uncharacteristic of Churchill who was normally over-prepared. Nor was Eden encouraged by Churchill's refusal to use a hearing aid despite his increasing deafness.

Churchill was driven to Bermuda's international airport on 3 December to meet French Prime Minister Joseph Laniel and Foreign Minister Georges Bidault. There were firm handshakes and smiles all round. The following day he returned to the airport for the arrival of President Eisenhower and Secretary of State Dulles. Eisenhower probably landed slightly on his guard. Although he greatly respected Churchill he knew the British leader could be very difficult if he did not get his own way. On a number of occasions during the Second World War Churchill had made Eisenhower's job as Allied Supreme Commander extremely unpleasant. Eisenhower was not prepared to put up with any of Churchill's tantrums. Nonetheless, he and Churchill lunched together alone much to the alarm of Dulles and Eden. Their topics of conversation were Korea, China and Europe. Eisenhower was not enthused by the idea of side-lining the French if they objected to including Germany in western Europe's defence arrangements. However, he was open to the idea of the four-power foreign ministers meeting with the Soviets. Churchill of course though really wanted a senior leadership summit involving himself, Eisenhower and Malenkov.

That afternoon the American, British and French leaders got together and Churchill invited Eisenhower to act as chairman. Eisenhower proposed that America, Britain and the Soviet Union make atomic energy material available for scientific research via the United Nations. They then discussed political developments in the Soviet Union. Bidault was of the opinion that it was largely business as usual in Moscow. Likewise, Eisenhower was unconvinced the Soviets had changed their ways and was very abusive towards the Soviet Union. This was not a good start for Churchill. The harsh views expressed in the meeting were leaked to the press much to his annoyance. Furthermore, he remained cross that America's refusal to share atomic bomb technology had forced Britain to develop its own costly weapon and the means to deliver it. To date Britain only had one operational bomb. Eisenhower declined to tell Churchill that America was now working on a vastly more destructive second-generation nuclear weapon, the hydrogen bomb.

The French found themselves coming under criticism over their intransigence with West Germany. 'The French government at that time,' Eisenhower later recalled, 'was passionately concerned lest the German strength become so powerful that it would take a dominant position in the Allied establishment.'[34] Churchill largely treated their delegation with rude indifference. James Hagerty, Eisenhower's press assistant, was appalled at how Churchill showed 'complete and utter distain' for them.[35] The American delegation on 5 December warned that their country would turn its back on Europe if France did not ratify the European

Defence Community. Churchill tried to placate Eisenhower and Laniel, but the truth was that it was a pointless creation that was seeking to duplicate NATO without American participation.

Churchill remained deluded in his optimistic vision of a European grand alliance minus Britain. 'There was no use in talking of the defence of Europe against Russia without Germany,' he warned.[36] Churchill then acknowledged that if the European Defence Community could not be made to work then NATO would need to be revised. He was concerned that the ongoing lack of unity over the inclusion of the West Germans would signal weakness to Moscow. Churchill said that the situation was urgent and now was not the time for further delays. The American solution was that Britain must guarantee France that it would leave its troops in Germany and if necessary join the community. This was a future expense and commitment Churchill did not want.

That evening Churchill, Eden, Eisenhower and Dulles over dinner discussed the thorny issue of a common atomic strategy. The French were excluded as they did not have nuclear weapons even though the discussions affected them. 'No atomic matters can be talked about to the French who are very sensitive at having no atomic piles or bombs,' John Colville noted in his diary.[37] At this point in the conference Laniel fell ill and was consigned to bed, leaving all the work to Bidault. Starkly Eisenhower repeated his position that if China violated the Korean armistice then America was prepared to use the bomb. The Americans were also prepared to consider using it against the Viet Minh in Indochina to help the French. In Eisenhower's mind there was no difference between atomic and conventional weapons, it was just a matter of escalation.

Neither Churchill nor Eden thought that this was remotely a good idea as it could spark a third world war. Churchill feared that although China did not have the bomb, the Soviet Union would leap to its defence and retaliate in kind against Europe. 'Even if some of us temporarily survive in some deep cellar under mounds of flaming and contaminated rubble,' said Churchill, 'there will be nothing to do but take a pill to end it all.'[38] He and Eden were so alarmed at the prospect of the atomic bomb being dropped on China that they subsequently presented their concerns to Eisenhower in writing. Churchill pointed out that the 1943 Quebec agreement signed by him and Roosevelt had granted Britain a veto over the use of the bomb. This argument did no good as Attlee's government had given up the veto. Eisenhower knew that he needed to keep the pressure up on Mao, because it was the nuclear option that had forced China and North Korea to the negotiating table in the first place.

'This morning everybody was rather in a state,' said Colville. 'First there is the momentous matter of last night's discussions which far outstrips in importance anything else at the conference.'[39] Nonetheless, on 6 December the agreed text proposing a foreign ministers' meeting with the Soviets in Berlin was sent to Konrad Adenauer. Churchill and Eisenhower were not shown the wording and Churchill was unhappy when he learned it mentioned German reunification. He thought this pointless in light of West Germany being a bulwark against Communist East Germany, but the reference nonetheless remained in. Adenauer advocated close ties with the western allies particularly America and France, even if that meant continued partition, in order to protect West Germany from the Cold War. He was also a supporter of the European Defence Community and NATO because of the security they offered. In contrast his political rival Kurt Schumacher favoured a neutral unified Germany free from western and Soviet military obligations. He felt only this would lessen the threat from Moscow.

That afternoon Churchill became increasingly frustrated over the French stance on the European Defence Community. It had been a French initiative and yet their subsequent dithering had delayed the creation of a West German army by over three years. A sticking point was the future of the Saar which France had claimed after the war, but the Saarlanders wanted to be part of Germany. Nor was Adenauer prepared to accept the integration of the Saar in to France. Churchill feared if the defence community failed and America withdrew from Europe then Britain would be left exposed and shouldering the burden. Eisenhower supported Churchill, pointing out to Bidault that without a new German army Europe's defence would inevitably be compromised. However, he did not support Germany joining NATO. Trying to sell the idea of America entering into a military alliance with a former adversary would be a controversial vote loser.

The next day the talks were dominated by Britain and France's positions in Egypt and Indochina respectively. Despite American views on empire, Churchill rather undiplomatically praised France for clinging on to Indochina and contrasted it with Britain's rushed abandonment of India. He also said how much he admired French actions in France's North African colonies. Neither comments went down well with Eisenhower and Dulles. Bidault tried to steer the conversation back to the Soviet Union. Churchill, forgetting his leading role in starting the Cold War remarked, 'If they had not been carried away by victory, something much better for all would have been feasible.'[40] Although he desperately wanted détente he knew European defence must come first.

Clementine wrote to her husband offering observations of the extensive press coverage of the conference back home. 'The general impression,' she noted, 'is that the French have been as tiresome and odious as usual.'[41] She and Mary were about to fly to Stockholm to accept the highly prestigious Nobel prize for literature on his behalf. Later Mary wrote with great pride, 'At a banquet for over 900 people Clementine read Winston's speech of thanks for this exceptional honour.'[42] Her father was also delighted with the tax-free monetary award that came with the prize, remarking cheekily, 'A little bit of sugar for the bird.'[43]

Dispiritingly Churchill came away from Bermuda on 10 December empty-handed. Eisenhower and Dulles made it clear they did not support his desire for a face-to-face with Malenkov. Churchill told Lord Moran, 'Russia, according to Ike, was out to destroy the civilised world.'[44] Nor did Eisenhower support Churchill's proposition that in return for Britain withdrawing from Egypt it should be brought under the NATO security umbrella. Churchill blamed himself, lamenting to Lord Moran, 'I have been humiliated by my own decay.'[45] He also blamed the US Secretary of State. 'Dulles is a terrible handicap,' he grumbled. 'Ten years ago I could have dealt with him.'[46] Likewise he lashed out at the French calling them 'Bloody Frogs'.[47]

Colville noted that day Churchill was 'in a cantankerous frame of mind'.[48] His aim of getting the 'Big Three' back together for an early Anglo-American-

Soviet summit had been dashed by America's understandable hostility towards the Soviet Union. Churchill observed despondently, 'They don't share my views about Russia.'[49] This was hardly surprising after Moscow crushed the East German uprising, furthermore Soviet-supplied tanks had spearheaded North Korea's opening assault. Back in London senior Conservatives, including Butler, Eden and Macmillan, began to mutter that Churchill should retire. Eden had been waiting since 1945 to take over, however, it fell to Macmillan to break the news. Elizabeth Gilliat thought this terribly unfair on Churchill, 'I felt he had so much still to give.'[50] Churchill's response was that he would not contemplate going before the next election, which could be scheduled as late as the end of 1956. 'He'd hate resigning and I thought it a pity that he shouldn't be allowed to carry on till he dropped,' adds Gilliatt. The Conservatives remained stuck with him unless his health finally gave out.

The Americans, like Churchill, were exasperated by the French and tried to keep the European Defence Community treaty alive. Dulles on 14 December, while addressing NATO, moved to reassure his audience that it would not signal an American withdrawal. Instead he warned its failure might have exactly that result. Eden was alarmed by this especially as Dulles had told him that their two countries 'were approaching a parting of the ways' and that 'the United States might swing over to a policy of western hemispheric defence'.[51] The last thing Churchill and Eden wanted in the face of the Cold War was a return to American isolationism.

Churchill's failure in Bermuda was mocked in the House of Commons by the Opposition on 17 December. He tried to put a brave face on things by declaring, 'I can assure the House that the first object of the Bermuda Conference was to nourish Anglo-American friendship and co-operation; and that, I am sure, has been achieved.'[52] It is doubtful that Eisenhower would have agreed with him. Lord Moran who was watching from the gallery recalled, 'He had nothing new to tell them, but it was done with verve and vigour.'[53] The gist of Churchill's speech was a warning about France rejecting the European Defence Community and the impact it would have on NATO. 'At Bermuda I made it clear that we should keep our troops on the Continent,' added Churchill, 'at least as long as the American troops were kept there.'[54]

In response Labour leader Clement Attlee scathingly called him 'a Father Christmas without any presents'.[55] This stung Churchill who regretted having told Attlee before the conference that Bermuda could be 'the definite step to a meeting of greater import'.[56] Referring to Eisenhower's initiative to share atomic energy Attlee further showed up Churchill's achievements. 'I think the right hon. Gentleman kept his only present until the end,' said Attlee grinning, 'and that was really President Eisenhower's.'[57]

Churchill was further disappointed when the Berlin conference, which commenced in late January 1954, achieved absolutely zilch regarding European security. Eden glumly reported, 'Opening was much as expected. Molotov produced nothing new.'[58] Molotov immediately opposed the idea of elections in Germany and reunification. He told Eden that Soviet security arrangements in eastern Europe were designed to protect the Soviet Union from Germany, whereas

NATO was clearly an anti-Soviet alliance. 'I am more than ever convinced that the sooner this conference ends its discussions of the German side of our affairs the better,' Eden advised Churchill.[59] The only positive outcome was that it was agreed the foreign ministers should reconvene in Geneva to settle the wars in Indochina and Korea. This would result in the birth of Cambodia, Laos and a partitioned Vietnam, unfortunately sowing the seeds for the Vietnam War.

Eisenhower had no intention of doing Churchill any favours, especially as he saw the conflicts in Kenya and Malaya as colonial wars that were needlessly tying down British troops. As far as he was concerned they would have been of greater value in Korea and western Europe. By this stage Britain had 800,000 men serving in the armed forces; around 300,000 of them were National Servicemen. This was a staggeringly large number for what was supposedly peacetime. Macmillan observed that 'this method of maintaining distant garrisons was becoming more and more expensive'.[60] Britain also had reserves of 600,000.

Ultimately the failure at Bermuda and Berlin to secure a meeting with Malenkov did British strategic interests no real harm. However, Churchill's failure to get Eisenhower's backing for Egypt to be encompassed under NATO's security blanket left Britain with no fall-back plan to safeguard the Suez Canal. Without international support Churchill was forced to agree to the Anglo-Egyptian Treaty of July 1954 which ended the British occupation of Egypt. Crucially this severed Britain's strategic hold on the lines of communication across the Mediterranean, the Red Sea and the Indian Ocean. It also precipitated the Suez Crisis. Churchill was right that in the event of a third world war NATO would need to hold Suez, but Eisenhower was just not interested in propping up Britain's position.

Eisenhower, pursing the usual American anti-British Empire policy, in July 1954 even suggested to Churchill that he make his legacy a declaration announcing self-determination within twenty-five years for all of Britain's remaining colonies. Churchill ever the die-hard imperialist responded acerbically, 'I am a bit sceptical about universal suffrage for hottentots.'[61] By which he meant Africans. Despite this the following month with the collapse of the European Defence Community, Churchill decided that the only way ahead was an Anglo-German-American alliance. He was prepared to pursue this even if it meant abandoning the French just as he had done in 1940. 'We picked them out of the gutter and now they think of nothing but themselves all the time,' he fumed.[62] Anthony Eden though moved to prevent the destruction of western European unity by setting in motion the acceptance of West Germany into NATO with French and American agreement. This diplomatic triumph was his alone not Churchill's. Under NATO's banner western Europe would continue to face down the Soviet Union and its satellite states for decades to come.

Unfortunately though Churchill and Eden's desire to see West German troops enrolled in the defence of Europe made matters far worse, not better. Even Eisenhower naively claimed 'it seemed impossible … that Germany could become a menace to the peace as a military entity.'[63] West Germany joining NATO and the ending of the occupation of Austria fuelled the Cold War even more. When all the former wartime Allied powers withdrew from Austria in 1955, it meant the Soviets needed a reason to continue stationing troops in Hungary and Romania.

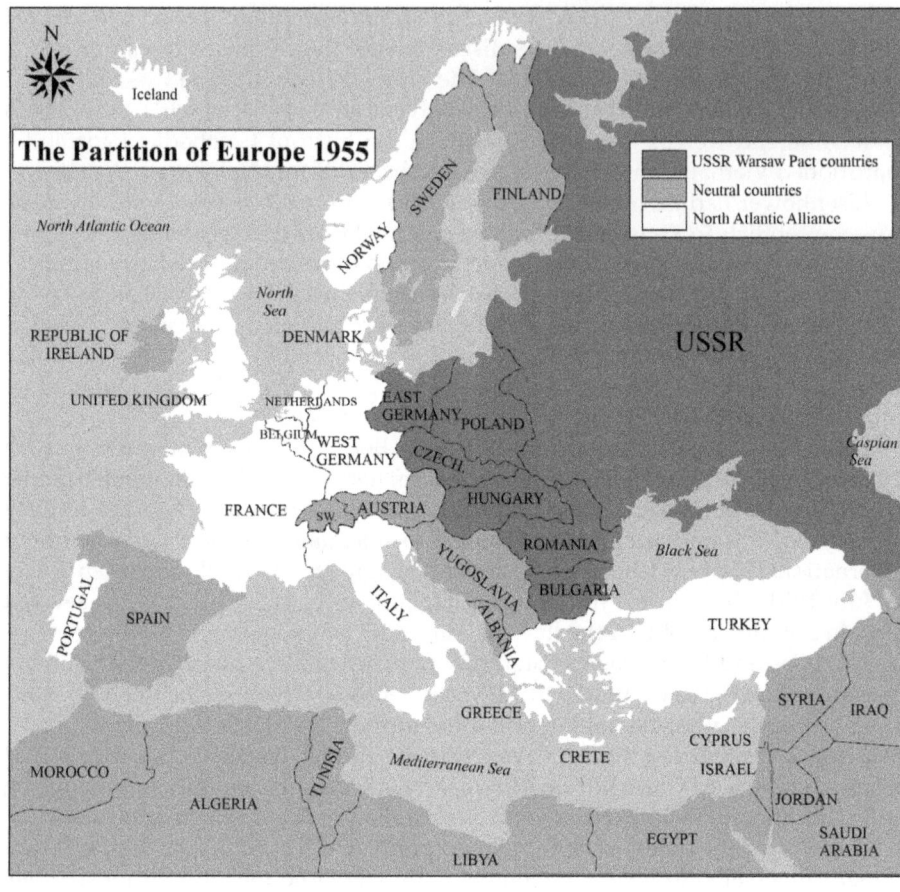

Previously they had been able to argue these deployments kept open Soviet lines of communication to their occupation forces in Austria. Moscow decided that the series of bilateral military pacts, which it had employed since the end of the Second World War to bind eastern Europe to the Soviet Union, were no longer sufficient. It wanted its own version of NATO. The leaders of Albania, Bulgaria, Czechoslovakia, East Germany, Hungary, Poland, Romania and the Soviet Union met in Warsaw on 14 May 1955, and fatefully signed a Treaty of Friendship, Co-operation and Mutual Support.

The creation of the Warsaw Pact occurred just one day before the conclusion of the Austrian State Treaty, which declared the country neutral territory. Moscow had hoped that West Germany would adopt a similar stance. Austria along with neutral Switzerland now split NATO in half cutting its lines of communication with Italy. Likewise, neutral Yugoslavia cut off Greece and Turkey from the rest of NATO. It's members were understandably alarmed that observer nations at the

Warsaw gathering included China, Mongolia, North Korea and North Vietnam, all Communist states with anti-Western agendas.

Although the Warsaw Pact was supposed to be a defensive alliance of equals there was no hiding its complete domination by Moscow. The Pact's commander-in-chief was a Soviet Marshal, while the military structure was headed by a Soviet deputy defence minister who was in charge of the Joint High Command. The latter's headquarters were conveniently located in Moscow and it had responsibility for training, tactics and weaponry. This meant that the non-Soviet Warsaw Pact members had to adhere to Soviet doctrine and employ Soviet arms. In the event of war all east European forces would come under Soviet commanders. Air defence was to be controlled by Moscow even in peace time. Overnight the Soviet Union solidified its hold on eastern Europe.

Inevitably this left the two halves of Europe in a permanent armed stand-off along the Iron Curtain, with either side regularly fearing attack by the other. This situation enflamed global Cold War paranoia. Ironically though the Warsaw Pact was to prove a greater menace to its members than NATO. When first Hungary and later Czechoslovakia tried to leave their aspirations for independence would be brutally crushed by the Warsaw Pact's tanks.

Chapter 16

The Bear and the Bomb

After the atomic bomb was dropped on Japan, Churchill knew it was only a matter of time before Stalin developed his own weapon. This would inevitably usher in a new era of warfare – one that could threaten the very future of the planet. The problem was that no one fully understood what had been unleashed. Journalist Malcolm Muggeridge who visited Hiroshima in 1946 recalled, 'I personally came across no one in any walk of life who had moral qualms at the time. Attlee subsequently disclosed the fact that he had never... heard talk of fall-out.'[1]

To make matters worse Britain and America fell out over the future of nuclear weapons. Churchill and Roosevelt had agreed during the Second World War that Britain and America would pool information on the bomb. However, at the end of 1945 Senator Brien McMahon, who was unaware of this, pushed a bill through Congress seeking to restrict the sharing of nuclear secrets. McMahon was Chairman of the US Atomic Energy Committee. His intention was that the development of nuclear power be kept out of the hands of the military and to prevent nuclear proliferation. This meant shutting out Britain and Canada who had been partners in the Manhattan project, which had led to the development of the American bomb. Attlee's Labour government failed to oppose this and the bill became law the following summer. Churchill was incensed and called it 'a breach of faith'.[2]

Although Churchill greatly valued the deterrence value of America possessing the atomic bomb, he knew the Americans would never be able to maintain their monopoly on such weapons. As far as Stalin was concerned America had developed a strategic advantage that could be used to keep Communist ambitions in check. 'We ought not to wait until Russia is ready,' Churchill told Lord Moran on 8 August 1946. 'I believe it will be eight years before she has these bombs.'[3] At the end of the year Churchill's son-in-law Duncan Sandys, who was a leading figure in the European Movement, briefed him following a trip to France. 'General de Gaulle considered that until such time as she developed the atomic bomb,' said Sandys, 'Russia would be most unlikely to provoke war.' However, de Gaulle's longer-term prognosis was not good. Sandys added, 'He was of the opinion that war between the Western Democracies and Soviet Russia was sooner or later a virtual certainty.'[4]

'America was conducting its foreign policy from a position of strength,' observed Nikita Khrushchev. 'The Americans had the atomic bomb, and they knew we didn't.'[5] Stalin, in light of the example set by the bombing of Hiroshima and Nagasaki had little reason to believe that America would not use the bomb against the Soviet Union. 'To make matters worse,' adds Khrushchev, 'The President was Truman, ...who was hostile and spiteful towards the Soviet Union.'[6] Certainly Truman made it no secret that he would not hesitate to use the bomb if the safety of America and democracy was in peril. However, he hoped that the creation of NATO to defend Europe would make such a decision unnecessary. Truman's stance alarmed Churchill because he feared America would deploy atomic bombs from British soil without British permission.

In some western circles it was felt the threat of nuclear war should be used to wring concessions from the Soviet leadership before the Soviet Union acquired the atomic bomb. Others postulated that perhaps the West should fight a preventative war while it still had the advantage. 'Western Nations will be far more likely to reach a lasting settlement, without bloodshed,' Churchill told the Conservative party conference on 9 October 1948, 'if they formulate their just demands while they have the atomic power and before the Russian Communists have got it too.'[7] Harold Nicolson observed in his diary on 29 November 1948, 'I think it is probably true that Russia is preparing for the final battle for world mastery and once she has enough bombs she will destroy Western Europe, occupy Asia and have a final death struggle with the Americas.'[8] It was a bleak prospect just three years after the end of the Second World War.

Churchill, in a letter to Field Marshal Montgomery in February 1949 which he decided not to send, speculated that the only way to stop a Soviet advance in Europe was by using the bomb. He made his views clear on its role while in America that year. The *New York Herald Tribune's* headline trumpeted, 'Churchill Declares Atom Bomb Alone Deters Russia from War'.[9] Not long after, Truman wrote to Churchill to praise his stance. 'I was deeply impressed by your statement about not fearing to use the atomic bomb if the need arose,' said the president. 'I am sure this will do more than anything else to ward off the catastrophe of a third world war.'[10]

The Soviets conducted their first successful atomic weapons test on 29 August 1949. Attlee and Truman did not make this public until 23 September. 'We are all feeling depressed about the Russian atomic bomb,' wrote Harold Nicolson the following day. 'We were told that they would not have one for five years, and they have got it in four.'[11] It would be another two years before they conducted two more tests. Significantly the latter included the first bomb delivered from the air. Churchill, during his speech in Zurich in 1946, warned, 'In these present days we dwell strangely and precariously under the shield and protection of the atomic bomb.'[12] Afterwards he informed Lord Moran, 'Only the atomic bomb keeps the Russians back.' Then in some alarm he claimed, 'They're making rockets to fire on us when they get to the coast.'[13] They now had the bomb.

General Eisenhower though was not impressed and greatly underestimated Soviet manufacturing capabilities. 'Although they were able to make an atomic bomb within four years of the time we first exploded one,' he noted in his memoirs, 'and although they had their scientific community pool of theoretical genius and engineering talent, the ingenuities of mass production... for the equipping of an army or for the convenience of a people were still a mystery.'[14]

However, Western intelligence was aware that in the late 1940s the Soviet Union had successfully reverse-engineered the American B-29 Superfortress bomber. A number of these had fallen into Soviet hands during the Second World War and Stalin put it into production as the Tu-4. The fact that it could reach Los Angeles understandably caused a sense of panic. By 1952 the Soviets had a fleet of 850 of them. It was followed by a whole series of Soviet strategic jet bombers all capable of reaching America. Further Soviet atomic bomb tests were conducted throughout the early 1950s.

Stalin's nuclear efforts were greatly assisted by spies in both Britain and America. Dr Klaus Fuchs, a German refugee, was arrested in Britain on 3 February 1950 for betraying atomic secrets to Stalin over a seven year period.[15] He had worked at Los Alamos and been closely involved with the Manhattan project. 'Our whole position in this atomic sphere has been worsened since the war by the fact that the Russians,' Churchill lamented to the House of Commons, 'unexpectedly as the Minister [of Defence] admitted, have acquired the secrets of the atomic bomb, and are said to have begun its manufacture.'[16] Fuchs' actions immediately impacted on Britain's efforts to develop an independent nuclear deterrent. America imposed a complete ban for nine years on sharing any atomic secrets despite Britain's leading role in the Manhattan project.[17]

'General Omar Bradly said that "in three or four years the Soviets would have a sufficient supply of these weapons to cause a major catastrophe"', noted Churchill in May 1950. 'At any rate they will have in three to four years both overwhelming military superiority in Europe and a formidable supply of atomic bombs.'[18] Attlee's government was so alarmed that it offered Truman a base in East Anglia from which to deploy nuclear weapons against the Soviet Union. 'We are therefore a prime target for attack,' concluded Churchill.[19] That summer Churchill criticised Attlee for failing to produce a single British atomic bomb. He could not understand why after Britain's involvement in the Manhattan project and all its subsequent research there was nothing to show for it. In contrast he pointed out the Soviet Union had overcome all its difficulties and had started production.

On 14 December he told the House of Commons that the idea of only using the atomic bomb in retaliation was silly. He reasoned that the Soviet Union would have no such scruples. 'Its potential use is,' said Churchill, 'the only lever by which we can hope to obtain reasonable consideration in an attempt to make a peaceful settlement with Soviet Russia.'[20] However, by the end of the year Churchill became increasingly worried by the prospect of Truman using atomic bombs to stop Chinese intervention in the Korean War.

During the general election of 1951 Churchill warned of the horrors of nuclear conflict. 'For another world war would not be like the Crusades or the romantic struggles in former centuries...,' he said at a rally in Plymouth. 'It would be nothing less than a massacre of human beings whether in uniform or out of uniform by the hideous forces of perverted science.'[21] He soon found that he had these 'hideous forces' at his disposal. When Churchill became Prime Minister he discovered that

Attlee's Labour government had in fact got to the point of producing an atomic bomb. 'Considerable if slow progress has been made,' Churchill informed the House of Commons on 6 December 1951. 'All that I will say is that we have taken over the very costly production of the Socialist Government. We have not decided on any important change in policy or principle.'[22] He planned to press on in order to give Britain its own independent nuclear deterrent.

First though Churchill sought agreement from Truman that America would not use the base in East Anglia to deploy the atomic bomb without British consent. A formal written arrangement was reached in January 1952 while Churchill was in Washington. The Korean War was at its height and when he addressed Congress he urged restraint. 'If I may say this, Member of Congress, be careful above all things, therefore,' he urged, 'not to let go of the atomic weapon until you are sure, …that other means of preserving peace are in your hands.' Looking round he added that it was imperative they 'ward off the fearful catastrophe'.[23] Churchill then met Senator McMahon who was still Chairman of the Senatorial Atomic Energy Committee. He showed him the terms of the original agreement with President Roosevelt about the atomic bomb. McMahon was aghast. 'If we had known this the Act would not have been passed,' he explained. 'Attlee never said a word.'[24]

Churchill announced on 17 February 1952 that Britain was ready to conduct its very first atomic bomb test. Nine days later he informed the House of Commons about America's undertaking regarding deployment of the American bomb from British soil. He also told the House, 'I was not aware until I took office that not only had the Socialist Government made the atomic bomb as a matter of research, … they had created… the important plant necessary for its regular production. This weapon will be tested in the course of the present year.'[25] The British test occurred on 3 October in the Monte Bello Islands, western Australia. This made Britain the third country to develop and test nuclear weapons. The first deployable weapon was a free-fall bomb dubbed Blue Danube, which was delivered to the Royal Air Force in late 1953. However, it would be another two years before the bombers capable of carrying it became available. The first Blue Danube was dropped in Maralinga in southern Australia in October 1956.[26]

Inevitably Britain's financial constraints impacted on vital policy decisions. Churchill instructed the chiefs of staff to formulate a global strategy paper in early 1952. Sir John Slessor, the Chief of the Air Staff, controversially argued that the Royal Air Force should now take priority because of its role in delivering the atomic bomb. He was alarmed to report that 'at the present time we held only four weeks' reserves of jet aviation fuel calculated at intensive rates.'[27] In other words the Royal Air Force could fight for a month and then would be grounded. As far as Slessor was concerned the existence of the bomb now vindicated the supremacy of air power.

When the chiefs of staff gathered at the Royal Naval College at Greenwich in July 1952 the army and navy heads reluctantly agreed to Slessor's proposals. Their tri-service 1952 Global Strategy Paper proposed three pillars comprising the defence of the British Isles; holding on to Suez to safeguard communications with the Far East and Australia and retention of the bases in Hong Kong and Singapore.

It also recognized the importance of the Persian Gulf. The paper emphasised placing less importance on conventional forces and greater reliance on nuclear deterrence. This was a seismic shift in military thinking. 'Unfortunately, we are faced with the ironical fact that while nuclear war seems capable of destroying society,' observed Field Marshal Montgomery, 'the means to avert it consist in building up the means to wage it.'[28]

Behind closed doors it was reasoned that this would increase Britain's standing with Washington while also lessening Britain's reliance on America's nuclear umbrella. A real concern remained that at some point America would pull out of Europe. The paper's proposals met with approval from Churchill and the cash-strapped Chancellor of the Exchequer. Slessor reasoned that a strategy of nuclear deterrence, backed by the development of tactical nuclear weapons to be deployed by the British Army of the Rhine, would greatly reduce defence costs particularly when it came to manpower. The army and the navy though were not convinced that the use of nuclear weapons would be decisive in any future global conflict. The army pointed out that nuclear weapons were of no help with counter-insurgency warfare in places like Kenya and Malaya. The threat of the bomb had little utility in deterring nationalist guerrillas. Likewise, the bomb could not effectively safeguard shipping lanes against enemy submarines and warships. Both services insisted that the Global Strategy Paper include a section highlighting that there would inevitably be a period of conventional fighting even after a nuclear exchange. This was done to protect their portions of the defence budget at a time when they were already facing overstretch.

In the case of the British army, it had the equivalent of five divisions deployed in Europe and almost six divisions elsewhere overseas. 'My first impression on looking round the scene at home in November as Minister of Defence,' Churchill told the House of Commons on 5 March 1952,' was a sense of extreme nakedness such as I had never felt before in peace or war – almost as though I was living in a nudist colony.'[29] He was so anxious about the threat of war and Britain's manpower problems that he called for the re-forming of the Home Guard and the creation of a Territorial Army. Some 30,000 men had been registered for the Home Guard at this point. Initially he was loathe to issue them with equipment, then ordered that 50,00 uniforms be made available from mobilization reserves. 'If war should come,' he warned the Commons, 'it will be with violent speed and suddenness... with almost all our regular Army overseas, we must rely to an unusual extent on the Home Guard.'[30] He also acknowledged, 'Today there is still in Europe and in the world a total lack of balance of power in conventional weapons, and this unbalance of power is only redressed by the terrible threat of the atom bomb.'[31]

When Slessor visited Washington to brief President Truman in the summer of 1952, he found the Americans were not receptive to an over-reliance on nuclear weapons. Truman suspected that this was a ploy by Churchill to save money and avoid boosting his conventional forces. This would be in defiance of a NATO agreement to strengthen their armies in Europe. Britain's decision to rely on deterrence though ended up swaying NATO. In December its members agreed to major reductions in planned troop levels. Ironically this was something that neither Churchill nor Truman really wanted. However, most NATO countries were reluctant to increase defence spending while they were still recovering from the Second World War. British thinking would also end up gaining traction in America. Slessor's ideas were adopted by Eisenhower when he became president the following year.

At the end of 1952 the Americans tested a hydrogen bomb, which was 450 times more powerful than the bomb used against Nagasaki. 'The atomic bomb,' said Churchill, 'with all its terrors, did not carry us outside the scope of human control.'[32] Once the hydrogen bomb had replaced the atomic bomb it meant America would have the ability to destroy not only entire cities but entire countries. This added a new urgency to the nuclear arms race. The Soviets announced on 12 August 1953 following a test detonation they had also developed a hydrogen bomb. 'That power could be developed into such a powerful offensive weapon,' noted Field Marshal Montgomery, 'that it was clear that no profit from war could come to any nation.'[33] Churchill warned John Colville, 'We must not go further on the path of war unless we are sure there is no other path to peace.'[34]

Churchill, in late 1953 while in Bermuda, grumbled to Lord Moran about the Soviets' growing nuclear capability. 'There was a time when the Western Powers could have used the atomic bomb without any reply by Russia,' he said. 'That time has gone.'[35] The threat of conventional and nuclear war in Europe meant that Britain and America were forced to turn their occupation zones in Germany into forward-operating bases. To counter the threat of Soviet air attack both the Royal Air Force and the United States Air Force deployed considerable forces to a whole series of airbases scattered across West Germany. At one point the RAF had almost 40; key amongst these was RAF Rheindahlen. British fighter pilots serving with the quick response squadrons trained to scramble within minutes to meet the Communist menace over central Europe. One of their main roles was to guard against Soviet bombers carrying nuclear weapons.

As the Cold War gathered pace it was decided that the RAF and the British Army of the Rhine needed a joint headquarters. Work began in the early 1950s at Rheindahlen in Mönchengladbach, North Rhine-Westphalia. RAF Rheindahlen came into being in 1954 as the headquarters for the 2nd Allied Tactical Air Force. Another key RAF station was Gütersloh, which was the nearest British airbase to the East German border. It had previously been home to Luftwaffe night-fighters that had fought to defend Hitler's Reich.

Just after the Second World War the first British Meteor and Vampire jet fighters were introduced into service. By 1950, although the RAF was rapidly becoming an all-jet force, it still had 600 Spitfires held in reserve. In May 1951 the RAF saw the arrival of its first jet bombers with the successful Canberra twin-jet aircraft. In contrast the swept-wing Hawker Hunter fighter proved a troubled aircraft and required considerable fine-tuning. As a stopgap Churchill's government purchased the American-built F-86 Sabre swept-wing jet fighter. From 1953 to 1956 Sabres equipped a total of twelve British squadrons. All of these, except for two, were stationed in Germany. The Hawker Hunter went into service with the RAF in July 1954. It would equip twelve squadrons in the UK and another twelve in Germany. Some 500 Hunters were delivered by September 1955.

The Americans occupied a number of former Luftwaffe bases in Bavaria, which was included in the American Occupation Zone. One of their key airbases was at Ramstein. In 1948 the Berlin Blockade by the Soviet Union made it evident that the location of United States Air Force Europe units so close to the East German and Czechoslovakian borders was not wise. After the creation of NATO the following year the Americans decided that their vulnerable fighter units should be redeployed west of the Rhine to ensure greater air defence warning times. This led to the creation of the base at Ramstein. France also agreed to provide airbase sites within the French Occupation Zone in the Rhineland-Palatinate.

The developing Soviet nuclear threat added an additional dimension to tensions not only in Europe but also North America. For America, Canada, Denmark, which is responsible for Greenland, and the Soviet Union the Arctic Circle became a new and vast frontline. The threat of a Soviet strategic bomber carrying an atomic bomb across the North Pole brought the Cold War to America's doorstep. Truman was obliged to create US Air Defense Command in 1946, which had responsibility for the integrated air defence of continental United States. For a brief period it was wound up, but with the outbreak of the Korean War was swiftly reactivated. To do its job effectively Air Defense Command had to be given plenty of warning that the enemy were on their way. Initially the USAF and the Royal Canadian Air Force created the Pinetree Line to provide early warning of Soviet bomber attacks. This consisted of a series of radar stations located across southern Canada on the 53rd and 50th parallels. Before it was even operational Pinetree was rendered obsolete by rapid advances in technology. The advent of the jet engine meant attackers would be well inside North American airspace before the defenders could react, also the pulse-based radars could not pick up targets close to the ground and were easy to jam.[36]

'I am more worried by the hydrogen bomb,' Churchill confided in Lord Moran after America's latest test in the Marshall Islands on 1 March 1954, 'than by all the rest of my troubles put together.'[37] His concerns were well-founded. After the scare over America potentially using nuclear weapons in the Korean War, this was swiftly repeated in Indochina. The French had known that they were facing defeat there since at least the end of the previous year. Their northern enclave around Hanoi was in grave danger from Ho Chi Minh's Viet Minh forces. Harold Nicolson dined at the French Embassy in London with Robert Schuman, the French Foreign Secretary. 'He speaks sadly to me afterwards about the disaster in Indochina,' Nicolson wrote in his diary. 'He fears that all these years of fighting will have been in vain, since France will have to abandon that empire.'[38] In a state of alarm John Foster Dulles, the US Secretary of State, informed Admiral Arthur Radford, chairman of the US Joint Chiefs of Staff, 'We could lose Europe, Asia and Africa all at once if we don't watch out.'[39]

France's position had become militarily and politically untenable. The French knew that if they were to withdraw from Indochina and avoid handing it over to Ho Chi Minh's Communists, they must first triumph over the Viet Minh. They foolishly decided to give battle at Dien Bien Phu in the heart of a long-isolated valley. By early 1954 thanks to Chinese military support the Viet Minh were on the verge of decisively defeating the French. In response Eisenhower and Dulles began to lobby Churchill and Eden to support international military intervention. Eisenhower wrote personally to Churchill on 4 April 1954 seeking to appeal to the Second World War's champion of democracy. 'If I may refer…,' he said, 'to history, we failed to halt Hirohito, Mussolini and Hitler by not acting in unity and in time. …May it not be that our nations have learned something from the lesson.'[40]

Churchill may have found this rather amusing as it was American non-interventionism which had prevented America's initial opposition to German, Italian and Japanese expansionism. Furthermore, he found it infuriating that America was prepared to rescue the French but would not tolerate British colonial policies. Regardless of the Communist threat to Malaya and Singapore, Churchill had no intention of intervening in Indochina. Attlee had rescued the French in Indochina in 1946, but now they were almost beyond help. Mao on 4 April ordered General Wei Guoqing, his military advisor to Ho Ch Minh, 'Try to complete the Dien Bien Phu campaign by… early May.'[41] Churchill's stance hardened even further when he learned that Eisenhower was considering the nuclear option to stop Ho Chi Minh.

Colonel Christian de Castries, the commandant at Dien Bien Phu, was desperate for someone, anyone, to blast the Viet Minh's guns off the surrounding hills. He did not care if this involved conventional or nuclear bombs as long as it had the desired effect. His own artillery and the French air force, despite the enormous volume of firepower they laid down, had singularly failed to do so. Ironically the Viet Minh's American-built 105mm howitzers had been supplied by Mao. His Communist forces captured large quantities of them during the Chinese Civil War and the Korean War. They were now being employed to relentlessly shell the exposed French airstrip. Slowly but surely the French were being cut off from all outside help.

Other than surrender the French had three choices. Firstly with Operation Condor they could fight a relief column through to the trapped garrison. At the same time the latter could fight its way out with Operation Albatross. The problem was that French forces were not strong enough to achieve either. Nor did they have sufficient air lift to maintain the base. The only remaining option, if Eisenhower would agree, was to pound the Viet Minh into withdrawing using American bombers. General Earle Partridge, commanding the US Far East Air Forces, arrived in Saigon on 14 April just as Condor was authorized, to prepare an American feasibility study. His bomber commander, General Joseph Caldera, flew over Dien Bien Phu three times and concluded that a daytime raid could be conducted successfully. Both generals, though, were concerned the French lacked comprehension of the destructive power of the B-29 Superfortress heavy bomber.

The Secretary of State for the French Air Force, M. Christiaens, very publicly announced on 15 April, that France had asked if it could borrow American B-29s that would be operated by French crews. Such a facade fooled no one, as the French had no experience operating this type of bomber. Eisenhower was presented with plans that envisaged deploying up to 200 American bombers from Manila and Okinawa to destroy the Viet Minh's positions around Dien Bien Phu. Proposals also considered deploying 150 fighter aircraft from the US Seventh Fleet to provide escort cover for 60 bombers.

It was now, much to Churchill's alarm, that the threat of nuclear war once again reared its ugly head. 'In Washington the Joint Chiefs of Staff devised a plan, known as Operation Vulture,' recalled Vice President Richard Nixon, 'for using three small tactical atomic bombs to destroy Viet Minh positions and relieve the garrison.'[42] French Foreign Minister Georges Bidault confirmed that Dulles had offered to make at least two such bombs available. Admiral Radford backed going nuclear. America had considered doing so in Korea to stop the Chinese, but decided that this would be a step too far in escalating the conflict. Besides which, the decision to authorize the atomic bombing of Japan continued to haunt many American policy-makers. South Korea had been saved without resorting to the bomb, but now northern Indochina faced being overrun by the Communists.

These public discussions about American bombers and nuclear weapons may have been part of a deliberate ploy to get Mao to pressure Ho Chi Minh to slacken his grip on Dien Bien Phu. Mao acquiesced to the status quo in Korea, partly due to Eisenhower's threats to use tactical nuclear weapons. Eisenhower now had to make a terrible decision over Indochina. It was the same dilemma he and Truman faced in Korea with not goading China into an all-out global war. If he agreed to help France, then his actions might save the French garrison, but there was no knowing how China or the Soviet Union might respond. Using American-crewed bombers to drop conventional or nuclear bombs would herald America's entry into the Indochina War. Mao might well react by committing ground forces. They would simply overwhelm the French in Hanoi if the Americans did not put boots on the ground as well.

Eisenhower desperately needed Churchill's backing with any sort of military action, but his old ally would simply not sanction it. Dulles on 20 April called a meeting in Washington of the ambassadors of Australia, Britain, Cambodia, France, Laos, New Zealand, the Philippines, Thailand and Vietnam to agree a united course of action. Churchill and Eden instructed Sir Roger Makins, the British Ambassador, not to attend. Eden said that Britain was not prepared 'to endorse a bad policy for the sake of unity'.[43] This made the conference a nugatory exercise.

Dulles met with Eden in the margins of a NATO meeting in Paris on 24 April. He informed the Foreign Secretary that with British support Eisenhower would seek permission from Congress for a large-scale intervention. Congress, after the losses of the Korean War, was in no mood for another major military adventure, however, Churchill might sway them. Eden immediately flew back to London to consult Churchill. He need not have bothered. 'Anthony says he won't agree,' Clarissa Eden noted in her diary, 'and if they go in it will mean fighting China and setting off a Third World War.'[44]

The British Cabinet and Chief of Staffs on 25 April agreed unanimously not to get involved. Eisenhower though was not done. That afternoon a message reached Churchill stating that the Americans were poised to bomb the Viet Minh within 72 hours of gaining British approval. Eden was furious as this would derail the Geneva Conference which was just about to start and escalate the Indochina War. 'What we are being asked to do,' Churchill told the reconvened Cabinet, 'was in effect to aid in misleading Congress into approving a military operation which would be ineffective and might well bring the world to the verge of a major war.'[45] The following day Admiral Radford arrived in London and painted a dire picture of what would happen if America and Britain did not step in. Churchill refused to budge from his position.

Eisenhower's proposals had made Churchill angry. 'The French want us to look after France in Europe while America watches over her Empire. It just won't do,' he grumbled to Lord Moran.[46] Britain's defence budget was stretched to the limit and the Korean War had proved very unpopular with the public. Furthermore, Churchill was well aware that British intelligence had cautioned against meddling in Indochina, assessing that, 'Any direct intervention by the armed forces of any external nation would probably lead to Chinese intervention, and there is a danger that it might ultimately lead to a global war.'[47]

Churchill was fearful that the use of nuclear weapons in Indochina may spark 'an assault by hydrogen bombs on these islands… and of all the nations involved, the United States would suffer the least.'[48] It was hard to conceive of a scenario where America dropped nuclear bombs on the Viet Minh without provoking China and the Soviet Union. American soil and American troops were not in danger so Eisenhower could not take the moral high ground with such an aggressive act. In the end, he prudently decided against implementing Operation Vulture. Dulles was furious because he believed that Eden had reneged on a joint commitment to help save the French.

What Churchill and Eisenhower did not know was that the battle being fought at Dien Bien Phu was all or nothing for the Viet Minh. It was a last roll of the dice for Ho Chi Minh who hoped to be able to negotiate a ceasefire at Geneva from a position of strength. He had warned Mao that if he lost at Dien Bien Phu his forces would have to retreat to the Chinese border. At that stage he wanted Mao to intervene against the French. In Geneva the Chinese Foreign Minister Zhou Enlai told Nikita Khrushchev that China had lost too many men in Korea. 'We simply can't grant Comrade Ho Chi Minh's request,' said Zhou. 'We're in no condition to get involved in another war at this time.'[49] Khrushchev cautioned him not to tell Ho Chi Minh for fear that the Viet Minh's morale might collapse if they knew the Chinese would not help. Zhou agreed to keep quiet. Mao had instructed Zhou that he 'definitely must have a settlement'.[50] He also ordered that after Geneva if the Viet Minh continued fighting they would be on their own.

It was made very evident in Paris and Hanoi that the Cold War and the nuclear deterrent did not extend to French colonial conflicts. The trapped French were left to fend for themselves. Foreign Minister Bidault in his memoirs later claimed that it was he who had rejected America's offer of nuclear weapons. He alleged that he had told Dulles the 'defenders will suffer as much as the assailants' and that if the bombs were used against China 'there's a risk of generalized war'.[51] This runs completely counter to France seeking help and Bidault probably said this to save his own political reputation. He did not want to go down in history as the man prepared to kill his own people in order to stop Communism.

Dien Bien Phu's garrison was finally overwhelmed on 7 May 1954 and 9,000 French troops, including Colonel de Castries, were captured. Overnight France lost control of northern Indochina. Shortly after, Harold Nicolson and historian Hugh Thomas arrived in Paris and received a frosty reception at the restaurant *Le Grand Véfour*. The French never forgave the British and Americans for their betrayal. Churchill though was just grateful that nuclear war had once again been averted. Twice now Eisenhower had narrowly avoided using nuclear weapons.

Churchill understood that, despite all the ongoing preparations in Europe and America, fighting a nuclear war was pointless. The end result would be mutually assured destruction as there was no way of winning. 'We cannot at present defend ourselves against an atomic attack,' he told Lord Moran in early May 1954. 'We should not even have time to evacuate the great cities.'[52] He tried to shape American perceptions of the most devastating weapon of all time. 'Churchill still wielded great influence in the United States,' said his daughter Mary, 'and had visited President Eisenhower in June 1954, when the full implications of the power of the hydrogen bomb were being appraised.'[53] He went armed with the British Chiefs of Staff paper on global strategy. 'His realistic understanding of the changed nuclear scene,' adds Mary, 'had a distinct impact on American attitudes and policy.'[54]

'In September 1954,' noted Field Marshal Montgomery, 'a Japanese fisherman died from jaundice brought on by radiation sickness caused by exposure to "fall-out" – and public opinion throughout the world became alarmed, demanding a suspension of testing in the atmosphere.'[55] A binding agreement between America and the Soviet Union proved almost impossible. Churchill's only real hope of ending the Cold War was through change within the Soviet Union. The Soviet bear now had the bomb and had to be treated even more carefully than ever. War needed to be avoided at all costs, or as Churchill put it, 'Europe would be shattered and subjugated'.[56] At the end of 1955 the Soviets tested their first true multi-stage hydrogen bomb. Churchill reasoned, 'The policy of deterrent cannot rest on nuclear weapons alone. We must, together with our NATO allies, maintain the defensive shield in Western Europe.'[57] Field Marshal Montgomery agreed with him. 'We now have the deterrent and it is a good one,' he wrote in his memoirs, 'it has prevented a major war. But it is doubtful the deterrent is also a good defence.'[58]

Four years later Eisenhower, defending spending cuts to the US armed forces, told Congress that a conventional ground war in Europe could not be won. Instead America would have to rely on other means. In response Clementine wrote to Winston on 13 March 1959 saying, 'Everyone I meet is shocked at Ike's statement about using the hydrogen bomb on Russia and dispensing with ground forces.'[59] Churchill never believed in the utility of the bomb except as part of a combined armed deterrent. 'Unless we were prepared to unleash a full-scale nuclear war as soon as some local incident occurs in some distant country,' he said, 'we must have conventional forces in readiness to deal with such situations as they arise.'[60] This measured view was to shape the defence of Western Europe by NATO over the decades. Despite the eventual introduction of tactical nuclear weapons into Europe, conventional forces remained the backbone of NATO's defensive measures.

Chapter 17

Petty Central American Issues

Churchill, apart from his visit to Havana in 1946 as a guest of the Cuban government, showed little interest in Latin America after the Second World War. During the conflict he had deliberately exaggerated the Nazi threat there as part of his campaign to get Roosevelt's support for Britain. Post-war Truman, and then Eisenhower, began to fear the emergence of Left-leaning governments hostile to extensive US business interests in the region. America had a track record of backing regime change in those countries formerly ruled by Spain that showed the slightest hint of Socialism. This was a policy it continued into the Cold War. Churchill, in the name of maintaining America's involvement in the defence of Western Europe, was prepared to turn a blind eye to this. When it came to Latin America he reasoned, 'It was important to keep a sense of proportion.'[1]

America bound the region together with the Rio Treaty in 1947. This defensive pact ensured that an attack on one was considered an attack on all. America's main priority was the security of the Panama Canal which links the Caribbean with the Pacific. Costa Rica was of concern as it had a long-running border dispute with Panama. This had not been settled by treaty until 1944. Four years later Costa Rica briefly fell into a state of civil war with the rebels winning. This was followed by an abortive invasion by right-wing Costa Ricans from neighbouring Nicaragua in December 1948. The latter country represented the only real major external threat to Costa Rica.

As the Cold War developed America increasingly saw the Rio Treaty an anti-Communist organisation. Members included its immediate southern neighbour. Mexico has a turbulent history but its shared border with America ensured it enjoyed a better level of economic stability than the rest of Latin America. In 1942 it sided with the Allies and sent a fighter squadron to take part in the closing stages of the Pacific campaign. The Mexicans always greatly benefitted from the supply of American weapons, investment and tourists. Although in the past Churchill had made disparaging remarks about the country, after the war the Mexican government invited him to visit. He politely declined on health grounds. 'It would not be good for me,' he wrote in a letter to President Truman, 'to live at such a height [in Mexico City] even for a week or ten days.'[2] He also passed on a trip to Brazil.

Across the Straits of Florida lay America's other southern neighbour, Cuba. Eisenhower was content for corrupt General Fulgencio Batista's regime to remain in power. America considered Batista an ally as he had signed up to the Rio Treaty. He was a beneficiary of the US military aid programme. In return Batista was happy to host major American business interests and organised crime. American investors dominated Cuba's economy as did America's unsatiable appetite for its sugar. The focus on growing the latter resulted in the production of basic food stuffs being neglected. This meant Cuba had to import its food and the sugar industry only provided employment for four months of the year. This made Cuba ripe for social revolution and ultimately susceptible to Communism. By the early 1950s resistance to Batista's brutal regime was growing. A young lawyer by the name of Fidel Castro was imprisoned following an attack on an army barracks in Santiago de Cuba. After his release he fled to Mexico to plot Batista's downfall.

Ever since Churchill's last visit to Cuba he had avoided criticising the Cuban government despite its terrible failings. These, coupled to America's financial interests, would create a terrible problem for Eisenhower and his successors. Eisenhower was completely ignorant of the emerging threat. Even the Soviet Union was unaware it was going to gain a new ally. 'We knew there were individual Communists participating in the movement which Castro led,' acknowledged Nikita Khrushchev, 'but the Communist Party of Cuba had no contact with him.'[3] However, Khrushchev also noted, 'We knew that Raúl Castro was a good Communist, but it appeared that he kept his true convictions hidden from his brother Fidel.'[4]

Britain's MI6 during the Second World War, thanks to Latin America's pro-Nazi sympathies, had maintained ten intelligence stations in the region at a cost of £200,000 (the equivalent of £6.6 million).[5] Afterwards the Attlee government, perceiving the Communist threat there to be minimal, reduced these to just three, in Buenos Aires, Mexico City and Rio de Janeiro.[6] What this meant was that Churchill inherited a greatly reduced intelligence gathering capability in Latin America. This was not helpful in light of the Latin Americans' extremely labyrinthine politics.

Although Churchill considered the threat of Communism in the western hemisphere fundamentally an American problem, it was not something he could entirely ignore. Britain had numerous footholds across the Americas. It had a chain of colonial possessions running through the Caribbean comprising British Honduras (Belize), Jamaica, Trinidad and Tobago and British Guiana (Guyana). Britain had taken control of Jamaica from Spain in the late 1650s and introduced self-government there in 1944. It was protected by the locally-raised West Indian Regiment but was reliant on the Royal Navy to patrol its waters. Churchill planned to visit Jamaica in 1949 to stay with Lord Beaverbrook but never made it. Beaverbrook was held responsible for Churchill's electoral defeat in 1945 and Clementine had cautioned him not to go for fear of upsetting his fellow Conservatives. Four years later he spent three weeks on the island at Prospect house near Ocho Rios on holiday.

The British, to the northeast of Jamaica and Cuba, also controlled The Bahamas as well as the Turks and Caicos islands. Churchill had exiled the Duke and

Duchess of Windsor to The Bahamas during the war. Off the coast of Venezuela Britain had taken the islands of Trinidad and Tobago from the Spanish and French respectively. In the late 1880s they became a British colony. British Honduras also became an independent colony at that stage. Both neighbouring Guatemala and Mexico had territorial claims on it. Although they initially renounced these following treaties in the late 1800s with Britain, the British never built a road linking Guatemala City with the Caribbean as promised. This led to renewed claims and regular tension along the border. Control of British Honduras would have given Guatemala a much greater Caribbean coastline. To confuse things, to the east of Guatemala former Spanish Honduras had declared independence in 1821, meaning there were two countries bearing the same name.

This external threat to British Honduras was very real. The Guatemalan Congress on 23 February 1948 suddenly called for an invasion with the intention of annexing it. There were provocatory reports in the Guatemalan press and the Guatemalan government withdrew police protection from the British embassy. For a moment it seemed as if war might be imminent. The 6,000 strong Guatemalan army could have easily overwhelmed the colony's meagre forces. British Honduras' only real defence were the Maya Mountains, which form a barrier with eastern Guatemala. Help was a long way away. The Royal Navy's America and West Indies Station headquarters was in distant Bermuda out in the Atlantic. The Jamaican naval command had been shut down way back in 1905.

Although this inflammatory resolution was rejected by the leader of the Guatemalan Congress, Attlee's government sent troops and two warships to make it clear Britain would fight. Foreign Secretary Bevin on 3 March 1948 gave reassurances to the House of Commons that the situation had been adequately dealt with. Opposition members of parliament were not entirely convinced. The hardline Colonel Francisco Arana, chief of the Guatemalan armed forces and a member of the military junta, may have been behind the rabble rousing. The following year he was killed in a shootout with supporters of President Juan José Arévalo. This sparked a brief military revolt that lasted a single day. One of Arana's key allies, Colonel Carlos Castillo Armas, was exiled.

From 1950 the People's United party in British Honduras then began to agitate for independence. They were partly spurred into action by the spectre of Guatemala taking over. No one wanted unification with their western neighbour. The governor and the colonial administration tried to paint the party as pro-Guatemalan and even Communist, neither of which were true although it had contacts with the new left-wing government in Guatemala. Much to Churchill's annoyance, when elections were held at the end of April 1954 the PUP won almost seventy per cent of the vote. The nationalists had achieved dominance peacefully. It would though be another decade before the colony achieved self-government and even longer before independence.[7]

Way down in the South Atlantic Churchill faced potential trouble because Argentina had long coveted the Falkland Islands. Britain annexed them in 1833 and the Argentines had claimed them ever since. Churchill was well aware of their strategic value following his stint as First Lord of the Admiralty during the First World War. To maintain access to Argentine beef and wheat during the

subsequent world war, Churchill had briefly considered recognising Argentina's sovereignty in return for Britain leasing them. Nothing though had come of this. Instead Churchill had maintained 2,000 troops on the islands. Argentina and Uruguay were given a graphic demonstration of British naval power during the Battle of the River Plate. The Royal Navy had forced the scuttling of the damaged German cruiser Admiral Graf Spee off Montevideo.

After the war Argentine ruler General Juan Domingo Perón renewed his country's claim to the Falklands but took no direct military action to force the issue. However, the Argentine armed forces and press regularly indulged in sabre-rattling. By the late 1940s the Argentine air force and navy were the most powerful in South America. Attlee's government found itself contending with an Argentine incursion in early 1947. The Argentine navy established a base on British-claimed territory, in the Melchior Islands, off Graham Land in the Antarctic. In response a British cruiser was sent from South Africa to the Falklands. The Royal Navy despite this show of strength took no action to expel the intruders.

That year Attlee offered to put the future of the Falklands, South Georgia Island, the South Sandwich Islands and the region now known as the British Antarctic Territory before the International Court of Justice at The Hague. Perón refused. Emboldened, the following year the Argentines set up a base in the South Shetland Islands, also in the Antarctic. Attlee's government in May 1948 in the name of saving money foolishly closed a naval facility on the Falklands. This was seen as a sign of weakness, and agitation over the Falklands was renewed in Argentina. Perón in November that year sent the largest Antarctic task force ever on its annual exercise. This included most of the fleet's active warships. British Foreign Secretary Ernest Bevin warned Argentina that any attempted invasion of the Falklands would be met with force. To defuse the situation both sides agreed to limit the number of warships deployed south of 60° South latitude.

Perón ratified the Rio Treaty in August 1950 largely with the intention of getting American weapons. Fortunately for Churchill, when he became prime minister again the Argentines were largely distracted at home by severe economic problems. These were as a result of Perón's policy of nationalisation and major concessions to the trade unions. This made him popular with the workers but caused a rift between the 'Peronistas' and the military. Perón further aggravated the military when he granted concessions to an American company in the Patagonian oilfields. Nonetheless, after Argentina received two American cruisers[8] in 1951 Churchill was taking no chances. He instructed the Chiefs of Staff on 20 February 1952 to ensure that Britain made a show of strength. Churchill wanted a frigate and a detachment of Royal Marines sent to the Falklands as soon as possible. A few weeks later Foreign Secretary Anthony Eden responded, 'It will no doubt be easy to arrange that the Marines are in evidence at Port Stanley from time to time.'[9] This seemed to do the trick.

Churchill and Eden were then amused when Perón's proposal to get involved in the Korean War made him even more unpopular. The Argentine government announced that it was prepared to send troops to fight in Korea if asked to do so by the United Nations. Colombia had already provided a frigate and a reinforced infantry battalion.[10] The latter was the only Latin America ground unit to ever fight in Asia and did so with distinction. This deployment was made despite Colombia being in a state of undeclared civil war. In Argentina the trade unions were incensed by the news and workers took to the streets, paralysing industry. The offer of military assistance was swiftly withdrawn. Argentina like most Latin American countries refrained from becoming embroiled in the Cold War. Luckily for Perón the young Argentine revolutionary Che Guevara, who was developing his theories for a united Latin America, was living in Guatemala. Nikita Khrushchev thought of Guevara as a Communist, but he personally preferred to be considered a Marxist.

Churchill continued to deploy two frigates to the Falklands annually and from 1954 based a Royal Marine detachment on Deception Island. Argentina soon fell into a period of political turmoil. The Argentine armed forces acted against Perón in September 1955 after it was rumoured he planned to supply weapons to the trade unions. The army marched on the capital Buenos Aires, while the navy blockaded the Plata estuary. Perón escaped on a Paraguayan gunboat and fled into exile. Britain submitted the territorial dispute to the International Court of Justice but Argentina made it known that it would not accept any decision.[11] It would be almost another three decades before Argentine troops briefly and ultimately unsuccessfully invaded the Falklands.

Churchill was aware of the potential Communist and nationalist threat to British interests in Latin America. The last thing he wanted was another Kenya or Malaya-type insurgency on his hands. British Guiana to the east of Venezuela came into being in 1831 and was granted limited self-government just before the Second World War. The extension of this in 1953 immediately led to an internal crisis. To complicate matters neighbouring Surinam and Venezuela laid claim to its territory. Dutch-owned Surinam was granted self-governing status in 1950, but did not gain full independence. Only the Dutch influence ensured the border did not become a flash point. Venezuela became a dictatorship under Colonel Marcos Pérez Jiménez after the military ousted the left-of-centre ruling party in 1948. However, America exerted considerable financial and political influence in Venezuela.

Notably, oil was first discovered in Venezuela in 1917 and by the mid-1950s it had almost 10,000 oil wells. This made the country of great strategic interest to America. As a result American business accounted for sixty-five per cent of foreign investment, controlled three fifths of the petroleum industry and all of the iron ore mining.[12] In fact Pérez Jiménez was such a friend to America that Eisenhower awarded him the Legion of Merit 'for exceptionally meritorious conduct in the performance of outstanding services to the Government of the United States'.[13]

Churchill in early October 1953 approved the suspension of the People's Progressive party's government in British Guiana for six months. This was supposedly done to stop Communist subversion. Cheddi Jagan, the newly elected Chief Minister, found himself unceremoniously sacked after just 133 days in office. His Socialist government's crime was agitating against British rule. This included supporting strike action and refusing to send a delegation to Queen Elizabeth II's coronation. There were suspicions that Jagan had attended the Soviet-backed World Federation of Trade Unions general council meeting in Berlin in November 1951, but British intelligence could not verify this. When he assumed office he wanted the formation of a 'People's Police'[14] and oversight of the school syllabus. This may have been because he did not trust the colonial authorities, but the governor saw more sinister forces at play. More alarmingly, according to local police sources, Jagan's supporters were planning arson attacks on the residences of Europeans and business property. Quite why Jagan would want to orchestrate anarchy after winning the election was unclear.

In response Churchill despatched a light cruiser and a battalion of men from the Royal Welch Fusiliers to the port of Georgetown to install an interim government on 9 October. Airborne troops flew in via Trinidad, catching the People's Progressive Party completely by surprise. Churchill had wanted Eisenhower's help but decided to go it alone. Quite what the Queen thought when she was asked to go through the formality of authorising the deployment of British forces overseas is anyone's guess. It was hardly an edifying day for democracy. It was also an example of British gunboat diplomacy at its worst.

Churchill was greatly preoccupied at this time. He was still recovering from his stroke that summer and dithering over whether to step down in favour of Anthony Eden. In addition he was preparing for the Conservative party Conference in Margate on 10 October. This involved writing 4,000 words for an hour-long speech. Churchill knew that his political future rested on a spirited performance. Lord Moran helpfully fortified him with amphetamine. Despite all these stresses and strains Churchill had endorsed the steps taken in British Guiana.

The rationale for regime change was extremely weak. The colony was not a priority for MI5, which had responsibility for intelligence gathering in Britain's overseas territories. The nearest security liaison officer was based in Trinidad and visited British Guiana reluctantly about once a month. Despite claims to the contrary there was no intelligence to show that Jagan was receiving funding from any external Communist organisations. Likewise, although Jagan and his wife were assessed to be Marxists, there was no intelligence to suggest they were Communists.[15] Churchill must have been well aware of this.

British paranoia over Communism taking root in the colony was long standing. In the early 1930s the governor had sent his counterpart in Barbados a plea for help, 'Have you any information Communist Agents to ferment labour troubles.' He then added, 'Shall be glad if you will keep me in touch with such movements if any suspected persons likely to visit this colony.'[16] Twenty years later it was reported at a Cabinet meeting that 'elected Ministers in British Guiana, who were under strong Communist influences, were taking every opportunity to undermine the constitution and to further the Communist cause.'[17] The Cabinet was also informed that following a strike in the sugar industry the People's Progressive Party was 'evidently seeking to establish a totalitarian dominance over the territory by penetrating the trade unions and local government'.[18] These claims seemed highly fanciful.

Jagan and his Education Minister Forbes Burnham travelled to London to plead their case. Churchill instructed the Cabinet on 13 October that 'it would hardly be appropriate for the Colonial Secretary to receive him immediately after he had been dismissed from office.'[19] The pair were spied on while they were staying at *The Royal Hotel* in London in case they had contact with the British Communist party or any other Communist groups. Intercepting their mail and telephone calls became more difficult after they relocated to the home of Dr K.D. Kumria, the General Secretary of the Council for Indians Abroad.

Jagan, far from consorting with Communists, conducted public talks at the London School of Economics and at Holborn Hall for Caribbean students and the migrant community. He approached Clement Attlee for help, but he claimed his hands were tied. Harold Wilson recalled that Aneurin Bevan welcomed Jagan and Burnham. 'Nye laid on a party for them at Cliveden Place,' noted Wilson. 'Seretse Khama, who had been ousted in an earlier coup de Whitehall [from Bechuanaland], was also present and full reports reached the press.'[20] The allegations of Jagan's links to Communism led to criticism of the Labour party. Churchill's government likewise came under attack by some elements of the press for sending in the troops.

Oliver Lyttelton, Secretary of State for the Colonies, on 22 October had to justify the government's actions in the House of Commons. He alleged the People's Progressive party was 'dominated by Communist ideas' intent on creating a totalitarian state.[21] Lyttelton also claimed Jagan had been denounced by leaders in Barbados and Jamaica as a troublemaker. 'Her Majesty's Government are not prepared to tolerate the setting up of Communist states in the British Commonwealth,' said Lyttelton firmly, 'and I have no doubt that, in taking up that position, we have the support of the overwhelming majority of the people of this country behind us.'[22]

The Secretary of State also announced, 'The Attorney-General of British Guiana is at this moment considering whether it is possible to prefer criminal charges against any of the persons concerned in the formulation of these [arson] plans.'[23] He then reassured the House that the deployment of troops had been necessary although they had not been needed. However, many Members of Parliament felt the government had been heavy-handed. Churchill was subsequently annoyed to learn that Jagan and Burnham travelled to India the following month seeking support from Prime Minister Nehru. When Jagan returned to Georgetown he was sentenced to six months in prison. Churchill's government had sent a firm message to Britain's Caribbean colonies.

Churchill, while in Washington in the summer of 1954, found American actions in Guatemala a potential problem for British Honduras. Amongst the topics discussed at the White House on 25 June was the ongoing Guatemalan anti-Communist revolution. Eisenhower's administration did not like the left-wing policies of President Jacobo Árbenz Guzmán. These included attempting to redistribute uncultivated land belonging to the US-based United Fruit Company, which was the largest landowner in the country. It dominated the banana economy.[24] The company also had a stranglehold on Guatemala's land and maritime lines of communication. United Fruit not only controlled the dock facilities at the Caribbean port of Puerto Barrios but also much of the shipping. On the western coast it had interests in the Pacific port of San José. It dominated the Guatemalan railways thanks to shares in International Railways of Central America. A subsidiary of the American and Foreign Power Company supplied most of Guatemala's electricity.

The Guatemalan Congress in May 1952 passed a law authorising the expropriation of uncultivated land from large estates to be redistributed to landless peasants. This was to be paid for using government bonds. Their actions actually did Churchill a favour. The ire of the Guatemalan public was switched from their traditional anger towards Britain for holding onto to British Honduras to the power and privilege of American big businesses. United Fruit was hit by a wave of strikes, to which the Guatemalan government turned a blind eye.

Alarm bells began to ring in Washington. The CIA was aware that Communists held positions within the Guatemalan government and headed the trade unions, some of whom were known to make regular trips to Moscow. When America refused to sell Arbenz weapons he turned to Czechoslovakia. In May 1953 2,000 tons of Czech arms were delivered, most of which dated from the Second World War. Nonetheless, this convinced the CIA even more that Communism had got a hold in Guatemala. In American eyes this posed a threat to Mexico and the Panama Canal. In the long term it also arguably posed a threat to British Honduras.

The CIA proceeded to provide Colonel Castillo Armas's anti-Communist rebels with arms via Honduras and Nicaragua. American instructors trained his men in Honduras. Castillo Armas' forces invaded Guatemala on 18 June 1954 just before Churchill departed for Washington. Arbenz thought his troops would easily defeat the rebels. However, he was concerned that if he won this would then spark an American invasion of his country. The Guatemalan Army though, after some initial fighting, simply melted away. Arbenz was forced to step down on 27 June and go into exile. Che Guevara, who supported Arbenz, fled to Mexico and then joined Castro. It did not escape Guevara's attention that US Secretary of State John Foster Dulles was both the attorney for the United Fruit Company and a stockholder. His brother, the CIA Director, Allen Dulles was on the company's board. As far as Guevara was concerned America was an imperialist power. He was not alone in such views.

Sir Pierson Dixon, the British representative at the United Nations in New York, was angry at how the Americans had behaved. He thought greed not ideology had driven them. When he dined with Churchill and Eden at the British Embassy in Washington on 28 June he made his feelings on the matter quite clear. This led to a heated argument. 'I'd never heard of this bloody place Guatemala,' responded Churchill, 'until I was in my seventy-ninth year.'[25] Dixon remonstrated with him, 'But Prime Minister, this is a moral issue. It is surely a question of right and wrong.'[26] America was in violation of the Rio Treaty as Guatemala was a signatory. Although Eden supported Dixon's stance he knew that it was pointless to argue. 'We ought not,' said Churchill, 'to allow Guatemala to jeopardise our relationship with the United States, for on them the safety of the world might depend.'[27] In light of Churchill's treatment of British Guiana he could hardly take the moral high ground.

Dixon found American actions in Latin America contradictory and perplexing. In May 1952, when Bolivian mine workers overthrew the ruling military junta, Eisenhower's administration did nothing to oppose President Victor Paz Estenssoro's new left-wing government. Instead it offered extensive economic aid. This was despite Paz Estenssoro's cabinet including Marxists plus the expropriation of foreign-owned tin mines. Remarkably this was the first occasion on which an American government had been prepared to assist a progressive Latin American regime.

John Colville was briefed by Sir Anthony Rumbold who was present at the embassy dinner. Colville noted in his diary that according to Rumbold, 'the F[oreign] S[ecretary] being all for caution and the PM being all for supporting the US in their encouragement of the rebels and their hostility to the Communist Guatemalan regime'.[28] Colville then spoke with Churchill when he went to bed. The Prime Minister was equally damning towards Eden and Guatemala. 'Eden was sometimes very foolish,' Churchill told Colville dismissively, 'He would quarrel with the Americans over some petty Central American issue which did not affect Great Britain.'[29] Churchill needed American support for the rehabilitation of West Germany to improve the defence of western Europe; he did not care about the fate of Guatemala. In Latin America the United States could do what it wanted.

While Communism would become an issue in the Caribbean thanks to Cuba, it was not such a problem in the rest of Latin America. Instead for much of the Cold War regional politics remained dominated by military coups and border wars. President Eisenhower continued to ensure nothing endangered the Panama Canal. General Anastasio Somoza, the Nicaraguan dictator, in January 1955 backed an attempted invasion of Costa Rica by supporters of former Costa Rican President Rafael Calderón Guardia. This was repelled by the democratic regime of President José Figueres with support from Eisenhower. Costa Rica and Nicaragua avoided going to war when Somoza, fearful of antagonising the Americans, stopped short of direct involvement with the rebels. Two years later Somoza turned westward and fought a brief and futile frontier conflict with Honduras.

When Harold Nicolson arrived by ship at Caracas in Venezuela in late January 1958, he was bemused to observe aircraft flying low over the harbour with frigates circling outside ready to open fire. He could also see on the road leading to the docks lorries full of workmen waving flags bearing 'Libertad'.[30] Nicolson recorded, 'The cool calm voice of the captain came over the loudspeakers to say it was a revolution, and that no passengers could be allowed on shore.'[31] A coup was underway to replace President Pérez Jiménez, who escaped to America where he lived for the next five years. It was clearly business as usual for Latin America.

PART SEVEN

ESCALATING TENSIONS

Chapter 18

Failing Warlord

Despite being surrounded by an excellent team of ministers, by the mid-1950s Churchill was regularly under enormous strain both physically and mentally. Harold Wilson recalled that, 'For those of us who knew and held him in high regard, there was the sad spectacle of the decline of Winston Churchill. His lapses were becoming more frequent.'[1] However, Churchill's wicked sense of humour showed no signs of diminishing. One day a young Conservative Member of Parliament spotted him leaving the lavatory with his fly buttons undone. The man coughed and said hesitantly, 'Prime Minister, the guardroom door is open.' Churchill glanced down and without missing a beat replied, 'And was the sentry standing to attention or lolling on a couple of sandbags?'[2]

Churchill struggled to manage Britain's enormously complex foreign policy. There was agitation against British rule in the likes of Cyprus, Kenya and Malaya and trouble was brewing in Rhodesia and Sudan. The latter fell into a state of civil war, which was to last sixteen years, and he failed to completely curtail the Mau Mau and Malayan risings. Likewise, closer to home Irish partition remained unresolved. In Europe the Soviets were an ever-present threat that seemed only to be kept in check by military force. There was little Churchill could do and it must have felt that he was constantly fighting a rearguard action against the vicissitudes of nationalism and Communism.

Domestically he was much more fortunate. Lord Butler assessed that Walter Monckton the Minister of Labour had done a particularly good job. 'He made it possible for Winston Churchill to rule in comparative peace during his last period of office,' recalled Butler.[3] Nigel Fisher, a Conservative Member of Parliament, noted of Monckton, 'I cannot remember any senior member of the Government who was more liked and respected.'[4] Monckton also ensured Butler's task as Chancellor of the Exchequer was easier. 'He made it possible for me to introduce good Budgets,' adds Butler, 'and he made it tolerable to proceed without an incomes policy.'[5] Monckton averted a major rail strike. In the winter of 1953 a railway workers' crisis loomed that threatened to paralyse the country over the Christmas period. Churchill thought this would be terrible and saw it in human terms whereas Butler was more worried about the impact on the economy if there were dramatic wage increases. When Churchill phoned Butler with good news, the latter asked, 'On what terms have you settled it?' Churchill cheerfully responded, 'Theirs, old cock!'[6]

Harold Macmillan also helped keep some of the pressure off Churchill. The Conservatives came to power in 1951 pledging to build 300,000 houses a year to try to remedy the post-war housing shortage. This task fell to Macmillan as the Housing Minister. When it came to arguments with Butler about financing he enjoyed the full backing of Churchill. By the end of 1952 Macmillan's department was overseeing the construction of 240,000 houses a year, this rose to 318,000 the following year. He had surpassed the government's target, meaning the Conservatives had more than delivered on their election pledge.

By 1954, because of Churchill's failing health, his ministers knew it was really time for him to step down. Clementine, who was not well either, had long wanted him to retire. John Colville was bemused because he recalled that when he rejoined Churchill in October 1951, 'Winston said it would probably be only for a year. He did not intend to remain in office.'[7] Some thought he might go following the Queen's coronation in 1953, especially after his acute stroke. Instead he continued to vacillate and struggled on. During the spring of 1954 Anthony Eden was confident that Churchill would go before the summer recess, which would enable him to form a new government. Churchill declined to cooperate, but then agreed to resign in September, only to change his mind.

Eden had his hands full with the Geneva conference, which was trying to decide the fate of Indochina after the French defeat at Dien Bien Phu. Churchill on 5 June 1954 following a briefing by Eden wrote to his wife complaining, 'The Communists are playing their winning hand with civility.'[8] He then claimed he and Eden had 'a very perfect understanding… about everything.'[9] On 24 August he wrote to Eden saying he intended to remain in office until the General Election in November 1955.

When Churchill addressed the Conservative party conference at Blackpool on 9 October, much to Eden's chagrin he made no mention of stepping down. 'Eden was dejected, but there was in fact nothing he could do about it,' observed John Colville, 'and the P.M. had great personal success at the Conservative Conference.'[10] At the end of the year on 22 December Lord Butler and other senior Conservatives confronted him and demanded he set a retirement date. Churchill knew it was coming. Earlier in the month he had told Lord Moran, 'I think I shall die quickly once I retire. There would be no purpose in living when there is nothing to do.'[11] Although Macmillan remained a loyal supporter, and Churchill dubbed him the Captain of the Praetorian Guard, even he thought Churchill should now resign.

The Conservative party were beginning to worry what would happen come the next General Election. When Lord Moran had lunch with Macmillan on 9 January 1955, the latter lamented how Churchill had treated Anthony Eden over the years. Then he announced, 'Winston ought to resign. …He can't do his job as Prime Minister as it ought to be done.'[12] Moran later noted in his diary, 'Plainly there is a growing feeling among Winston's friends that the time has come for him to go. But only Harold Macmillan has had the guts to say so.'[13] Churchill clung to his unrealised dream of meeting the Soviet leadership and brokering an end to the Cold War. He confided in the French Prime Minister Pierre Mendès France on 12 January that he had 'for some time felt a strong desire to establish a direct personal contact with the new leaders of the Soviet Government such as might lead to a fruitful Four-Power Conference'.[14]

By early February 1955 Churchill finally made the decision to go on 5 April that year. He decided to keep his departure a secret apart from telling his inner circle which included Eden, Macmillan and Moran. Churchill had found the challenges of the latest Commonwealth Prime Ministers' conference particularly tiring. During this he sought to persuade Australia and New Zealand to commit troops to Malaya. To Churchill's disappointment the Pakistani Prime Minister Mohammad Ali Bogra announced that his country would become a republic and no longer recognise the British monarchy. The sudden resignation of Soviet Premier Georgy Malenkov and the Chinese shelling of islands held by Taiwan were also hot topics of discussion.

The Queen hosted a lunch at Buckingham Palace on 18 February for the Shah of Iran and Queen Soraya who were on a State visit. 'In come Winston and Clemmie, looking grand,' recalled Harold Nicolson who was also attending. 'He looks far, far better than when I last saw him.'[15] The Shah was in London to discuss amongst other things Middle Eastern security. Evelyn Shuckburgh, Eden's Principal Private Secretary, was amongst the guests and raised the Commonwealth Prime Ministers' Conference with Churchill. 'I have worked very hard with [Prime Minister] Nehru [of India],' Churchill informed Shuckburgh. 'I told him he should be the light of Asia, to show all those millions how they can shine out, instead of accepting the darkness of Communism.'[16] He also suggested to Shuckburgh rather fancifully that Israel should be granted membership of the Commonwealth. Three days later Churchill hosted the Shah and Queen Soraya at No.10 Downing Street.

At the end of the month Iraq and Turkey signed the Baghdad Pact which was modelled on NATO and designed to protect the Middle East from the Soviet Union. They were subsequently joined by the United Kingdom, Pakistan and Iran. Britain's membership increased the importance of the British bases in Cyprus as valuable staging posts. Eisenhower did not sign up America due to the pro-Israel lobby and the resulting difficulties in getting approval from Congress.

Churchill delivered his last major speech in the House of Commons on 1 March 1955 with a sober warning. 'There is widespread belief throughout the free world that, but for American nuclear superiority,' he told his fellow Members of Parliament, 'Europe would already have been reduced to satellite status and the Iron Curtain would have reached the Atlantic and the Channel.'[17] The following day he took exception to Aneurin Bevan in the Commons, who said he wanted talks with Russia but these had been stymied by America. Churchill said this was not true, he had planned to meet Malenkov but had been struck down by ill-health.

Through early March Churchill suffered from a cold and was depressed about his impending resignation. Nonetheless, on 8 March he confirmed to Eden that he would resign on 5 April. Then three days later he received a telegram suggesting that he and Eisenhower go to Paris on 8 May 1955 for the tenth anniversary of Victory in Europe Day. This was intended to get the French to ratify the London-Paris Agreements which had replaced the troubled European Defence Community.

Churchill was immediately re-invigorated because he saw this as a way to achieve his long-cherished three-power summit. Shortly after, Churchill wrote to Eden informing him that he was not stepping down. Eden was furious. On 14 March he angrily said to Macmillan, 'I have been Foreign Secretary for ten years. Am I not to be trusted?'[18] Churchill three days later, after lunch with Macmillan and Field Marshal Montgomery, announced his chosen date was now definite. 'PM seems rather low,' Macmillan wrote in his diary. 'It is now certain that the crisis of indecision is over.'[19]

'From his own point of view it would have been better,' Mary Soames said to Lord Moran on 17 March, 'if he had gone on till he dropped in his tracks, ...but when he resigns I think his "lust for life" will keep him going.'[20] Churchill had backtracked once it was clarified that Eisenhower had no intention of meeting the Soviet leadership. He then changed his mind yet again when the Soviets let it be known they were amenable to four-power talks. After Churchill and Clementine dined with the Edens at the end of the month he decided not to press the point. Instead he asked the Queen's private secretary to inform her of his intentions. 'From now till the "day" it will be hard going,' observed Mary. 'He minds so much.'[21] At No.10 Downing Street on 1 April, at a birthday party marking Clementine's seventieth, Churchill told Moran sadly, 'I don't want to go, but Anthony wants it so much.'[22]

As the date approached Churchill's spirits lifted. He invited the Queen and Prince Philip to dine with him at Downing Street on 4 April on the very eve of his departure. The party initially intended as a small affair involved fifty people. John Colville noted, 'It was a splendid occasion.'[23] The guests had either guessed its significance or already knew. 'Winston, in proposing the Queen's health, made a touching, graceful and debonair speech,' recalled Mary, 'reminding the company that it was a toast "which I used to enjoy drinking during the days when I was a cavalry subaltern in the reign of Your Majesty's great-great-grandmother, Queen Victoria"'.[24] Churchill, facing his monarch added, 'Madam, I should like to express the deep... sense of gratitude... for all the help and inspiration... which spreads with ever-growing strength throughout the British realm and the Commonwealth and Empire.'[25] The Queen then rose and proposed a toast to 'My Prime Minister'.[26] Afterwards a smiling Churchill was photographed gallantly escorting the Queen to her car.

The following day Churchill formally informed his Cabinet that he intended to step down and would present himself to the Queen that afternoon. 'At 4.30 Winston handed his resignation to the Queen, who was graciously pleased to accept it,' Harold Nicolson wrote in his diary. 'I suppose she will send for Anthony [Eden] tomorrow.'[27] The Queen offered Churchill a dukedom but he declined saying he 'would prefer to remain in the Commons till he died'.[28] On 6 April Churchill told Moran, 'I am going to bury myself at Chartwell. I shall see no one.'[29] Nicolson added, 'There are fine tributes to him in both Houses. Bless his heart.'[30]

Churchill though did not immediately bury himself at home. Instead he and Clementine flew to Sicily for a well-earned rest. On the flight he read a letter from the Queen in which she thanked him for his wise guidance over the past three years. The Queen also astutely wrote, 'During the more recent years you have had to face the Cold War and with it threats and dangers which are more awe-inspiring than any which you have had to contend with before, in war or peace.' By this she no doubt meant the threat of nuclear war. The Queen concluded, 'You will take with you into retirement a deep fund of affectionate goodwill.'[31] Churchill wrote back to her on 18 April and thanked her for her kindness. He also lamented Britain's lost prestige, 'Our Island no longer holds the same authority or power that it did in the early days of Queen Victoria.'[32] Unfortunately their three-week break in Syracuse at the Villa Politi was marred by bad weather and they came home early.

Just before Churchill departed he acquiesced to Mountbatten becoming First Sea Lord. This was a job that he had long coveted. The current incumbent Sir Rhoderick McGrigor had offered Mountbatten the job in September 1954 once his term in office ended. When Churchill was informed of this he tried to obstruct his appointment presumably because he still bore Mountbatten a grudge over India. Eventually Churchill changed his mind and Mountbatten's selection was met with approval from both the Conservatives and Labour. Conveniently Mountbatten's first day in office was on 18 April 1955, so after Churchill had gone. Subsequently Mountbatten joined Macmillan and a few others at Churchill's London house for lunch. Churchill was in a bad mood throughout the meal, perhaps annoyed that Mountbatten had finally got his way. When they had almost finished Mountbatten said, 'I'm so sorry, but I have to go to a Chiefs of Staff meeting.'[33] Churchill suddenly cheered up and seemed amused by this. 'Who is that man?' he asked with a grin after Mountbatten had left, 'Ought I to know him?'[34]

A month after Churchill's resignation West Germany joined NATO though it had yet to form an army. Further afield progress was finally being made in Malaya which held its first general election in July 1955. The ground war there had firmly turned against the Communist insurgency. That summer the Mau Mau were decisively defeated in Kenya. In contrast the Irish Republican Army was poised to launch a terror campaign against British rule in Northern Ireland. Eden found he inherited many of Churchill's ongoing foreign policy problems, notably the future of the colonies. In the eastern Mediterranean he was forced to declare a state of emergency in Cyprus which would last four years. At home, once more Britain's railway workers threatened action and Monckton did what he could to head off industrial unrest. By the end of the year Monckton was thinking of resigning when Eden offered him the role of Minister of Defence. He would last just ten months in the job.

Eden then found himself hosting Khrushchev and Soviet Premier Nikolai Bulganin when they came to London for talks in the spring of 1956. 'We considered Eden relatively progressive for a Conservative,' said Khrushchev mischievously.[35] He had recently denounced Stalin in a speech to the Communist party Congress. Churchill did not see this as progress. 'I am sure it is a great blunder which will markedly hamper the Communist Movement,' he said in a letter to Eisenhower. Then without seeing the irony of his remarks added, 'Stalin always kept his word to me. I remember particularly saying to him when I visited Moscow in 1944, "You keep Romania and Bulgaria... but let me have Greece." To this bargain he scrupulously adhered.'[36] In London the topic of conversation as always was the future of Germany. The Soviets understandably were not happy about West Germany's membership of NATO.

Eden generously invited Churchill to dinner with the Soviet delegation on 17 April at Downing Street. This presented Winston with a golden opportunity to try to influence Soviet policy, but he did not take it. 'I sat next to Khrushchev,' Churchill informed Lord Moran. 'The Russians were delighted to see me. Anthony told them I had won the war.'[37] Khrushchev though was far from complimentary about the former Prime Minister remarking, 'He was very old and fat and doddering.'[38] Their conversation was stilted and Churchill not only ate his own portion of oysters but also Khrushchev's. 'Churchill was obviously making an effort to avoid business talk,' concluded Khrushchev. 'He wasn't head of the government anymore, and he left serious matters for Eden to discuss.'[39] Khrushchev saw Churchill a second time in the House of Commons where he observed him fall asleep on the back benches.

The Soviet delegation did not make a good impression with the British Opposition. 'My Labour friends tell me that the dinner given by the Labour Executive to Bulganin and Khrushchev was a ghastly failure,' reported Harold Nicolson.[40] In his speech Khrushchev stated that Russia alone had won the Second World War. Labour Member of Parliament George Brown was outraged and remonstrated with the Soviet leader. 'He delivered a speech that was absolutely scandalous and completely unacceptable,' recorded Khrushchev angrily.[41] The offended Soviet delegation immediately left. Tempers had further been enflamed by Hugh Gaitskell, leader of the Labour party, handing Khrushchev a list of missing East European politicians wanting to know what had happened to them. Brown later tried to apologise but Khrushchev would not accept his apology. A puzzled Khrushchev concluded, 'We found that the Labourites were consistently more hostile toward us than the Conservatives.'[42] Churchill later told Moran, 'I should not be in favour of Bulganin and Khrushchev going to the States.'[43] He felt that it would only make things worse.

During the autumn of 1956 Churchill went on a working holiday to La Pausa in the south of France. His focus was his *History of the English Speaking Peoples.* Unfortunately he suffered a stroke on 20 October and was unconscious for twenty minutes. Many felt that he should have retired sooner, especially as Eden was now plunged into the Suez Crisis. Monckton, who opposed Eden's course of action, was sacked. That winter Britain and France invaded Suez to a chorus of international disapproval. On 22 November at John Colville's urging, Churchill, after some initial reluctance in the name of trying to save the special relationship, wrote to Eisenhower. 'There is not much left for me to do in this world and I have neither the wish nor the strength to involve myself in the present political stress and turmoil.' He then added, 'But I do believe, with unfaltering conviction, that the theme of the Anglo-American alliance is more important today than at any time since the war.' He signed it, 'Your old friend Winston S. Churchill.'[44] It was the last time Churchill made such a direct intervention in international affairs. Eisenhower did not seem to hold him responsible for the Suez fiasco and bore him no grudge.

Eisenhower continued to take a hard line with the spread of Communism. In January 1957 he announced the Eisenhower Doctrine which was intended to protect the Middle East from the Soviet threat. This was partly in response to Egyptian nationalism and Britain's disastrous withdrawal from Suez. It was also fuelled by the fear of a Communist take-over in Syria. Most Arabs though saw this latest American initiative as an excuse to try and contain Arab nationalism in the wake of Britain and France's humiliating departure from the region. Churchill felt that Eisenhower's undertaking was a bit late. Eisenhower was not pleased to learn that the French had finished fencing in Algeria by the summer of 1957, cutting it off from neighbouring Morocco and Tunisia. That winter Algerian guerrillas started launching desperate attacks trying to break through from the Tunisian side. Eisenhower felt Algeria should be given independence regardless of what the French settlers wanted.

Churchill's old wartime ally Charles de Gaulle became the Prime Minister of France in June 1958. He was voted into office because of the insurgency in Algeria and political instability in Paris. During the early part of the Second World War Churchill had valiantly championed de Gaulle and his Free French forces with President Roosevelt. Once it became apparent that the Frenchman's sole goal was the restoration of French authority and the French Empire to the exclusion of all else, their relationship became more acrimonious. Now though after all these years de Gaulle wanted to honour Churchill, who was delighted.[45] On 6 November 1958 he arrived in Paris to be awarded the Croix de la Libération. This was France's highest award given to those who had fought with the Free French and the Resistance.

After the ceremony in the garden of Hôtel Matignon, Churchill declared, 'I thank you all for the honour you have done me. Vive la France!'[46] The only other Briton to receive this accolade was King George VI. 'Whatever had been the differences between these two men over the years,' wrote Mary, 'only the strong link which bound them – a fierce love of liberty and of France – was remembered on this day.'[47] Afterwards Winston and Clementine had lunch with de Gaulle and his wife. He was on best behaviour and avoided the vexed issues of Algeria, NATO and West Germany. By this point the French had decisively won the Battle of the Morice Line, which prevented Algerian guerrillas infiltrating from Tunisia.[48] De Gaulle though knew France could not hold Algeria much longer. The white colonists were outnumbered and the war was simply too costly to carry on indefinitely.

Much to Eisenhower's alarm in early 1959 the Soviet Bloc moved into the western hemisphere, more specifically the Caribbean. In January the US-backed government of General Batista in Cuba collapsed and Fidel Castro's left-wing guerrillas took power in Havana. In the face of America sanctions Castro quickly aligned himself with Moscow and announced Cuba would become a Socialist state. Khrushchev recalled, 'We gave them tanks and artillery... In addition we sent them anti-aircraft guns and some fighter planes.'[49] The Cold War was now in America's backyard. Eisenhower and his advisors feared that Castro would export Communism throughout Latin America. In Asia that March, Mao Zedong's Communist forces ruthlessly crushed an uprising against Chinese rule in Tibet. He had annexed the country nine years earlier after brief resistance by the outnumbered Tibetans. The uprising lasted less than two weeks and the Dalai Lama, Tibet's Buddhist spiritual leader, was forced to flee to India.

Churchill, at the age of eighty-four, suffered another small stroke on 13 April 1959 and was subjected to numerous tests by his doctors. At the end of the month Montgomery did what Churchill had failed to achieve; he flew to Moscow for talks with the Soviet leadership. Although he went in a private capacity as he was now retired, the Foreign Office and the British press were outraged at what they saw as his unofficial and potentially dangerous meddling. In response Montgomery said, 'This East-West tension is just no good. I want to find out what causes it.'[50] When Churchill heard of Montgomery's plans he must have felt a little envious. Khrushchev gave Montgomery the full red carpet treatment as if it were a State visit.

Montgomery and Khrushchev had two days of talks, during which Monty sensibly suggested that to lessen tensions Berlin should be made the responsibility of the United Nations. He then reasoned that once there was a treaty recognising the two Germanys, NATO and Soviet troops could then be withdrawn from German soil. Remarkably Khrushchev publicly agreed to all this, although nothing was to come of it.[51] 'If it could be agreed that national forces should return to their own countries,' said the Soviet leader, 'then Russia would accept a very comprehensive plan of inspection and control of national territories.'[52]

Montgomery saw China as a powerful counterweight to the Soviet Union. When he got home he concluded, 'I don't believe the Soviet Union would enter into an all-out nuclear war with the West, and be left devastated and prostrated, with a thousand million Chinese on her Eastern flank.'[53] His visit, though well-intentioned, did him no favours. 'There is no doubt that this kind of action did not improve the Field Marshal's standing in the eyes of the British Government,' wrote Montgomery's younger brother Brian.[54] Not to be outdone Macmillan travelled to Moscow that summer, but the only agreement he got was for more talks. There could be no concealing Britain's weakening influence in the East-West détente negotiations.

Whereas Churchill remained extremely popular in America, Montgomery's criticism of Eisenhower's wartime leadership in his memoirs published in 1958 and on American television won him no friends. He foolishly pushed the President too far. 'I eventually just stopped communicating with him,' said Eisenhower crossly. 'I was just not interested in keeping up communications with a man that just can't tell the truth.'[55] Montgomery, realising he had been cut off lamented, 'If I've lost the friendship of that great and good man, it would be very distressing to me.'[56] Eisenhower though was not prepared to forgive Montgomery's injudicious remarks about America's efforts during the Second World War and its role in NATO.

After his stroke Churchill desperately wanted to visit America, and when this became known he was offered full VIP treatment by Eisenhower. 'He was determined to go and would not take Lord Moran,' explained Mary Soames, 'as he did not wish to appear an invalid; he was accompanied by [private secretary] Anthony Montague-Browne and his valet-nurse.'[57] The following month he arrived as Eisenhower's personal guest. For the very first time he crossed the Atlantic to Washington by jet plane and later flew by helicopter with Eisenhower to his Gettysburg farm. 'All goes well and the President is a real friend,' Churchill wrote to Clementine on 5 May 1959. 'We had a most pleasant dinner last night.'[58] While at the White House he was reunited with General Clark. The latter was dismayed to see how frail the former prime minister had become. 'I was sad to see this great man with an impediment in his speech,' recalled Clark, '…and when it came time and I called on him for a few words, it was very noticeable.'[59]

Inevitably Churchill and Eisenhower discussed conflict. Eisenhower was not happy that de Gaulle, who was now the French President, whilst insisting the war against Algerian nationalists was an internal French affair, wanted NATO backing. Eisenhower saw what was happening in Algeria as a war of independence that had nothing to do with the Cold War. Just before Churchill arrived in Washington the French military had commenced Operation Courroie to clear the mountains to the southwest of Algiers. De Gaulle, in a bid to end the conflict, had also offered amnesty for surrendering guerrillas, a halt to judicial executions and started releasing detainees. On the ground the French military seemed to be winning, but completely clearing the mountains of guerrillas was an impossible task. Eisenhower was of the view that African colonies should be given independence before the inhabitants took it forcibly. This clearly was a criticism of Britain as much as France. Regarding NATO the President remarked, 'The big question is, will the West have the endurance and the tenacity and the courage to keep up the struggle long enough?'[60]

At Gettysburg Churchill and Eisenhower, both wearing hats, were photographed grinning like school boys taking a ride together in a golfcart. Not all the reunions were so joyous. Churchill also met with John Foster Dulles who was dying from cancer and General George Marshall who was unable to speak following a stroke. Both would be dead before the year was out. Travelling to the airport to fly home Churchill turned to Sir Harold Caccia, the British Ambassador to the US, and said, 'I hope you will give the Prime Minister a good report of my visit.' Then with a glint in his eye he added, 'and say that I behaved myself.'[61] Caccia had been sent to Washington by Macmillan to try and mend the special relationship following the Suez Crisis and Eden's downfall.

In early September Churchill met with Eisenhower again when he came to London for a dinner marking the twentieth anniversary of the outbreak of the Second World War. Once more they were photographed sitting together smiling amiably. Churchill may have felt a twinge of jealousy when Khrushchev finally visited America for the first time on 15 September. This could have been his long cherished 'Big Three' summit, but by this stage his concentration and stamina were rapidly waning. There would though be no rapprochement. 'You know,' said Eisenhower to the Soviet leader, 'we really should come to some sort of an agreement in order to stop this fruitless, really wasteful rivalry.'[62] Although Khrushchev agreed with him, no settlement was reached and the Cold War continued unabated. The day after Khrushchev arrived in Washington de Gaulle, in a broadcast to France, spoke of self-determination for Algeria. The French colonists were outraged.

Churchill made his final political speech to his home constituency at Woodford on 29 September 1959 in the run-up to the General Election. 'I played a part in awakening free Europe to the need to join together with the United States and the British Commonwealth to protect their freedom,' he told his audience, 'but the Cold War was none of my seeking, and I have never sought to perpetuate or prolong it.'[63] In his supporting literature he focused on Britain's international standing. 'We must never forget our unique position,' he said, 'as the heart and centre of the British Commonwealth and Empire and a leading partner in the Atlantic Alliance.'[64] This was Winston and Clementine's fifteenth election campaign together and their very last. On 8 October the Conservatives were returned to power for a third time with Macmillan as Prime Minister. Churchill easily retained Woodford with a majority of 14,797. This showed a reduction of over 1,000 from 1955, which was a protest by those who felt he was long overdue to retire as their Member of Parliament. When he unveiled a statue of himself in Woodford on 31 October this was to be his last public speech. In November Churchill had another stroke.

He returned to America one last time in early April 1961 on board the yacht of Greek tycoon Aristotle Onassis. He saw his old friend Bernard Baruch in New York, but was not strong enough to travel to Washington to meet President John Kennedy. Shortly after, the latter was embroiled in controversy over the failed CIA backed invasion of Cuba by exiles hoping to topple Castro. The *Daily Mirror* reported, 'Rebel forces in Cuba are being heavily attacked by Soviet-built MiG jet fighters and tanks.'[65] The Cold War had reached boiling point.

Churchill's fears about Egypt falling into the Soviet camp were reinforced that summer. President Nasser's internal campaign against Communism plus the benefits of American economic aid had temporarily disrupted Egypt's relationship with the Soviet Union. However, in 1960 the two countries concluded a new arms supply agreement. On 2 June 1961 Churchill met with the Israeli Prime Minister David Ben-Gurion and the Israeli Ambassador to London Arthur Lourie. Ben-Gurion told him that Moscow was supplying Egypt with MiG-19 fighter jets that were superior to anything the Israeli air force had. There were also about 200 Soviet instructors in Egypt. This was a worrying development that posed a threat to Israel. Ben-Gurion then informed Churchill that he had asked Macmillan for air defence weapons. He also thanked Churchill for his unwavering support for Israel over the years.

The following summer the Soviet Union began supplying Egypt with the newer MiG-21 fighter and Tu-16 medium bomber. This continual build-up made another Arab-Israeli war inevitable. Furthermore, Egyptian plotting triggered the downfall of the royal house of Yemen in September 1962. Nasser despatched 20,000 troops to support the new republican regime. Saudi Arabia was alarmed by the Egyptian and Communist penetration of the Arabian peninsula. In response the Saudis backed the Yemeni Royalists resulting in a five-year war forcing Egypt to commit yet more troops. Egyptian air power played a role but it was unable to defeat the royalists.

During his retirement Churchill watched the Cold War gather pace while the last of Britain's colonial possessions slipped away with British Somaliland, Cyprus, Kenya, Kuwait, Ghana, Malaysia, Malta, Nigeria, Sudan and Zambia all gaining independence. After the Korean War ended the country remained partitioned in armed deadlock. Following the departure of the French from Indochina the region was blighted by conflict with the outbreak of the Vietnam War in the 1960s. Neighbouring Laos remained in a state of civil war between the government forces and the Communist Pathet Lao. In Angola and Mozambique Communist-backed nationalist guerrillas rose up against Portuguese rule. To the north of Angola the Congo, which gained independence from Belgium, fell into a state of prolonged civil war. Communist China fought a brief border war with India in the Himalayas in 1962, which the Chinese won. It proved an unwelcome wake-up call for the Indian military who were also in an armed stand-off with Pakistan.

Churchill was dramatically distracted from international affairs in the summer of 1962. Whilst at the Hôtel de Paris in Monte Carlo he fell and broke his left hip. This was immediately immobilised with a huge plaster cast to protect it. He instructed Anthony Montague Browne, 'Remember, I want to die in England. Promise me that you will see to it.'[66] Montague Browne called No.10 and Harold Macmillan sent a Royal Air Force air ambulance to collect Churchill. He required surgery and was kept in hospital in London for almost two months. Mary Soames noted sadly that 'it marked a definite further stage in his slow decline.'[67] Nonetheless, Sarah Churchill wrote, 'My father was now in his eighty-eighth year, but still retained his capacity for recovery.'[68] Churchill was not quite ready to give up the good fight. 'Winston recovered slowly from his last accident,' said Mary, but added, 'and his general mobility was considerably affected.'[69]

Despite Khrushchev's attempts to reform the totalitarian Stalinist model of government, his final years witnessed the height of the east-west confrontation. Under his rule there was the Sino-Soviet split in 1960, the physical partition of East and West Berlin with the construction of the Berlin Wall the following year and the Cuban Missile Crisis in 1962. The latter brought the Soviet Union and America to the very brink of nuclear war – the one thing that Churchill had always feared.[70] Although he had fond memories of the island, his failing health meant he was unable to take an active interest in events. In the summer that year after much bloodshed de Gaulle declared Algeria independent. The assassination of President Kennedy in November 1963 sparked conspiracy theories that the Soviet bloc might have been involved in his death.

When Macmillan and Mountbatten dined with Churchill and Clementine in 1963, they sadly found Winston much diminished. Mountbatten recalled that 'he sat there huddled up and not speaking.'[71] When he did talk about Mountbatten's exploits during the Second World War he was confused about the details. 'He had reached the age when memory played him tricks,' noted Mountbatten.[72] It was an altogether unhappy meeting as Macmillan was nearing the end of his political career. He was suffering from ill-health and resigned as prime minister on 18 October that year to be succeeded by Alec Douglas-Home.

Churchill attended the House of Commons for the last time on 27 July 1964. The next day Prime Minister Douglas-Home, the Leader of the Opposition Harold Wilson and the Leader of the Liberal party Jo Grimond presented him with a resolution thanking him for over fifty years of public service in Parliament and to the nation. That October Leonid Brezhnev replaced Khrushchev as Soviet leader after the failure of his economic liberalisation programme. This made no difference to the Cold War. The US Congress approved military support for South Vietnam in its struggle against the Communist North. The following year American troops began to arrive, dramatically escalating the conflict.

In his final years Churchill was constantly surrounded by his family and was content to be doted over. 'But sometimes he withdrew a great distance from us,' said Mary, 'and who knows what thoughts or images moved across the screen of his consciousness from the long saga of life, so crowded with events and people?'[73] The *Evening Standard* headline on 15 January 1965 warned 'Sir Winston is Seriously Ill.' Nine days later Churchill at the age of ninety died. His state funeral took place on 30 January. 'We had been told it was not necessary to curtsey to the Queen and her family,' said Sarah Churchill. 'They were already in their pews. For the first time in English history, the monarch waived her prerogative and waited for her humble servant.'[74] Such was her high esteem for her former Prime Minister.

Amongst those paying their respects were Attlee, Eden, Macmillan, Wilson, Eisenhower and de Gaulle. Montgomery was recovering from prostate surgery in South Africa so was unable to attend. Many of the Commonwealth nations sent representatives as did the European monarchy. Notably American President Lyndon Johnson did not attend due to ill-health, though it has been alleged he did not come because of Prime Minister Harold Wilson's refusal to support America in Vietnam. Hubert Humphrey the vice president did not attend either.

Churchill's dream of defusing east-west tensions remained unrealised. Although known as the Cold War, armed proxies ensured it remained hot around the world until 1991 with the collapse of the Soviet Union. In November 1965 Britain's colonial presence in Africa came to an end when the white minority government in Rhodesia announced a unilateral declaration of independence. Britain would cling on in the Middle East until the early 1970s when the last flickering embers of the Empire were finally extinguished.

Chapter 19

Winston's Post War Legacy

In comparison to his first premiership Churchill's second stint in Downing Street is often unfairly seen as lacklustre. What though even possessed him to want to be Prime Minister again? After the enormous pressures of the Second World War it would have been perfectly understandable if he had stepped down from politics and retired. He could have indulged his passions of writing, painting and travelling – after all he had been commissioned to write his six-volume history *The Second World War* and his four-volume *A History of the English Speaking Peoples*. These tasks were mammoth undertakings in themselves without continuing to lead the Conservatives. Clementine and his family would certainly have preferred it if he had settled down to a quiet life, but that was not how he operated. Churchill was a driven man looking for the next challenge and he loved the international limelight. Furthermore, he wanted to prove a political point.

His electoral defeat in 1945 left him feeling that he had unfinished work to do. After successfully leading the wartime coalition government his very public rejection was hard to take. Labour's sweeping victory was a personal blow to him even though the election was about policies and not personalities. This made him more determined than ever to win the role just to show that he could. The Conservative party in 1945, 1950 and again in 1951 knew their best path to power lay with Churchill at the helm. Even if some felt that they should have a younger, more vigorous leader such as Anthony Eden, Churchill's standing as a war leader and a charismatic figure was a vote winner. Although the Conservatives slipped in with a small majority in 1951, he had shown he was electable and laid firm foundations for the future success of his party. Both Anthony Eden and Harold Macmillan were able to substantially build on the Conservative majority in the next two general elections. This was one of the greatest legacies of his second term in office.

The problems faced by Churchill during his second term, although still global, were of a completely different nature to those of the Second World War. Fighting Nazi Germany and its Axis allies was not the same as countering the ideologies of Communism and nationalism. There was no grand alliance committed to fighting a common enemy. After the war every country looked to its own recovery and wanted no more talk of war. China and the Soviet Union were able to export

Communism without recourse to a third world war. America understandably was reluctant to be dragged into yet another major conflict and NATO was formed solely to protect western Europe. However, events in Germany, China, Korea, Indochina and even Malaya showed that the Cold War was anything but cold.

Fortunately Churchill never saw the Soviet Union or Communist China in the same light as Nazi Germany. He always felt that both countries would see reason if they were brought to the negotiating table. Thankfully he had mellowed from his vehemently anti-Bolshevik days when he championed intervention in the Russian Civil War in a bid to strangle Communism at birth. He understood that nothing could be achieved by continually threatening the Communist bloc. Despite his warlord tendencies, although Churchill supported a united front in the face of Communist expansionism, he realised all-out war would achieve nothing but the destruction of the planet. Furthermore, Britain's steady decline meant inevitably he had to accept that America would have to continue to be the defender of democracy with very limited British help. This though did not mean that Britain should agree to everything America wanted.

To the very end of his second premiership Churchill hoped that the Soviet Union might somehow mellow. Just before Harold Wilson travelled to Moscow on private business in 1954 he saw Winston. 'What we want,' Churchill informed him, 'you tell them – is easement.'[1] Wilson recalled, 'Then the old statesman told me what to look for: consumer goods. If they were allocating more materials for the production of consumer goods... it was a sign they were looking for a peaceful solution... that they were taking more notice of ordinary people.'[2] Churchill had no way of knowing that the western democracies and NATO would ultimately win the Cold War by outspending the Soviet Union.

Eisenhower though did not share Churchill's optimistic idealism. Going on best available evidence, following events in China, Germany, Korea and Indochina, he felt the Communists would only respond to military strength. This included using the atomic bomb if necessary. He was an advocate of the domino theory, in which the spread of Communism caused a deadly knock-on effect. As far as he was concerned being conciliatory would achieve nothing. In Europe Churchill struggled to balance the interests of America, Britain, France and Germany. His support for the integration of West Germany into first the European Defence Community and then NATO inadvertently fuelled the Cold War by contributing to the creation of the Warsaw Pact. The irony of this was that it tied Britain and America very firmly to the defence of Europe.

The rise of Communism and the end of empire was met by Britain piecemeal. The country's post-war shrinking resources meant that these issues had to be dealt with in an ad hoc fashion by both Attlee and Churchill. Attlee felt that it was only right Britain should grant Burma, Ceylon and India independence as quickly as possible. He was backed up in this by Lord Mountbatten, his man on the spot. Spiralling costs and the threat of violence towards British rule made this a very sensible decision. It also won American approval. Attlee in the case of Europe was happy to commit Britain to NATO and the defence of the continent. He never seemed to bear a grudge against Churchill for sowing the seeds of the Cold War by granting Stalin a free hand in eastern Europe. Even so Churchill's desire to save

Greece from Communism meant that the former Axis states ended up becoming the Warsaw Pact.

Once Churchill was in office again the spread of Communism and the fear of a third world war encouraged him to retain Britain's remaining colonial possessions. This was a stance that America thoroughly disapproved of. Field Marshal Montgomery and his contemporaries though saw such places as Aden, Cyprus, Gibraltar, Malta and Suez as vital strategic stepping stones for any future global conflict. If Britain relinquished control then that would impede its ability to fight the Soviet Union should the need arise. Furthermore, Churchill was not prepared to abandon Malaya in the face of a Communist insurgency that did not represent the population. Singapore remained a cornerstone in British strategic interests in the Far East.

His retention of Kenya as well as Northern and Southern Rhodesia was much more problematic. 'He deeply distrusted the proliferation of states in Africa,' explained Anthony Montague Browne, 'with their democratic political slogan so often – ...in his words: "One man, one vote, once"'.[3] Churchill feared that the creation of such states as Malawi and Zambia would result in anarchy. 'He felt that in the broader sweep of history,' added Montague Browne, 'the breaking up of units like the Central African Federation was a terrible mistake leading, possibly, to the barbarism and anarchy of the Dark Ages.'[4]

Whereas Churchill had often been autocratic during his first stint as prime minister, during his second he relied much more on his ministers. 'It is idle to pretend that Winston himself was not, at times, maddening,' observed Mary Soames. 'He could on occasion, behave like a spoilt and naughty child. A loyal and affectionate staff often managed so that these usually brief outbursts passed unnoticed.'[5] Nonetheless, his advancing years and health problems forced him to mellow his leadership style. It was sheer will power that kept him in office in the face of regular calls to retire. Even so he no longer had the drive or energy to micro-manage policy as he had once done. 'I joined the cabinet as his [defence] minister at the beginning of 1952,' recalled Field Marshal Alexander, 'and found Sir Winston had gathered around him all his old friends and colleagues who had served him, or had been associated with him, in war years.'[6] Notably Churchill was ably assisted by four men in particular, Lord Butler, Anthony Eden, Oliver Lyttelton and Harold Macmillan, two of whom were future prime ministers.

Lord Butler helped to protect Churchill domestically by rescuing the economy. Churchill chose well when he opted for Butler rather than Lyttelton as his Chancellor of the Exchequer. He knew that it was vital to orchestrate an economic recovery within two or three years if Britain was to fund its re-armament. Butler inherited the post-war balance of payments crisis that had been exacerbated by the Korean War and Britain's ongoing colonial commitments. Butler's budget proved a triumph and ensured that by May 1952 calls for Churchill's early retirement had been silenced thanks to the country's recovering finances. Macmillan ensured that the Conservatives lived up to their house building pledge.

Despite their differences Churchill relied on Eden and trusted his judgement. 'As Foreign Secretary, Churchill was prepared to leave more to his discretion,' noted Harold Wilson, 'than either Chamberlain before him or Macmillan after him would have been prepared to do.'[7] Wilson speculated that Eden's illness in 1953 was one of the reasons that Churchill did not step down then. Instead he gallantly hung on 'when he was also seriously ill, but waited to give Eden time to complete his recovery'.[8] This situation prompted Macmillan to hope that he might replace Churchill. 'As we talked,' recalled historian Sir Martin Gilbert, 'it became clear to me just how much Macmillan had hoped to succeed Churchill as Prime Minister in 1955. He had been encouraged in this hope by Eden's recurrent illness, and his own promotion to Defence Minister in the last months of Churchill's premiership.'[9] In the end Macmillan patiently waited his turn.

Lyttelton helped with the inordinately difficult and complex task of disengaging Britain from the Empire. One of Churchill's lasting regrets was Attlee's handling of Indian independence and partition. If he had won the election in 1945 he would certainly have tried to slow it down with potentially catastrophic consequences for the British administration there. Rather unfairly Churchill blamed Mountbatten and not Attlee for the rushed nature of Britain's departure from India. 'The only part of my father's extraordinary career,' recalled Patricia Mountbatten, 'that Churchill did not agree with was his service as Viceroy of India.'[10] She felt that this was because Churchill was firmly a child of the empire and an ardent imperialist, 'This disapproval arose because Churchill... could not bear to think that the new post-war Labour Government... was "giving away India and the British Empire," and my father was aiding and abetting.'[11] If Churchill had become prime minister again in 1945 it is very doubtful that Mountbatten would have been appointed the last Viceroy.

Mountbatten called Churchill a 'great man'[12] but whether they truly settled their differences is open to debate. In the summer of 1952 while Churchill was on holiday in the South of France he invited Mountbatten to dine with him. The latter at the time was commanding the Mediterranean Fleet. To Mountbatten's alarm Churchill became quite emotional. 'With tears in his eyes,' Mountbatten told his daughter, 'he kept repeating how much he loved me, that he had quite forgotten and forgiven me about India... Quite embarrassing.'[13] As far as Mountbatten was concerned there was nothing to forgive.

Harold Wilson was full of praise for Attlee's handing of India. 'For none will deny that he was the statesman who transformed, irrevocably,' wrote Wilson generously, 'the British Empire into the Commonwealth of Nations.'[14] However, it was Lyttelton who did much to implement Churchill's desire to remould the Empire into the Commonwealth. Anthony Montague Browne recalled, 'He once summed up to me his political aims in life as follows: "A strong and united Commonwealth and a happy and peaceful world"'.[15] Churchill wanted to head off the spread of republicanism and declarations of independence, which would have seen a complete break from British influence and the monarchy.[16] 'To my mind Oliver [Lyttelton] has been underestimated in modern history,' wrote Lord Butler in his memoirs, 'he was a man of immense ability who shone in everything which he undertook.'[17]

Churchill and Lyttelton helped to sow the seeds for independence and democracy in both Kenya and Malaya, which like India were wholly British constructs. By resisting the Mau Mau and the Malayan Communists they ensured the eventual emergence of stable modern unitary states with the creation of the republics of Kenya and Malaysia. Churchill cannot be held solely responsible for some of the more unsavoury methods used to achieve this. He did not create the strategy and tactics employed to defeat the insurgents. If there was one thing he understood it was that sectarian violence had to be overcome before democracy could flourish. Ireland and India were proof of this. The birth of Rhodesia and Zambia from the two Rhodesias proved even more troubled affairs, but Churchill had no hand in that.

Churchill's well-intentioned attempts to cling on in Egypt in order to keep control of the Suez Canal simply made things worse. It not only greatly antagonised the Egyptians, it displeased the Americans who saw it as flagrant imperialism. The Anglo-French attempt to retake Suez was the high watermark of British military power and imperial ambition. The enormous diplomatic outcry signalled the international community would not tolerate such adventurism by two of the world's leading democracies. Eden, with Churchill behind the scenes, gravely misjudged the situation and did irreparable harm to Britain's reputation. The Soviet Union was grateful because Suez distracted attention from what it had done in Hungary. Likewise, Britain's attempts to retain Aden and Cyprus simply fuelled insurrection, which ultimately resulted in independence anyway.

Churchill's second premiership inevitably lacked the dynamism and the iconic moments of his first. It was a different time and he was much older. Would, though, Eden have done a better job had Churchill stepped aside in 1945? Chances are the Conservatives would still not have got back in power. Both Eden and Macmillan were highly experienced and very competent politicians, but they did not have the charisma and appeal of Churchill. Ironically they became prime ministers by default, much as Churchill had done first time, not through the ballot box.

Churchill always denied that he was partly the architect of the Cold War. 'I am certainly responsible for pointing out to the free world...' he said in a speech at Woodford on 20 April 1959, 'the perils inherent in complacently accepting the advance of Communist imperialism. But apart from this, my conscience is clear.'[18] He preferred to forget that in a moment of bonhomie he had greenlit Stalin's occupation of Eastern Europe. Churchill should have known better.

Perhaps Churchill's greatest post-war legacy was helping to steer the world away from nuclear Armageddon. He had fully supported the Manhattan project and the use of the atomic bomb against Japan in order to end the Second World War. Never again though was he an advocate for the employment of nuclear weapons. Churchill was horrified that Attlee acquiesced to the McMahon Act and surrendered Britain's veto on the use of the American bomb. He fought to get this reversed at least when it came to its deployment from British soil. American nuclear threats against China had filled him with dread.

It was American intransigence that forced him to press on with building Britain's independent nuclear deterrent. Nonetheless, the development of the hydrogen bomb convinced him that fighting a nuclear war would be madness. He understood that the western democracies must maintain strong conventional armed forces, because it was still possible to fight a war without resorting to the bomb. NATO's strategy came to epitomise that sentiment despite the eventual deployment of tactical nuclear weapons.

Although Eisenhower did not always see eye to eye with Churchill, he nonetheless greatly respected him. Eisenhower wrote, 'I found him, despite the weight of years, still a source of inspiration, of wisdom, and above all of faith that right and justice firmly maintained will ever triumph.'[19] This seems a very fair summation of Churchill's outlook and his intentions. In a broadcast as Churchill's coffin was carried up the Thames in 1965 Eisenhower said, 'Winston Churchill was Britain – he was the embodiment of British defiance to threat, her courage in adversity, her calmness in danger, her moderation in success.'[20] In the face of Communism and the end of Empire Churchill always tried to do what he believed was right and for the good of humanity. Such was his selfless devotion to public service even in his twilight years.

Epilogue

The Unthinkable

It is important to acknowledge that Churchill at the end of the Second World War briefly considered doing the unthinkable. While his role in the Cold War is well known, what is not generally appreciated is that before it began he briefly contemplated deliberately starting the Third World War. The British Chiefs of Staff had discussed the future threat posed by the Soviets to Europe as early as July and October 1944. 'Churchill was concerned that the [Allied] attacks on Europe were too confined to Western Europe,' recalled Harold Wilson, '...the victorious Russians were not only driving the defeated Germans through Poland back to Berlin, they were enveloping most of Eastern Europe.'[1] It was accepted the Soviet Union at some point would go from being a key ally to a threat. This was an unpalatable prospect and something the Foreign Office had not wanted to countenance at the time. Certainly it wanted no talk of choosing sides after the war.

Churchill had been angered by the Red Army's failure, deliberate or otherwise, to save the Polish Home Army from annihilation in 1944. It was this that had given Stalin a free hand in Warsaw. Churchill, alarmed by the prospect of 'that Russian bear sprawled over Europe'[2], had to examine every option. This was especially the case once the Red Army had full control of Poland and eastern Germany. His inability to influence the political future of Poland greatly frustrated him, but was he ever prepared to fight for its freedom? The Soviets also seemed to have designs on Denmark. 'It looks as if the Germans opposite Monty may surrender en masse,' observed John Colville, 'but there is a threat of the Russians trying to get to Denmark first by parachute, and thus control the Kattegat.'[3]

Churchill, just as Hitler was committing suicide in Berlin, had written to Stalin highlighting the perils of Europe being partitioned between the victorious western Allies and the supporters of Communism. 'It is quite obvious that their quarrel would tear the world to pieces,' warned Churchill, 'and all of us leading men on either side... would be shamed before history.'[4] What he said publicly and what he did privately proved to be two different things. By the end of the war the British armed forces were at the height of their power. This would have been the prime time to confront Stalin. It was essentially a one-shot deal. The Red Army had suffered the most appalling casualties taking Berlin and was at the very end of its supply lines. In early May 1945 Churchill controversially instructed the

222

British Chiefs of Staff to draw up plans for a military operation to drive the Red Army from Germany and Poland. To spearhead an attack towards Berlin he had the 7th Armoured Division deployed at Hamburg, the 3rd Division at Bremen and the 51st Highland Division at Bremerhaven. To the south at Magdeburg was the US 2nd Armored Division.[5] All were tough highly combat-experienced units.

On 12 May, just four days after VE Day, he sounded out President Truman over how best to stand up to the Soviet Union. 'If it is handled firmly before our strength is dispersed, Europe may be saved another bloodbath,' said Churchill. 'Otherwise the whole fruits of our victory may be cast away.'[6] Unknown to Churchill he was not alone in his desire to confront Communism head on. US General George Patton in Bavaria was all for taking on the Red Army as soon as possible. Patton, like Field Marshal Montgomery, received complaints from the Soviets about his slowness in disbanding German units. Over an open telephone line he told Eisenhower's deputy, General Joseph McNarney, 'We are going to have to fight them sooner or later... We can do it ourselves easily with the help of the German troops.'[7] Eisenhower responded to this and Patton's slowness in de-Nazifying Bavaria by sacking him. This was clearly a measure of America's aversion to showing any hostility towards the Soviet Union.

Churchill's proposal to the Chiefs of Staff was to attack on 1 July 1945 before the General Election, the Potsdam Conference, the atomic bombing of Japan and crucially before the British and American armies began to demobilise in Europe. The far-reaching ramifications of this were simply appalling. 'I asked him if he took charge of all the political aspects of launching a war on our ally!' recalled an alarmed Field Marshal Brooke. 'He said we could leave that aspect and concentrate on the military problem.'[8] Brooke knew that the chances of President Truman ever agreeing to such a course of action, especially with the war still going on against Japan, were non-existent.

Nevertheless, on 22 May 1945 the Joint Planning Staff produced the highly appropriately named Operation Unthinkable.[9] This was put together on the basis of the involvement of British, American, Polish and even German troops. In the case of the latter, prisoners of war were to be armed. According to Field Marshal Montgomery's figures there were some twenty million Germans in the British Zone, which included two and a half million German military personnel. Many German soldiers assumed it would only be a matter of time before they joined Britain and America to fight the Soviet Union. Major General Lewis Lyne, the commander of the 7th Armoured, had no inkling that Churchill might order him to rearm the prisoners he had been busy rounding up.

Crucially the plan assessed that in order to safeguard Poland it would be necessary to occupy western Russia. In other words the Allies would have to replicate Hitler's Operation Barbarossa. The flaw in this strategy, just as Hitler discovered and the Joint Planning Staff pointed out, was that Soviet forces could withdrew beyond the Ural Mountains. 'There was virtually no limit to the distance to which it would be necessary for the Allies to penetrate into Russia in order to render further resistance impossible,' warned the planners.[10]

If this Top Secret plan had been leaked to the press there would have been enormous international outrage. Having fought a bloody world war to defeat

Hitler and end Nazi control of the occupied territories, Britain was now in turn advocating the occupation of the Soviet Union. For Churchill public knowledge of this would have meant political suicide. It would have caused such a scandal that not even he could have survived and it would have left his international reputation in tatters.

Furthermore, for Unthinkable to defeat the Soviet Union it would have required a global war. 'The result of a total war with Russia is not possible to forecast,' concluded the joint planners. They also noted, 'Owing to the special need for secrecy, the normal staff in Service Ministries have not been consulted.'[11] The only slim chance of success was that an initial victory in Europe might force Stalin to accept terms. However, his military superiority in eastern Europe meant that such a scenario was highly unlikely. After the fall of Berlin the Soviets were increasingly suspicious of British and American intentions so were hardly likely to be taken completely by surprise.

Stalin was far from pleased how the British were treating their defeated enemy. When Marshal Zhukov was summoned to the Kremlin on 20 May the Soviet leader aired such concerns. 'While we have disarmed all the officers and men of the German army and placed them in prisoner-of-war camps, the British are keeping the German troops in a state of combat readiness,' alleged Stalin.[12] He also noted that Field Marshal Montgomery was stockpiling German weapons. 'I think,' he continued, 'the British seek to retain the German troops so that they can be used later.'[13] This was counter to Montgomery's orders which were 'to disarm and disband the German armed forces'.[14]

Soviet suspicions were confirmed when Montgomery kept 700,000 former German personnel in concentration areas waiting to be disbanded. 'Montgomery took them all,' complained Stalin to Nikita Khrushchev, 'and he took their arms.'[15] Furthermore, German military headquarters were maintained to administer them and around 100,000 German personnel were organised into a corps. Montgomery saw no reason to establish a British administration when a German one already existed. Although the German units were all disarmed Montgomery argued he had nowhere to put them if they were dispersed. In his memoirs he avoided admitting that he had kept them in place for any other reason. This situation led to public accusations being made by Zhukov, and Montgomery was obliged to order the forces to be disbanded. However, by the time this took place Churchill was out of office.

Churchill's actions are surprising in light of Clementine having just returned from a five-week goodwill tour of Soviet cities as a guest of the Soviet Red Cross, during which she had presented Stalin with a gold fountain pen. 'My husband wishes me to express the hope that you will write him many friendly messages with it,' she had told her host.[16] Nor was Churchill ever in a position to enact such a harebrained scheme as Unthinkable. His Coalition government came to an end on 23 May leaving him Prime Minister of a Conservative caretaker government until the General Election on 5 July.

Nonetheless, the day after the Coalition dissolved the Chiefs of Staff gathered to assess the Unthinkable plan. Field Marshal Brooke was horrified, noting, 'The idea is of course fantastic and the chances of success quite impossible.'[17] No one round the table was convinced that a pre-emptive war was remotely a good idea. 'The result of this study made it clear that the best we could hope for,' concluded Brooke gloomily, 'was to drive the Russians back to about the same line as the Germans had reached. And then what?'[18] Furthermore, many senior British commanders in Germany knew it would be unwise to underestimate the Soviets. 'The Russian Army of May, 1945, may have been young, may have been uneducated, may have been uncouth,' observed Lieutenant General Brian Horrocks, 'but it was a truly formidable fighting machine.'[19] Brooke was just grateful that Churchill was now distracted. 'For the present he is absorbed in this mad election,' noted Brooke gratefully in his diary, 'and for the next few months he will be unable to devote much attention to war plans!'[20]

The Chiefs of Staffs' findings were relayed back to Churchill. Thankfully he appreciated that even contemplating launching the Third World War was sheer lunacy. 'The Operation Unthinkable documents do not imply that Churchill was an inveterate anti-Communist warmonger,' argues historian Andrew Roberts, 'but show that he was preparing for every eventuality, however unlikely or unwelcome.'[21] Furthermore, he did not have the authority to act on it. Instead the following month the plan morphed into the basis for defending the British Isles in the event of a Soviet attack. This contingency planning was spurred on by the fear that the Soviets might take advantage of American troops relocating from Europe to the Pacific.

Although the offensive version of Operation Unthinkable was little more than a paper exercise, it is still very sobering to know that Churchill toyed with the idea of attacking his wartime ally. If this had happened there would have been no Cold War and his legacy would have been completely ruined. Furthermore, with the Soviet Union at war there is a good chance that China, Indochina and North Korea might not have been lost to Communism. Instead throughout the Cold War Churchill very wisely tried not to 'be shamed before history'. His plan to attack the Soviet Union would remain a closely guarded secret for over fifty years.

Cold War Timeline

1944 Churchill agrees with Stalin that Eastern Europe, apart from Greece, should become a Soviet sphere of influence, sowing the seeds for the partition of Europe

1944 Churchill intervenes in Greece in support of the Royalists against the Communists. Stalin refrains from backing the Greek Communists

1945 Churchill loses General Election to Clement Attlee and the Labour party

1945 Partition of Korea as a result of the Soviet and US occupation zones in the North and South

1945 Britain helps France reassert control of Indochina after the Japanese occupation ends

1945 Britain helps the Netherlands reassert control of the Dutch East Indies after the Japanese occupation ends

1946 Churchill makes his 'Iron Curtain' speech in Fulton, Missouri referring to the partition of Europe, heralding the Cold War between Communism and Democracy

1946 The Chinese Civil War recommences after a hiatus during the Second World War. Stalin arms Mao Zedong's Chinese Communists. Nationalists under Chang Kai-Shek are backed by America

1946 French Indochina War commences with Vietnamese Communists led by Ho Chi Minh trying to take power from France

1947 India gains independence heralding the beginning of the end for the British Empire. India partitioned with the creation of Pakistan

1947 Kashmir's hopes of independence dashed after partition by India and Pakistan

1948 Burma and Ceylon gain independence from Britain

1948 Britain withdraws from Palestine and the State of Israel is created

1948 Berlin Blockade, Soviets sever access to West Berlin (administered by America, Britain and France) sparking fears of a third world war

1948 Soviet, Czech and Polish operations conducted to destroy the anti-Communist Ukrainian Insurgent Army in Ukraine; resistance continues until the mid-1950s

1948 Hyderabad's hopes of independence dashed after invasion by India

1948 Malayan Campaign starts – Chinese Communist revolt against British rule

1949 Berlin Blockade is defeated by a massive airlift which keeps West Berlin resupplied and forces Stalin to backdown

1949 Formation of NATO to protect Western Europe

1949 Greek Civil War comes to an end with the defeat of the Communists

1949 Indonesian War of Independence ends - Netherlands relinquishes control of the Dutch East Indies with the creation of Indonesia

1949 Mao Zedong's Communists take power in China. Nationalists under Chiang Kai-shek flee to Taiwan

1950 China invades and annexes neighbouring Tibet

1950 Korean War – Communist North invades the South using Soviet-supplied weapons. United Nations sends troops, including American and British, to save the South. In response China intervenes in support of the North

1951 Churchill becomes Prime Minister for a second term. He continues Britain's involvement in the Korean War (which drags on until 1953) and continues to resist the Communists in Malaya (campaign drags on until 1960)

1951 Unrest in Tibet against Chinese rule

1952 Mau Mau Revolt against British rule in Kenya (drags on until 1960)

1953 Churchill suspends the new government in British Guiana, fearing a Communist takeover

1953 Stalin dies and is succeeded by Georgy Malenkov. Churchill wants a three-power summit

1953 Uprising in East Berlin against Soviet rule which spreads to the rest of East Germany, but is swiftly crushed

1953 Cuban Civil War commences with a Communist rising

1953 Civil War in Laos (formerly part of Indochina) commences

1954 Growing unrest against British rule in Cyprus after Britain announces it will never be independent

1954 America backs a rebel invasion of Guatemala to oust a pro-Communist government

1954 French Indochina war ends with Communist victory after French defeat at Dien Bien Phu. Vietnam is partitioned leaving the Communists controlling the North

1954 Algerian Revolution begins against French rule sparking war in North Africa

1954 Britain signs new Anglo-Egyptian treaty agreeing to withdraw troops from the Suez Canal

1955 Due to ill-health Churchill resigns as Prime Minister and is succeeded by his protégé Anthony Eden

1955 Albania, Bulgaria, Czechoslovakia, East Germany, Hungary, Poland and Romania are tied to the Soviet Union by the Warsaw Pact

1955 Greek Cypriot revolt against British rule, state of emergency declared

1955 Vietnam War commences – America steps in to help defend the South, Britain remains on the side-lines

1955 Ukrainian insurgents finally overwhelmed by the Soviet Army

1955 First Sudanese Civil War commences

1956 Sudan gains independence from Britain

1956 Last British forces withdraw from the Suez Canal

1956 Eden and Churchill meet Soviet leader Nikita Khrushchev in London

1956 Arab-Israeli War – Israel overruns Sinai to reach Suez

1956 Britain and France occupy the Suez Canal after the Egyptians nationalise it. International uproar, Eden forced to resign and Britain and France withdraw

1956 Hungarian Revolt against Soviet rule is swiftly crushed by the Soviet Army

1959 Castro's Communists take power in Cuba and align with the Soviet Union

1962 Cuban Missile Crisis threatens nuclear war between the Soviet Union and United States

1962 Indo-Chinese Border War sparks fear of a wider war

1964 America escalates its involvement in the Vietnam War by sending troops while the Soviet Union and China back the North with weapons. Britain still refrains from getting involved

1965 Churchill dies at the age of 90

1989 Fall of the Iron Curtain which leads to German reunification

1991 Collapse of the Soviet Union finally ending the Cold War

Acknowledgements

I must confess after *Churchill Master and Commander: Winston Churchill at War 1895-1945* I never intended writing another volume on Churchill. Indeed its reception rather took me by surprise. I was inordinately grateful to Justin Reash at the International Churchill Society; Gregg Collins, Christopher Tidmore and Walter Wolf at the Churchill Society of New Orleans; David Wynne at the North Florida Churchill Society; Craig Horn and Rick Hudson at the Churchill Society of North Carolina; Elisebeth Checkel, Stan Guszczewski and Will Randall at the Sir Winston Spencer Churchill Society of Edmonton, Dr Robert Citino and Jeremy Collins at the National WWII Museum, New Orleans, Barry Singer at Chartwell Booksellers, New York, John Q Adams and Dan Reinbold at Valour Canada, Jackie Jansen van Doorn at The Military Museums Foundation, Calgary, and Lord Andrew Roberts for so generously embracing and championing *Churchill Master and Commander*.

It was the gallant Christopher Tidmore who was insistent that as a Churchillian I should continue the journey and follow Winston's life to the end. Why had I not covered his second premiership and the Cold War years he asked? Being a former Cold War warrior myself this got me thinking that perhaps there was more to say on Churchill's military exploits. I am therefore grateful to Tara Moran at Frontline Books for so readily giving *Churchill Cold War Warrior* a home. As a commissioning editor her support went way above and beyond the call of duty. My thanks to the rest of the team, Olivia Camozzi-Jones, Harriet Fielding and Jon Wilkinson for doing such an excellent job and to fellow writer Gerry van Tonder for producing the fine maps. Also thanks to Matt Lowing at Bloomsbury for his sterling assistance with reference material. Likewise, my thanks to Lizzie Rowles at William Collins for early sight of Emeritus Professor David Reynolds' *Mirrors of Greatness: Churchill and the Leaders Who Shaped Him*. Finally my gratitude to fellow Churchillian Professor Richard Toye for kindly writing the foreword. His formidable expertise on the life and career of Churchill easily precedes him.

Bibliography

Date of publication is the edition consulted.

Books

Alao, Abiodun & Hook, Christa, *Mau-Mau Warrior*, Oxford: Osprey, 2006

Alexander, Bevin, *Korea: The Lost War*, London: Arrow, 1989

Alexander, Field Marshal, *The Alexander Memoirs 1940-1945*, London: Cassell, 1962

Andrew, Christopher, *The Defence of the Realm: The Authorized History of MI5*, London: Allen Lane, 2009

Archard, Louis, *Hungarian Uprising: Budapest's Cataclysmic Twelve Days, 1956*, Barnsley: Pen & Sword, 2018

Arthur, Max, *Churchill The Life: An Authorised Pictorial Biography*, London: Cassell, 2017

Auton, Jim, *The Secret Betrayal of Britain's Wartime Allies: The Appeasement of Stalin and its Post-War Consequences*, Barnsley: Pen & Sword, 2014

Avnery, Uri, *1948: A Soldiers Tale – The Bloody Road to Jerusalem*, Oxford: Oneworld, 2008

Avon, The Rt. Hon. The Earl of, *The Eden Memoirs: The Reckoning*, London: Cassell, 1965

Ball, S.J., *The Cold War: An International History 1947-1991*, London: Bloomsbury, 2011

Barker, Brian, *When the Queen was Crowned*, London: Routledge & Kegan Paul, 1976

Bartel, Fritz, *The Triumph of Broken Promises: The End of the Cold War and the Rise of Neoliberalism*, Cambridge, MA: Harvard University Press, 2022

Beckett, Ian (ed.), *Communist Military Machine*, London: Hamlyn, 1985

Bence-Jones, Mark, *The Viceroys of India*, London: Constable, 1984

Best, Geoffrey, *Churchill: A Study in Greatness*, New York: Oxford University Press, 2003

Black, Jeremy, *The Cold War: A Military History*, London: Bloomsbury, 2015

Blakemore, Harold & Smith, Clifford T., *Latin America: Geographical Perspectives*, London: Methuen, 1974

Brogan, Patrick, *World Conflicts: Why and Where They Are Happening*, London: Bloomsbury, 1989

Burleigh, Michael, *Small Wars, Far Away Places: The Genesis of the Modern World 1945-65*, London: Macmillan, 2013

Bury, Helen, *Eisenhower and the Cold War Arms Race: 'Open Skies' and the Military-Industrial Complex*, London: Bloomsbury, 2020

Butler, Lord, *The Art of Memory: Friends in Perspective*, London: Hodder & Stoughton, 1982

Bryan III, J. & Murphy, Charles J.V., *The Windsor Story*, London: Granada, 1979

Caine, Michael, *The Elephant to Hollywood*, London: Hodder & Stoughton, 2010

Carew, Tim, *The Korean War: The Story of the Fighting Commonwealth Regiments*, London: Pan, 1970

Carradice, Phil, *The Cuban Missile Crisis: Thirteen Days on an Atomic Knife Edge October 1962*, Barnsley: Pen & Sword, 2017

Catchpole, Brian, *The Korean War 1950-53*, London: Constable, 2000

Catherwood, Christopher, *Churchill: The Story of the Greatest Briton in Words, Photographs and Documents*, London: SevenOaks, 2018

Chalfont, Alun, *Montgomery of Alamein*, London: Weidenfeld & Nicolson, 1976

Chang, Jung & Halliday, Jon, *Mao: The Unknown Story*, London: Jonathan Cape, 2005

Chant, Christopher, *War: Armed Conflicts of the 20th Century Outside the Two World Wars*, London: Hamlyn, 1988

Charlwood, David, *Suez Crisis 1956: End of Empire and the Reshaping of the Middle East*, Barnsley: Pen & Sword, 2019

Charmley, John, *Churchill's Grand Alliance: The Anglo-American Special Relationship 1940-57*, New York: Harcourt Brace, 1995

Chaudhuri, Nirad C., *Thy Hand, Great Anarch! India 1921-1952*, London: Chatto & Windus, 1987

Churchill, Randolph S., *Winston S. Churchill, Volume II, Young Statesman 1901-1914*, London: Heinemann, 1967

Churchill, Sarah, *A Thread in the Tapestry*, London: Andre Deutsch, 1967

Churchill, Sarah, *Keep on Dancing: An Autobiography*, London: Weidenfeld & Nicolson, 1981

Churchill, Winston S., *Frontiers and Wars: His Four Early Books covering his Life as Soldier and War Correspondent*, New York: Smithmark, 1995

Churchill, Winston S., *The Story of the Malakand Field Force*, Barnsley: Leo Cooper, 2002

Churchill, Winston S., *The Second World War: Closing the Ring*, London: Cassell, 1952

Churchill, Winston S., *The Second World War: Triumph and Tragedy*, London: Cassell, 1953

Churchill, Winston S., (grandson – ed.), *Never Give In! The Best of Winston Churchill's Speeches*, New York: Hyperion, 2003

Cimino, Al, *Roosevelt and Churchill: A Friendship that saved the World*, New York: Chartwell Books, 2018

Collier, Richard, *The War that Stalin Won*, London: Hamish Hamilton, 1983

Clarke, Peter, *Hope and Glory: Britain 1900-2000*, London: Penguin, 2004

Clarke, Peter, *Mr Churchill's Profession: Statesman, Orator, Writer*, London: Bloomsbury, 2013

Cohen, Ronald I. (ed), *The Heroic Memory: The Memorial Addresses to the Rt. Hon. Sir Winston Spencer Churchill Society Edmonton, Alberta, 1990-2014*, Edmonton: The Churchill Statue and Oxford Scholarship Foundation, 2016

Colville, John, *The Fringes of Power: 10 Downing Street Diaries 1939-1955*, New York: W.W. Norton, 1985

Crawley, Aidan, *De Gaulle*, London: William Collins, 1969

Crowder, Richard, *Aftermath: The Makers of the Postwar World*, New York: I.B. Tauris, 2015

Cullimore, Charles, *The Last Days of Empire and the Worlds of Business and Diplomacy: An Inside Account*, Barnsley: Pen & Sword, 2021

Cunningham-Boothe, Ashley & Farrar, Peter, *British Forces in the Korean War*, Leamington Spa: The British Korean Veterans Association, 1988

Danchev, Alex & Todman, Daniel (ed.), *War Diaries 1939-1945: Field Marshal Lord Alanbrooke*, London: Phoenix Press, 2002

D'Este, Carlo, *Patton: A Genius for War*, New York: Harper Perennial, 1996

Dewar, Lieutenant-Colonel Michael, *The British Army in Northern Ireland*, London: Arms & Armour Press, 1985

Dockrill, Michael, *British Defence since 1945*, Oxford: Basil Blackwell, 1988

Dockrill, Michael L. & Hopkins, Michael F., *The Cold War: 1945-1991*, London: Red Globe Press, 2006

Eisenhower, Dwight D., *At Ease: Stories I Tell to Friends*, London: Robert Hale, 1968

English, Adrian J., *Armed Forces of Latin America*, London: Jane's, 1984

Eprile, Cecil, *War and Peace in the Sudan 1955-1972*, Newton Abbot: David & Charles, 1974

Fall, Bernard B., *Hell in a Very Small Place: The Siege of Dien Bien Phu*, Cambridge, MA: Da Capo Press, 2002

Faught, C. Brad, *Churchill and Africa: Empire, Decolonisation and Race*, Barnsley: Pen & Sword, 2023

Fazan, S.H., *Colonial Kenya Observed: British Rule, Mau Mau and the Wind of Change*, London: Bloomsbury, 2020

Ferrier, Neil, (ed.), *Churchill: The Man of the Century*, London: Robinson, 1955

Fischer, Louis, *The Life of Mahatma Gandhi*, London: Harper Collins, 1997

Fisher, Nigel, *Harold Macmillan*, London: Weidenfeld & Nicolson, 1982

French, Patrick, *Liberty or Death: India's Journey to Independence and Division*, London: Harper Collins, 1997

French, Paul, *North Korea: State of Paranoia*, London: Zed, 2015

Gaddis, John Lewis, *The Cold War*, London: Penguin, 2007

Gilbert, Martin, *Churchill: A Life*, London: Pimlico, 2000

Gilbert, Martin (ed.), *Churchill: The Power of Words - His remarkable life recounted through his writings and speeches*, London: Bantam, 2014

Gilbert, Martin, *Descent into Barbarism: A History of the 20th Century 1933-1951*, London: Harper Collins, 1999

Gilbert, Martin, *In Search of Churchill*, London: Harper Collins, 1994

Gilbert, Martin, *Winston S. Churchill: Never Despair 1945-1965*, Boston: Houghton Mifflin, 1988

Gilbert, Martin, *Road to Victory: Winston S. Churchill 1941-1945*, London: William Heinemann, 1986

Gibson, Carrie, *Empire's Crossroads: A History of the Caribbean from Columbus to the Present Day*, London: Macmillan, 2014

Grehan, John, *The Berlin Airlift: The World's Largest Ever Air Supply Operation*, Barnsley: Air World, 2019

Grunwald, Henry Anatole, *Churchill The Life Triumphant: The Historical Record of Ninety Years*, New York: American Heritage Publishing, 1965

Hagedorn, Dan & Overall, Mario, *The Caribbean Legion and its Mercenary Air Forces 1947-1950*, Stroud: Lime Tree, 2021

Halliday, Jon & Cumings, Bruce, *Korea: The Unknown War*, London: Viking, 1988

Hamilton, Nigel, *Monty: The Field-Marshal 1944-1976*, London: Hamish Hamilton, 1986

Hardman, Robert, *Queen of our Times: The Life of Elizabeth II 1926-2022*, London: Macmillan, 2022

Hart-Davis, Duff (ed.), *King's Counsellor – Abdication and War: The Diaries of Sir Alan Lascelles*, London: Weidenfeld & Nicolson, 2006

Harte, John, *The Race for the Atom Bomb: How Soviet Russia Stole the Secrets of the Manhattan Project*, Barnsley: Pen & Sword, 2023

Hastings, Max, *Abyss: World on the Brink, The Cuban Missile Crisis 1962*, London: William Collins, 2023

Hastings, Max, *Finest Years: Churchill as Warlord 1940-45*, London: Harper Press, 2009

Hastings, Max, *The Korean War*, London: Michael Joseph, 1987

Hatch, Alden, *The Mountbattens*, London: W. H. Allen, 1966

Heritage, Andrew, *The Cold War: An Illustrated History*, Sparkford: Haynes, 2010

Hermiston, Roger, *All Behind You, Winston: Churchill's Great Coalition 1940-45*, London: Aurum Press, 2017

Holmes, Richard, *In the Footsteps of Churchill*, London: BBC Books, 2005

Hough, Richard, *Mountbatten Hero of Our Time*, London: Weidenfeld & Nicolson, 1981

Hough, Richard, *Winston and Clementine: The Triumphs and Tragedies of the Churchills*, London: Bantam, 1991

Horne, Alistair, *Macmillan 1894-1956*, London: Macmillan, 1988

Horrocks, *Lieutenant General Sir Brian, A Full Life*, London: Collins, 1960

Jackson, Julian, *Charles de Gaulle*, London: Cardinal, 1990

Jackson, Robert, *The Malayan Emergency & Indonesian Confrontation: The Commonwealth's Wars 1948-1960*, Barnsley: Pen & Sword, 2021

James, Lawrence, *Churchill and Empire: Portrait of an Imperialist*, London: Weidenfeld & Nicolson, 2014

Jeffery, Keith, *MI6: The History of the Secret Intelligence Service 1909-1949*, London: Bloomsbury, 2011

Jenkins, Roy, *Churchill A Biography*, New York: Farrar, Straus & Giroux, 2001

Jowett, Philip, *Chiang Kai-shek versus Mao Tse-tung. The Battle for China 1946-1949*, Barnsley: Pen & Sword, 2018

Judt, Tony, *Postwar: A History of Europe Since 1945*, London: Pimlico, 2007

Keay, John, *India: A History*, London: William Collins, 2022

Kennedy, Robert F., *13 Days: The Cuban Missile Crisis*, London: Pan, 1969

Khan, Sulmaan Wasif, *Haunted by Chaos: China's Grand Strategy from Mao Zedong to Xi Jinping*, Cambridge, MA: Harvard University Press, 2022

Khrushchev, Nikita, *Khrushchev Remembers*, London: Andre Deutsch, 1971

Kitson, Major Frank, *Gangs and Counter-gangs*, London: Barrie & Rockliff, 1960

Kurzman, Dan, *Genesis 1948: The First Arab-Israeli War*, New York: Signet, 1972

Kyle, Keith, *Suez*, London: Weidenfeld & Nicolson, 1991

Lacey, Robert, *Royal: Her Majesty Queen Elizabeth II*, London: Time Warner, 2002

Laffin, John, & Chappell, Mike, *Arab Armies of the Middle East Wars 1948-73*, London: Osprey, 1982

Laffin, John & Chappell, Mike, *The Israeli Army in the Middle East Wars 1948-73*, London: Osprey, 1982

Lamb, Richard, *Churchill as War Leader: Right or Wrong?* London: Bloomsbury, 1993

Lamb, Richard, *The Macmillan Years 1957-1963: The Emerging Truth*, London: John Murray, 1995

Langley, Michael, *Inchon Landing: MacArthur's Last Triumph*, London: Batsford, 1979

Larman, Alexander, *The Windsors at War: The Nazi Threat to the Crown*, London: Weidenfeld & Nicolson, 2023

Lash, Joseph P., *Eleanor and Franklin*, London: Andre Deutsch, 1971

Leaming, Barbara, *Churchill Defiant: Fighting On 1945-1955*, New York: Harper Perennial, 2011

LeBor, Adam, *City of Oranges: Arabs and Jews in Jaffa*, London: Bloomsbury, 2007

Linklater, Eric, *The Campaign in Italy*, London: Her Majesty's Stationery Office, 1977

Lloyd, Selwyn, *Suez 1956: A Personal Account*, London: Jonathan Cape, 1978

Lownie, Andrew, *The Mountbattens*, London: Blink, 2019

Lownie, Andrew, *Traitor King: The Scandalous Exile of the Duke and Duchess of Windsor*, London: Blink, 2021

Mackintosh, Malcolm, *Juggernaut: A History of the Soviet Armed Forces*, London: Secker & Warburg, 1967

Macmillan, Harold, *The Blast of War 1939-1945*, London: Macmillan, 1967

Macmillan, Harold, *Tides of Fortune 1945-1955*, London: Macmillan, 1969

Mason, Philip, *A Matter of Honour: An Account of the Indian Army, its Officers and Men*, London: Jonathan Cape, 1974

Malkasian, Carter, *The Korean War 1950-1953*, Oxford: Osprey, 2001

Maxwell, Neville, *India's China War*, Harmondsworth: Pelican, 1972

McHugo, John, *A Concise History of the Arabs*, London: Saqi, 2016

McKay, Sinclair, *Berlin: Life and Loss in the City that shaped the Century*, London: Viking, 2022

McKinstry, Leo, *Attlee and Churchill: Allies in War, Adversaries in Peace*, London: Atlantic Books, 2019

Midgley, Peter (ed.), *The Heroic Memory: The Memorial Addresses to the Rt. Hon. Sir Winston Spencer Churchill Society Edmonton, Alberta, 1965-1989*, Edmonton: The Churchill Statue and Oxford Scholarship Foundation, 2005

Mollo, Boris, *The Indian Army*, Poole: Blandford, 1981

Montgomery, Brian, *A Field-Marshal in the Family*, London: Constable, 1973

Montgomery, Field Marshal the Viscount, *A Concise History of Warfare*, London: Collins, 1972

Montgomery, Field-Marshal the Viscount, *The Memoirs*, London: Collins, 1958

Moran, Lord, *Winston Churchill: The Struggle for Survival 1940-1965*, London: Constable, 1966

Morris, James, *Farewell the Trumpets: An Imperial Retreat*, London: Penguin, 1979

Morrow, Ann, *The Queen*, London: Granada, 1983

Morton, Andrew, *The Queen*, London: Michael O'Mara, 2022

Morton, Andrew, *Elizabeth & Margaret: The Intimate World of the Windsor Sisters*, London: Michael O'Mara, 2021

Mountbatten, Earl, *Mountbatten: Eighty Years in Pictures*, London: Macmillan, 1979

Moynahan, Brian, *The Claws of the Bear: A History of the Soviet Armed Forces from 1917 to Present*, London: Hutchinson, 1989

Muggeridge, Malcolm, *Chronicles of Wasted Time, Volume 2, The Infernal Grove*, London: Collins, 1973

Murray-Brown, Jeremy, *Kenyatta*, New York: E.P. Dutton, 1973

Nel, Elizabeth, *Mr Churchill's Secretary*, London: Hodder & Stoughton, 1961

Nester, William, *Winston Churchill and the Art of Leadership: How Winston Changed the World*, Barnsley: Frontline Books, 2020

Nicolson, Nigel (ed.), *Harold Nicolson: Diaries and Letters 1945-62*, London: Collins, 1968

Nicolson, Nigel (ed.), *Vita and Harold: The Letters of Vita Sackville-West and Harold Nicolson*, London: Weidenfeld & Nicolson, 1992

Norman, Dr Andrew, *Winston Churchill: Portrait of an Unquiet Mind*, Barnsley: Pen & Sword, 2012

O'Ballance, Edgar, *The Wars in Vietnam 1954-1973*, Shepperton: Ian Allan, 1975

Ovendale, Ritchie, *The Origins of the Arab-Israeli Wars*, Harlow: Longman, 1985

Owen, Frank, *Tempestuous Journey: Lloyd George his Life and Times*, London: Hutchinson, 1954

Parritt, Brigadier Brian, *Chinese Hordes and Human Waves: A Personal Perspective of the Korean War 1950-1953*, Barnsley: Pen & Sword, 2020

Pelling, Henry, *Winston Churchill*, London: Macmillan, 1974

Pendle, George, *A History of Latin America*, London: Penguin, 1990

Percox, David, *Britain, Kenya and the Cold War: Imperial Defence, Colonial Security and Decolonisation*, London: I.B. Tauris, 2012

Pimlott, Ben, *The Queen: A Biography of Elizabeth II*, London: Harper Collins, 1996

Pimlott, John (ed.), *Guerrilla Warfare*, London: Bison, 1985

Pivka, Otto von, *Armies of the Middle East*, Cambridge: Patrick Stephens, 1979

Ponting, Clive, *Churchill*, London: Sinclair-Stevenson, 1994

Purnell, Sonia, *First Lady: The Life and Wars of Clementine Churchill*, London: Aurum Press, 2015

Raghavan, Srinath, *India's War: The Making of Modern South Asia 1939-1945*, London: Penguin, 2017

Read, Simon, *Winston Churchill Reporting: Adventures of a Young War Correspondent*, Boston: Da Capo, 2015

Rees, Laurence, *World War Two Behind Closed Doors: Stalin, the Nazis and the West*, London: BBC Books, 2008

Reynolds, David, *Mirrors of Greatness: Churchill and the Leaders Who Shaped Him*, London: William Collins, 2023

Ridgway, Matthew B., *The War in Korea*, London: Barrie & Rockliff, 1968

Roberts, Andrew, *A History of the English-Speaking Peoples Since 1900*, London: Weidenfeld & Nicolson, 2006

Roberts, Andrew, *Churchill: Walking with Destiny*, London: Penguin, 2019

Roberts, Andrew, *Eminent Churchillians*, London: Weidenfeld & Nicolson, 1994

Robinson, Derek, *Just Testing*, London: Collins Harvill, 1985

Robinson H., *Latin America*, London: MacDonald & Evans, 1970

Roosevelt, Eleanor, *The Autobiography of Eleanor Roosevelt*, New York: Da Capo Press, 1992

Roskill, Stephen, *Churchill and the Admirals*, Barnsley: Pen & Sword, 2013

Rottman, Gordon L. & Dennis, Peter, *Inch'on 1950: The Last Great Amphibious Assault*, Oxford: Osprey, 2006

Ruane, Kevin, *Churchill and the Bomb: In War and Cold War*, London: Bloomsbury, 2018

Ryder, Chris, *The Fateful Split: Catholics and the Royal Ulster Constabulary*, London: Methuen, 2004

Sandys, Celia, *Churchill: By His Granddaughter*, London: Imperial War Museum, 2010

Schiff, Ze'ev, *A History of the Israeli Army: 1874 to the Present*, London: Sidgwick & Jackson, 1987

Schofield, Victoria, *Wavell: Soldier & Statesman*, London: John Murray, 2006

Scurr, John, & Chappell, Mike, *The Malayan Campaign 1948-60*, London: Osprey, 1982

Sebag Montefiore, Simon, *Stalin: The Court of the Red Czar*, London: Weidenfeld & Nicolson, 2003

Service, Robert, *Stalin: A Biography*, London: Pan, 2005

Shawcross, William, *Queen Elizabeth The Queen Mother: The Official Biography*, London: Macmillan, 2009

Sherwen, Nicholas (ed.), *NATO's Anxious Birth: The Prophetic Vision of the 1940s*, London: Hurst, 1985

Shlaim, Avi, *The Iron Wall: Israel and the Arab World*, London: Penguin, 2001

Simons, Graham M., *The Secret US Plan to Overthrow the British Empire: War Plan Red*, Barnsley: Frontline, 2020

Slim, Field Marshal Sir William, *Defeat into Victory*, London: Cassell, 1956

Snow, Peter & MacMillan, *Ann, Kings & Queens: The Real Lives of the English Monarchs*, London: Welbeck, 2022

Soames, Mary, *Clementine Churchill*, London: Cassell, 1979

Soames, Mary, *Family Album: A Personal Selection from Four Generations of Churchills*, Boston: Houghton Mifflin, 1982

Soames, Mary (ed.), *Speaking for Themselves: The Personal Letters of Winston and Clementine Churchill*, London: Black Swan, 1999

Soames, Mary, *Winston Churchill His Life as a Painter: A Memoir by his Daughter*, London: Collins, 1990

Spector, Ronald H., *Eagle Against the Sun: The American War with Japan*, London: Cassell, 2000

Spurr, Russell, *Enter the Dragon: China at War in Korea*, London: Sidgwick & Jackson, 1989

Stelzer, Cita, *Working with Winston: The Unsung Women Behind Britain's Greatest Statesman*, New York: Pegasus, 2019

Stephenson, Charles, *Stalin's War on Japan: The Red Army's Manchurian Strategic Offensive Operation 1945*, Barnsley: Pen & Sword, 2021

Stewart, Jules, *The Savage Border: The Story of the North-West Frontier*, Stroud: Sutton, 2007

Summer, Ian, Vauvillier, François & Chappell, Mike, *The French Army 1939-45 (2): Free French, Fighting French & the Army of Liberation*, London: Osprey, 1998

Sutherland, Jonathan & Canwell, Diane, *Berlin Airlift: The Salvation of a City*, Barnsley: Pen & Sword, 2007

Tatlock Miller, Harry & Sainthill, Loudon, *Churchill: The Walk with Destiny*, London: Hutchinson, 1959

Thomas, Nigel, Abbott, Peter & Chappell, Mike, *The Korean War 1950-53*, London: Osprey, 1986

Thompson, Major General Julian (ed.), *The Imperial War Museum Book of Modern Warfare: British and Commonwealth Forces at War 1945-2000*, London: Sidgwick & Jackson, 2002

Thompson, Sir Robert (ed.), *War in Peace: An Analysis of Warfare Since 1945*, London: Orbis, 1981

Thomson, Malcolm, *Churchill: His Life and Times*, London: Odhams, 1965

Tolstoy, Nikolai, *Victims of Yalta*, London: Corgi, 1979

Toye, Richard, *Age of Hope: Labour, 1945, and the Birth of Modern Britain*, London: Bloomsbury, 2023

Toye, Richard, *Churchill's Empire: The World that Made Him and the World He Made*, London: Pan Books, 2011

Trevelyan, Humphrey, *The Middle East in Revolution*, London: Macmillan, 1970

Tucker-Jones, Anthony, *Churchill Master and Commander: Winston Churchill at War 1895-1945*, Oxford: Osprey, 2021

Tucker-Jones, Anthony, *Dien Bien Phu: The First Indochina War 1946-1954*, Barnsley: Pen & Sword, 2017

Turbett, Colin, *A People's History of the Cold War: Stories from East and West*, Barnsley: Pen & Sword, 2023

Turner, Barry, *Suez 1956*, London: Hodder & Stoughton, 2006

Tynan, Elizabeth, *Atomic Thunder: British Nuclear Testing in Australia*, Barnsley: Pen & Sword, 2018

Vale, Allister & Scadding, John, *Winston Churchill's Illnesses 1886-1965: Courage, Resilience and Determination*, Barnsley: Frontline Books, 2020

van der Bijl, Nick, *The Cyprus Emergency: The Divided Island 1955-1974*, Barnsley: Pen & Sword, 2021

van der Bijl, Nick, *The Mau Mau Rebellion: The Emergency in Kenya 1952-1956*, Barnsley: Pen & Sword, 2017

van Tonder, Gerry, *Berlin Blockade: Soviet Chokehold and the Great Allied Airlift 1948-1949*, Barnsley: Pen & Sword, 2017

van Tonder, Gerry, *Irgun: Revisionist Zionism 1931-1948*, Barnsley: Pen & Sword, 2019

van Tonder, Gerry, *Korean War Allied Surge: Pyongyang Falls, UN Sweep to the Yalu October 1950*, Barnsley: Pen & Sword, 2019

van Tonder, Gerry, *Korean War Chinese Invasion: People's Liberation Army Crosses the Yalu October 1950-March 1951*, Barnsley: Pen & Sword, 2020

van Tonder, Gerry, *Malayan Emergency: Triumph of the Running Dogs 1948-1960*, Barnsley: Pen & Sword 2017

van Tonder, Gerry, *Red China: Mao Crushes Chiang's Kuomintang, 1949*, Barnsley: Pen & Sword, 2018

Varble, Derek, *The Suez Crisis 1956*, Oxford: Osprey, 2003

Walker, Jonathan, *Aden Insurgency: The Savage War in Yemen 1962-67*, Barnsley: Pen & Sword, 2021

Walker, Jonathan, *Churchill's Third World War: British Plans to Attack the Soviet Empire, 1945*, Stroud: The History Press, 2017

Webb, Simon, *British Concentration Camps: A Brief History from 1900-1975*, Barnsley: Pen & Sword, 2022

Werth, Alexander, *Russia at War 1941-1945*, London: Pan, 1965

Wheeler-Bennett, John W., *King George VI: His Life and Reign*, London: The Reprint Society, 1959

Whicker, Alan, *A Journey of A Lifetime*, London: Harper Collins, 2009

Whicker, Alan, *Whicker's War*, London: Harper Collins, 2005

Whiting, Charles, *Patton's Last Battle*, Staplehurst: Spellmount, 2002

Wilson, Harold, *A Prime Minister on Prime Ministers*, London: Michael Joseph, 1977

Wilson, Harold, *Memoirs 1916-1964: The Making of a Prime Minister*, London: Weidenfeld & Nicolson and Michael Joseph, 1986

Windrow, Martin, *The Algerian War 1954-62*, London: Osprey, 1997

Windrow, Martin, *The Last Valley: Dien Bien Phu and the French Defeat in Vietnam*, London: Cassell, 2005

Wintle, Justin, *The Viet Nam Wars*, London: Weidenfeld & Nicolson, 1991

Wynn, Stephen, *Churchill's Flawed Decisions: Errors in Office of the Greatest Briton*, Barnsley: Pen & Sword, 2020

Ziegler, Philip, *Mountbatten: The Official Biography*, London: William Collins, 1985

Zhisui, Dr Li, *The Private Life of Chairman Mao*, New York: Random House, 1994

Zhukov, Marshal of the Soviet Union G., *Reminiscences and Reflections, Volume 2*, Moscow: Progress, 1985

Journals

Daily Express
East African Standard
Evening Standard
Hansard
New York Herald Tribune
Northern Daily Mail
Pravda
The Canberra Times
The Times
The West Australian
Time
Western Morning News

Online Resources

Blenheim Palace
www.blenheimpalace.com
Churchill Central
www.churchillcentral.com
International Churchill Society
www.winstonchurchill.org

International Churchill Society Partners
Chartwell, The National Trust, England, UK
www.nationaltrust.org.uk/chartwell
Churchill Archives Centre, Churchill College, Cambridge, UK
www.churchillarchive.com
Churchill War Rooms
www.iwm.org.uk/visits/churchill-war-rooms
Imperial War Museum, London UK
www.iwm.org.uk
National Churchill Leadership Center, Washington, DC
www.winstonchurchill.org/visit/national-churchill-leadership-center
America's National Churchill Museum, Fulton, Missouri
www.nationalchurchillmuseum.org
The Queen Mary, Long Beach California
Winston Churchill Memorial Trust, London, UK

Notes and References

Prologue

1. Mary Soames, *Clementine Churchill*, London: Cassell, 1979, p.437
2. Mary Soames, *Winston Churchill: His Life as a Painter*, London: Collins, 1990, p.178
3. Ibid.
4. Sarah Churchill, *A Thread in the Tapestry*, London: Andre Deutsch, 1967, p.24
5. Peter Clarke, *Mr Churchill's Profession: Statesman, Orator, Writer*, London: Bloomsbury, 2013, p.283
6. Martin Gilbert, *Winston S. Churchill: Never Despair 1945-1965*, Boston: Houghton Mifflin, 1988, p.1166
7. Lord Moran, *Winston Churchill: The Struggle for Survival 1940-1965*, London: Constable, 1966, p.660
8. Soames, *Clementine Churchill*, p.432
9. Harold Wilson, *Memoirs: The Making of a Prime Minister 1916-64*, London: Weidenfeld & Nicolson and Michael Joseph, 1986, p.148
10. Cita Stelzer, *Working with Winston: The Unsung Women Behind Britain's Greatest Statesman*, New York: Pegasus, 2019, p.179
11. Wilson, *Memoirs*, p.148
12. John Colville, *The Fringes of Power: 10 Downing Street Diaries 1939-1955*, New York: W.W. Norton & Company, 1985, p.705
13. Moran, *Winston Churchill: The Struggle for Survival 1940-1965*, p.523
14. Malcolm Muggeridge, *Chronicles of Wasted Time, Volume 2, The Infernal Grove*, London: Collins, 1973, p.45
15. Ibid.
16. David Charlwood, *Churchill and Eden: Partners through War and Peace*, Barnsley: Pen & Sword, 2020, p.208
17. Gilbert, *Never Despair*, p.1126
18. These led to Operation Black Arrow on 28 February 1955 when Israeli paratroops attacked an Egyptian military base in Gaza. Israel subsequently supported the British and French assault on the Suez Canal.
19. Mary Soames (ed.), *Speaking for Themselves: The Personal Letters of Winston and Clementine Churchill*, London: Black Swan, 1999, p.585

20. Mary Soames, *Family Album: A Personal Selection from Four Generations of Churchills*, Boston: Houghton Mifflin, 1982, p.393
21. Moran, *Winston Churchill*, p.630
22. Colville, *The Fringes of Power*, p.706
23. Moran, *Winston Churchill: The Struggle for Power*, p.634
24. Sarah Churchill, *Keep on Dancing*, London: Weidenfeld & Nicolson, 1981, p.150
25. Soames, *Speaking for Themselves*, p.590
26. Nigel Fisher, *Harold Macmillan*, London: Weidenfeld & Nicolson, 1982, p.146
27. Alistair Horne, *Macmillan 1894-1956*, London Macmillan, 1988, p.352
28. Gilbert, *Never Despair*, p.1126
29. Horne, *Macmillan 1894-1956*, p.352

Chapter 1: A Deal With The Devil

1. Moran, *Winston Churchill: The Struggle for Survival*, p.173
2. Field Marshal Alexander, *The Alexander Memoirs 1940-1945*, London: Cassell, 1962, p.132
3. Ibid., p.172
4. Harold Macmillan, *The Blast of War 1939-1945*, London: Macmillan, 1967, p.711
5. Colville, *The Fringes of Power*, p.506
6. The Rt. Hon. The Earl of Avon, *The Eden Memoirs: The Reckoning*, London: Cassell, 1965, p.470
7. Ibid., p.470-1
8. Alex Danchev and Daniel Todman (ed.), *War Diaries 1939-1945: Field Marshal Lord Alanbrooke*, London: Phoenix Press, 2002, p.585
9. Macmillan, *The Blast of War*, p.576
10. The first Quebec conference had been held in August 1943
11. Martin Gilbert, *Road to Victory: Winston S. Churchill 1941-1945*, London: William Heinemann, 1986, p.963
12. Macmillan, *The Blast of War*, p.576
13. Avon, *The Eden Memoirs: The Reckoning*, p.475
14. Colville, *The Fringes of Power*, p.513
15. Ibid.
16. Avon, *The Eden Memoirs: The Reckoning*, p.477
17. Moran, *Winston Churchill: The Struggle for Survival*, p.191
18. Ibid.
19. Al Cimino, *Roosevelt and Churchill: A Friendship that saved the World*, New York: Chartwell Books, 2018, p.159
20. Colville, *The Fringes of Power*, p.523
21. Avon, *The Eden Memoirs: The Reckoning*, p.459
22. Ibid.
23. Gilbert, *Road to Victory*, p.786
24. Ibid., p.832
25. Ibid., p.490
26. Moran, *Winston Churchill: The Struggle for Survival*, p.161

27. Duff Hart-Davis (ed.), *King's Counsellor – Abdication and War: The Diaries of Sir Alan Lascelles*, London: Weidenfeld & Nicolson, 2006, p.261

28. Elizabeth Nel, *Mr Churchill's Secretary*, London: Hodder & Stoughton, 1961, p.152

29. Simon Sebag Montefiore, *Stalin: The Court of the Red Tsar*, London: Weidenfeld & Nicolson, 2003, p.421

30. This was the eastern border for Poland proposed at the Paris Peace Conference in 1919-20 by the British Foreign Secretary Lord Curzon. The Allies agreed at the Tehran Conference that this would be the new post-war border for Poland without the agreement of the Poles.

31. Estonia, Latvia and Lithuania.

32. Avon, *The Eden Memoirs: The Reckoning*, p.481

33. Colville, *The Fringes of Power*, p.524

34. Gilbert, *Road to Victory*, p.991

35. Ibid., p.992

36. Ibid., p.993

37. Ibid.

38. Max Hastings, *Finest Years: Churchill as Warlord 1940-1945*, London: Harper Press, 2009, pp.514-5

39. In Albania indigenous Communist forces numbered 70,000, in Greece 125,000 and in Yugoslavia 390,000. In Bulgaria the 55,000 strong Bulgarian Workers Party took a leading role in the new anti-Nazi government, positioning the Communists to take power.

40. Martin Gilbert, *Churchill: A Life*, London: Pimlico, 2000, p.796

41. Avon, *The Eden Memoirs: The Reckoning*, p.483

42. Ibid.

43. John Charmley, *Churchill's Grand Alliance: The Anglo-American Special Relationship 1940-57*, New York: Harcourt Brace, 1995, p.112

44. Ibid.

45. Danchev and Todman, *War Diaries*, pp.603-4

46. Gilbert, *Churchill: A Life*, p.797

47. Gilbert, *Road to Victory*, p.992

48. Soames, *Speaking for Themselves*, p.506

49. Ibid.

50. Cimino, *Roosevelt and Churchill*, p.159

51. Cita Stelzer, *Working with Winston: The Unsung Women Behind Britain's Greatest Statesman*, New York: Pegasus, 2019, p.149

52. Gilbert, *Road to Victory*, p.1015

53. Ibid., p.991

54. Gilbert, *Churchill: A Life*, p.799

55. Charmley, *Churchill's Grand Alliance*, p.109

56. Moran, *Winston Churchill: The Struggle for Survival*, p.204

57. Roy Jenkins, *Churchill: A Biography*, New York: Farra, Straus & Giroux, 2001, p.758

58. Moran, *Winston Churchill: The Struggle for Survival*, p.203

59. Ibid.

60. Danchev and Todman, *War Diaries*, p.604

61. Avon, *The Eden Memoirs: The Reckoning*, p.488

62. Colville, *The Fringes of Power*, p.526

63. Soames, *Speaking for Themselves*, p.506
64. Hart-Davis, *King's Counsellor*, p.266
65. *Hansard, Columns 490-8*, 27 October 1944
66. Martin Gilbert (ed.), *Churchill: The Power of Words – His remarkable life recounted through his writings and speeches*, London: Bantam, 2014, p.489
67. Cimino, *Roosevelt and Churchill*, p.160
68. Hart-Davis, *King's Counsellor*, p.269
69. Ibid.
70. Gilbert, *Road to Victory*, p.1056
71. The Allies continued to arm the partisans and in March 1945 alone delivered over 500 tons of supplies. By this stage they numbered some 50,000, organised into battalions and brigades, which spent their time harassing German garrisons and lines of communication; see Eric Linklater, *The Campaign in Italy*, London: Her Majesty's Stationery Office, 1977, pp.419-20
72. Avon, *The Eden Memoirs: The Reckoning*, p.503

Chapter 2: We Seemed to be Friends

1. Colville, *The Fringes of Power*, p.551
2. Cimino, *Roosevelt and Churchill*, p.162
3. Soames, *Speaking for Themselves*, p.513
4. Sarah Churchill, *A Thread in the Tapestry*, p.76
5. Nel, *Mr Churchill's Secretary*, p.166
6. Gilbert, *Road to Victory*, p.1167
7. Moran, *Winston Churchill: The Struggle for Survival*, p.226
8. Avon, *The Eden Memoirs: The Reckoning*, p.512
9. Ibid.
10. Ibid.
11. Sarah Churchill, *A Thread in the Tapestry*, p.76
12. Gilbert, *Road to Victory*, p.1171
13. Ibid., p.1172
14. Moran, *Winston Churchill: The Struggle for Survival*, p.219
15. Jenkins, *Churchill: A Biography*, p.781
16. Ibid.
17. Alexander Werth, *Russia at War 1941-1945*, London: Pan, 1965, p.750
18. In 1942 the Germans formed eight Tartar self-defence companies totalling some 3,000 men for anti-partisan operations in the mountains, and others cooperated with the Gestapo. However, Tartars also fought with the partisans.
19. Werth, *Russia at War*, p.750
20. Sarah Churchill, *A Thread in the Tapestry*, p.77
21. Nel, *Mr Churchill's Secretary*, p.167
22. Ibid., p.168
23. Gilbert, *Churchill: A Life*, p.817
24. Alexander, *The Alexander Memoirs*, p.134
25. Ibid.
26. Cimino, *Roosevelt and Churchill*, p.162

27. Moran, *Winston Churchill: The Struggle for Survival*, p.226
28. Jenkins, *Churchill: A Biography*, p.780
29. Werth, *Russia at War*, p.871
30. Gilbert, *Road to Victory*, p.1186
31. Werth, *Russia at War*, p.870
32. Richard Collier, *The War that Stalin Won*, London: Hamish Hamilton, 1983, p.240
33. Werth, *Russia at War*, p.874
34. Gilbert, *Churchill: A Life*, p.820
35. Danchev and Todman, *War Diaries*, p.660
36. Stalin claimed elections could be held in Poland within a month. They took place twenty-three months later on 19 January 1947 and were not free elections by any Western standard.
37. Collier, *The War that Stalin Won*, p.239
38. Nikolai Tolstoy, *Victims of Yalta*, London: Corgi, 1979, p.120
39. Moran, *Winston Churchill: The Struggle for Survival*, p.230
40. Avon, *The Eden Memoirs: The Reckoning*, p.513
41. Joseph P. Lash, *Eleanor and Franklin*, London: Andre Deutsch, 1971, p.717
42. Gilbert, *Churchill: The Power of Words*, p.499
43. Moran, *Winston Churchill: The Struggle for Survival*, p.232
44. Ibid., p.1209
45. Avon, *The Eden Memoirs: The Reckoning*, p.518
46. Sarah Churchill, *A Thread in the Tapestry*, p.83
47. Lash, *Eleanor and Franklin*, p.717
48. Colville, *The Fringes of Power*, p.560
49. John W. Wheeler-Bennett, *King George VI: His Life and Reign*, London: The Reprint Society, 1959, p.618
50. Sarah Churchill, *A Thread in the Tapestry*, p.81
51. Eleanor Roosevelt, *The Autobiography of Eleanor Roosevelt*, New York: Da Capo Press, 1992, p.274
52. Avon, *The Eden Memoirs: The Reckoning*, p.520
53. Horne, *Macmillan*, p.241
54. Macmillan, *The Blast of War*, p.661
55. Ibid., p.678
56. Clive Ponting, *Churchill*, London: Sinclair-Stevenson, 1994, p.683
57. Wheeler-Bennett, *King George VI*, p.618
58. Ibid.
59. Ponting, *Churchill*, p.684
60. Ibid.
61. Colville, *The Fringes of Power*, p.587
62. Soames, *Speaking for Themselves*, p.525
63. Wheeler-Bennett, *King George VI*, p.620
64. Avon, *The Eden Memoirs: The Reckoning*, p.529
65. *The Times*, 3 May 1945
66. Gilbert, *Never Despair*, p.6
67. Ibid., p.7

68. Danchev and Todman, *War Diaries*, p.690
69. Macmillan, *The Blast of War*, p.194
70. Danchev and Todman, *War Diaries*, p.685
71. To avoid a border war between Italy and Yugoslavia, during 1947-54 Trieste was a free zone under United Nations protection. Afterwards Trieste and the territory to the north was returned to Italy, while the territory to the south became Yugoslavian.
72. Danchev and Todman, *War Diaries*, p.691
73. Hastings, *Finest Years*, p.581
74. Ibid.
75. Ibid., p.583
76. Ibid.
77. Sarah Churchill, *A Thread in the Tapestry*, p.85
78. Lord Butler, *The Art of Memory: Friends in Perspective*, London: Hodder & Stoughton, 1982, p.21
79. Winston S. Churchill, *The Second World War: Triumph and Tragedy*, London: Cassell, 1953, p.545
80. Max Arthur, *Churchill The Life: An Authorised Pictorial Biography*, London: Cassell, 2017, p.220
81. Soames, *Speaking for Themselves*, p.532
82. Gilbert, *Never Despair*, p.63
83. Ibid., p.76
84. Avon, *The Eden Memoirs: The Reckoning*, p.547
85. Danchev and Todman, *War Diaries*, p.709
86. Ibid.
87. Marshal of the Soviet Union G. Zhukov, *Reminiscences and Reflections, Vol 2*, Moscow: Progress, 1985, p.449
88. Ibid.
89. Colville, *The Fringes of Power*, p.611
90. Wheeler-Bennett, *King George VI*, p.636
91. Nel, *Mr Churchill's Secretary*, p.184
92. Wheeler-Bennett, *King George VI*, p.637
93. Zhukov, *Reminiscences and Reflections, Vol 2*, p.449
94. Moran, *Winston Churchill: The Struggle for Survival*, p.289
95. Nikita Khrushchev, *Khrushchev Remembers*, London: Andre Deutsch, 1971, p.224

Chapter 3: Harbinger of Doom

1. Nigel Nicolson (ed.), *Harold Nicolson: Diaries and Letters 1945-1962*, p.31
2. Soames, *Winston Churchill: His Life as a Painter*, p.138
3. Field Marshal the Viscount Montgomery, *A Concise History of Warfare*, London: Collins, 1972, p.350
4. For more on this campaign see Charles Stephenson, *Stalin's War on Japan: The Red Army's Manchurian Offensive Operation 1945*, Barnsley: Pen & Sword, 2021
5. Danchev and Todman, *War Diaries*, p.716

6. See Philip Jowett and Stephen Walsh, *Japan's Asian Allies 1941-45*, Oxford: Osprey, 2020
7. Gilbert, *Never Despair*, p.120
8. Ibid.
9. Wheeler-Bennett, *King George VI*, p.645
10. Avon, *The Eden Memoirs: The Reckoning*, p.555
11. Soames, *Winston Churchill: His Life as a Painter*, p.138
12. Moran, *Winston Churchill: The Struggle for Survival*, p.289
13. Nigel Nicolson (ed.), *Harold Nicolson: Diaries and Letters 1945-1962*, p.36
14. This got him in trouble with the influential Conservative 1922 Committee, which felt Churchill did not spend enough time in the House of Commons.
15. Christopher Catherwood, *Churchill: The Story of the Greatest Briton in Words, Photographs and Documents*, London: SevenOaks, 2018, p.139
16. Soames, *Winston Churchill: His Life as a Painter*, p.150
17. See Ian Sumner, François Vauvillier and Mike Chappell, *The French Army 1939-45 (2): Free French, Fighting French & the Army of Liberation*, London: Osprey, 1998
18. Gilbert, *Never Despair*, p.170
19. Soames, *Family Album*, p.360
20. Although Cuba declared war on the Axis following Pearl Harbor, its role in the Second World War was extremely limited. Nonetheless it had benefitted from US Lend Lease military assistance and subsequently from the US Military Aid Programme.
21. Gilbert, *Churchill: A Life*, p.864
22. Ibid.
23. Antonio Giraudier supplied Churchill with cigars free of charge for the next twenty years.
24. Dwight D. Eisenhower, *At Ease: Stories I Tell to Friends*, London: Robert Hale, 1968, p.317
25. Ibid., 319
26. Horne, *Macmillan 1894-1945*, p.306
27. Khrushchev, *Khrushchev Remembers*, p.361
28. Gilbert, *Never Despair*, pp.195-6
29. Gilbert, *Churchill: A Life*, p.865
30. Gilbert, *Never Despair*, p.200
31. Moran, *Winston Churchill: The Struggle for Survival*, p.610
32. Gilbert, *Never Despair*, p.202
33. Stelzer, *Working with Winston*, p.123
34. Gilbert, *Churchill: The Power of Words*, p.540
35. Ibid, p.541
36. Colville, *Fringes of Power*, p.636
37. *Pravda*, 14 March, 1946
38. Khrushchev, *Khrushchev Remembers*, p.361
39. Jenkins, *Churchill: A Biography*, p.811
40. Gilbert, *Never Despair*, pp.209-10
41. Ibid., p.215

42. Soames, *Family Album*, p.360
43. Gilbert, *Never Despair*, p.232
44. Ibid.
45. The last British troops left Indonesia in November 1946. The Dutch government refused to recognise Indonesian independence until 1949.
46. Gilbert, *Churchill: The Power of Words*, p.542
47. Ibid.
48. Moran, *Winston Churchill: The Struggle for Survival*, p.316
49. Soames, *Winston Churchill: His Life as a Painter*, p.154
50. Gilbert, *Churchill: The Power of Words*, p.546
51. Ibid.
52. Ibid., p.547
53. Ibid.
54. Soames, *Winston Churchill*, p.155
55. Zhukov, *Reminiscences and Reflections, Vol 2*, p.479
56. Ponting, *Churchill*, p.735
57. Moran, *Winston Churchill: The Struggle for Survival*, p.315
58. Ibid., p.316
59. Zhukov, *Reminiscences and Reflections, Vol 2*, p.479
60. Khrushchev, *Khrushchev Remembers*, p.361
61. Gilbert, *Never Despair*, p.286
62. Colville, *The Fringes of Power*, p.618
63. Ibid.
64. Nigel Nicolson (ed.), *Vita and Harold: The Letters of Vita Sackville-West and Harold Nicolson*, London: Weidenfeld & Nicolson, 1992, pp.377-8
65. Ibid., p.378

Chapter 4: End of Empire

1. Nirad C. Chaudhuri, *Thy Hand, Great Anarch! India 1921-1952*, London: Chatto & Windus, 1987, p.794
2. Ibid.
3. Lawrence James, *Churchill and Empire: Portrait of an Imperialist*, London: Weidenfeld & Nicolson, 2014, p.343
4. These were the 31st Punjab and 35th Sikh Infantry Regiments. For more on Churchill's adventures on the North-West Frontier see Anthony Tucker-Jones, *Churchill: Master and Commander*, London: Osprey, 2021 pp.40-7
5. Winston S. Churchill, *Frontiers and Wars: His Four Early Books covering his Life as Soldier and War Correspondent*, New York: Smithmark, 1995, p.114
6. The mutiny affected 20 shore bases, 78 ships and 20,000 sailors; see Srinath Raghavan, *India's War: The Making of Modern South Asia 1939-1945*, London: Penguin, 2017, p.448
7. Pakistan was conceived by Indian students at Cambridge University in 1932. P stood for Punjab, A for the Afghan areas of the North-West Frontier, KI

for Kashmir, S for Sind and TAN for Baluchistan. PAK also meant pure in a Muslim sense.

8. Hindus numbered over 225 million compared to 92 million Muslims; there were also 5.5 million Sikhs mostly in the Punjab.
9. Quoted numbers seem to vary, but by 1947 only 21 of these had state governments; there were also thousands of titled landowners.
10. For more on the development and complex structure of the British Raj see John Keay's revised and updated *India: A History*, London: William Collins, 2022, pp.383-414
11. James Morris, *Farewell the Trumpets: An Imperial Retreat*, London: Penguin, 1979, p.480
12. Richard Hough, *Mountbatten: Hero of our Time*, London: Weidenfeld & Nicolson, 1981, p.212
13. Morris, *Farewell to Trumpets*, p.481
14. Gilbert, *Never Despair*, p.233
15. Ibid., p.277
16. Ponting, *Churchill*, p.740
17. Louis Fischer, *The Life of Mahatma Gandhi*, London: Harper Collins, 1997, p.550
18. Horne, *Macmillan 1894-1956*, p.309
19. Ibid., p.310
20. Ibid., 311
21. Ibid.
22. Ibid., p.312
23. Alden Hatch, *The Mountbattens*, London: W.H. Allen, 1966, p.333
24. Ibid.
25. Wheeler-Bennett, *King George VI*, pp.710-11
26. Patrick French, *Liberty or Death: India's Journey to Independence and Division*, London: Harper Collins, 1997, p.276
27. Mark Bence-Jones, *The Viceroys of India*, London: Constable, 1984, p.302
28. Mountbatten, *Mountbatten: Eighty Years in Pictures*, p. 170
29. Bence-Jones, *The Viceroys of India*, p.302
30. Mountbatten, *Mountbatten: Eighty Years in Pictures*, p. 170
31. Hough, *Mountbatten: Hero of our Time*, p.210
32. Victoria Schofield, *Wavell: Soldier & Statesman*, London: John Murray, 2006, p.373
33. Ibid., p.372
34. Ibid.
35. Richard Hough, *Winston and Clementine: The Triumphs and Tragedies of the Churchills*, London: Bantam, 1991, p.602
36. Moran, *Winston Churchill: The Struggle for Survival*, p.328
37. Schofield, *Wavell: Soldier & Statesman*, p.390
38. Wheeler-Bennett, *King George VI*, p.709
39. Ponting, *Churchill*, p.740
40. Ibid., p.741
41. Schofield, *Wavell: Soldier & Statesman*, p.377
42. Hough, *Mountbatten: Hero of our Time*, p.214
43. Morris, *Farewell the Trumpets*, p.484

44. Fischer, *The Life of Mahatma Gandhi*, p.587
45. Hatch, *The Mountbattens*, pp.340-1
46. Hough, *Mountbatten: Hero of our Time*, p.219
47. Richard Holmes, *In the Footsteps of Churchill*, London: BBC Books, 2005, p.49
48. Winston S. Churchill, *The Story of the Malakand Field Force*, Barnsley: Leo Cooper, 2002, p.215
49. Hough, *Mountbatten: Hero of our Time*, p.218
50. Andrew Lownie, *The Mountbattens*, London: Blink, 2019, p.205
51. Hatch, *The Mountbattens*, p.341
52. Ibid., p.344
53. Nigel Nicolson (ed.), *Harold Nicolson: Diaries and Letters 1945-1962*, p.100
54. Gilbert, *Never Despair*, p.334
55. Ibid.
56. Fischer, *The Life of Mahatma Gandhi*, p.585
57. Chaudhuri, *Thy Hand, Great Anarch!* p.826
58. Fischer, *The Life of Mahatma Gandhi*, p.587
59. Gilbert, *Never Despair*, p.334
60. After independence about 30,000 British and 35,000 Gurkha troops remained in the Indian subcontinent. Had they been deployed they were too few to keep the peace. The Gurkhas were not recruited in India but from Nepal, so four Gurkha regiments were transferred to the British Army and six to the new Indian Army.
61. Lownie, *The Mountbattens*, p.226
62. Philip Mason, *A Matter of Honour: An Account of the Indian Army, its Officers and Men*, London: Jonathan Cape, 1974, p.525
63. The 1st, 8th, 14th, 15th and 16th Punjab Regiments were allocated to Pakistan. The 2nd Punjab Regiment went to India. The 6th Rajput and 7th Rajput Regiments and the 17th Dogra Regiment went to India and the 10th Baluch Regiment to Pakistan. The Sikh units were also divided up. See Boris Mollo, *The Indian Army*, Poole: Blandford, 1981, pp.177-79
64. Lownie, *The Mountbattens*, p.228
65. Estimates have put the dead as high as two million.
66. Butler, *The Art of Memory*, p.69
67. Ibid., p.63
68. Philip Ziegler, *Mountbatten: The Official Biography*, London: William Collins, pp.504-5
69. This figure was according to the official Indian report, but other sources have put the dead at 200,000 or higher.
70. Butler, *The Art of Memory*, p.130
71. Gilbert, *Never Despair*, p.431
72. Morris, *Farewell the Trumpets*, p.495
73. Gilbert, *Churchill: A Life*, p,877
74. Ibid.
75. Stephen Roskill, *Churchill and the Admirals*, Barnsley: Pen & Sword, 2013, p.281
76. Hough, *Mountbatten: Hero of our Time*, p.232

77. Ronald I. Cohen (ed.), *The Heroic Memory: The Memorial Addresses to the Rt. Hon. Sir Winston Churchill Spencer Society Edmonton, Alberta, 1990-2014*, Edmonton: The Churchill Society Statue and Oxford Scholarship Foundation, 2016, p.4
78. Gilbert, *Churchill: The Power of Words*, p.559
79. Gilbert, *Never Despair*, p.439
80. Ibid.
81. Moran, *Winston Churchill: The Struggle for Survival*, p.328
82. Nigel Nicolson (ed.), *Harold Nicolson: Diaries and Letters 1945-1962*, p.170
83. Wheeler-Bennett, *King George VI*, p.731

Chapter 5: The Promised Land

1. In 1922 Churchill produced a white paper that offered British support for a Jewish homeland in Palestine. However, it set economic conditions on Jewish immigration, it suggested elected institutions on the basis of proportional representation rather than parity and excluded Transjordan from Jewish settlement. See Avi Shlaim, *The Iron Wall: Israel and the Arab World*, London: Penguin, 2001, p.10
2. For more on the development of Irgun see Gerry van Tonder, *Irgun: Revisionist Zionism 1931-1948*, Barnsley: Pen & Sword, 2019
3. Ritchie Ovendale, *The Origins of the Arab-Israeli Wars*, Harlow: Longman, 1985, p.78
4. Between 1880-1924 and the imposition of restrictive US immigration quotas over two million European Jews went to America. The total annual quota was then set at about 164,000 people a year, though was often much lower especially during the 1930s-40s.
5. Wilson, *Memoirs: The Making of a Prime Minister 1916-64*, p.125
6. Leo McKinstry, *Attlee and Churchill: Allies in War, Adversaries in Peace*, London: Atlantic Books, 2019, p.476
7. Between 1933 and 1945 America admitted 275,000 refugees, including 180,000 Jews. In contrast between May and September 1945 only 5,718 Jewish refugees were admitted. Britain took over 300,000 refugees, including 70,000 Jews; see Ovendale, *The Origins of the Arab-Israeli Wars*, p.95
8. Ibid., p.84
9. Gilbert, *Churchill: The Power of Words*, p.467
10. Gilbert, *Never Despair*, pp.210-11
11. Ibid., p.231
12. Ibid., p.244
13. Ibid.
14. Winston S. Churchill (grandson - ed.), *Never Give In! The Best of Winston Churchill's Speeches*, New York: Hyperion, 2003, p.425
15. Ibid., p.426
16. Gilbert, *Never Despair*, p.251
17. Ibid

18. Field Marshal the Viscount Montgomery, *The Memoirs*, London: Collins, 1958, p.423
19. Ibid.
20. Nigel Hamilton, *Monty: The Field Marshal 1944-1976*, London: Hamish Hamilton, 1986, p.637
21. Montgomery, *The Memoirs*, p.427
22. Ovendale, *The Origins of the Arab-Israeli Wars*, p.97
23. Ibid, p.469
24. *Hansard*, Palestine Conference (Government Policy), Volume 433, 18 February 1947
25. Gilbert, *Never Despair*, p.336
26. Churchill (ed.), *Never Give In!* p.434
27. Ibid.
28. Hamilton, *Monty: The Field Marshal 1944-1976*, p.696
29. Uri Avnery, *1948: A Soldier's Tale – The Bloody Road to Jerusalem*, Oxford: Oneworld, 2008, p.9
30. Ibid., p.12
31. Dan Kurzman, *Genesis 1948: The First Arab-Israeli War*, New York: Signet, 1972, p.46
32. Adam LeBor, *City of Oranges: Arabs and Jews in Jaffa*, London: Bloomsbury, 2007, p.114
33. Ibid., p.115
34. Ibid., p.120
35. Ibid.
36. Kurzman, *Genesis 1948: The First Arab-Israeli War*, p.220
37. Nigel Nicolson (ed.), *Harold Nicolson: Diaries and Letters 1945-1962*, p.139
38. Ibid., p.140
39. Kurzman, *Genesis 1948: The First Arab-Israeli War*, p.778
40. Nigel Nicolson (ed.), *Harold Nicolson: Diaries and Letters 1945-1962*, p.140
41. Haganah numbered almost 30,000. Although the Egyptian army was 50,000 strong it could only muster 10,000 for the attack on Israel. Jordan fielded 4,500, but by the time of the armistice this force had doubled. At the start of the war Syria had 8,000 men under arms. This meant that including the small Iraqi and Lebanese contingents the Israeli and Arab forces were roughly evenly matched. Israel though did not have the manpower to fight a prolonged war. After the first truce the Egyptians boosted their assault force to 18,000; the Iraqis increased theirs to 15,000. However, the Jordanians only numbered 4,000 as they had to deploy forces for an internal security problem and the Arab Liberation Army had shrunk to just 2,000. See John Laffin & Mike Chappell, *Arab Armies of the Middle East Wars 1948-73*, London: Osprey, 1982, John Laffin & Mike Chappell, *The Israeli Army in the Middle East Wars 1948-73*, London: Osprey 1982 and Otto von Pivka, *Armies of the Middle East*, Cambridge: Patrick Stephens, 1979
42. Pelling, *Winston Churchill*, p.572
43. Nigel Nicolson (ed.), *Harold Nicolson: Diaries and Letters 1945-1962*, p.149

44. Selwyn Lloyd, *Suez 1956: A Personal Account*, London: Jonathan Cape, 1978, p.79
45. Ibid.

Chapter 6: Berlin-the First Test

1. Gilbert, *Never Despair*, p.400
2. Ibid., pp.509-10
3. Nicholas Sherwen (ed.), *NATO's Anxious Birth: The Prophetic Vision of the 1940s*, London: Hurst, 1985, p.49
4. Gerry van Tonder, *Berlin Blockade: Soviet Chokehold and the Great Allied Airlift 1948-1949*, Barnsley: Pen & Sword, 2017, p.49
5. Hamilton, *Monty: The Field Marshal 1944-1976*, p.714
6. Ibid.
7. There were also around 4,000 British and French military personnel in the city.
8. Richard Crowder, *Aftermath: The Makers of the Postwar World*, New York: I.B. Tauris, 2015, p.223
9. The signatories were America, Belgium, Britain, France, the Netherlands and Luxembourg.
10. Soames, *Winston Churchill: His Life as a Painter*, p.164
11. Brian Moynahan, *The Claws of the Bear: A History of the Soviet Armed Forces from 1917 to Present*, London: Hutchinson, 1989, p.279
12. Hamilton, *Monty: The Field Marshal 1944-1976*, p.713
13. Colville, *The Fringes of Power*, p.626
14. Martin Gilbert, *In Search of Churchill*, London: Harper Collins, 1994, p.249
15. Ibid., p.250
16. Ibid.
17. Ibid.
18. Harold Wilson recounted this incident verbally to Martin Gilbert. Ibid., p.249. Wilson made no mention of it in his memoirs published in 1986.
19. Montgomery, *The Memoirs*, p.482
20. Ibid., p.483
21. Gilbert, *Never Despair*, p.421
22. Eisenhower, *At Ease*, p.311
23. Hamilton, *Monty: The Field Marshal 1944-1976*, p.715
24. The Red Army at its height in 1945 had 500 divisions, these had been reduced to 175 by the end of 1947. By this stage the Soviet Army still had 3.2 million men under arms not including the air force and navy. Regarding the change in terminology see note 35.
25. Ibid.
26. Nigel Nicolson (ed.), *Harold Nicolson: Diaries and Letters 1945-1962*, p.146
27. Ibid.
28. Gilbert, *Churchill: A Life*, p.881
29. Montgomery, *The Memoirs*, p.483
30. These were the US 28th and 307th Bombardment Groups.

31. He wrote this on 24 September 1946 and it was published in February 1947 in the *Bolshevik*, Moscow, No.3 February 1947; see Malcolm Mackintosh, *Juggernaut: A History of the Soviet Armed Forces*, London: Secker & Warburg, 1967, p.278
32. Soames, *Winston Churchill: His Life as a Painter*, p.165
33. Ibid.
34. Gilbert, *Churchill: A Life*, p.882
35. On 25 February 1946 the Red Army was officially renamed the Soviet Army.
36. For more on Churchill's relationship with the Duke of Windsor see Andrew Lownie, *Traitor King: The Scandalous Exile of the Duke and Duchess of Windsor*, London: Blink, 2021 and Alexander Larman, *The Windsors at War: The Nazi Threat to the Crown*, London: Weidenfeld & Nicolson, 2023
37. Soames, *Speaking for Themselves*, p.549
38. Nigel Nicolson (ed.), *Harold Nicolson: Diaries and Letters 1945-1962*, p.150
39. Ibid., p.151
40. Ibid.
41. Gilbert, *Never Despair*, p.437
42. Soames, *Speaking for Themselves*, p.551
43. Horne, *Macmillan 1894-1956*, p.307
44. Ibid.
45. Butler, *The Art of Memory*, pp.27-8
46. Ibid., p.29
47. Gilbert, *Never Despair*, p.475
48. John Grehan, *The Berlin Airlift: The World's Largest Ever Air Supply Operation*, Barnsley: Air World, 2019, p.163
49. Ibid., p.162
50. By the time the airlift stopped the aircrews of the American, Australian, British, Canadian, New Zealander and South African air forces had flown almost 278,000 sorties delivering 2.3 million tons of supplies to Berlin.
51. S.J. Ball, *The Cold War: An International History 1947-1991*, London: Bloomsbury, 2011, p.11
52. Khrushchev, *Khrushchev Remembers*, pp.452-3
53. Gilbert, *Never Despair*, p.483
54. Soames, *Winston Churchill: His Life as a Painter*, p.169
55. Barbara Leaming, *Churchill Defiant: Fighting On: 1945-1955*, New York: Harper Perennial, 2011, pp.100-1
56. Stelzer, *Working with Winston*, p.190
57. Moran, *Winston Churchill: The Struggle for Survival*, p.334
58. Ibid.
59. Allister Vale and John Scadding, *Winston Churchill's Illnesses 1886-1965: Courage, Resilience and Determination*, Barnsley: Frontline Books, 2020, p.191. Their clinical assessment is that Churchill did have a stroke.
60. Moran, *Winston Churchill: The Struggle for Survival*, p.335
61. Leaming, *Churchill Defiant*, p.110
62. Macmillan, *Tides of Fortune 1945-1955*, London: Macmillan, 1969, p.179
63. Soames, *Winston Churchill: His Life as a Painter*, p.169

Chapter 7: Mao Triumphant

1. Gilbert, *Churchill: The Power of Words*, p.450
2. Winston S. Churchill, *The Second World War: Closing the Ring*, London: Cassell, 1952, p.290
3. Ibid., p.289
4. Macmillan, *The Blast of War*, p.430
5. Soames, *Speaking for Themselves*, p.487
6. Sarah Churchill, *Keep on Dancing*, p.69
7. Hart-Davis, *King's Counsellor*, pp.124-5
8. Lash, *Eleanor and Franklin*, p.678
9. Ibid., p.681
10. Roosevelt, *The Autobiography of Eleanor Roosevelt*, p.249
11. Churchill, *The Second World War: Closing the Ring*, p.290
12. Avon, *The Eden Memoirs: The Reckoning*, p.424
13. Churchill, *The Second World War: Closing the Ring*, p.290
14. Moran, *Winston Churchill: The Struggle for Survival*, p.131
15. Dr Li Zhisui, *The Private Life of Chairman Mao*, New York: Random House, 1994, p.52
16. Pontin, *Churchill*, p.678
17. Ibid.
18. Soames, *Speaking for Themselves*, p.501
19. Moran, *Winston Churchill: The Struggle for Survival*, p.232
20. Pontin, *Churchill*, p.691
21. Gilbert, *Road to Victory*, p.1183
22. Ibid.
23. Avon, *The Eden Memoirs: The Reckoning*, p.514
24. Jung Chang and Jon Halliday, *Mao: The Unknown Story*, London: Jonathan Cape, 2005, p.295
25. Ibid., p.292
26. Ibid., p.300
27. Sir Robert Thompson (ed.), *War in Peace: An Analysis of Warfare Since 1945*, London: Orbis, 1981, p.3
28. Ronald H. Spector, *Eagle Against the Sun: The American War with Japan*, London: Cassell, 2000, p.560
29. These were the 1st and 4th Tank Divisions. The latter was formed from Japanese training units in July 1944. There was a third tank division in Japan but this remained a training unit.
30. According to Anthony Eden a number of units escaped, as one or two divisions from Korea were sent back to Japan along with one from Manchuria before the Soviet invasion. Avon, *The Eden Memoirs: The Reckoning*, pp.530-1
31. Gilbert, *Never Despair*, p.166
32. Ibid.
33. Charmley, *Churchill's Grand Alliance*, p.185
34. America trained and equipped the Nationalist New 1st and New 6th Armies, the 14th Armoured Army and the 92nd Airborne Army.

35. Gilbert, *Never Despair*, p.205
36. Zhisui, *The Private Life of Chairman Mao*, p.117
37. Ibid.
38. Gilbert, *Never Despair*, p.437
39. Ibid., p.437
40. Gerry van Tonder, *Red China: Mao Crushes Chiang's Kuomintang, 1949*, Barnsley: Pen & Sword, 2018, p.93
41. Sulmaan Wasif Khan, *Haunted by Chaos: China's Grand Strategy from Mao Zedong to Xi Jinping*, Cambridge, MA: Harvard University Press, 2022, p.35
42. Zhisui, *The Private Life of Chairman Mao*, p.117
43. Chang and Halliday, *Mao: The Unknown Story*, p.362
44. Ibid.
45. Ibid.
46. Gilbert, *Never Despair*, p.474
47. Churchill, *The Second World War: Closing the Ring*, p.291
48. Roosevelt, *The Autobiography of Eleanor Roosevelt*, p.343
49. Ball, *The Cold War: An International History 1947-1991*, pp.37-8
50. Hamilton, *Monty: The Field-Marshal 1944-1976*, p.832
51. Khrushchev, *Khrushchev Remembers*, p.463
52. Gilbert, *Never Despair*, p.495
53. Ibid.

Chapter 8: Troublesome Neighbour

1. Danchev and Todman, *War Diaries*, p.579
2. Hart-Davis, *King's Counsellor*, p.320
3. Andrew Roberts, *Churchill: Walking with Destiny*, London: Penguin, 2019, p.877
4. Hart-Davis, *King's Counsellor*, p.95
5. Gilbert, *Never Despair*, p.231
6. Ibid., p.12
7. Ibid.
8. Hart-Davis, *King's Counsellor*, p.324
9. Danchev and Todman, *War Diaries*, p.220
10. Ibid., p.518
11. Colville, *The Fringes of Power*, p.306
12. Churchill, *The Second World War: Closing the Ring*, p.615
13. Ibid., p.614
14. Moran, *Winston Churchill: The Struggle for Survival*, p.304
15. Gilbert, *Never Despair*, p.237
16. Ibid., p.238
17. Wheeler-Bennett, *King George VI*, p.718
18. Hart-Davis, *King's Counsellor*, p.52
19. Ibid., p.372
20. Ibid.

21. Ibid.
22. Nicolson, *Vita and Harold*, p.290
23. The Duke of Windsor also considered settling in America, Spain and Switzerland; see Lownie, *Traitor King*, p.263.
24. In 1936 de Valera had been in favour of Edward VIII's abdication; with a constituency of ninety percent Roman Catholics he did not support the King's marriage to American divorcee Wallis Simpson.
25. J. Bryan III and Charles J.V. Murphy, *The Windsor Story*, London: Granada, 1979, p.508
26. Wheeler-Bennett, *King George VI*, p.718
27. Gilbert, *Never Despair*, pp.439-40
28. Pim commanded twenty small boats that took 3,500 men off the beaches.
29. Asquith's Liberal government passed an Irish Home Rule Bill in 1912. Although it offered only limited authority to a Dublin parliament it was decisively rejected by the House of Lords. The Bill did not become law until 1914 but was then derailed by the First World War.
30. Frank Owen, *Tempestuous Journey: Lloyd George, his Life and Times*, London: Hutchinson, 1954, p.580
31. Ibid., p.578
32. Gilbert, *Never Despair*, p.443
33. Ibid.
34. Nigel Nicolson (ed.), *Harold Nicolson: Diaries and Letters 1945-1962*, pp.152-3
35. Maffey epitomised the British colonial service and everything de Valera despised. He had served as the Private Secretary to the Viceroy of India from 1916-20, Governor-General of Sudan from 1926-33 and was Permanent Under-Secretary of State for the Colonies from 1933-37. He was UK representative to Eire from 1939-49.
36. Nigel Nicolson (ed.), *Harold Nicolson: Diaries and Letters 1945-1962*, p.153
37. Ibid.
38. Ibid.
39. Ibid.
40. Ibid.
41. Wheeler-Bennett, *King George VI*, p.719. Although Irishmen from both the north and the south fought for the British Army, they were never formed into divisions in the same manner that the Scots and the Welsh were. For example in Europe the Irish Guards were assigned to the Guards Armoured Division and battalions from the Royal Ulster Rifles served with the 3rd Infantry Division and the 6th Airborne Division. The 38th (Irish Brigade) raised in Northern Ireland fought in North Africa and Italy with the 6th Armoured and 78th Infantry Divisions. This undoubtedly was a political move as there were sufficient recruits to form at least several Irish divisions.
42. Wheeler-Bennett, *King George VI*, p.719
43. Gilbert, *Never Despair*, p.432
44. Ibid., p.521
45. Moran, *Winston Churchill: The Struggle for Survival*, p.473

Chapter 9: Return of the Bulldog

1. Wheeler-Bennett, *King George VI*, p.771
2. Soames, *Speaking for Themselves*, p.553
3. Soames, *Winston Churchill: His Life as a Painter*, p.183
4. Gilbert, *Never Despair*, p.502
5. Ibid., p.503
6. Moran, *Winston Churchill: The Struggle for Survival*, p.336
7. Ibid.
8. Ibid., p.337
9. Gilbert, *Never Despair*, p.508
10. Ibid., p.509
11. Ibid., p.510
12. Ibid.
13. Ibid.
14. Nigel Nicolson (ed.), *Harold Nicolson: Diaries and Letters 1945-1962*, p.186
15. Gilbert, *Churchill: A Life*, p.889
16. Wilson, *Memoirs*, p.110
17. Gilbert, *Churchill: A Life*, p.890
18. Gilbert, *Never Despair*, p.512
19. Horne, *Macmillan 1894-1956*, p.326
20. Wheeler-Bennet, *King George VI*, p.772
21. To be fair only two of these were British, the rest were Indian and African units.
22. At the start of the conflict the South Koreans could muster seven weak divisions, by the end this number had doubled.
23. Gilbert, *Never Despair*, p.565
24. Horne, *Macmillan 1894-1956*, p.326
25. Hamilton, *Monty: The Field Marshal 1944-1976*, p.832
26. Wilson, *Memoirs*, p.135
27. Butler, *The Art of Memory*, p.89
28. Ibid.
29. Soames, *Clementine Churchill*, p.428
30. Jenkins, *Churchill: A Biography*, pp.837-8
31. Ibid., p.838
32. Ibid.
33. Nigel Fisher, *Harold Macmillan*, London: Weidenfeld & Nicolson, 1982, p.132
34. Jenkins, *Churchill: A Biography*, p.838
35. Ibid.
36. Moran, *Winston Churchill: The Struggle for Survival*, p.340
37. Ibid., p.341
38. Soames, *Winston Churchill: His life as a Painter*, p.180
39. Montgomery, *A Field Marshal in the Family*, p.33
40. Ibid.
41. Soames, *Winston Churchill: His Life as a Painter*, p.182
42. Wilson, *Memoirs*, p.130
43. Moran, *Winston Churchill: The Struggle for Survival*, p.339

44. Ibid., p.345
45. Soames, *Clementine Churchill*, p.429
46. Gilbert, *Churchill: A Life*, p.897
47. Ponting, *Churchill*, p.753
48. Gilbert, *Never Despair*, p.643
49. Ibid.
50. Wilson, *Memoirs*, p.134
51. Arthur, *Churchill: The Life*, p.237
52. Nigel Nicolson (ed.), *Harold Nicolson: Diaries and Letters 1945-1962*, p.211
53. Ibid.
54. *Evening Standard*, 26 October 1951
55. Wheeler-Bennett, *King George VI*, p.796
56. Gilbert, *Never Despair*, p.649
57. Moran, *Winston Churchill: The Struggle for Survival*, p.349
58. Soames, *Clementine Churchill*, p.429
59. Montgomery, *The Memoirs*, p.491
60. Colville, *The Fringes of Power*, p.633
61. Ibid.
62. Soames, *Speaking for Themselves*, p.562
63. Soames, *Clementine Churchill*, p.412
64. This did Sandys political career no harm as he went on to serve as Minister of Housing and Local Government, Minister of Defence, Minister of Aviation, Secretary of State for Commonwealth Relations and Secretary of State for the Colonies.
65. Moran, *Winston Churchill: The Struggle for Survival*, p.349
66. Nigel Nicolson (ed.), *Harold Nicolson: Diaries and Letters 1945-1962*, p.212
67. Ibid.
68. Colville, *Fringes of Power*, p.632
69. Ibid.
70. Ibid., p.633

Chapter 10: Seeing Old Friends

1. Moran, *Winston Churchill: The Struggle for Survival*, p.353
2. Colville, *The Fringes of Power*, p.637
3. Sarah Churchill, *Keep on Dancing*, p.142
4. Jenkins, *Churchill: A Biography*, p.847
5. Hough, *Mountbatten: Hero of Our Time*, p.234
6. Colville, *The Fringes of Power*, p.637
7. Ibid.
8. Ziegler, *Mountbatten: The Official Biography*, p.503
9. Churchill and Mountbatten fell out yet again in 1953 during the Coronation Naval Review. Mountbatten ignored the Prime Minister's invitation to meet, so Churchill summoned him. By Mountbatten's own admission their get-together did not go well; see Peter Midgley (ed.), *The Heroic Memory: The Memorial Addresses to the Rt. Hon. Sir Winston Spencer Churchill Society*

Edmonton, Alberta, 1965-1989, Edmonton: The Churchill Statue and Oxford Scholarship Foundation, 2005, pp.30-31

10. Moran, *Winston Churchill: The Struggle for Survival*, p.353
11. Colville, *The Fringes of Power*, p.637
12. Ibid.
13. Moran, *Winston Churchill: The Struggle for Survival*, p.353
14. Ibid., p.355
15. Gilbert, *Never Despair*, p.676
16. Colville, *The Fringes of Power*, p.637
17. Gilbert, *Never Despair*, p.677
18. Colville, *The Fringes of Power*, p.638
19. Ibid.
20. Gilbert, *Never Despair*, p.680
21. Colville, *The Fringes of Power*, p.638
22. Pelling, *Winston Churchill*, p.600
23. Moran, *Winston Churchill: The Struggle for Survival*, p.373
24. Afterwards the couple travelled to America and met President Truman. This led to a comedy moment when Truman introduced Princess Elizabeth to his elderly mother-in-law. She congratulated the Princess on the re-election of her father – referring to Churchill! See Robert Hardman, *Queen of Our Times: The Life of Elizabeth II 1926-2022*, London: Macmillan, 2022, p.113
25. Moran, *Winston Churchill: The Struggle for Survival*, p.363
26. Hamilton, *Monty: The Field Marshal 1944-1976*, p.817
27. Moran, *Winston Churchill: The Struggle for Survival*, p.363
28. Hamilton, *Monty: The Field Marshal 1944-1976*, p.817
29. Moran, *Winston Churchill: The Struggle for Survival*, pp.363-5
30. Ibid., p.365
31. Sarah Churchill, *Keep on Dancing*, p.143
32. Colville, *The Fringes of Power*, p.639
33. Gilbert, *Never Despair*, p.688
34. Sarah Churchill, *Keep on Dancing*, p.143
35. Ibid.
36. Gilbert, *Never Despair*, p.688
37. Ibid., p.689
38. Ibid.
39. Moran, *Winston Churchill: The Struggle for Survival*, p.367
40. Gilbert, *Never Despair*, p.689
41. Moran, *Winston Churchill: The Struggle for Survival*, p.367
42. Gilbert, *Never Despair*, p.690
43. Churchill (ed.), *Never Give In!*, p.475
44. Moran, *Winston Churchill: The Struggle for Survival*, p.367
45. *The Times*, 14 January 1952
46. Pelling, *Winston Churchill*, p.599
47. Moran, *Winston Churchill: The Struggle for Survival*, p.369
48. Colville, *The Fringes of Power*, p.639
49. Soames, *Speaking for Themselves*, p.563

50. Ibid., p.564
51. Moran, *Winston Churchill: The Struggle for Survival*, p.372
52. Robert Lacey, *Royal: Her Majesty Queen Elizabeth II*, London: Time Warner, 2002, p.166
53. Andrew Morton, *The Queen*, London: Michael O'Mara, 2022, p.116
54. William Shawcross, *Queen Elizabeth The Queen Mother: The Official Biography*, London: Macmillan, 2009, p.653
55. Hardman, *Queen of our Times*, p.117
56. Colville, *The Fringes of Power*, p.640
57. Soames, *Clementine Churchill*, p.432
58. Sarah Churchill, *Keep on Dancing*, p.142
59. Nigel Nicolson (ed.), *Harold Nicolson: Diaries and Letters 1945-1962*, p.219
60. Stelzer, *Working with Winston*, p.247
61. Moran, *Winston Churchill: The Struggle for Survival*, p.372
62. Churchill (ed.), *Never Give In!* p.476
63. Ibid., p.479
64. Andrew Morton, *Elizabeth & Margaret: The Intimate World of the Windsor Sisters*, London: Michael O'Mara, 2021, p.127
65. Colville, *The Fringes of Power*, p.641
66. Soames, *Clementine Churchill*, p.432
67. Peter Snow and Ann MacMillan, *Kings & Queens: The Real Lives of the English Monarchs*, London: Welbeck, 2022, p.255
68. Lownie, *The Mountbattens*, p.257
69. Nigel Nicolson (ed.), *Harold Nicolson: Diaries and Letters 1945-1962*, p.223
70. Ibid., p.222
71. Ibid.
72. Gilbert, *Never Despair*, p.705
73. Nigel Nicolson (ed.), *Harold Nicolson: Diaries and Letters 1945-62*, p.222
74. Ibid.
75. Moran, *Winston Churchill: The Struggle for Survival*, p.379
76. Colville, *The Fringes of Power*, p.642

Chapter 11: Emergency in Malaya

1. Gilbert, *Never Despair*, p.660
2. Pelling, *Winston Churchill*, p.563
3. Gilbert, *Never Despair*, p.666
4. Ibid
5. Peter Midgley (ed.), *The Heroic Memory: The Memorial Addresses to the Rt. Hon. Sir Winston Spencer Churchill Society Edmonton, Alberta, 1965-1989*, Edmonton: The Churchill Statue and Oxford Scholarship Foundation, 2005, p.201
6. Michael Burleigh, *Small Wars, Far Away Places: The Genesis of the Modern World 1945-1965*, London: Macmillan, 2013, p.171
7. Field Marshal Sir William Slim, *Defeat into Victory*, London: Cassell, 1956, p.145
8. Ibid.
9. *Western Morning News*, 22 June 1950

10. Ibid.
11. Horne, *Macmillan 1894-1956*, p.329
12. Dewey also visited Australia, Hong Kong, Indochina, Indonesia, Japan, Korea, New Zealand, the Philippines and Taiwan.
13. *The Canberra Times*, 25 June 1951
14. *The West Australian*, 20 August 1951
15. Ibid.
16. *Northern Daily Mail*, 6 October 1951
17. Moran, *Winston Churchill: The Struggle for Survival*, p.451
18. Ibid., p.363
19. Ibid., p.364
20. *Hansard, The Situation in Malaya*, Volume 175, 27 February 1952
21. Ibid.
22. Gilbert, *Never Despair*, p.716
23. *Hansard, Malaya (Decapitation)*, Volume 500, 7 May 1952
24. Ibid.
25. Simon Webb, *British Concentration Camps: A Brief History from 1900-1975*, Barnsley: Pen & Sword, 2022, p.149
26. Chang and Halliday, *Mao: The Unknown Story*, p.387
27. Gilbert, *Never Despair*, p.839
28. Robert Jackson, *The Malayan Emergency & Indonesian Confrontation: The Commonwealth's Wars 1948-1960*, Barnsley: Pen & Sword, 2021, pp.102-3
29. Moran, *Winston Churchill: The Struggle for Survival*, p.423
30. Ibid.
31. Anthony Tucker-Jones, *Dien Bien Phu: The First Indochina War 1946-1954*, Barnsley: Pen & Sword, 2021, p.113
32. Patrick Brogan, *World Conflicts: Why and Where they are Happening*, London: Bloomsbury, 1989, p.190
33. Gerry van Tonder, *Malayan Emergency: Triumph of the Running Dogs 1948-1960*, Barnsley: Pen & Sword, 2017, p.103

Chapter 12: Korean Impasse

1. Nigel Nicolson (ed.), *Harold Nicolson: Diaries and Letters 1945-1962*, p.116
2. Khrushchev, *Khrushchev Remembers*, p.372
3. Max Hastings, *The Korean War*, London: Michael Joseph, 1987, p.72
4. Ibid. p.75
5. *Reynolds News*, 9 July 1950
6. The Australian and New Zealand fleets sent seventeen ships. Australia, Canada and South Africa also sent air force units.
7. Nigel Nicolson (ed.), *Harold Nicolson: Diaries and Letters 1945-1962*, p.191
8. Hastings, *The Korean War*, p.72
9. Gilbert, *Never Despair*, p.546
10. Alan Whicker, *Journey of a Lifetime*, London: Harper Collins, 2009, p.57
11. Ibid. p.56
12. Gilbert, *Never Despair*, p.552-3

13. Ibid., p.547
14. Ibid., p.554
15. Jenkins, *Churchill: A Biography*, p.834
16. Churchill, *The Second World War: Closing the Ring*, p.432
17. Churchill (ed.), *Never Give In!*, p.342
18. Gerry van Tonder, *Korean War Allied Surge: Pyongyang Falls, UN Sweep to the Yalu October 1950*, Barnsley: Pen & Sword, p.36
19. Gerry van Tonder, *Korean War Chinese Invasion: People's Liberation Army Crosses the Yalu October 1950-March 1951*, Barnsley: Pen & Sword, 2020, p.26
20. Andrew Roberts, *Eminent Churchillians*, London: Weidenfeld & Nicolson, 1994, p.214
21. Nigel Nicolson (ed.), *Harold Nicolson: Diaries and Letters 1945-1962*, p.195
22. *Liverpool Echo*, 29 November 1950
23. Paul French, *North Korea: State of Paranoia*, London: Zed, 2015, p.332
24. Wilson, *Memoirs*, p.114
25. Van Tonder, *Korean War Allied Surge*, p.117
26. Matthew B. Ridgway, *The War in Korea*, London: Barrie & Rockliff, 1968, p.xi
27. Ibid.
28. Russell Spurr, *Enter the Dragon: China at War in Korea*, London: Sidgwick & Jackson, 1989, p.221
29. Chang and Halliday, *Mao: The Unknown Story*, p.382
30. Gilbert, *Never Despair*, p.580-1
31. Ibid., p.581
32. Ibid., p.583
33. Nigel Nicolson (ed.), *Harold Nicolson: Diaries and Letters 1945-62*, p.197
34. Wilson, *Memoirs*, p.114
35. Gilbert, *Never Despair*, p.593
36. Tim Carew, *The Korean War: The Story of the Fighting Commonwealth Regiments*, London: Pan, 1970, p.181
37. Ponting, *Churchill*, p.754
38. Wilson, *Memoirs*, p.135
39. Ibid., p.134
40. Ibid., p.135
41. Ibid.
42. Peter Midgley (ed.), *The Heroic Memory: The Memorial Addresses to the Rt. Hon. Sir Winston Spencer Churchill Society Edmonton, Alberta, 1965-1989*, Edmonton: The Churchill Statue and Oxford Scholarship Foundation, 2005, p.101
43. Gilbert, *Never Despair*, p.737
44. Alan Whicker, *Whicker's War*, London: Harper Collins, 2005, p.184
45. Gilbert, *Never Despair*, p.747
46. *Hansard, Korea (Military Situation)*, Volume 504, 28 July 1952
47. Ibid.
48. The Commonwealth Division was deployed on an eight mile front west of the Imjin river, where it repulsed numerous Chinese attacks; see Ashley Cunningham-Boothe and Peter Farrar (ed.), *British Forces in the Korean War*, Leamington Spa: The British Korean Veterans Association, 1988, pp.8-11

49. Brigadier Brian Parritt, *Chinese Hordes and Human Waves: A Personal Perspective of the Korean War 1950-1953*, Barnsley: Pen & Sword, 2020, p.54
50. Michael Caine, *The Elephant to Hollywood*, London: Hodder & Stoughton, 2010, p.53
51. Ibid.
52. Ibid., p.52
53. Nigel Nicolson (ed.), *Harold Nicolson: Diaries and Letters 1945-1962*, p.230-1
54. Gilbert, *Never Despair*, p.814
55. Nigel Nicolson (ed.), *Harold Nicolson: Diaries and Letters 1945-1962*, p.238
56. Gilbert, *Never Despair*, p.812
57. Ponting, *Churchill*, p.770
58. Zhisui, *The Private Life of Chairman Mao*, p.643
59. Jon Halliday and Bruce Cumings, *Korea: The Unknown War*, London: Hamish Hamilton, 1986, p.195
60. Moran, *Winston Churchill: The Struggle for Survival*, p.423
61. Colville, *The Fringes of Power*, p.672
62. Moran, *Winston Churchill: The Struggle for Survival*, p.465
63. Churchill (ed.), *Never Give In!*, p.485

Chapter 13: Clinging to Suez

1. Gilbert, *Never Despair*, p.230
2. Ibid., p.231
3. Ibid.
4. Ibid., p.252
5. Ibid, p.658
6. Ibid., p.659
7. Ibid., p.679
8. Ponting, *Churchill*, p.774
9. Gilbert, *Never Despair*, p.774
10. Ibid., p.781
11. Ponting, *Churchill*, pp.774-5
12. Nigel Nicolson (ed.), *Harold Nicolson: Diaries and Letters 1945-1962*, pp.236-7
13. Ponting, *Churchill*, p.775
14. Hamilton, *Monty: The Field-Marshal 1944-1976*, p.853
15. Gilbert, *Never Despair*, p.945
16. Ibid., p.946
17. Selwyn Lloyd, *Suez 1956: A Personal Account*, London: Jonathan Cape, p.17
18. Moran, *Winston Churchill: The Struggle for Survival*, p.527
19. Lloyd, *Suez 1956: A Personal Account*, p.19
20. Ponting, *Churchill*, p.788
21. Ibid.
22. *Daily Express*, 28 July 1954
23. Lloyd, *Suez 1956: A Personal Account*, p.20
24. Khrushchev, *Khrushchev Remembers*, p.433

25. Ibid.
26. Ibid.
27. Lloyd, *Suez 1956: A Personal Account*, p.28
28. Nigel Nicolson (ed.), *Harold Nicolson: Diaries and Letters 1945-1962*, p.261
29. *Hansard, Cyprus (Incidents)*, Volume 539, 6 April 1955
30. Ibid.
31. Soames, *Speaking for Themselves*, p.597
32. Ibid.
33. Lloyd, *Suez 1956: A Personal Account*, p.154
34. Soames, *Speaking for Themselves*, p.609
35. Ibid.
36. Gilbert, *Never Despair*, p.1203
37. Keith Kyle, *Suez*, London: Weidenfeld & Nicolson, 1991, p.173
38. Horne, *Macmillan 1894-1956*, pp.404-5
39. Moran, *Winston Churchill: The Struggle for Survival*, p.702
40. Ibid.
41. Ibid., p.703
42. Kyle, *Suez*, p.242
43. Humphrey Trevelyan, *The Middle East in Revolution*, London: Macmillan, 1970, p.126
44. Ibid., pp.126-7
45. Nigel Nicolson (ed.), *Harold Nicolson: Diaries and Letters 1945-1962*, p.311
46. Trevelyan, *The Middle East in Revolution*, p.129
47. *Evening Standard*, 5 November 1956
48. Nicolson (ed.), *Vita and Harold*, p.421
49. Colville, *The Fringes of Power*, p.719
50. Ibid., p.721
51. Ibid.
52. Gilbert, *Never Despair*, p.1224
53. Nigel Nicolson (ed.), *Harold Nicolson: Diaries and Letters 1945-1962*, p.324

Chapter 14: East African Revolution

1. Randolph Churchill, *Winston S. Churchill, Volume II, Young Statesman 1901-1914*, London: Heinemann, 1967, p.234
2. Jeremy Murray-Brown, *Kenyatta*, New York: E.P. Dutton, 1973, p.73
3. Horne, *Macmillan 1894-1956*, p.148
4. Mau Mau was a term only used by the British authorities and its origin is unclear. The rebels variously called themselves the Kenya Land and Freedom Army, The Movement or The Unifier. Mau Mau may have been an anagram of 'Uma Uma', which meant 'Get out, get out!' More precisely Mzungu Aende Ulaya – Mwafrica Apete Uhuru, which translated from Swahili means 'Let the white man go back abroad so that Africa can get its independence.' See Biodun Alao and Christa Hook, *Mau-Mau Warrior*, Oxford: Osprey, 2006, p.5
5. In 1952 the population numbered just under 6 million: 5.5 million Africans, 165,000 Indians and 55,000 Europeans.

6. *East African Standard*, 16 June 1950
7. Surprisingly biographies on Queen Elizabeth II do not mention the threat posed by the Mau Mau. The only exception is Robert Lacey, *Royal: Her Majesty Queen Elizabeth II*, London, Time Warner, 2002, p.176, who makes a passing reference to the danger at Treetops.
8. Ben Pimlott, *The Queen: A Biography of Elizabeth II*, London: Harper Collins, 1996, p.174
9. Ann Morrow, *The Queen*, London: Granada, 1983, p.47
10. Ibid.
11. Andrew Morton, *The Queen, London*: Michael O'Mara, 2022, p.120
12. S.H. Fazan, *Colonial Kenya Observed: British Rule, Mau Mau and the Wind of Change*, London: Bloomsbury, 2020, p.195
13. Ibid.
14. Burleigh, *Small Wars, Far Away Places*, p.371
15. David Percox, *Britain, Kenya and the Cold War: Imperial Defence, Colonial Security and Decolonisation*, London: I.B. Tauris, 2012, p.51
16. Andrew, *The Defence of the Realm: The Authorized History of MI5*, p.457
17. Percox, *Britain, Kenya and the Cold War*, p.51
18. 'Kenya: Panga War,' *Time magazine*, 10 November 1952
19. Ibid.
20. Andrew, *The Defence of the Realm: The Authorized History of MI5*, p.455
21. Ibid., p.454
22. Murray-Brown, *Kenyatta*, p.315
23. Ibid., p.316
24. 'Kenya: Panga War,' *Time Magazine*, 10 November 1952
25. Ibid.
26. Major Frank Kitson, *Gangs and Counter-gangs*, London; Barrie & Rockliff, 1960, p.47
27. Andrew, *Defence of the Realm: The Authorized History of MI5*, p.456
28. Kitson, *Gangs and Counter-gangs*, p.92
29. Ibid., p.xii
30. Gilbert, *Never Despair*, p.803
31. Ibid., p.834
32. Kitson, *Gangs and Counter-gangs*, p.131
33. Moran, *Winston Churchill: The Struggle for Survival*, p.528
34. Fazan, *Colonial Kenya Observed*, p.193
35. Moran, *Winston Churchill: The Struggle for Survival*, p.528
36. Kitson, *Gangs and Counter-gangs*, p.132
37. Ibid.
38. Fazan, *Colonial Kenya Observed*, p.213
39. Ibid.
40. Nick van de Bijl, *The Mau Mau Rebellion: The Emergency in Kenya 1952-1956*, Barnsley: Pen & Sword, 2017, p.151
41. Burleigh, *Small Wars, Far Away Places*, p.379
42. Alao and Hook, *Mau-Mau Warrior*, p.40
43. Kitson, *Gangs and Counter-gangs*, p.xi

44. For more on this issue see Webb, *British Concentration Camps: A Brief History from 1900-1975*
45. Nigel Nicolson (ed.), *Harold Nicolson: Diaries and Letters 1945-1962*, p.369
46. Butler, *The Art of Memory*, p.103
47. Moran, *Winston Churchill: The Struggle for Survival*, p.758
48. Nigel Nicolson (ed.), *Harold Nicolson: Diaries and Letters 1945-1962*, p.369
49. Butler, *The Art of Memory*, p.104
50. Kitson, *Gangs and Counter-gangs*, p.xii

Chapter 15: Rendezvous in Bermuda

1. Colville, *The Fringes of Power*, p.654
2. Moran, *Winston Churchill: The Struggle for Survival*, p.508
3. Ibid., p.662
4. Eisenhower, *At Ease*, p.374
5. Ibid.
6. Lacey, *Royal: Her Majesty Queen Elizabeth II*, p.179
7. Nigel Nicolson (ed.), *Harold Nicolson: Diaries and Letters 1945-1962*, pp.241-2
8. Malcolm Thomson, *Churchill: His Life and Times*, London: Odhams, 1965, p.445
9. Colville, *The Fringes of Power*, p.715
10. Ibid., p.713
11. They were from Australia, Canada, Ceylon, India, New Zealand, Pakistan, Rhodesia and South Africa.
12. Gilbert, *Never Despair*, p.837
13. Ibid.
14. Ibid., p.838
15. Moran, *Winston Churchill: The Struggle for Survival*, p.406
16. Gilbert, *Never Despair*, p.845
17. Moran, *Winston Churchill: The Struggle for Survival*, p.406
18. Gilbert, *Never Despair*, p.850
19. Ibid., p.851
20. Khrushchev, *Khrushchev Remembers*, p.343
21. Ibid., pp.322-3
22. Moran, *Winston Churchill: The Struggle for Survival*, p.504
23. Ponting, *Churchill*, p.790
24. Ibid., p.791
25. Some units of the Lithuanian Activists Front continued to resist the Soviet Army until 1952, survivors of the Ukrainian Insurgents Army held out until 1955. Likewise the Chechen insurgency operating from the Caucasus mountains lasted till the mid-1950s.
26. Moran, *Winston Churchill: The Struggle for Survival*, p.493
27. Ibid., p.494
28. Gilbert, *Never Despair*, p.910
29. Moran, *Winston Churchill: The Struggle for Survival*, p.497
30. Ibid.
31. Gilbert, *Churchill: A Life*, p.920

32. Stelzer, *Working with Winston*, p.255
33. Ibid., p.254
34. Eisenhower, *At Ease*, p.374
35. Horne, *Macmillan 1894-1956*, p.349
36. Gilbert, *Never Despair*, p.926
37. Colville, *The Fringes of Power*, p.684
38. Leaming, *Churchill Defiant*, p.244
39. Colville, *The Fringes of Power*, p.685
40. Gilbert, *Never Despair*, p.935
41. Soames, *Speaking for Themselves*, p.577
42. Soames, *Clementine Churchill*, p.440
43. Soames, *Winston Churchill: His Life as a Painter*, p.190
44. Moran, *Winston Churchill: The Struggle for Survival*, p.505
45. Ibid., p.508
46. Ibid.
47. Ibid.
48. Colville, *The Fringes of Power*, p.689
49. Moran, *Winston Churchill: The Struggle for Survival*, p.515
50. Stelzer, *Working with Winston*, p.179
51. Charmley, *Churchill's Grand Alliance*, p.274
52. *Hansard, Foreign Affairs*, Volume 522, 17 December 1953
53. Moran, *Winston Churchill: The Struggle for Survival*, p.514
54. *Hansard, Foreign Affairs*, Volume 522, 17 December 1953
55. Pelling, *Winston Churchill*, p.608
56. McKinstry, *Attlee and Churchill*, p.590
57. *Hansard, Foreign Affairs*, Volume 522, 17 December 1953
58. Charlwood, *Churchill and Eden*, p.192
59. Ibid.
60. Horne, *Macmillan 1894-1956*, p.345
61. Ponting, *Churchill*, p.761
62. Ibid., p.791
63. Eisenhower, *At Ease*, p.374

Chapter 16: The Bear and the Bomb

1. Muggeridge, *The Infernal Grove*, p.263
2. Moran, *Winston Churchill: The Struggle for Survival*, p.359
3. Ibid., p.315
4. Gilbert, *Never Despair*, p.286
5. Khrushchev, *Khrushchev Remembers*, p.361
6. Ibid.
7. Churchill (ed.), *Never Give In!*, p.448
8. Nigel Nicolson (ed.), *Harold Nicolson: Diaries and Letters 1945-1962*, p.155
9. *New York Herald Tribune*, 1 April 1949
10. Gilbert, *Never Despair*, p.468
11. Nigel Nicolson (ed.), *Harold Nicolson: Diaries and Letters 1945-1962*, p.175

12. Gilbert, *Never Despair*, p.266
13. Moran, *Winston Churchill: The Struggle for Survival*, p.316
14. Eisenhower, *At Ease*, p.309
15. Although Dr Klaus Fuchs was sentenced on 1 March 1950 to fourteen years in prison, he was released in 1959.
16. *Hansard, Defence*, Vol 472, 16 March 1950
17. For more on Soviet espionage activities see John Harte, *The Race for the Atom Bomb: How Soviet Russia Stole the Secrets of the Manhattan Project*, Barnsley: Pen & Sword, 2023
18. Gilbert, *Never Despair*, p.530
19. Ibid., p.531
20. Gilbert (ed.), *Churchill: The Power of Words*, p.573
21. Churchill (ed.), *Never Give In!*, p.470
22. *Hansard, Defence*, Vol 494, 6 December 1951
23. Gilbert (ed.), *Churchill: The Power of Words*, p.578
24. Moran, *Winston Churchill: The Struggle for Survival*, p.359
25. *Hansard, Defence*, Vol 496, 26 February 1952
26. For more on these tests see Elizabeth Tynan, *Atomic Thunder: British Nuclear Testing in Australia*, Barnsley: Pen & Sword, 2018
27. Gilbert, *Never Despair*, p.709
28. Field Marshal Montgomery, *A Concise History of Warfare*, London: Collins, 1972, p.355
29. *Hansard, Defence*, Vol 497, 5 March 1952
30. Ibid.
31. Ibid.
32. Churchill (ed.), *Never Give In!*, p.492
33. Montgomery, *The Memoirs*, p.516
34. Colville, *The Fringes of Power*, p.675
35. Moran, *Winston Churchill: The Struggle for Survival*, p.503
36. Both the subsequent Mid-Canada Line and Distant Early Warning Line suffered the same fate and were overtaken by technological advances making them redundant before they were ever completed.
37. Moran, *Winston Churchill: The Struggle for Survival*, p.530
38. Nigel Nicolson (ed.) *Harold Nicolson: Diaries and Letters 1945-1962*, pp.247-8
39. Kevin Ruane, *Churchill and the Bomb in War and Cold War*, London: Bloomsbury, 2018, p.254
40. Ibid., pp.256-7
41. Chang & Halliday, *Mao: The Unknown Story*, p.596
42. Tucker-Jones, *Dien Bien Phu*, p.100
43. Bernard B. Fall, *Hell in a Very Small Place: The Siege of Dien Bien Phu*, Cambridge, MA: Da Capo Press, 2002, p.308
44. Ruane, *Churchill and the Bomb in War and Cold War*, p.258
45. Ibid.
46. Moran, *Winston Churchill: The Struggle for Survival*, p.543
47. Ibid., p.101
48. Horne, *Macmillan 1894-1956*, p.346

49. Khrushchev, *Khrushchev Remembers*, p.482
50. Chang & Halliday, *Mao: The Unknown Story*, p.596
51. Fall, *Hell in a Very Small Place*, p.475
52. Moran, *Winston Churchill: The Struggle for Survival*, p.544
53. Soames, *Winston Churchill: His Life as a Painter*, p.195
54. Ibid.
55. Montgomery, *A Concise History of Warfare*, p.354
56. Moran, *Winston Churchill: The Struggle for Survival*, p.503
57. Churchill (ed.), *Never Give In!*, p.497
58. Montgomery, *The Memoirs*, pp.517-8
59. Soames, *Speaking for Themselves*, p.631
60. Churchill (ed.), *Never Give In!*, p.497

Chapter 17: Petty Central American Issues

1. Moran, *Winston Churchill: The Struggle for Survival*, p.568
2. Gilbert, *Never Despair*, p.172
3. Khrushchev, *Khrushchev Remembers*, p.488
4. Ibid.
5. Keith Jeffery, *MI6: The History of the Secret Intelligence Service 1909-1949*, London: Bloomsbury, 2011, p.456
6. Ibid., p.688
7. British Honduras was renamed Belize in 1973 and finally became independent in 1981.
8. These were the Second World War vintage light cruisers USS Boise and Phoenix. They were renamed Nueve de Julio and Diez y Siete de Octubre; the later subsequently became the General Belgrano which was sunk by the Royal Navy during the Falklands War in 1982.
9. Gilbert, *Never Despair*, p.708
10. A total of four Colombian battalions served in Korea, along with a nine-piece Latin band, resulting in 4,000 soldiers gaining valuable combat experience; see Adrian J. English, *Armed Forces of Latin America*, London: Janes, 1984, p.171 and Nigel Thomas & Peter Abbott, *The Korean War 1950-53*, London: Osprey, 1986, p.24
11. After Churchill retired he was not happy when he heard that Argentina had become the first country in Latin America to operate an aircraft carrier in 1958. To make matters worse it was a British one sold to the Argentine navy by Harold Macmillan's government. It was decommissioned before the Argentine assault on the Falklands in 1982.
12. George Pendle, *A History of Latin America*, London: Penguin, 1990, p.169
13. Legion of Merit, Department of the Army, General Orders No.11, 8 February 1955
14. Lawrence James, *Churchill and Empire: Portrait of an Imperialist*, London Weidenfeld & Nicolson, 2014, p.384
15. Andrew, *The Defence of the Realm*, p.477

16. Carrie Gibson, *Empire's Crossroads: A History of the Caribbean from Columbus to the Present Day*, London: Macmillan, 2014, p.271
17. Ibid., p.272
18. Ibid.
19. Gilbert, *Never Despair*, p.898
20. Wilson, *Memoirs: The Making of a Prime Minister 1916-1964*, p.140
21. *Hansard*, British Guiana, Volume 518, 22 October 1953
22. Ibid.
23. Ibid.
24. The United Fruit Company also had extensive interests in Costa Rica, Cuba, Honduras and Nicaragua. Along with the Standard Fruit Company they dominated 90 per cent of the banana market in the United States. These companies came to epitomise negative US influence in Latin America and the Caribbean and led to the derogatory term 'Banana Republic'; see Harold Blakemore and Clifford T. Smith, *Latin America: Geographical Perspectives*, London: Methuen, 1974, p.155
25. Moran, *Winston Churchill: The Struggle for Survival*, p.568
26. Ibid.
27. Ibid.
28. Colville, *The Fringes of Power*, p.694
29. Ibid.
30. Nigel Nicolson (ed.), *Harold Nicolson: Diaries and Letters 1945-62*, p.346
31. Ibid.

Chapter 18: Failing Warlord

1. Wilson, *Memoirs: The Making of a Prime Minister 1916-1964*, p.147
2. Ibid., p.148
3. Butler, *The Art of Memory*, p.141
4. Roberts, *Eminent Churchillians*, p.268
5. Butler, *The Art of Memory*, p.141
6. Ibid., p.137
7. Colville, *The Fringes of Power*, p.704
8. Soames, *Speaking for Themselves*, p.582
9. Ibid.
10. Colville, *The Fringes of Power*, p.705
11. Moran, *Winston Churchill: The Struggle for Survival*, p.623
12. Ibid., p.626
13. Ibid., p.628
14. Gilbert, *Churchill: A Life*, p.934
15. Nigel Nicolson (ed.), *Harold Nicolson: Diaries and Letters 1945-1962*, pp.276-7
16. Gilbert, *Never Despair*, p.1095
17. Gilbert, *Churchill: The Power of Words*, pp.591-2
18. Horne, *Macmillan 1894-1956*, p.354
19. Gilbert, *Never Despair*, p.1111
20. Moran, *Winston Churchill: The Struggle for Survival*, p.640

21. Soames, *Clementine Churchill*, p.451
22. Moran, *Winston Churchill: The Struggle for Survival*, p.643
23. Colville, *The Fringes of Power*, p.708
24. Soames, *Clementine Churchill*, p.452
25. Churchill, (ed.), *Never Give In!*, pp.498-9
26. Soames, *Clementine Churchill*, p.453
27. Nigel Nicolson (ed.), *Harold Nicolson: Diaries and Letters 1945-1962*, p.281
28. Colville, *The Fringes of Power*, p.709
29. Moran, *Winston Churchill: The Struggle for Survival*, p.649
30. Nigel Nicolson (ed.), *Harold Nicolson: Diaries and Letters 1945-1962*, p.281
31. Gilbert, *Never Despair*, p.1127
32. Ibid., pp.1127-8
33. Hough, *Mountbatten: Hero of Our Time*, p.257
34. Ibid.
35. Khrushchev, *Khrushchev Remembers*, p.402
36. Gilbert, *Never Despair*, p.1192
37. Gilbert, *Churchill: A Life*, p.947
38. Khrushchev, *Khrushchev Remembers*, p.410
39. Ibid.
40. Nigel Nicolson (ed.), *Harold Nicolson: Diaries and Letters 1945-1962*, p.300
41. Khrushchev, *Khrushchev Remembers*, p.413
42. Ibid., p.412
43. Moran, *Winston Churchill: The Struggle for Survival*, p.695
44. Colville, *The Fringes of Power*, p.719
45. The French Prime Minister Paul Ramadier had awarded Churchill with the Médaille Militaire in 1947.
46. Gilbert, *Never Despair*, p.1280
47. Soames, *Clementine Churchill*, p.467
48. According to French figures the Algerians lost over 6,000 men trying to break through the Morice Line.
49. Khrushchev, *Khrushchev Remembers*, p.491
50. Hamilton, *Monty: The Field Marshal 1944-1976*, p.913
51. Notably Khrushchev makes no mention of this meeting with Montgomery in his memoirs.
52. Hamilton, *Monty: The Field Marshal 1944-1976*, p.914
53. Ibid.
54. Brian *Montgomery, A Field Marshal in the Family*, London: Constable, 1973, p.344
55. Alun *Chalfont, Montgomery of Alamein*, London: Weidenfeld & Nicolson, 1976, p.323
56. Ibid.
57. Soames, *Winston Churchill: His Life as a Painter*, p.208
58. Soames, *Speaking for Themselves*, p.633
59. Midgley (ed.), *The Heroic Memory*, p.101
60. Gilbert, *Never Despair*, p.1295
61. Ibid., p.1296

62. Khrushchev, *Khrushchev Remembers*, p.520
63. Gilbert, *Churchill: The Power of Words*, p.609
64. Roberts, *Churchill: Walking with Destiny*, p.959
65. 'Castro's MiGs Gun Rebel Army,' *Daily Mirror*, 19 April 1961
66. Soames, *Speaking for Themselves*, p.639
67. Ibid., p.640
68. Sarah Churchill, *Keep on Dancing*, p.199
69. Soames, *Family Album*, p.412
70. The Soviets not only deployed nuclear ballistic missiles to Cuba, but they also sent nuclear tactical cruise missiles to use against any American invasion. In the Western Atlantic Soviet submarines secretly patrolled, armed with nuclear tipped torpedoes. There are numerous studies on the crisis, amongst the most comprehensive is Max Hasting's *Abyss: World on the Brink, The Cuban Missile Crisis 1962*, London: William Collins, 2023
71. Midgley (ed.), *The Heroic Memory*, pp.31-32
72. Ibid., p.32
73. Soames, *Family Album*, p.412
74. Sarah Churchill, *A Thread in the Tapestry*, p.99

Chapter 19: Winston's Post War Legacy

1. Gilbert, *In Search of Churchill*, p.253
2. Ibid.
3. Midgley (ed), *The Heroic Memory*, p.274
4. Ibid.
5. Soames, *Clementine Churchill*, p.441
6. Midgley (ed), *The Heroic Memory*, p.50
7. Wilson, *Memoirs*, p.158
8. Ibid.
9. Gilbert, *In Search of Churchill*, p.246
10. Cohen (ed.), *The Heroic Memory*, p.4
11. Ibid.
12. Midgley (ed.), *The Heroic Memory*, p.11
13. Gilbert, *Never Despair*, p.762
14. Harold Wilson, *A Prime Minister on Prime Ministers*, London: Michael Joseph, 1977, p.301
15. Midgley (ed.), *The Heroic Memory*, p.274
16. Of the 56 members of the Commonwealth only 14 recognise the British monarchy
17. Butler, *The Art of Memory*, p.133
18. Gilbert, *Never Despair*, p.1290
19. Henry Anatole Grunwald, *Churchill: The Life Triumphant: The Historical Record of Ninety Years*, New York: American Heritage Publishing, 1965, p.5
20. Ibid., p.143

Epilogue: The Unthinkable

1. Wilson, *A Prime Minister on Prime Ministers*, p.264
2. Danchev & Todman, *War Diaries*, p.693
3. Colville, *The Fringes of Power*, p.597
4. William Nester, *Winston Churchill and the Art of Leadership: How Winston Changed the World*, Barnsley: Frontline Books, 2020, p.186
5. In total the Allies had available about 100 divisions facing over 260 Soviet divisions in the summer of 1945.
6. Gilbert, *Never Despair*, p.8
7. Carlo D'Este, *Patton: A Genius for War*, New York: Harper Perennial, 1996, p.763 & Charles Whiting, *Patton's Last Battle*, Staplehurst: Spellmount, 2002, pp.213-4
8. Danchev & Todman, *War Diaries*, p.693
9. The National Archives, Operation "Unthinkable", Report by the Joint Planning Staff, 22 May 1945, Ref: CAB120/691. This document was not released until 1998.
10. Ibid.
11. Ibid.
12. Zhukov, *Reminiscences and Reflections*, Vol 2, p.429
13. Ibid.
14. Hamilton, *Monty: The Field Marshal 1944-1976*, p.542
15. Khrushchev, *Khrushchev Remembers*, p.222
16. Soames, *Speaking for Themselves*, p.524
17. Danchev & Todman, *War Diaries*, p.693
18. Ibid., p.694
19. Lieutenant General Sir Brian Horrocks, *A Full Life*, London: Collins, 1960, p.275
20. Danchev & Todman, *War Diaries*, p.693
21. Roberts, *Churchill: Walking with Destiny*, p.879

Index